# Freedom and Modernity

SUNY Series in Philosophy

George R. Lucas, Jr., Editor

# Freedom and Modernity

Richard Dien Winfield

State University of New York Press

Published by
State University of New York Press, Albany



Printed in the United States of America



For information, address State University of New York
Press, State University Plaza, Albany, N.Y., 12246

Production by M.R. Mulholland
Marketing by Fran Keneston

Library of Congress Cataloging in Publication Data

Winfield, Richard Dien, 1950-
Freedom and modernity / Richard Dien Winfield.
p. cm. — (SUNY series in philosophy)
Includes bibliographical references and index.
ISBN 0-7914-0809-4 (alk. paper). — ISBN 0-7914-0810-8 (pbk. : alk. paper)
1. Reason. 2. Act (Philosophy) 3. Autonomy (Philosophy)
I. Title. II. Series.
BC177.W57 1992
128'.3—dc20 90-22216
CIP

10 9 8 7 6 5 4 3 2 1

For my son,
Manas Samuel

# Contents

Introduction ix

A Note on the Text xv

Part I: Autonomous Reason

1. The Method of Autonomous Reason 3
2. The Ordeal of Self-Critical Critical Philosophy: Reflections on Husserl and Wittgenstein 15
3. Is Systematic Logic a Transcendental Ontology? 19
4. Conceiving Reality without Foundations 33
5. On Individuality 51

Part II: Autonomous Action

6. Morality without Community 61
7. The Injustice of Human Rights 77
8. Freedom as Interaction: Hegel's Resolution to the Dilemma of Liberal Theory 89
9. Hegel and the Legitimation of Modernity 107
10. The Dilemma of Labor 137
11. The Young Hegel and the Dialectic of Social Production 155
12. The Logic of Marx's *Capital* 169
13. The Social Determination of the Labor Process from Hegel to Marx 203
14. Hegel's Challenge to the Modern Economy 227
15. Rethinking Politics: Carl Schmitt versus Hegel 261
16. Political Freedom and Territorial Rights 283

Index 305

# Introduction

The autonomy of reason and the autonomy of action, once so prized as emblems of knowledge and ethics, have become objects of ridicule and disbelief. On the one extreme, their very existence is denied. Reason and action, we so often hear, are inextricably caught in the web of desire, language, culture, and history. Held hostage by conceptual frameworks specific to different communities, and then further entrapped by standpoints within each relative to gender, sexual orientation, race, ethnicity, class, and the like, knowing and conduct must allegedly forfeit all claim to independence. On this view, autonomous reason and self-determined action are but delusions of those who have yet to awaken to the cage they inhabit. When, by contrast, rational autonomy and autonomous conduct are begrudgingly granted any reality, they are unmasked as historical conventions of value only for the particular culture in which they thrive. Or, just as commonly, freedom of thought and action are denounced as modes of domination, sacrificing the particular on the altar of the universal, strangling feeling with abstractions, reducing nature to a vessel of manipulation, subduing and devouring every incongruent culture, all in a logocentric, phallocentric frenzy of modernization, Westernization, rationalization, liberation.

Compounding the rampant devaluation of theoretical and practical autonomy is the parallel discrediting of modernity and of the West from which modernization has sprung as an irrepressible contagion. The ills of modernity and Westernization, so deserving of condemnation, have become identified with the affirmation of freedom, recognized to be so central to the modern project with which the West has stricken the East. Everything modern and Western that lays claim to universal validity has come under suspicion, and this suspicion has extended itself to the claims of autonomy in theory and practice, as if both sets of claims were one. Yet, just as modernity and its Western womb have been battlegrounds of competing tendencies as opposed as liberalism, fascism, and Marxist-Leninism, so the understanding of just what autonomous reason and action are has assumed diametrically opposed forms.

This diversity raises a suspicion of its own that the critique of modernity, Westernization, and autonomy in theory and practice may suffer from a failure of discrimination. It might just be that those who repudiate modernity and Westernization have failed to differentiate the competing aspects of each, blanketly rejecting the whole, when only parts are at blame. By the same token, those who devalue the freedom of thought and conduct may well have the wrong vision of autonomy before them, flailing away at a straw man called the "Enlightenment project," "reification," "logocentrism," "phallocentrism," or "the problem of technology," to name but a few variants.

Yet the most vexing problem may lie in how a critique of the autonomy of reason and action can provide any affirmative doctrine of knowledge or ethics, or, for that matter, any normative critique of modernity, without embracing the independence of thought and conduct it spurns. Can autonomy in theory and practice be just cultural givens, of local value or global contamination, or must all thought and action derive legitimacy from the freedom they exhibit?

The following essays challenge the fashionable discrediting of autonomy in theory and practice by investigating how self-determination has normative validity and, indeed, is the very substance of legitimacy for both knowledge and conduct. In arguing this claim, these essays equally challenge the prevailing view of what autonomous reason and autonomous action actually comprise. It will be shown that self-determination in both theory and practice has been misconstrued as the determining of a given determiner, where objectivity and value are constructs of some subject or other. Foisting a false logic upon freedom, this has not only obscured the legitimacy of rational autonomy and autonomous action but has robbed us of the conceptual tools needed to evaluate modernity. Nevertheless, what we need to surmount these confusions is already at hand in the work of the thinker of freedom par excellence, Hegel. However incomplete, inconsistent, and misunderstood his efforts may often be, Hegel has provided the strategy and basic categories for remedying the dilemmas of postmodern thought. For this reason, the following investigations address autonomous reason and self-determined action in constant dialogue with Hegel.

The five essays of Part I set the stage for what follows by examining the self-legitimating process of autonomous reason. The first essay, "The Method of Autonomous Reason," investigates the convergent demands inherent in logic's project of thinking valid thinking and in philosophy's quest for a nonarbitrary starting point. It is argued that what alone resolves the quandaries of logic and of philosophy's beginning is a radically autonomous conceptual development, achieving a liberation from the hold of givenness with a self-generating, self-ordered system of categories.

Such a categorial development may be required, but can it avoid turning into another version of transcendental argument, where various guiding assumptions must be introduced to insure that any content and ordering emerge? "The Ordeal of Self-Critical Critical Philosophy: Reflections on Husserl and Wittgenstein" underscores the impasse that would result if we were to be left with no alternative to transcendental inquiry than dogmatism or the abandonment of philosophy. Although, as the essay suggests, Husserl and Wittgenstein are both intent on overcoming the residues of dogmatism within transcendental philosophy, the foundering of their complementary strategies reveals how critical philosophy cannot be self-critical enough.

"Is Systematic Logic a Transcendental Ontology?" confronts the skeptical challenge that would condemn autonomous reason to such dilemmas, doing so in reference to Alan White's analysis of Schelling's critique of Hegel. In answer to Schelling, the essay shows how the categorial development that Hegel presents can begin without presuppositions and still generate specific concepts with an ordering of their own. Such a logic of categories can do so precisely by comprising the self-determination of autonomous reason, rather than a transcendental argument.

Yet, if the self-ordered categories of autonomous reason are not transcendental, how can they provide knowledge of reality? "Conceiving Reality without Foundations" examines this problem in light of Hegel's strategy for moving from the self-thinking thought of logical science to the thinking of nonlogical entities. The essay argues that only by maintaining the rational autonomy of immanent categorial development can reality be conceived without falling into the complementary dilemmas of correspondence and coherence theories of truth.

A further support for overcoming foundations in conceiving reality is provided by the categorial analysis of "On Individuality." Drawing upon Hegel's ground-breaking theory of the relation of the universal, the particular, and the individual, the essay establishes how the universal and the particular cannot be conceived apart from individuality and how individuality cannot be determined independently of universality and particularity. This interconnection undermines the opposition of universal and individual commonly upheld by Platonism and nominalism, gives reason access to existence, and indicates how the dilemma of reconciling individual freedom and the common good is a false problem resting on the mistaken assumptions of ethical atomism.

Part II addresses the parallel issues underlying the legitimacy and structure of autonomous action. "Morality without Community" calls into question the contemporary dogma that utilitarianism, deontology, and communitarianism exhaust the three incompatible options from which ethical theory must choose. Contrary to the self-understandings of each of these positions, it is argued that utilitarianism and deontology capture different aspects of moral agency, which comprises a mode of autonomous interaction distinct from, yet reconcilable with, the institutions of ethical community. Once these are properly conceived as universal structures of freedom rather than particular givens of historical convention, the diversity of ethical life can be duly comprehended.

So long, however, as the liberal natural right conception of agency is retained as the exclusive model of freedom, the legitimacy of self-determination will remain problematic and the vision of liberation will suffer from the truncations analyzed in "The Injustice of Human Rights." By rooting rights in natural givens, the human rights conception both misconstrues the intersubjective character of self-determination and ends up reducing the scope of entitled freedoms to those of personhood and moral accountability, ignoring the institutional freedoms of ethical community, without reference to which a critique of modern regimes is sorely hobbled.

To advance beyond the incoherences of human rights, it is necessary to conceive self-determination not as something given by nature or defined in terms of an individual self, but as a self-ordered system of modes of free interaction of a plurality of agents. "Freedom as Interaction: Hegel's Resolution to the Dilemma of Liberal Theory" critiques the liberal reduction of freedom to a natural liberty of the individual and then develops the basic interactive structure of self-determination.

"Hegel and the Legitimation of Modernity" moves beyond the minimal interaction of freedom to outline the system of the structures of self-determination, following Hegel's treatment in his *Philosophy of Right*. The essay then examines, in light of Joachim Ritter's interpretation, how Hegel applies the concept of this system to evaluate the justice of modernity, focusing upon the relation between civil society and the state.

If conceiving the structures of self-determination comprising the system of justice provides the needed yardstick for evaluating modernity, it is equally true that the current state of social freedom cannot be understood without examining what is essential to commodity relations, capital, and their role in civil society. "The Dilemma of Labor" broaches this investigation by questioning the analyses of labor made by the young Marx and Habermas. Whereas both conceive labor in contrast to interaction as something either anthropologically or monologically defined, the essay argues that the laboring specific to markets and capital is not a form of instrumental action, but rather a component of a structure of interaction. Only when this is duly recognized can the nature of economic autonomy be understood.

"The Young Hegel and the Dialectic of Social Production" pursues the analysis of the interactive character of modern production in light of the social theory of the young Hegel and its interpretation by Georg Lukács. Although Hegel's early writings on commodity relations are marred by an inability to conceive of the economy within a civil society fully demarcated from the state, he does begin to introduce the categories with which a socially determined production process can be conceived, contrary to Lukács, who remains bound to the monological conception of the young Marx.

"The Logic of Marx's *Capital*" prepares the ground for a systematic conception of capital by investigating the categorial structure of Marx's analysis of capital in general. To this end, particular attention is paid to how categories from Hegel's *Logic* underlie Marx's argument.

"The Social Determination of the Labor Process from Hegel to Marx" investigates the way in which Marx's analysis of capital's labor process extends the interactive conception of production that Hegel introduces in his *Philosophy of Right*. The essay shows how Marx's argument in *Capital* and the *Grundrisse* moves beyond the monological and anthropological threatments of his early writings, though remaining marred by the retention of the labor theory of value.

"Hegel's Challenge to the Modern Economy" takes Hegel's analysis of civil society as a point of departure in order to rethink the problems of justice afflicting the modern economy. The essay shows how Hegel's analysis provides the conceptual tools for conceiving what is inherent in market relations and capital, grasping their universal structure instead of conflating it with particular historical forms that they have taken. Once this is done, the realization of economic autonomy can be properly posed, freed of the false reductions that have blinded the antagonists of left and right.

"Rethinking Politics: Carl Schmitt versus Hegel" extends the evaluation of modernity to the state by examining Schmitt's critique of liberalism and modern politics in view of Hegel's conception of political association. It is argued that, contrary to Schmitt, sovereignty does not reside in a friend-foe distinction or the power to declare and preside over emergency situations, and that democracy, parliamentarism, and constitutionality are not incompatible, but can be reconciled provided that civil society and the state are kept in the proper relationship.

The structure of self-determination constitutive of just political association may be, as "Rethinking Politics" argues, determined independently of the interaction of states, yet the theory of autonomous action would not be complete without a consideration of the normative principles governing international relations. "Political Freedom and Territorial Rights" addresses this topic by investigating the basis of territorial rights. Although the relationship between different states might seem similar to the state of nature of individuals as described by liberal theory, there are fundamental differences that call into question the application of liberal principles to international relations as well as the liberal application of atomism to domestic justice. It is argued, contrary to liberal theory, that the requirements of domestic self-government are the basis for territorial rights and that the rights of nations are accordingly relative to their domestic justice, rather than subject to any formal principles of equality.



# A Note on the Text

These essays were written between 1970 and 1990. Their publication details are listed below.

''The Method of Autonomous Reason,'' a slightly enlarged version of the essay ''The Method of Hegel's Science of Logic,'' published in *Essays On Hegel's Logic*, ed. by George di Giovanni (Albany, NY: SUNY Press, 1990), pp. 45–57.

''Is Systematic Logic a Transcendental Ontology?'' published under the title ''Is Hegel's Logic a Transcendental Ontology?'' *Man and World*, Vol. 20, No. 3 (August 1987), pp. 337–349.

''Conceiving Reality without Foundations'' published with the subtitle: ''Hegel's Neglected Strategy for *Realphilosophie*'' in *The Owl of Minerva*, Vol. 15, No. 2 (Spring 1984), pp. 183–198.

''Morality without Community,'' *Praxis International*, Vol. II, No. 1 (April 1991).

''The Injustice of Human Rights,'' *Philosophy and Social Criticism*, Vol. 9, No. 1 (1982), pp. 81–96.

''Freedom as Interaction: Hegel's Resolution to the Dilemma of Liberal Theory,'' in *Hegel's Theory of Action*, ed. by Lawrence S. Stepelevich and David Lamb (Atlantic Highlands, NJ: Humanities Press, 1983), pp. 173–190.

''Hegel and the Legitimation of Modernity,'' published in abbreviated form as the introduction, pp. 1–34, in my translation of Joachim Ritter's *Hegel and the French Revolution: Essays on the Philosophy of Right* (Cambridge, MA: MIT Press, 1982), and incorporating material published in ''The Legitimacy of Freedom and The Quest For Justice'' (*Social Concept*, Vol. 2, No. 1, September 1984, pp. 3–24).

"The Dilemma of Labor," *Telos*, No. 24 (Summer 1975), pp. 115–128.

"*The Young Hegel* and the Dialectic of Social Production," *Telos*, No. 26 (Winter 1975–1976), pp. 184–194.

"The Logic of Marx's *Capital*," a slightly revised version of the essay published under the same title in *Telos*, No. 27 (Spring 1976), pp. 111–139.

"The Social Determination of the Labor Process from Hegel to Marx," *The Philosophical Forum*, Vol. 11, No. 3 (Spring 1980), pp. 250–272.

"Hegel's Challenge to the Modern Economy," in both *History and System*, ed. by Robert L. Perkins (Albany: SUNY Press, 1984), pp. 219–253, and *Hegel on Freedom and Economics*, ed. by William Maker (Macon, GA: Mercer University Press, 1987), pp. 29–63.

"Rethinking Politics: Carl Schmitt versus Hegel," *The Owl of Minerva*, Vol. 22, No. 2 (Spring 1991), pp. 209–225.

"Political Freedom and Territorial Rights," an expanded version of the essay "Territorial Rights," in *The Territorial Rights of Nations and Peoples*, ed. by John R. Jacobson (Lewiston, NY: Edwin Mellen Press, 1989), pp. 187–210.

# Part I

# Autonomous Reason

# 1

# The Method of Autonomous Reason

The most vexing problem facing any reader of Hegel's *Science of Logic* is penetrating the method of its advance. Although Hegel continually intones the necessity of the passage from one category to the next, it is tempting to throw up one's hands and decry the arbitrariness of every move.

Hegel invites much of this frustration by failing to supply in advance a unitary doctrine of method. Instead he offers fragmentary accounts at different points along the way, accounts whose compatibility, let alone justification, is far from obvious.[1] Perhaps the most familiar of these is the introductory description of six general features of method, according to which (1) the form of logical development is in unity with its content; (2) the subject matter unfolds immanently, as a self-development; (3) the science proceeds by means of determinate negation; (4) the movement of categories is circular, such that the advance from the starting point is equally a regress towards the true ground on which the development rests; (5) the determination of categories is neither merely analytic nor synthetic, but both at once; and (6) the development has its own method as its final result.

Although these characterizations are first listed without much ado, Hegel does outline a dual strategy for confirming whether they are the fundamental features of valid method. This lies in the twin discussions that introduce the systematic argument of the *Science of Logic*. In the first, entitled "Notion of Logic in General," Hegel considers the nature of logic and examines what method must be adopted to permit logical science to achieve its aims. In the second, entitled "With What Must the Science Begin?" he analyzes how philosophy can be undertaken without being burdened by foundations. As Hegel shows, these problems have one and the same solution, whereby the discourse satisfying the demands of logic equally allows philosophy to overcome foundationalism. This convergence not only makes intelligible why Hegel calls that with which philosophy begins a "Science of Logic," but also provides the key arguments for judging the legitimacy of his descriptions of method.

Let us consider each converging path in turn.

## i) The Determination of Method out of the Demands of Logic

Logic consists in the thinking of thinking. Although logic may be called a formal science, in that it is not a thinking about particular objects of thought, Hegel aptly points out that logic has a subject matter all its own: the determination of thought.[2] For just this reason, the form of logic has a special relation to its content, setting logical science apart from other disciplines.

Since all other sciences conceive something other than thinking, the form in which their content is presented, namely, scientific thought, is different from their subject matter. Insofar as this leaves their method something that cannot be established within their own investigations, nonlogical sciences are compelled to take their method for granted, as something that must already be at hand in order for their investigations to proceed. However, because the method of nonlogical sciences must be determined independently of the investigation of their particular subject matters, having the method in hand does not bring with it any content. Hence, the subject matter other sciences address must equally be given by an acceptance of some concepts or other, since otherwise there would be no determinate content for their given method to address.[3]

In logic this distinction between form and content is overcome to the degree that logic consists in the thinking of thinking, or self-thinking thought. Whereas in other inquires form and content fall asunder, the form and content of logical science appear to be one and the same: thinking that thinks itself.

In this respect, logic proceeds upon the overcoming of the distinction of consciousness that Hegel claims is the prerequisite for systematic philosophy.[4] This distinction, whose overcoming is purportedly achieved by the *Phenomenology of Spirit*'s immanent critique of consciousness's foundational knowing,[5] consists in the differentiation of knowing from its object, where the standard of truth resides in the independent given comprising knowing's referent. If in logic the object of inquiry, pure thought (that is, thought that thinks itself), is indistinguishable from the thinking cognition in which logic engages, then logical science will lack the appeal to independent givens constitutive of the representational framework of consciousness. Given how the thoughts of logic refer to nothing but themselves, there can be no question of logic seeking their truth in some distinct criteria. For just this reason there is nothing logical at hand to refer to until logical thinking has gotten under way. Since this eliminates any possibility of drawing a distinction between reference and referent, logical thought is nonrepresentational, lacking the constitutive distinction defining representational cognition.

Hence, if the method of logic is the ordering of the content of logic, then the logical method will be at one with what it presents, in expression of the unity of form and content in logic. Because of this underlying unity, the methodological form of the thinking of thinking is only established in the determination of what thinking is by and within logical science. Consequently, the method of logic will not be conceivable apart from the content it orders. If anything like a doctrine of logical method were to be sought, it could only be obtained from the completed development of logic's subject matter. Since the logical unfolding of thought presents what is at one with its mode of presentation, only with completion of logic is the form in which thinking is thought fully at hand. Instead of being given at the start, as something distinct and independent of its topic, the method of logic can only be determinable as a result of the full exposition of the content logic presents.

This allows logical science to make an absolute beginning, avoiding the dependence upon a given method and content characterizing other sciences. Because the unity of form and content in logic prevents logical method from having its proper determination prior to the completed exposition of the content of logical thought, logic begins without any antecedently determined method. Similarly, since what logic is about has no independent being apart from logical thought, logic begins without any antecedently determined subject matter. By contrast, other sciences cannot make an absolute beginning. Because what they address is different from their theorizing, the form of their theorizing can no more provide the content it addresses than the subject matter examined can provide the form of its own theoretical presentation. As a result, the subject matter of other sciences must be independently given at the outset in order to be available, just as their method must be independently determined apart from thinking the subject matter of their particular science.[6] Logic, by contrast, begins absolutely in the sense that neither its content nor its method has any given character at the outset of logical investigation. Not before and outside but only in and through its thinking of thinking do logic's unitary topic and procedure get determined.

As a consequence, logic must proceed immanently, as a self-development. Since it has no given form or content, logic must generate its own subject matter and ordering, unless external interventions supply it with either along the way. The latter option, however, is ruled out by the unity of form and content defining logic's thinking of thinking. If any terms were externally introduced or externally ordered, the thought under examination would no longer be undertaking its own investigation. Instead, the train of logical thought would be broken and destroyed by a thinking that determines the content and/or order of the science yet stands outside its purview. To escape this outcome, logic must have an immanent development, where both what is thought and how it is thought are determined by nothing but the course of logical thinking itself. Insofar as logic develops a thinking that thinks itself, its development cannot fail to be immanent, for it is nothing but a self-development, where what is presented provides its own exposition.

It follows that logic is circular in the sense that each advance represents a regress towards the ground on which the whole development rests. As a self-development uniting form and content, logical thinking only arrives at the completed determination of both what is under way developing itself and the order of its exposition at the conclusion of its working. Only then is the subject matter of the development determined, just as only then is the ordering principle or method of the advance at hand. As we have seen, both are what they are only as results of the development leading to and constituting them. Since the preceding development is nothing more than the succession of stages by which logical thought both constitutes and orders itself, each advance is a move towards the ground that determines and contains the prior stages as what they are: elements in the self-constitution of logical thought. This ground is, of course, the totality of logic, which only arises as a result of the completed development.

Hence, logic is not caught in a holism of coherence, where the truth of each category is defined in terms of the given totality within which it resides. Nor is logical thought involved in rebuilding the ship in which it is already afloat. In either case, the content of logic would be determined by a framework encompassing and lying beyond it, leaving categories always determined by something falling outside them all. This would once again disrupt the unity of form and content because the determining of logic would not reside in its own exposition but in an external context that could never become subject to logical investigation, since it would always be presupposed by any logical thought.

Logical thought escapes the dilemmas of holism because the whole to which the categories belong is not something given at the outset of the development, providing an omnipresent determining context, but rather a result that only contains and orders them at the end of its self-development. On the one hand, the totality that proves itself to be the ground of the preceding development can be completely transparent to logical thought, for it is precisely what that development has consisted of thinking through. On the other hand, this totality is not some irreducible given that thought must accept as its unquestionable foundation. Because logical thought arrives at the conception of this totality without submitting its labors to any external guide, this resultant whole is not an ungrounded assumption. On the contrary, it owes every aspect of itself to the development leading to it. However, because this development is the self-constitution of self-thinking thought in its entirety, neither resting on anything else nor following any foreign principle, the totality of logical thought is self-grounding, mediated by nothing but its own unfolding.

Hence, the pure thought of logic is just as much unmediated as mediated. It is unmediated to the extent that, as a whole, nothing else determines it. On the other hand, it is equally mediated, since, instead of being given, in the manner of a static form that requires an independent thinker to posit it and relate it to others, self-thinking thought is what it is only through the mediation of the categorial development of logic.

Similarly, logical thought is at once analytic and synthetic. The self-thinking of thought is analytic insofar as every logical category is contained in the resultant totality comprising both the ordering principle and subject of logical science. At the same time, self-thinking thought is synthetic in that each new category is not contained in those that precede it. If it were, the order and content of the ensuing development would already be given in the first category, rendering the method and topic of logic matters that logical science must take for granted rather than establish. Self-thinking thought is able to avoid presupposing both, and thereby retain a synthetic dimension, precisely because its pure thinking arrives at a complete determination of its method and subject matter only as the result of its labors. This equally allows self-thinking thought to retain an analytic dimension because, in arriving at its method and content, it incorporates the entire preceding development.

Finally, in following an advance no less analytic than synthetic, self-thinking thought can be said to proceed by means of determinate negation. Insofar as each successive category supplants its predecessor with a nonderivative content, it negates what precedes it. Yet, to the degree that it equally incorporates its predecessors as constitutive elements of its nonderivative determination, its negation of its predecessor is determinate, in that the otherness it opposes to the former is equally determined in reference to it. Since each successive category leading to the final totality of self-thinking thought undergoes this dual negation and incorporation by what follows it, logical development can thus be described as being ordered by determinate negation.

This might suggest that logic is subject to a formal ordering principle distinct from its content of self-thinking thought. However, the prior analysis of how determinate negation rests on the equally analytic and synthetic character of the advance should indicate that this unity of form and content is the very precondition for determinate negation playing any role. In effect, because determinate negation ties how categories succeed one another to what they are, it is an ordering principle that cannot be detached from a development where form and content are thoroughly intertwined.[7]

### ii) Pure Thought and Prescriptive Logic

All these ramifications of the demands of logic very neatly correspond to the six features cited in Hegel's first account of the method of his *Science of Logic*. But do they really follow from the concept of logic itself? After all, many different types of logic have been pursued. Some are merely descriptive, restricted to describing how thought in general has factually operated, whereas others are prescriptive, seeking to prescribe how valid thought should proceed. And within this broad division, logics have been developed that are formal, transcendental, or dialectical. Although in every case logic involves a thinking about thinking, it is far from true that the thinking each logic engages in is identical to the thinking it is describing or prescribing.

In fact, formal logic and transcendental logic, to take the most widely practiced types, cannot possibly achieve a unity of form and content. The rules of inference that formal logic provides as the canon of thought cannot be described or prescribed by their own laws of entailment. Formal logic cannot practice what it preaches, both because all entailment ultimately proceeds from some indemonstrable given premise, which accordingly can only be known by some nondemonstrative knowing, and because establishing rules of inference by means of themselves would beg the question. Similarly, transcendental logic cannot transcendentally constitute its own transcendental arguments. Because transcendental logic seeks to determine some privileged structure comprising the prior conditions by which objectivity is known, transcendental logic must always define those structures directly rather than conceive them as determined by themselves like all other objects of knowledge. If it tried the latter route, it would either have to take what they are for granted or transform them into self-determined structures, eliminating the distinction between knowing and its object that first allows for the conditions of knowledge to be examined prior to an examination of particular objects of knowledge.[8]

However, if an identity of form and content is not and cannot be achieved by formal and transcendental logics, this does not mean that it is not entailed by the concept of logic, understood as a prescriptive science of valid thought. For if logic is taken to be a science concerned, not with describing how individuals think, but with prescribing how they should think, then logic will itself be valid only if what it establishes as the logic of valid thought is equally the logic ordering its own investigation. If, on the contrary, the thinking logic employs is not one with the logic of valid thought it presents, the exposition of thought by logic will not be valid. In other words, logical science cannot be valid unless it achieves a unity of form and content. Since such a unity escapes every effort of formal and transcendental logics, it follows that they can never successfully prescribe how we should think.

A true science of logic, however, must exhibit all the ramifications of this unity that have so far been discussed. First, since a properly prescriptive logic aims at establishing what valid thinking is, its own method cannot be taken for granted at the start. Instead, it falls within the science of logical investigation, comprising none other than its ultimate subject matter. Since the method of logic is therefore at once the form and content of its investigation, logical science must begin with no antecedently given method or subject matter. If either just its method or just its content were given, the offered candidate of valid thought would differ from its exposition, undermining the legitimacy of each. If, on the other hand, both its method and subject matter were antecedently determined, the science of logic would accomplish nothing in its own right, leaving the putative form and content of valid thinking arbitrary assumptions, postulated outside of scientific investigation. To be worthy of the name, logical science must rather arrive at both its method and subject matter as a result of its own labors. Hence, the very concept of prescriptive logic does indeed entail that it begin absolutely, without any preconception of its form or content, establishing its own method and subject matter at the very end of its investigation, at which point it completes what could best be called its self-exposition of valid thinking.

It might well seem paradoxical that the idea of prescriptive logic could entail a development of thought whose theme and ordering are yet totally free of determination by any antecedent, independently given principle. How can a logic whose form and content must have no prior determination be entailed by anything at all? The paradox disappears once it is recognized that the concept of prescriptive logic has no further positive filling apart from the preconception-free conceptual development that alone can bring it to realization, or, more properly speaking, to self-realization. This recognition need not be at hand in order to legitimate the science of logic. Rather, it is something the science itself establishes at its end by fully determining the idea of prescriptive logic and demonstrating that it is an idea that determines itself.

These considerations of the demands inherent in logic thus give support to Hegel's claims that the form of logical development is in unity with its content, that the science of logic consists in an immanent self-development, that it exhibits determinate negation and is equally analytic and synthetic, and that its movement of categories takes the form of a circle, where every advance is a retreat to the ultimate ground having the determination of method as its final result.

Let us grant that these strictures of method are all necessary fulfillments of the demands of logical science. Are they, however, methodological features, not just of logic, but of philosophical thought in general? As Hegel makes clear in his other introductory discussion, "With What Must the Science Begin?" the *Science of Logic* is concerned not just with bringing logic to completion but with allowing philosophy per se to achieve its constitutive aims. Do philosophy's requirements entail the very same methodological prescriptions inherent in logical science?

### iii) The Method of Philosophy as the Method of Logic

In asking, with what must the science of philosophy begin?, Hegel ponders how philosophy can overcome foundationalism, that is, begin without presuppositions and achieve the complete theoretical self-responsibility that philosophical thought needs to rise above doxology. The challenge is twofold. Negatively speaking, philosophy must liberate itself from reliance upon dogmatic givens, be they contents or procedures that have not already been established within and by philosophical investigation. Positively speaking, philosophy must ground itself, legitimating its subject matter and method by its own means alone. These demands are two sides of the same coin, for in order to proceed without foundations, philosophy must independently establish all its own terms and method, just as to be self-grounding and self-justifying, philosophy must be thoroughly free of foundations.

If we examine these dual requirements in light of Hegel's analysis of the starting point of philosophical discourse, we find two coordinate features. On the one hand, to proceed without foundations, philosophy must start with no givens, since to start with any determinate content or method involves presuppositions whose legitimacy has not been established within philosophy. Hence, philosophy can only begin with indeterminacy or being, signifying the exclusion of any assumptions concerning either the subject matter or procedure of philosophy.

On the other hand, if philosophy is to proceed from indeterminacy and ground itself, its conceptual development must be self-determining. Since the content philosophy presents cannot derive from any source other than what philosophical thinking sanctions and since the method by which its content is ordered must equally be established by philosophy, both what and how philosophy thinks must be determined in and through philosophical thought. Hence, philosophical reason must be genuinely autonomous, achieving not just the negative freedom of liberty from external ordering but also the positive freedom of self-determination.

Taking these coordinate features together, whereby philosophy starts with indeterminacy and then exhibits self-determination, it follows that philosophy will commence by presenting nothing but self-determination per se, which, it should already be clear, amounts to the logic of self-grounding. Because philosophy must begin with indeterminacy, its ensuing self-determination cannot be the self-determination of some further substrate, such as any independently given notions of reality or thought. If it were, philosophy would rest upon prephilosophical assumptions and fail to achieve either its negative freedom of presuppositionlessness or its positive freedom of self-grounding. Hence, the very autonomy of reason requires that it proceed from indeterminacy rather than from any determinate foundation. Little else could be expected, given how what is genuinely self-determined has no determination prior to what it determines itself to be.

Granted that the answer to how philosophy must begin is that philosophical reason starts with indeterminacy and presents self-determination per se, it remains to be shown how this dual prescription entails the six features of Hegel's introductory account of method.

To begin with, does it entail a unity of form and content? Is foundation-free discourse, proceeding from indeterminacy and presenting the logic of self-determination or self-grounding, a conceptual development whose content and ordering coincide? Hegel suggests as much in observing how philosophers had first considered the principle of philosophy as if it merely concerned what content should be conceived but had now recognized that the act of knowing was essential to truth, requiring the method of philosophy to be united with its content and its form united with its principle, so that what is first for thinking also be first in the path of thinking.[9] If philosophy begins with indeterminacy to be free of foundations and to provide the only admissible commencement for a development determined by nothing but itself, then, indeed, the indeterminate content with which philosophy begins is equally indeterminate in form, insofar as no determinate method can already be operative. Hence, contra Kierkegaard,[10] the beginning not only begins with immediacy but begins immediately.[11]

Moreover, insofar as what proceeds from indeterminacy is and can only be self-determination per se, its ordering is a self-ordering, where the succession of categories is equally rooted in what they present. Hence, the content of the ensuing development just as much determines the form of its own presentation as its ordering is inseparable from its content. Since what is being determined is self-determination per se, how it is being determined is identical to what it is. If, on the contrary, the form of exposition were distinct from its content, the content would be ordered by something else, undermining its self-determined character, just as the determining principle of the content would not longer coincide with the identity or "self" of the latter, as self-determination requires.

If this suggests how the demands of philosophy entail the same unity of form and content required by logic, it equally entails that the method emerge as the final term of philosophy's initial undertaking. The ordering principle or method of self-determination per se consists in nothing less than the "self" or subject matter that is under way determining itself. Consequently, the ordering of what philosophy first presents is not at hand until self-determination has completed its own development, at once establishing what it is and how it is determined. As the unity of form and content already implies, only when the content of self-determination has constituted itself is its form or method equally established.

This means that philosophical discourse, like logic, will proceed immanently as a self-development whose every advance is equally a retreat towards its ground. Insofar as philosophy must begin with indeterminacy and offer self-determination per se, it consists in a self-development whereby the subject matter provides for its own exposition, generating its own content and ordering. In order for this to occur, each new determination must be incorporated into the self-constitution of the subject matter whose self-determination is under way. Otherwise, the connection between terms would depend upon something outside their development. Since what each new determination is a determination of is only established at the end of the development, every advance beyond the indeterminate beginning represents a closing in on the whole that will end up containing every preceding determination as an element in its own constitution. Thus, although the resulting whole is not a given foundation, antecedently underlying the development, it turns out to be the ground supporting each category, providing the sole basis for determining of what they are part.

This allows the ensuing movement to be analytic and synthetic at once. As was the case with logic's self-thinking of thought, here each advance is synthetic by presenting something not already contained in what precedes it, yet analytic insofar as it provides nothing that is not contained within the whole that is in the process of determining itself.

Similarly, the development could be said to proceed by determinate negation. Each new term does represent a negation of what proceeds it because it has an irreducible otherness. If it lacked that element and were merely contained in its predecessor, the movement would not be self-determining but would instead be determined by contents given prior to the ensuing development. However, because each term ends up integrated within the whole of self-determined determinacy, the otherness differentiating the terms from their predecessors equally incorporates the former terms as constitutive elements of the determination under way. Consequently, each term arises through a determinate negation, negating the preceding term by comprising something other to it yet incorporating this predecessor as an element of its own determination.

In sum, then, the requirements of philosophy in general entail the same methodological prescriptions that are required by logic. As we have seen, if logic is to achieve its constitutive goals, it must achieve precisely what philosophy turns out to demand. In fact, the self-thinking thought that logic should comprise is identical to the presuppositionless self-determined discourse to which philosophy must aspire. This is why Hegel has good reason to call the discourse with which philosophy must begin a science of logic and to introduce it with parallel discussions of the methodological problems of logic and of philosophy in general. Perhaps their convergence also gives us good reason to endure our frustrations and buckle down to the toils of speculative thought.

## Notes

1. The first of these accounts, scattered in the two introductory discussions, "General Notion of Logic" and "With What Must Science Begin?" lists general features that apply throughout the method's application. A second account, surfacing in the remarks preceding the Logics of Being, of Essence, and of The Concept, describes how each section has its own manner of advance, suggesting that the method operates differently in each logical sphere. Finally, Hegel provides a third account at the very end of the Logic, where he first addresses the method in a self-consciously systematic fashion as a topic falling within logic under the heading of the Absolute Idea. This final analysis describes a three-stage method, unrelated to the division into logics of being, essence, and the concept, that hardly seems to correspond to either of the two earlier accounts.

2. G.W.F. Hegel *Wissenschaft der Logik*, ed. by Georg Lasson (Hamburg: Felix Meiner Verlag, 1975), Vol. 1, p. 23.

3. *Ibid.*, Vol. 1, p. 23.

4. *Ibid.*, Vol. 1, p. 30.

5. *Ibid.*, Vol. 1, p. 30.

6. *Ibid.*, Vol. 1, p. 23.

7. This is largely what Hegel's analysis of the method in the Absolute Idea demonstrates when it shows how the determinate negation by which logic advances expands into the whole system of logical determination.

8. For a more detailed discussion of this problem, see Richard Dien Winfield, *Reason and Justice* (Albany, NY: SUNY Press, 1988), Chapter 3.

9. Hegel, *op. cit.*, Vol. 1, p. 52.

10. Soren Kierkegaard, *Concluding Unscientific Postscript* (Princeton, NJ: Princeton University Press, 1974), pp. 101–102.

11. For a discussion of why this immediacy is not disrupted by the mediation of the *Phenomenology of Spirit*, see Richard Dien Winfield, "The Route to Foundation-Free Systematic Philosophy," *Philosophical Forum*, Vol. 15, No. 3 (Spring 1984), p. 337ff.

# 2

# The Ordeal of Self-Critical Critical Philosophy: Reflections on Husserl and Wittgenstein

Since Kant, transcendental philosophers have grappled with the problem of accounting for the possibility of transcendental knowledge. Calling into question the dogmatic assumption of the correspondence of knowing and its objects, refraining from making immediate reference to what is true and instead investigating the conditions by which objectivity is construed as a necessary preliminary for making knowledge claims of any sort, critical philosophers have had to face the question of by what right they can know the transcendental conditions of knowing and certify the privileged role and the particular description they ascribe to them. Although Kant notoriously ignores this issue, subsequent thinkers have been more self-critical. Of those who refuse to revert to dogmatism but see no other alternative than transcendental philosophy, Husserl and Wittgenstein stand out for pioneering the two options between which a self-critical critical philosophy must choose.

Unlike Kant, Husserl is acutely aware that all reference to the transcendental conditions of knowing must be accounted for in the same way that all other knowledge claims are established: not by immediate reference to what is assumed to be given, but through a transcendental constitution, identifying the cognitive acts by which the object of knowing is determined to be what it is for the knowing that addresses it. Whereas Kant limits his analysis of transcendental constitution to the synthesizing processes by which empirical objects are given to experience, regulative ideas are given to theoretical reason, ethical laws are given to practical reason, and aesthetic and teleological ideas are given to judgment, Husserl extends transcendental constitution to the conditions of knowing themselves. However, in so doing, Husserl retains the distinction between constituting act and constituted object of knowledge. That distinction is basic to transcendental investigation, since without it the conditions of knowing could not be investigated apart from making knowledge claims about an object. Consequently, when Husserl reflects upon how the transcendental conditions are themselves given to knowing and attempts to specify the acts by which these conditions are themselves constituted, he must admit that whatever constituting acts are identified must themselves be subject to a further reflection that seeks to identify the acts making the former possible as objects of knowledge. Yet, because at each stage of constitution the constituting act, as object of reflection, is something different from the act constituting it, it is impossible to ever account for the ultimate determining condition of knowing. Every time a consituting act is uncovered, its own givenness as an object of discourse depends upon a further constituting act that has yet to be made thematic. As Husserl acknowledges, transcendental investigation remains an infinite task, condemned to a striving that can never consummate itself and achieve the thorough self-responsibility to which transcendental phenomenology aspires. Although Husserl accepts this outcome as inescapable, it provides a lesson that suggests an alternative. Husserl's self-critical turn indicates that so long as the conditions of knowing remain irrevocably separated from the objects of knowing, transcendental inquiry arrives at an impasse. This suggests abandoning the distinction between transcendental knowledge and the knowing it investigates, a distinction that not only divides knowing into two irreconcilable levels but equally introduces two incommensurate fields to be known: the domain of transcendental conditions and that of the objects they structure.

Wittgenstein's later writings represent an attempt to achieve such a solution without abandoning transcendental argument. Whereas Husserl seeks to account for his knowledge of the transcendental conditions by a reflection retaining the distinction between constitued object and constituting act, Wittgenstein removes the barrier between the two. He does so by characterizing the determining conditions of objectivity as actual linguistic practices, identifying them as language games that, as such, are historically given, particular conventions, knowledge of which can be neither a priori nor necessary. Just as these conditions of discourse are as empirically given as the objects they determine, so knowledge of them is of no other character than the knowledge of the objects they make possible. In this way, Wittgenstein may be seen to escape the uncritical residue of Kantian transcendental philosophy, which made knowledge claims about transcendental conditions even though those conditions were excluded from the domain of objects of experience to which knowledge was equally limited. Whereas this exclusion left transcendental knowledge inexplicable and rendered the transcendental conditions equivalent to things in themselves, Wittgenstein's construal of the conditions of objectivity as actual language games sets them within the same horizon to which empirical knowledge applies. Consequently, Wittgenstein can presumably reflect upon language games without falling into the infinite striving that paralyzes Husserl's attempt to make transcendental argument self-critical.

Yet has Wittgenstein really escaped the difficulties of Kant and Husserl? From the Kantian and Husserlian points of view, Wittgenstein's gambit of treating the transcendental conditions as actual practices would well be denounced as a regression to dogmatism and psychologism, respectively. Wittgenstein would be held to have committed the fatal blunder of describing the conditions of objectivity in objectlike terms, thereby employing precisely what are in need of an account as elements of the conditions that are to provide their basis. It is to escape this very problem that Kant distinguishes the processes of transcendental synthesis from any empirically given physiological, psychological, linguistic, or otherwise objective phenomena, just as Husserl demarcates the acts of transcendental constitution from any actual activities falling within the horizon of constituted objects. Both are aware that if they fail to uphold this divide between the conditions of knowing and known phenomena they will have either made direct, metaphysical reference to the transcendental conditions, describing them as immediately given things, or fallen into the vicious circularity of describing the conditions of knowing by means of what these conditions alone supposedly make possible. In Wittgenstein's case this signifies that if language games are actual conventions, whose particular character is neither a priori nor necessary, then they cannot play the constitutive role they are assigned. This would be precluded since their own specification falls within an already given horizon, which, if it is constituted by any prior condition, must be constituted by something other than what that horizon contains.

Such criticism provides at most a very Pyrrhic victory, for if Wittgenstein's gambit of eliminating the divide between transcendental and non-transcendental knowledge is repudiated, transcendental philosophers find themselves back in the same dilemma that gave rise to Wittgenstein's strategy in the first place. If the transcendental conditions are not to have any objectlike character yet are still determinate, their specification becomes an enigma. It introduces an entity, the transcendental structure and its processes, lying beyond the horizon of known objects and about which every claim is a product of direct reference from a standpoint of transcendental knowing whose authority defies explanation. In a word, simply by making any determinate claims about the transcendental conditions of knowing, Kant and Husserl fall into the same problems of dogmatic reference and psychologism that they denounce.

Self-critical critical philosophy thereby offers the spectacle of an oscillation between the Scylla and Charybdis of an infinite series of self-reflective constitutions and an appeal to practices whose objectlike characterization ill suits the privileged role they are ascribed. Wittgenstein may well be the more self-critical thinker for recognizing how transcendental argument has no right to refer to unworldly conditions of knowing and assign them an a priori and necessary status. Yet, in bringing the conditions of reference down to earth,

Wittgenstein needs to ask himself how he has access to what language games are themselves and by what right he can assign them their privileged role. Although the move to eliminate the gulf between transcendental conditions and objects of reference is intended to circumvent such reflections, it does not reduce philosophy to silence and assign all questions about language games to empirical reportage. Wittgenstein may plead ignorance of any philosophical knowledge of the particular content of specific language games because it always resides in a given practice, whose conventions, like those of any game, are arbitrary. Yet he still makes universal claims about them in general and about the corresponding context-dependency of discourse. In particular, he continually advances two correlative theses: (1) that all justification ultimately rests upon groundless activities that posit ultimate yet arbitrary standards of adjudication, and (2) that language games, identified as just such groundless practices, thereby not only determine the conventional meaning of the terms they encompass but further determine what counts as true or false employment of these terms. In other words, Wittgenstein presumes that all discourse is foundational and thereby arbitrarily grounded, and that this is so precisely because language games function as transcendental conditions of knowledge. If these claims are made independently of any language games, then they violate the very idea of knowledge that Wittgenstein is advocating. If, however, they issue from a further language game, then they rest upon a particular, given practice whose very contingency makes their authority purely local and fleeting.

To escape such puzzles, Wittgenstein may, and of course does, deny possessing any general knowledge of language games, claiming that we never have direct reference to them insofar as they are always already at work in any reflection we make. This, however, is a universal, incorrigible claim in its own right. Moreover, it only reintroduces the infinite regress into which Husserl fell, where the underlying structure by which objectivity is construed is an object of reference, yet always beyond reach, like some thing in itself.

If this does not silence philosophy, it does suggest that whichever option is followed, self-critical critical philosophy is not, and cannot be, self-critical enough.

# 3

# Is Systematic Logic a Transcendental Ontology?*

With post-analytic philosophy sounding the tocsin for foundationalism, Hegel's project of a systematic philosophy without foundations has attracted renewed attention as an alternative to the edifying deconstruction sweeping the academy. Alan White's *Absolute Knowledge: Hegel and The Problem of Metaphysics* represents a timely contribution to this latest turn to Hegel. What distinguishes White's book from much other Hegel scholarship is its concentration upon the focal issues that make or break Hegel's attempt to escape foundationalism without relinquishing philosophy's traditional quest for truth.

White organizes his study as a dialogue between Schelling and Hegel, where White presents Schelling's critique of Hegel's system and then shows how this critique can be parried if and only if Hegel be interpreted as a transcendental ontologist. There are two reasons for why the controversy between Schelling and Hegel is of utmost contemporary interest. First, Schelling's criticisms raise all the central issues on which the Hegelian project rests. Thus it is no surprise that Schelling's critique contains virtually every objection that has subsequently been made against Hegel's effort to develop a foundation-free systematic philosophy. Secondly, the opposition between Schelling and Hegel presents a theoretical divide, which, in our 'post-foundationalist' age, may well offer the two remaining routes for philosophical investigation.

Schellings' critique focuses upon Hegel's *Science of Logic*, and the three themes that have always raised the most questions: 1. the character of the logical beginning, 2. the nature of the logical development following from the initial category of being, and 3. the conclusion of logic with its transition to the concept of nature. As White documents, Schelling's scrutiny of these problem areas involves a twofold critique. On the one hand, Schelling maintains that Hegel violates his own tenets in dealing with each of these three issues. On the other hand, Schelling argues that even if one could correct Hegel's inconsistencies and carry through the Hegelian project, it would still fail to meet the fundamental demands of philosophy.

In order to assess White's own resolution of the Hegel-Schelling controversy, it is worth turning to each of these three matters of debate.

### i) The Starting Point of Logic

Hegel, as is well known, characterizes the starting point of philosophical investigation in a dual way: (1) as a presuppositionless beginning that must start with indeterminacy or being in order to refrain from making any assumptions about method or content, and (2) as the starting point of logic, which, in so far as logic is self-thinking thought, must begin such that what comes first in thinking is equally what is first for thought.

In acknowledging both these characterizations, White adds a third, that what Hegel launches in his *Science of Logic* is a first philosophy, i.e. metaphysics, whose task is to ground itself and all other fields of knowledge. Although White regards Hegel to be the last thinker to advocate a first philosophy or metaphysics, instead of mathematics or physics, as the ground of all other theoretical endeavor,(1) this does not deprive Hegel's thought of contemporary significance. As White maintains, there remains a need for first philosophy in so far as the methods of physics and mathematics can neither be deductively or empirically established, and in so far as abandoning metaphysics is tantamount to admitting that our knowledge of facts and values cannot be rationally grounded.(3) The question is whether or not Hegel's version of metaphysics, namely, his *Science of Logic*, is capable of fulfilling its self-grounding role as first philosophy. White's fundamental claim is that only if Hegel's *Logic* is interpreted as a transcendental ontology, can it succeed as first philosophy. On this interpretation, the Logic would be ontological, rather than theological, by comprising a doctrine of categories rather than one of supersensible entities, and transcendental by presenting the conditions of the possibility of experience.(6)

These interpretative claims leave us with two questions: do Hegel's own characterizations of the Logic's starting point conform to White's understanding, and is Schelling's critique of Hegel's starting point disarmed by White's Hegel interpretation?

What then are Schelling's criticisms of Hegel's starting point? Contrary to Hegel's claim of beginning presuppositionlessly, Schelling argues that the *Logic*'s starting point is actually conditioned in three ways: (1) by Hegel's assumption that philosophy is a science of essences, concerning the what, not the that of things, (2) by the unacknowledged presence of the thinking subject, and (3) by the experiential and intellectual capacities making possible the very thinking of the *Logic*.(24) In regard to the first point, Schelling maintains that Hegel offers no more justification for excluding problems of existence from his system, than for why the absolute is found in and by pure thought. These remain unargued assumptions from beginning to end.(16) As for the second two points, Schelling argues that it makes no sense for a science of concepts to come first in a system of philosophy. Since concepts exist only for consciousness, Schelling holds that the development of consciousness out of nature should be analyzed prior to any consideration of concepts. Hence, the subject must be posited at the beginning. Although Hegel refuses to acknowledge the subject's presence, the Logic's beginning is actually a constructed one, dependent upon the abstracting of the logician.(18) For this reason, not only is the beginning arbitrary, but it is nonsensical to regard it as the starting point of a self-moving development of thought. The latter is precluded, since any exposition of concepts always presupposes the subject who thinks them, the concepts themselves, and the laws of logic by which they are interrelated. Consequently, no system of categories can be presuppositionless. Hegel's own claim to presuppositionlessness presupposes the concept of presupposition, as well as language, and every other condition underlying his thought. Hence, Schelling concludes, philosophy is actually the science that presupposes everything.(19)

White attempts to answer all three of these objections in Hegel's behalf. He dismisses the first objection, that the Logic is conditioned by Hegel's assumption that philosophy is a science of essences, by arguing that Schelling fails to take into account the mediating role of the *Phenomenology of Spirit*. Once the logical beginning is understood to be phenomenologically mediated, White maintains, it can appear in advance as the only possible beginning for philosophy as science, while still not resting on a presupposition about the nature of philosophy.(24) This anticipatory suitability of the logical beginning does not confirm it as the starting point of a successful absolute science. The latter confirmation can occur only at the end of the system when the logical beginning can be retrospectively grasped as that from which the whole system develops.(25) Nevertheless, the *Phenomenology* serves to introduce the logical beginning as an unavoidable starting point without providing a preconception of philosophy undermining the presuppositionlessness that the category of being is supposed to enjoy.

How this can be accomplished is something that White accounts for by offering a capsule interpretation of the *Phenomenology*. In the *Phenomenology*, White maintains, the phenomenologist, the reader, considers successive knowledge claims made by natural consciousness, i.e. the human subject. The process ends when a stance is reached where the phenomenologist confirms that the subject knows what it claims to know. This comprises the standpoint of pure or absolute knowledge, where the subject knows that the absolute is truly articulated in thought that succeeds in thinking itself. In this fashion, the *Phenomenology* leads its reader to the standpoint at which absolute knowledge is possible. However, White argues, the *Phenomenology* does not include that knowledge. Rather, the account of the absolute itself is given in the *Logic* and further developed in the systematic sciences of nature and spirit.(22–23) Although White asserts that the *Phenomenology* is only one among many possible introductions, it is the only one that is scientifically structured and that provides presystematic proof that Hegel's standpoint of pure knowing is absolute. What allows the *Phenomenology's* introduction to operate without counting as a presupposition is that the start with being remains what comes first in the course of the logical thinking of pure concepts.

Does White's account really remove Schelling's objection or conform to Hegel's own argument? Like many Hegel interpreters, White regards the concluding shape of consciousness described in the *Phenomenology* to be a determinate standpoint which has privileged access to the absolute by realizing the identity of thought and being. Although White maintains that reaching this standpoint does not already involve the thinking of the absolute that self-thinking thought supposedly entails, the very fact that such a standpoint is identified as the standpoint of logic predetermines the logical beginning in a dual way: as the first thought of a given absolute standpoint of self-thinking thought and equally as the first determination of the absolute. If the logical beginning is to have this character, then Schelling is quite right to charge Hegel with loading his starting point with added determinations that are not already argued for within the systematic science that is about to get underway. White wishes to dispel this objection by maintaining that the *Phenomenology* provides proof of these qualifications even though its proof is presystematic. What knowledge, however, can a presystematic proof pretend to establish, if, as White himself maintains, *Logic* is to provide the system of categories on which the validity of all positive theory depends? What White has inadvertently shown is that so long as the *Phenomenology* is interpreted as a doctrine of knowing, establishing a privileged determinate standpoint from which knowledge of the absolute is immediately accessible, Hegel's *Logic* cannot be defended from Schelling's critique.

Does this failure signify the collapse of the Hegelian project? Hegel himself provides us with ample resources to escape Schelling's objection. First of all, Hegel does not present the concluding shape of consciousness described in the *Phenomenology* as a determinate standpoint from which knowledge of the absolute is at hand. On the contrary, what he there describes is the collapse of the foundational project which takes consciousness as the determining structure of all knowledge claims, accepting the representational model of knowing where some given always counts as the standard of truth. What Hegel attempts to show is that representational knowing can never succeed in grounding its truth claims, and that when consciousness finally comes to consider how its constitutive appeal to givens is ultimately its own arbitrary posit, the whole structure of reference on which it depends gets eliminated. In arriving at this result, the *Phenomenology* does not leave us with any positive preconception of systematic science, but only testimony to how foundational knowing undermines itself when it becomes self-reflective. This phenomenological mediation of Logic undermines Schelling's critique, for it leaves the logical beginning saddled with neither any determinate standpoint nor any reference to the absolute. Although Schelling maintains that the category of being already involves reference to the essence of things, it would be more accurate to observe that being simply presents the sheer indeterminacy that results when all foundational claims are laid aside and nothing is assumed regarding method or subject matter. Once this is understood, the logical starting point no longer stands immersed within an antecedently assumed framework of reference. White's interpretation of the *Phenomenology*, on the contrary, sets the logical beginning in relation to the absolute, as if the category of being were a thought determination about the most elementary feature of reality. When this is done, it is impossible for the development of categories to avoid presupposing the conceptual scheme in which concepts figure as determinations of the absolute.

White's dismissal of Schelling's second objection, that the subject must be the starting point of philosophical argument, is more felicitous. To begin with, Hegel's *Logic* does not comprise a pre-Kantian metaphysics in which thought is derived from non-thought, since from the outset the development of categories remains within the element of thought.(25) However, this does not mean that the subject of thought must be the first logical category, since, as Hegel maintains, the category of subject is intelligible only if that of object is already understood. Nevertheless, there is no need to deny that the thinking subject is present at the beginning, nor to consider it a logical defect that the subject is ignored in the logical beginning. The beginning, taken alone, is necessarily incomplete, since what it is a beginning of can only be established in the course of the succeeding development. The success of *Logic* does depend on thought's ability to thematize its own essential content in which it as thinker is included, but the subject can be thematized only later on when its own conceptual prerequisites have been developed.(25)

White's rebuttal is to the point, provided the subject that is thematized within *Logic* is understood to be the category of subjectivity and not the real conscious subject of thought who becomes Hegel's theme in the Philosophy of Spirit. Although the presence of the living thinker, be it as writer, reader or critic of the development of categories, need not be disputed, what must be denied is that the nature of the subject's presence plays any juridical role in determining what content and order the categories should have. The moment the subjective conditions of discourse are treated as juridical conditions of knowledge, the problems of transcendental argument are reintroduced, leaving inexplicable how one is to know before knowing, that is, how transcendental knowledge is possible. If, for example, the logical beginning were saddled with a constitutive reference to a knowing subject, the concept and primacy of that subject would have to figure as an unaccountable presupposition simply because all categorial discourse would already rest upon it. Hence, ignoring the subject at the logical beginning is a methodological necessity, which Hegel observes by starting with indeterminacy per se without further qualifying it as a category thought by a given thinker in reference to any given object. That Hegel or we the reader are engaged in thinking the logical beginning is no more part of what is first analyzed than something bearing upon the legitimacy of the starting point.

Although White is not unaware of the self-referential difficulties of transcendental argument, he tends to retain reference to the thinking subject as if its presence ultimately were and need be part and parcel of the subject matter of Hegel's *Logic*. It is this residual reference that underlies White's understanding of Logic as a transcendental ontology.

This is apparent in White's answer to Schelling's third objection, that the logical beginning cannot be presuppositionless since it is conditioned by experiential and intellectual capacities. White responds in a familiarly transcendental way, maintaining that although philosophical reflection is temporally posterior to sensible experience, it is logically prior because the forms of thought are presupposed by experience.(26) This way of putting things might seem innocent enough, especially when White maintains that the logical independence of the categories from sensory experience is only established if Logic overcomes the dogmatism of Kant's metaphysical deduction of the categories by organizing and determining them through their own purely ideal interrelations.(27) However, White construes this requirement as equivalent to the demand that the categories must arise in the course of the speculative experience of the thinker who thinks thought itself. This suggests that the interrelations of the categories are not the only source of their content and order, but that a privileged structure of "speculative" experience methodologically underlies their exposition, as Schelling critically maintains.

Moreover, White sets speculative experience in a transcendental relation to mundane experience, whereby the absolute content of logic is not just internally and independently structured, but further qualified as grounding the intelligibility of feelings, representations and intuitions.(31) This suggests that the logical beginning and all that follows from it proceeds in terms of a given contrast between the privileged standpoint of speculative experience and the standpoint of everyday experience. On this basis, the categories of logic figure much as Kant's pure categories, as functions grounding the intelligibility of experience.

Although much in White's account of the logical beginning mitigates against any such references, when he turns to Schelling's critique of Hegel's move from being to nothing and becoming, his solution remains equivocal. According to Schelling, the logical beginning cannot be made with being, since what is objective is necessarily posited by the subject and hence not a real first. The first thought must therefore be the mere subject, or being determined as subject.(32) Hence, when Hegel purports to move from the category of being to that of nothing, all that is exhibited is the subjective arbitrariness and unintelligibility of the first concept. Pure being cannot become aware of itself as nothing, as Hegel's argument seems to require. Rather, the thinker discovers being to be nothingness and then claims that being is nothing. In so doing, the thinker makes a discovery that is not a real development, inherent in the starting point, but a fundamental question-begging. Further, Schelling points out, when Hegel connects being and nothing by the copula 'is', he does so without explaining what the copula means. Yet, since the copula in non-tautological propositions sets the subject as the ground of the predicate, Hegel's statement, 'being is nothing', either posits being as the ground of nothing, or is a tautology.(33) Furthermore, Schelling argues, Hegel's move to becoming rests on the unjustified qualification that pure being is 'still' nothing, in the determinate sense of not-yet-actual-being. This means that being is not indeterminate as Hegel pretends, but already determined as potency, just as becoming does not unify being and nothing but rather consists in a transition from potential to actual being.(34)

To refute Schelling's assertion of the primacy of the subject, White reflects upon Hegel's characterization of logic as self-thinking thought to show how it need not condition the logical beginning with any determinate reference to a given subject of thought. Pure thinking, which Hegel calls the element of logic, is thought thinking itself. Although it will indeed become knowing, at first pure thinking is without any distinctions since at the beginning of *Logic*, pure thinking does not yet know anything, nor have any determinate thought of itself. Hence only immediacy is present. Yet since thought, to remain pure, must think only itself, it must first think this immediacy, for that is all it is at the start. Consequently, White concludes, Schelling's 'subject' cannot be the first thought.(35)

This argument seems to imply that logic is subject to the prior methodological principle that all its categories be determined in terms of the self-thinking of thought. White claims that this has been already established by the *Phenomenology's* demonstration that only self-knowledge can be absolute knowledge.(35) If this were so, the method of logic would not be a topic for logical investigation and logic would rest upon a 'pre-scientific' inquiry, contrary to Hegel's demand that logical method be established within logic as its final result. Indeed, Hegel's own characterization of logic as self-thinking thought seems to contradict his claim of presuppositionlessness by framing all categorial development within the structure of self-knowledge. However, to the extent that self-thinking thought can only begin with immediacy, that is, with an absence of all thinking and all objects of thought, it does not figure as a given foundation but rather has neither any determinate role nor character at the outset. For this reason, it is appropriate to characterize the starting point of philosophy as the beginning of the science of logic. Since logic is self-thinking thought and self-thinking thought, unlike the thinking of anything other than thought, can only begin with no determinate method or subject matter, thinking without foundations is equivalent to fulfilling the constitutive project of logic. Accordingly, when Hegel introduces the starting point of systematic philosophy he can do so in two parallel ways: by discussing what is required for logical science to be coherently developed, and by discussing with what science, i.e. philosophy in general, must begin.

If this disarms Schelling's claim that the subject is irreducibly primordial, it still leaves suspect the moves from being to nothing and from nothing to becoming. Schelling has argued that the move from being to nothing is an arbitrary contribution of the logician, who relates them by a copula signifying tautological identity or predication. Either way, the subsequent transition to becoming requires treating being as an already determinate potentiality. White responds first by arguing that the move from being to nothing is not an external arbitrary move. Pure being can only have its indeterminacy explicated in terms of nothing, just as nothing can be thought only as pure being. However, this thinking of being and nothing, each in terms of the other, involves more than these two thoughts. It consists in a movement in thought from being to nothing and back again, a movement which must be categorially specified if thought is to continue thinking itself. This produces the category of becoming, not through any appeal to potentiality, but simply through the thinking of being and nothing themselves.(36)

According to White, this categorial thinking involves judgments that are both synthetic and a priori.(40) Sounding a Kantian note, White maintains that these judgements are known only through experience, yet are necessary because the experience in question is speculative logical experience. Unlike the experience to which Kant limited objective knowledge, logical experience consits in the thinking about thought determinations rather than about things either sensible or supersensible.(41) Significantly, Hegel does not characterize the categorial development of logic as being synthetic and a priori. Making no reference to any given framework of experience, he instead describes the logical advance as being both synthetic and analytic. The advance is synthetic not because it falls within the given standpoint of the speculative logician, but because the prior categories figure as presupposed components of further terms irreducible to them. The advance is at the same time analytic because the resultant categorial whole can only be constituted through the succession of categories which has led to it as their encompassing principle. This discrepancy between Hegel's self-understanding and White's interpretation raises the issue of what exactly is the character of logical development, an issue to which White focuses attention by returning to Schelling's Hegel critique.

## ii) The Character of Logical Development

To satisfy Hegel's own criteria, Schelling observes, the logic must develop its categories so that they are ordered in and of themselves and so that their order is accessible to the speculative philosopher.(44) Schelling maintains that the *Logic* violates these requirements in several ways. First, its development is guided by an illicit anticipation of a contingent goal relative to Hegel: namely the world as Hegel perceives it to be. Secondly, the logical categories are ordered through the external application of an independently given method. This cannot be avoided, for there simply is no single order in which the logical categories must be presented, especially when logic begins with pure being, ignoring the absolute subject that alone provides the principle for generating any real development.(50)

White first responds to these objections by citing the unity of form and content that Hegel considers the hallmark of any foundation-free systematic argument. If, as presuppositionlessness demands, logical development must be dictated by the categories themselves, then the method of logic cannot be described in isolation from its application, as is the case with the experimental-scientific method. Since there is no access to the form of logical development except through the movement of categories themselves, no adequate description of the path of the *Logic* can be given either in advance or retrospectively.(51) By the same token, as the content is the means to consciousness of the method or form, the only justification for the development is the *Logic* itself in its entirety.(52) Appeal to any other standard would introduce extraneous assumptions undermining Hegel's turn away from given foundations. As White points out, only because the categories are interrelated by their own determination can the *Logic* free the logician of having to apply an external method or to appeal to any other presuppositions.(58)

Accordingly, logical method can be articulated only at the end of the categorial development, at which point the unfolded content has provided the full ordering in which its self-ordered movement consists. When Hegel describes the method of logic in analyzing the final logical category, the Absolute Idea, the general features he outlines cannot comprise a revelation after the fact of a concealed motor of development. As White maintains, any reviewing of the path now retrospectively visible in its entirety must be demanded by the course of speculative thought itself. Only then, when the categories become so self-reflective that they determine their own nature and interconnection, can the method be accounted for without any extralogical categories.(58) As White points out, because there can be no method generating the categories in independence from the categories themselves, any formalization of systematic logic is impossible.(65)

Granted these consequences of the unity of form and content in logical development, it makes little sense to maintain that categories cannot be discursively developed or that their development is not unique. Since the ordering of speculative logic is a determination of its content, the development of categories is necessarily categorially determinate, that is, discursive. Similarly, since the order of the categories is wedded to their content, so long as their content is univocal, so must be their development. Only if logic resulted from the application of a contingent method to a given content could there by any possibility of multiple orderings.(66)

Although these points sufficiently underline how systematic logic cannot involve an external method or governing telos, White adds some transcendental moves to counter Schelling's critique. He maintains that the independence of logical development from nonspeculative influences guarantees that the categories are presupposed by experience rather than derived from it.(60) This is further insured by the move to the Idea, where the ability of concepts to determine objectivity is logically confirmed. Further, White argues, the Logic of the Concept establishes that consciousness does not receive ready-made givens and that the speculative standpoint is reached only by those who realize that thought is ingredient in reality.(61) With each of these claims, White inserts extralogical terms into the logical development, as if the categories referred not just to themselves, but transcendentally to knowing and the objects of consciousness.

Hence, when White addresses Schelling's critical point that the subject plays a guiding role in the logical development, White readily assents, arguing that the Logic of the concept shows that determinacy is dependent upon the subject who determines it. According to White, the Absolute Ideas brings closure to logical development by determining the subject as the principle of all determination. Accordingly, the Logic itself turns out to be a science of the subject's functional determinations, or in other words, a transcendental ontology.(62)

White holds that this disarms Schelling's objection that the absence of the subject from the logical beginning and its presence at the end proves the arbitrariness of the development. At the same time, White maintains that Hegel's enterprise does not thereby collapse into Schelling's theological idealism. Contrary to Schelling, the logical development does not reconstruct any real process, ending with a world, either experienced or ideal. It simply establishes the principle of determination, the Absolute Idea.(63) Yet can logic independently establish the principle of not just logical, but all determination without violating the methodological proscription of extralogical reference? By the same token, can the role of the category of subjectivity in logical development determine the structure of the real subjectivity of consciousness without presupposing a parallel between logical and extralogical determinacy?

These questions center upon the relation between logic and reality, a relation that becomes thematic when Hegel makes his transition from the Science of Logic to the Philosophy of Nature. Schelling's critique of this transition and White's response bring these questions to a head.

### iii) The Transition from Logic to Reality

Schelling judges Hegel's transition from logic to nature to be unintelligible, whether the Absolute Idea be considered a theological or ontological principle. Either way, it is complete in itself as the end of Logic leaving any move to Nature dependent upon some external impetus, which in Hegel's case is the covert intervention of the philosophizing subject.(73) Furthermore, Hegel characterizes the transition to Nature as if the Idea were God the creator, whereas nothing in logic establishes the divinity of the Idea.(74)

White's response to these criticisms has two sides. On the one hand, he grants that logic cannot establish a theological principle of reality with which nature can be understood to arise from a divine idea. If Hegel's first philosophy is metaphysical theology, then it succumbs to Schelling's objections.(75) But, White alternately argues, the logic is purely idea, comprising a transcendental ontology whose dialectic remains ideal throughout the realms of nature and spirit. Instead of providing an account of the emanation of beings from a transcendent source, the move from logic to reality rather involves a move of transcendental constitution, where the categories determine the possible structure of reality. The reason for this, according to White, is that one cannot say what things might be like independent of the subject. Hence, the determinations of thought, united in the Absolute Idea, ground truth in the real as well as in the ideal realm. The Absolute Idea is thus not God before creation, but the absolute ontological principle, containing the categories by which anything, ideal or real, can be determinate.(76) In so far as White retains the subject as the foundation of determinacy, he characterizes the categories encompassed by the Absolute Ideas as all of consciousness's determinative functions.(78)

What then distinguishes Hegel's development of categories from that of Kant? White's answer is that Hegel presents the categories fundamental to the thinking of not just perceived objects, but anything determinate. Whereas Kant neglected to transcendentally constitute the concepts of reflection and account for transcendental knowledge, Hegel systematically relates objective categories and categories of reflection, thereby grounding transcendental as well as empirical thought.(82)

However, even if Hegel does in this way develop transcendental theory more consistently than Kant, can his move from Logic to Nature still escape Schelling's objections? First, if logic is interpreted as transcendental ontology, then the move to Nature can neither be an emanation from a supersensible entity nor the afterthought of the finite subject who realizes the incompleteness of logical determinacy. Instead of having the cosmological, psychological or theological character that Schelling finds incoherent, the transition will amount to conceiving the necessary features of any possible world, leaving unaccounted for the contingent aspects of factical reality that can only be encountered empirically.(85–86)

On these terms, White maintains, the relation of logic to the extralogical neither compromises logical purity nor introduces any extrasystematic impetus. Logical purity is maintained because the distinct determinacy of each category does not depend upon reference to a factical realm.(85) Further, the determination of the extralogical is implicit in logic, first since most categories are applicable not to other categories but to things, secondly in so far as the subject is Idea rather than mere concept by being able to determine a reality different from itself, and thirdly because the method established in logic consists in developing categories in the order of their increasing richness of determination.(86–87) For White, these points are confirmed in how the resulting philosophies of nature and spirit are categorial sciences thematizing the categories fundamental to all possible worlds and to subjects confronted with worlds.

Nevertheless, it warrants asking whether the categories of logic can have a content establishing their applicability to noncategorial determinations, whether the objectivity to which the subject is related within the Idea is something other than logical objectivity, and whether the increasing richness in categorial development provides enough of a reason for moving from the Absolute Idea to something categorizable as Nature. Leaving the conceptually overdetermined contingencies of factical reality outside the concepts of nature and spirit does not remove the problem of establishing how these two noncategorial realms are categorially determinate in a way irreducible to logical determination. On the other hand, introducing into logic a subject that figures as a constituting foundation identified with consciousness seems to violate the strictures of categorial immanence with which Hegel seeks to surmount the self-referential dilemmas of transcendental argument. Given these problems, does it make sense to characterize Hegel's logic as a transcendental ontology?

## iv) Hegel's Philosophical Project

One way of answering this question is to consider White's defense of the Hegelian project from Schelling's charge that even if the Logic satisfied its own requirements it would fail to meet those of philosophy in general. Schelling's chief objection against Hegel, the transcendental ontologist, is that the Logic's retreat to pure thought provides access only to the essential realms of the possible and necessary, leaving out of account philosophy's most important subject matter: the contingent facticity of existence.(145) For Schelling anthropological problems, both existential and political, are vital to philosophy, and Hegel's failure to address them shows the limitations of his system, limitations that no mere doctrine of categories can avoid.(154)

But, as White responds, it is no problem for Hegel that anthropological issues fall outside the scope of his system. They are beneath philosophical investigation since the merely factical is no more a matter for conceptual analysis than the contingently non-existent. Philosophy can only address what is rational, and what is rational is what cannot be other wise. One may obtain 'correct' beliefs about 'what the case is' through empirical study, but incorrigible truth can only be had in reasoning about what is constitutive for any possible world. If the philosopher examines the factical, it is only to recognize traces of the rational and answer the demands of reason rather than those of life.(150, 154)

Accordingly, White maintains, Hegel does not attempt to construct an ideal state. This would not be possible within a transcendental ontology, since the factical can never fully correspond to the pure possibilities in which the rational consists.(157) White admits that Hegel does conceptually analyze what is essential to political structures, but these can only provide the ground for an evaluative account of any given state. Because the factical is burdened with contingencies that can only be empirically ascertained, the Hegelian sage cannot employ his wisdom to write codes of law, construct a real state in which actual individuals would attain total satisfaction or make any practical suggestions. The Hegelian philosopher cannot move from the ideal and necessary to the real but contingent in search of further truth. The transition from essence to existence can only be made in search of amusement.(159) Does this mean that the account of the factical is not grounded in that of the categorial? Not at all, White answers, for transcendental ontology does not allow any direct passage from the purely possible to the factical. A direct transition from categorial to factical discourse would be possible only if dialectical relations were real rather than ideal, that is, if the categories belonged to a transcendent idealism or realism rather than a transcendental ontology.(159)

Paradoxically, White concludes that Hegel's attempt to exhaust the categorial realm can at best provide a completed first philosophy. In completing metaphysics with a transcendental ontology, Hegel provides philosophical anthropology with the point from which it can begin.(160) Perhaps Hegel's *Logic* can stand as a first philosophy from which concepts of nature and spirit can be developed without taking for granted the categories of determinacy. Yet can it be maintained that the philosophies of nature and spirit are just propadeutics to further philosophical investigations of human nature?

Certainly Hegel himself regards the philosophies of nature and spirit as the one and only place where the various dimensions of human existence can be examined with philosophical rigor. Significantly, it is within the philosophy of spirit and not within logic that Hegel sees fit to analyze the structure of consciousness and the actual reasoning of living individuals. These topics must be treated within the philosophy of reality because they no more than any other extralogical condition can have bearing upon the development of categories. For this reason, Hegel does not begin philosophy with epistemology, developing logic as a treatise on how the knowing subject determines the object of knowing. He instead examines categories in their own right, as topics of a theory of determinacy that, as such, can take no determinacy for granted. How these categories can be thought by living subjects or applied to things are problems that can only be dealt with in the philosophy of reality after the categories of determinacy have been determined in and of themselves. By characterizing Hegel's logic as a transcendental ontology, White loses sight of these points, so fundamental for developing philosophy without foundations.

## Notes

* Alan White, *Absolute Knowledge: Hegel and the Problem of Metaphysics* (Athens, OH: Ohio University Press, 1983). Numbers in parenthesis refer to pages in the White text.

# 4

# Conceiving Reality without Foundations

Although Hegel has frequently been granted felicitous insight into the rich detail of known facts, his strategy for conceiving reality has been roundly dismissed as a relic of philosophical hypertrophy. Such dismissal is certainly understandable considering how often Hegel's theory of reality has been interpreted to be the child of either a leviathan metaphysical construction or a demonically inventive transcendental constitution. Unfortunately, the weight of these interpretations has not just led to the general discrediting of Hegel's system. It has also virtually banished from view a central strand in Hegel's argument which suggests an entirely different approach offering a viable, yet ignored strategy for conceiving reality without falling prey to the foundational dilemmas afflicting metaphysical and transcendental argument. There is no better way of comprehending the significance and neglected promise of this strategy than first following in broad outline the path of inquiry which has led to the quagmire in which thought today confronts reality.

## i) The Flight from Reality of Positive Science

In an age when philosophers proclaim their own inability to conceive reality, nothing seems more appropriate than simply taking up what is given and examining it as offered. With philosophical thought abandoning the real, and resigning itself to exercises in logical consistency and edification, positive science would seem to have been granted the domain of truth for its own. Since positive scientists address their subject matter only in so far as it can be taken for granted, they have felt little need to doubt its reality for science any more than science's access to it.

Nevertheless, however positive science rises to the task of enjoying the self-evidence of its subject matter, the result can be no more than the very same formal consistency to which an obliging philosophy stands condemned. Since positive science immediately considers a given subject matter, its analysis is relative to both the particular content it puts under investigation and its own given relation to this object. Whether it begins by turning to certain facts, meditating upon an inner experience, or simply defining its terms, positive science can never claim an absolute knowledge of reality as it is in itself, but only an understanding of what it assumes to be given for it. Since its object is just as much an unjustified postulate as the validity of its knowing of it, positive science can arrive at no truth, but only the formal consistency of properly deriving conclusions from a given assumption according to some accepted procedure.

Thus positive science is left with the very same inability to know reality that has been ascribed to philosophy. This leveling of the two disciplines can hardly exclude the possibility of conceiving reality, however, for just as positive science cannot get at the truth of what is real, so it cannot legitimately claim that there be no other knowing than its own. The attempt of skeptical positivists such as Quine[1] to reduce philosophy to positive science founders on this very point. They have ignored that the doubly conditioned standpoint of positive science cannot be asserted to be the inescapable predicament of all discourse, since the acknowledged relativity of positive science leaves it itself unable to ground the universality they claim for it.

### ii) Metaphysics and the Dilemma of First Asking, ''What Is?''

Despite the recurring temptation, philosophy has never been able to restrict itself to the relative understanding which positive science properly pursues. From the start, philosophy has instead sought to conceive reality without forsaking truth.

When this calling emerged from passive wonder by asking, ''What is?'', it immediately took the form subsequently both hailed and branded as metaphysics. Given its constitutive question, this approach has inveterately conceived reality by first presenting some specific content and immediately claiming that it is not something merely stipulated by the philosopher as an object for his or her own knowing, but something in itself, given *in res* independently of any reference to it.

Since whatever thus gets taken to be true in itself is so by virtue of being immediately given, there can be no mediating principle by which the claimed reality of different contents can be judged. On these terms any given content is just as susceptible of being presented as something in itself as any other. Consequently metaphysics could not help but offer a sorry parade of completely different competing systems of reality, each equally claiming immediate and unqualified truth.

Of course, such conflict could not escape the eyes of metaphysicians themselves, and attempts were made to surmount the dilemma. Some thinkers sought an absolute first principle of reality which would overcome the competing claims of different given contents by deriving them all out of itself in an ordered construction of the totality of reality. However, once engaged, their attempts necessarily fell prey to disputes concerning not only what was the first principle, but also what constituted the criteria for the completeness and validity of its presumed derivation of all reality. A vicious circle always seemed to arise, where in order to judge the truth of the stipulated first principle, one already had to have true knowledge of the scope and interconnection of the full content of reality, something that should be unattainable without relying upon the first principle, if the latter were truly the basis of everything else.

In response to these difficulties, Socrates argued alternately that in order to answer the question, "What is?", one first had to call opinion into question, purge oneself of all assumptions concerning reality and reach the state of knowing nothing at all, where the quest for truth generically begins. From that putatively presuppositionless standpoint one could then directly proceed to know reality as it is in itself.

The problem with this alternative becomes clear when Plato takes up the Socratic program in the discussion of the divided line in the *Republic*, moving beyond the negative outcome of the dialectic of Socratic questioning. There Plato describes how, upon reaching that point beyond all assumption, one faces a content presupposing no other, out of which all true reality gets determined. This unconditioned givenness is the Good, and from it one can proceed without reference to anything else to conceive one idea after another of things as they are in themselves. Although Plato nowhere shows how the specific ideas immanently emerge from the Good, even if one allows that they do, the Platonic approach can never account for how one can decide what is the valid givenness beyond all assumption from which all reality derives, without already taking for granted what can and cannot be presuppositionless in itself. So long as *any* specific content is ascribed immediate and unconditioned reality, there is nothing that can legitimate it against the opposing claim of any other arbitrary assumption. Whether it be a particular fact, an all encompassing first principle, or the determining source of everything real, whatever is immediately put forward as true in itself can comprise no true reality, but only the referent of a knowing that takes the content of reality for granted.

This holds, even if one were to follow Aristotle, and undertake a study of being qua being, in recognition that being must first be conceived in its own right in so far as nothing real can lack being nor therefore be conceived without a prior understanding of being itself. Again, arbitrary assumptions would undermine the whole enterprise, for how could the study of being qua being stand as first philosophy without assuming in reality the primacy and elemental character ascribed to being?

By asking "What is?" as the first question of philosophy, metaphysics thus perenially commits the error of making immediate reference to reality. No matter what it gives in answer, metaphysical discourse is always left presupposing the correlation between the content of its conception and that of the real. The arbitrariness of such postulated congruence is insurmountable. Because metaphysics constitutively begins its inquiry with some presumed knowledge of what is in itself, it can never establish the correspondence of thought and reality which its own truth claims depend upon. As a result, the metaphysical conception of reality can never be more than a mere stipulation.

If this leaves metaphysics without any knowledge of what is, it does not mean that reality can not be known. On the contrary, the failure of metaphysics to know the real casts in doubt the presumed correspondence of thought and reality while indicating that all immediate reference to reality must be ruled out.

Given, however, that all reference to reality occurs within knowing, the experience of metaphysics would seem to leave philosophy with not only doubt and suspicion, but also the positive task of first investigating the character and limits of knowing before asking, "What is?"

### iii) The Self-Elimination of All Transcendental Theory of Reality

Once this now familiar trancendental turn is taken, the problem of conceiving reality is not simply put off till after knowing is certified ready and able. Rather, the conception of reality falls itself within the consideration of knowing—on two accounts.

To begin with, if the correspondence of thought and reality be called into question and all immediate reference to reality be proscribed, then an examination of the full character and limits of true knowing will have to consider the knowledge of reality to be determined in terms of the structure of knowing itself.

Furthermore, since the knowing under investigation claims truth for its knowledge only by both distinguishing and comparing its concepts with the objects to which they are to correspond, the critical assessment of true knowing will involve considering what knowledge refers to, and how it can be in accord with its concept.

Although this posing of the matter is predicated upon a rejection of all direct reference to reality, it would seem to involve metaphysical claims of its own concerning what knowing itself is, and do so in such a manner that any knowledge of reality would be precluded from the start.

If knowing can be investigated in its own right, independently of any particular knowledge of reality, this would seem to assume that knowing is either an instrument or medium through which reality is encountered, or a structure of referring which constitutes the very object to which it refers.

In the first case, knowledge of reality as it is in itself would be impossible since what would be obtained by the act of the instrument or the transmission of the medium would be something already worked upon and distorted by knowing's process. If one attempted to get at the unaltered reality by somehow subtracting the effects of such knowing, one would only be left where one was before knowing, namely, with no knowledge of reality at all.[2]

If, on the other hand, one eliminates all reference to something in itself, and instead conceives knowing as referring to an object generated in the act of knowing itself, then one seems condemned to solipsism, where knowledge can never be of anything more than one's own subjective stipulation.

In face of these difficulties, any trancendental conception of reality would necessarily require solving a problem first posed, if not satisfactorily answered, by Kant in his trancendental deduction of the categories.

As Kant recognizes, once metaphysical reference is excluded and objective knowledge is seen as something to be determined in terms of the structure of knowing itself, then solipsism can be avoided and knowledge of reality redeemed if two conditions be fulfilled.

First, the knowing in terms of which all reference proceeds must be such that what it refers to as the object of its knowledge is not merely its own subjective stipulation, but something given independently of its reference to it. Of course, if the referent of knowledge is just knowing's own stipulation, then one is left with the solipsism of positive science, where the known object has no more reality than what the knower assumes it to have.

Secondly, even if the object of knowledge be something in itself, and no mere stipulation of the knower, there will be no knowledge of reality unless knowing be such that its knowledge corresponds to what it knows. Since, however, all immediate reference to reality is illegitimate, the corespondence at issue cannot be validated by any comparison falling outside the structure of knowing, that is, between it and some thing in itself. Rather, the only way trancendental philosophy can escape solipsism and achieve knowledge of reality is if it demonstrates that the conditions for the conception of what is given at the same time provide the conditions under which objects can be given in correspondence with those concepts.

In the "Transcendental Deduction of the Categories," Kant rightfully raises this very problem as the touchstone of his entire philosophical project. His particular solution, however, immediately goes awry due to the complementary metaphysical assumptions upon which it depends.

Through his openly "metaphysical" deduction of the categories (B95–B116), Kant supplies the content of these most essential elements of knowing's own structure by immediately referring to the cognitive reality of certain functions handed down traditionally from Aristotelian logic.

Then, having determined the conditions knowing through a metaphysical reference, Kant proceeds to characterize the conditions of the objects of its knowledge in the same manner. What knowing refers to as its object is claimed to be an appearance of some thing in itself which is not known in terms of the knowing under critique, but in virtue of an immediate reference to reality.

Therefore, when Kant shows how the categories allow the conditions of a possible experience to coincide with the conditions for the possibility of the appearances to which knowing adequately refers, his argument is already undermined by the same metaphysical stipulation it seeks to avoid.

Clearly, if the problem of the transcendental deduction of the categories is to be resolved, with knowledge of reality secured, both the conditions of knowing and the conditions of what it knows must be determined independently of all immediate reference to reality. In face of this challenge, thinkers such as Fichte, the young Schelling, and Husserl have attempted to purge transcendental inquiry of all metaphysical vestiges by seeking to eliminate all immediate reference to a thing in itself and to derive the entire content of the conditions of knowing through its transcendental critique.

However persistently such attempts be pursued, they cannot possibly redeem any knowledge of reality nor any valid knowledge of knowing, for once transcendental philosophy becomes self-critical its own constitutive framework collapses.

To see this, all one need do is consider what would happen if transcendental philosophy were to forsake all metaphysical reference to its own object of inquiry. For this to occur, the knowing which performs the critique of knowing would itself have to fulfill the conditions of the knowing under investigation. This means that if the transcendental philosopher is to avoid stipulating the conditions of knowing in a metaphysical manner, that philosopher must relate to the subject matter in just the same way that the knowing under critique properly relates to its object. Since what is to be known by the transcendental philosopher is the structure of knowing in terms of which all true knowledge of reality is possible, the transcendental inquiry can legitimately determine what such true knowing is only if its own discourse refers to true knowing just as true knowing refers to what is for it.

This requirement immediately offers its own solution. Because the knowing under critique is to be the knowing whose knowledge corresponds to its object and is certain thereof, while the critique of knowing is to have such true knowing as its object, the two can only coincide if true knowing *is* a knowing of true knowing. In that case, what the transcendental inquiry performs is precisely what it investigates, just as knowing is itself self-critique. Nevertheless, when transcendental discourse thus becomes fully consistent, with metaphysical reference giving way to a knowing which does its own critique, the achieved equalization of transcendental argument with the knowing it investigates has just as much eliminated all distinction between knowing and its object.

Knowing and the object of knowing are here identical because true knowing, the object known through transcendental investigation, is itself a knowing of true knowing, whereas the knowing exercised by the transcendental philosopher is nothing other than a knowing of true knowing as well. Since transcendental knowing is therefore no different than its object, true knowing, the former's identity with its object equally signifies that true knowing is indistinguishable from its object.

This resulting solipsism is of fatal consequence, for the ability to make a distinction between reference and referent, knowing and object known, is what first allows for true knowing and transcendental philosophy itself. If knowing and its object cannot be differentiated, knowing lacks the independent referent it needs to contrast against its knowledge, if the latter is to be the knowledge of something real, and not just of its own representation. In effect, the absence of such distinction leaves no knowing at all, for without any referent to refer to, there is no reference, nor any knowledge to be had.

Similarly, only insofar as knowing can be considered separately from its specific object can the conditions for knowing and its object be investigated at all. When, on the contrary, knowing and its object have collapsed into identity, as happens when transcendental inquiry becomes self-referentially consistent, no *epochē* or transcendental reflection can be made. At one with its object, knowing can no longer be grasped by itself, for not only does it have no structure apart, but none whatsoever, insofar as its constitutive relation of reference has been eliminated.[3]

As a result, transcendental philosophy ultimately fails to secure the conditions for its own quest, just as much as the conditions for knowledge of reality.

### iv) The Transcendental Impasse of Holism

In recent years, it has become increasingly recognized that the dilemma of transcendental argument does not concern the particular content ascribed to the transcendental condition, but rather the foundational claim of a transcendental condition in general. Whether the ground of objective discourse is characterized as Kantian noumenal subjectivity, an ideal speech situation of non-distorted communication, or the given practice of ordinary language, the same fatal problem arises of having to equalize the transcendental standpoint with its object in order to avoid metaphysical stipulation and achieve self-referential consistency.

Currently the program of philosophical holism has been drawing adherents as a solution to the foundational dilemmas of transcendental argument.

Advanced in varying forms by such thinkers as Hans-Georg Gadamer, Richard Rorty, Alasdair MacIntyre, and Hilary Putnam,[4] the holist strategy seeks to extricate philosophy from metaphysical and transcendental problems, by affirming that all truth claims proceed from pragmatic decisions that stipulate norms for justification and thereby provide the commensurable framework allowing for meaningful argument once they are accepted as a practice agreed upon by those in conversation. These underlying pragmatic decisions may already be enshrined in the normal discourse of a shared culture and tradition, or they may frame a new paradigm of science challenging the old. Whatever the case, holism argues, objectivity always consists in agreement rather than in the accurate mirroring of nature or in the constituting activity of a transcendental subject. Accordingly, the holist would argue, philosophy must restrict itself to interpreting and contrasting the different conventions of discourse, without imposing any preferred set of terms of its own. Instead of seeking a true knowledge of reality, philosophy can only aim at an edification which fosters a self-conscious awareness of the practices through which objectivity is construed.

By limiting philosophy to such edification, the holist claims to have avoided all reference either to reality or to transcendental conditions in his or her own discourse. However, precisely by making this claim, holism does not advance its own pragmatic characterization of knowing as a mere matter of agreement, as arbitrary as any other description. Rather, holism asserts it as a juridical conception that accurately represents the universal predicament of discourse and, on that basis, precludes the legitimacy of any systematic philosophy with truth as its aim. In so doing, holism ends up making a metaphysical claim concerning the reality of conversation, only to revert to transcendental foundationalism by treating this putative reality of conversation as the ultimate context in which justifications are constituted. In other words, holism's affirmation of the universality of its pragmatic description of discourse renders the latter a preferred set of terms, and thereby reintroduces the very same dilemmas it seeks to avoid.

Consequently, holism presents no alternative to the problems of metaphysical and transcendental argument, but only one more example of their well-traveled path.

### v) Starting with Nothing: The Development from Being to Categorial Totality

Can there then be any non-positive, non-metaphysical, non-transcendental conception of reality? In view of the encompassing character of these three failed approaches, it would be hard not to reject any affirmative answer out of hand. For if one is not to stipulate any content, nor make any immediate reference to what is, nor finally determine reality in terms of some conception of knowing, what is one left with but nothing at all?

Strange as it may sound, if there is anything that can lead to a true determination of reality, it will have to be nothing: nothing that is stipulated, nothing that is real in itself, nothing that can be claimed about knowing. The experience of positive science, metaphysics and transcendental philosophy leaves this one alternative, an alternative of simply considering the empty indeterminacy one is left with, when all stipulation is ruled out and all immediate truth claims about reality and knowing have revealed their bankruptcy and been eliminated.

The figure in the history of philosophy who has raised this alternative is Hegel. Although interpreters from Schelling, Marx and Kierkegaard onward have judged and condemned him to be the last great metaphysical system-builder who conceives reality as it is in itself from an absolute standpoint of subject-object identity, there is a neglected current in Hegel's thought which actually offers a unique attempt to forego metaphysical and transcendental arguments and instead begin philosophy without any specific preferred set of terms with regard either to method or to subject matter. With due attention to the systematic issues, his *Science of Logic* and *Encyclopedia* can be seen to take this radically anti-foundational course, and provide the basic outline of its strategy, if not its adequate realization. Although Hegel makes many a remark that can be taken metaphysically according to standard interpretations, what makes his work so philosophically significant for advancing the present state of thought are those of his arguments which break new ground for a non-foundational theory of reality.

Hegel recognizes that when ontological and epistemological truth claims are completely discarded in virtue of their own internal untenability,[5] what is left is an absence of all reference and referent, and not any reality or knowledge. Because there is no stipulated content, nor anything in itself, nor any determination of knowing, the indeterminacy resulting from their exclusion has no internal distinctions, no relation to anything else, and no quality of any sort. It is therefore not indeterminacy *in res* or a category of some knowing, but unanalyzable, undifferentiated, uncontrasted indeterminacy about which nothing specific can be said. Hegel calls this "being" and aptly points out that, in contrast to the traditional metaphysical usage of the term, such "being" has no ontological status, nor any status as a primitive term which receives further determination through other terms or provides the privileged principle for their specification.[6] The being in question can play no such foundational role, for it would cease to be indeterminacy if it were further qualified as a foundation of something else, be it epistemically as a category of thought, or ontologically as the totality of all that is. Even if one were to take being to be merely indeterminate reality this would still involve beginning with more than just indeterminacy. Indeed, what allows the consideration of being to escape the pitfalls of positive science, metaphysics, and transcendental philosophy is precisely the utter indeterminacy at hand, which simply can contain no stipulated content or claims about reality or knowing.

Nevertheless, it is tempting to object that any attempt to begin philosophy with being involves stipulating its specific determinacy, and in doing so, presupposes that the category of being is the privileged starting point of philosophical investigation. This objection fails to recognize that indeterminacy is not the same thing as stipulated indeterminacy or indeterminacy taken as the immediate givenness addressed by the quest for truth. If one were to begin with stipulated being, and consider it as such, what would lie at hand would be the topic with which Hegel begins his *Phenomenology of Spirit*, namely, sense-certainty. There, what is observed is precisely knowing's stipulation of being as what is immediately given for knowing. Hegel is fully aware that such a beginning cannot qualify as the starting point of philosophy, but rather comprises the most elementary shape of consciousness, whose knowing remains burdened by reference to some in-itself which it posits as the given standard of its knowledge. By contrast, being in its own right involves no stipulated content, nor any assumption concerning philosophy or reality simply because its indeterminacy would be violated if it contained any such further relations.

Be this as it may, the very indeterminacy of being would still appear to render it a dead end for all inquiry since it seems inexplicable how anything, let alone anything real, could arise from it. Because such being can only be considered if nothing else is admitted, any further determination would have to emerge from it alone, independently of any outside reference, be it to some given method or to some given content. Otherwise, the problems attending metaphysical reference and transcendental constitution would be reintroduced. On the other hand, since this being lacks all difference and relation to be what it is, it cannot be a ground or cause or determiner of anything, nor can it give rise to something whose own character involves difference or relation to something determinate.

Consequently, if anything were to arise from being, it could only do so in an utterly groundless manner and be just as uncontrasted and unmediated as being itself. In other words, nothing can arise from being.

Hegel recognizes that this does not mean that there can be no non-foundational development from being. Instead, it spells out the very terms of the advance, indicating that nothing does arise from being without any ground at all, that, in other words, a second indistinguishable indeterminacy follows as being's only possible successor, and does so without any cause or reason.

Being, which is neither something in itself nor a category of reason, but completely indeterminate, *is immediately* nothing, just as nothing *is immediately* the same absence of all determinacy that being comprises.[7]

Thus, instead of precluding further development, the very indeterminacy of being immediately allows the rise of a contrast that is no contrast at all, of being that is nothing and nothing that is being, where each is the groundless becoming of the other. With this passage that immediately cancels itself as a passage insofar as being and nothing are indistinguishable, being has in fact given rise to something other than itself, namely, the process of becoming within which being and nothing continually resolve themselves into one another.[8]

To the degree that this becoming is contrastable to the aspects of being and nothing contained within it, it comprises a specific determinacy which stands developed without reference to any determinate foundations. In effect, what Hegel offers in these considerations, in contrast to the foundational assumptions of metaphysical and transcendental thought, is a development of determinacy which takes no determinacy for granted.

Nonetheless, if this emergence of becoming indicates how being can be a starting point of further determination, it does not in any way signify that anything real will result. In fact, when one simply considers the character of the advance, one sees that the development from being has a radical formality allowing of no distinction between what would be a determination *per se* as opposed to one in reality or one in thought for that matter.

Since whatever here develops does so in complete absence of all positing of a given content, all reference to reality, and any predetermined notion of what constitutes true knowing, it must follow from being in a wholly immanent manner. Instead of arising through the application of some given method or the direct introduction of what is claimed to be, the development from being must be determined through nothing other than itself, that is, it must be self-developing.

Furthermore, because such development proceeds from nothing determinate, its process cannot be a self-determination of some content, such as thought, will, or reality. It must rather be self-determination *per se*. This means that the foundation-free theory of determinacy which issues from being is a theory of self-determined determinacy, with no immediate ontological or epistemological application.

Admittedly, even if the dilemmas of basing the quest for truth upon some givenness are patent enough, it is difficult to imagine how the development of self-determination would not either collapse into nothing, due to the absence of any foundation to support it, or involve a completely arbitrary, open-ended series of determinacies.

That these alternatives do not apply becomes evident once it is recognized that *what* determines itself from being can only be manifest at the conclusion of the development, for only at its end does the self-determination fully determine its subject, namely itself, in its totality. Being is thus not the substrate of development, ever acquiring new determination for itself in the manner of fundamental ontology. On the contrary, being does not even stand as the beginning of what finally results until the very conclusion of the entire development where that of which being is a beginning first comes into view.

This signifies that the development of self-determined determinacy does in fact have a non-collapsing structure, which, however, is not immediately given, but produced through the mediation of its own self-determination. This structure is not arbitrary, for it does not issue from the arbitrariness of any given determiner. Precisely by comprising a self-development starting from nothing, it avoids all arbitrary assumptions as well as all arbitrary orderings. So, too, its self-development is not open-ended, for the unity of self-determination entails that that unity provide closure for itself.

It may be that not till the end can it be manifest what the determinations following from being are determinations of, but the character of the conclusion can still be anticipated. Since no other content or any separate knowing can be relied upon to establish the relation between the stages in the development from being or what certifies its completion, the development must itself come to a determination that presents the interconnection of all the categories and grasps them as a totality determined in and through itself. Only in this way will our exposition and reflection have no constitutive role to play in placing the different categories in relation to one another as elements of a whole.

Consequently, if the self-development is to come to any conclusion at all, this will have to comprise a final determination so structured as to relate all the preceding ones together as the specific components of the self-determined totality which is their result as well as their encompassing unity. Hegel recognizes, however, that, as such, the last category becomes their totality itself, precisely by being the entire retrospective ordering of all that has preceded in which every category figures as a constitutive stage in the concluded self-determination containing them all and to which they have led.[9]

This resultant self-ordering whole is then the actual subject of the development following from being to which Hegel devotes his *Science of Logic*. Insofar as the very totality of this resultant subject provides the ordering principle of its own developed content, it no less comprises the method by which all the categories are determined. Conversely, because it forms the ultimate subject of the development, this totality is what each and every category is a determination of. Hegel calls this categorial totality the "Absolute Idea," and he appropriately concludes the *Science of Logic* with it, characterizing it as the method of the self-determined development of determinacy it itself comprises.[10]

In effect, both method and subject matter have here emerged at the end of the development, instead of being presupposed at the start in the fashion of positive science, metaphysics, and transcendental philosophy. Because such a development of categories proceeds with no primitive terms, no logical operators, and no foundations of any sort, it is genuinely self-grounding, exhibiting a self-ordered content relying on no exogenous criteria for its justification.

For just this reason, the categorial totality involves no referral of categories to anything distinguishable from them as reality, a knowing subject, or a thing in itself. Being, for example, is constitutively not a determination existing *in res*, nor something thought as a category of reason, but simply indeterminacy without further qualification than that it retrospectively be revealed to be the component starting point in the self-determination of categorial totality. Even the categorial totality itself refers to nothing given in reality, nor anything thought, but only to its own system of categories *per se*.

Consequently, what one is left with when one eliminates all positive science, metaphysics and transcendental inquiry is a development of categories more formal than any formal logic could be. For whereas formal logic proceeds by assuming certain logical operators and functions, as well as the logician in person, the categories following from being depend for their development upon no given knower nor any given content, be it a methodological principle or a reference *in res*.

Although they therefore provide no conception of reality, their concluded development does leave open one possible solution to the problem, a solution which Hegel briefly sketches in moving from his *Science of Logic* to his *Philosophy of Nature*.

### vi) The Transition from Categorial Totality to Reality

Having come this far, if there is to be no return to the errors committed by positive science, metaphysics and transcendental philosophy, then the determination of reality must somehow follow from the categorial totality alone. Because the latter has so far shown itself to be the sole content to which reference can legitimately be made without recourse to presupposed foundations, any determination of reality will have to emerge immanently from the complete development of categories which Hegel calls the Absolute Idea.

If one were, for instance, to undertake a ''logic of discovery'' where one turns to what is given to one and conceives reality by finding the categories as they are there purportedly embodied, then the dilemma of metaphysical reference would reassert itself. Once again, one would be assuming the correspondence of categories and reality, while making immediate truth claims for which any adjudication would be excluded from the start.

To avoid this trap by following an immanent development from categorial totality does not mean, however, that reality is to be conceived as something determined *by* categorial totality. Although at one point Hegel himself lapses into characterizing the Absolute Idea as God before Creation,[11] giving much cited fuel to metaphysical misinterpretations, his whole argument runs counter to any such suggestion that categorial totality be thought of as the determiner of reality. If this be done, the system of categories gets illicitly assigned a primacy foreign to its own special uncontrasted formality. Instead of being taken as the *self*-determined whole it is, categorial totality would here be made the determiner of something other than itself. As such, it would effectively become a transcendental structure contrasted to ''reality'' as a positor stands related to what it posits. With this the case, one falls back into the dilemmas of transcendental argument, where ''reality'' can no more escape being a solipsist construction, than the constitution of reality in terms of the categories can escape being a subjective positing.

What saves an immanent transition beyond categorial totality from all these problems are the two sides of self-determination already revealed through the concluded development from being.

On the one hand, if categorial totality were to develop immanently into reality, this would involve no immediate reference to anything in itself. The transition would be made entirely on the basis of what categorial totality itself comprises, without any outside intervention. Consequently, the problem of metaphysics would not arise.

On the other hand, what results from immanent development is not determined *by* what it arises from. On the contrary, a fully independent development is a self-determination, and what determines itself is not already given at the start, but only comes to be at the end as the result. Thus, if reality emerges immanently from categorial totality, the actual subject of the self-development will not be the system of categories, but rather the completely determined reality. As a result of the development, reality will be what has actually determined itself in the process, whereas categorial totality will stand not as reality's determiner or as God before creation, but as the component starting point from which the determinacy of reality develops itself. Only in this way will reality be as free of foundations as the theory which conceives it. Furthermore, the relation of categorial totality and reality can not be based upon our reflection, but must be made within the development itself at the point it achieves its final and full totality.

On these terms, the possibility of a non-positive, non-metaphysical and non-transcendental conception of reality lies open. Given the nature of the problem, the first task is determining how categorial totality can result immanently in something which is other than itself and which actually is.

To begin with, what emerges from categorial totality must be irreducible to all and any of its constitutive categories. Otherwise it will simply fall back within categorial totality as a purely formal determination. Irreducibility must be achieved, however, without any introduction of stipulations, immediate references to reality, or acts of knowing. Because all there is is categorial totality itself, the only otherness that could possibly emerge would have to be a pure other of categorial totality, pure in that it would refer to nothing else and nevertheless would rely on the content of categorial totality for its otherness. Furthermore, this pure other would have to be such as a self-development from categorial totality. Otherwise the required immanence would be broken.

The only way all these conditions can be met is if categorial totality develop into what is its own content external to itself. If what emerges be, in other words, the entirety of categorial totality related to itself as something given, then one will have what is specifically other to categorial totality, without entailing either a return to any particular categories or an illicit introduction of extraneous content.

At the very end of the *Science of Logic*, Hegel offers this insight, and observes that just such a transition immediately occurs once categorial totality itself emerges as the concluding determination of the development from being.[12] To be concluding, this final category is itself a retrospective ordering of all preceding ones as component stages in the development of the whole which incorporates them all by determining itself through them. Thus, the moment categorial totality arises, the entire development stands as something given to it, presenting it as something that has run its course, been achieved, and thus come into being. In other words, as soon as it has developed, categorial totality stands external to itself. Consequently, what one has is no longer categorial totality in all its radical formality, but rather the self-externality of categorial totality, or the self-externality of the Idea, to use Hegel's expression.[13]

Although this new structure incorporates nothing but the determinations of categorial totality, it does so as something given, and not in a manner which is itself a category, as was the case with the purely formal ordering comprising the concluding category of the system of categories. As a result, for the first time there is not just determinacy without further qualification, but a given determinacy. The latter is given not to some presupposed structure of knowing, but rather to the groundless, presuppositionless totality of determinacy it contains within itself as its structural element. Since such given determinacy is neither stipulated, nor metaphysically referred to, nor transcendentally constituted, it provides a reality free of the dilemmas confronting all past candidates for what is.

Needless to say, the self-externality of categorial totality does not exhaust the determination of reality, but at best supplies the minimal threshhold of given determinacy required for any further real structure. Hegel accordingly characterizes it as the most rudimentary and immediate content of natural givenness, which all others must presuppose and incorporate.[14] What reality as a whole actually is must await the completion of a further development which can only arise out of reality's initial specification as the self-externality of categorial totality.

With all external stipulation still excluded, the real can come to its full determination only on the basis of self-development. Its self-determining process, however, like self-determination *per se*, can only reach a conclusion by arriving at a final determination relating all those that preceded as elements in the development of the whole. Just as the development from being had to arrive at its own method to achieve closure, so the development from the self-externality of categorial totality must reach a real determination providing that ordering principle for all reality which allows it to seal its own totality.

If we are to follow Hegel's indications,[15] such a consummating entity would seem to be nothing other than philosophy itself, taken as the real phenomenon it is appearing in the world with a history of its own. It could provide the element within reality determining how all structures of givenness are constitutive components in the self-determined totality of the real. In so doing, philosophy would not only allow reality to achieve totality by determining itself as a whole independently of anything else. Philosophy would further secure the truth of the conception of reality which must be distinguished from what reality is itself.

This would be accomplished on two fronts, both of which are internal to reality's own development, as they would have to be, if external stipulations were to be avoided.

On the one hand, the completed determination of reality would establish the full relation between categories *per se* and real determinations. This would happen not simply because the concluded development of reality would provide what is to be contrasted to categories, but rather because reality would make the contrast itself. Since the development from being to categorial totality would proceed no less immanently to a self-development from categorial totality to the whole of reality, there would actually be one continuous self-determination which runs from being through to the summit of reality. Consequently, at the very end of all this, the actual subject of the entire self-determination would first stand complete and show itself to be that totality of reality made manifest with philosophy's appearance.

On this basis, then, the entire sphere of categories would no longer be just an uncontrasted whole proceeding from being, but a categorial totality which figures as the component element for the minimal structure of the real. The application of the categories within the determination of reality would here lie established entirely in virtue of reality's own development, rather than in virtue of some given foundation. Hegel, who calls the totality of reality "spirit," suggests as much by arguing that the Idea is spirit in itself, that is to say, spirit implicit, insofar as spirit's self-determination incorporates the categorial totality of the Idea as the basic element of all its real aspects.[16]

As Hegel recognizes, what would permit knowledge of this relation between reality and categorial determinacy without recourse to a transcendent standpoint is the role philosophy would play as reality's own comprehending component. In virtue of the retrospective ordering achieved by a philosophical thought unencumbered by ontological or epistemological assumptions, the relation of reality to categorial determinacy, that lies within the self-determination of reality, would also be conceived as such within that same self-determination. Through this real act of foundation-free philosophy, the non-positive, non-metaphysical, non-transcendental conception of reality would then secure truth for itself, not by presupposing the correspondence of thought and reality, but by arriving at it, no less in reality than in thought, as the final result of its labor. Without any immediate reference to reality, or any transcendental grounding of its knowledge, philosophy would here conceive reality as containing its own philosophical activity. In so doing, philosophy would conceive its own conceptions in distinction from both categories *per se* and reality as a whole, while grasping the unitary process in which all are bound together.

If this opens the possibility of a true knowing of what is, that must still remain only a possibility until the full development leading to this point has actually been given. No stipulated anticipatory schema can substitute for the immanent determining at issue.

Consequently, the strategy Hegel has offered for conceiving reality without metaphysical or transcendental arguments requires nothing less than first showing in full detail how indeterminacy does in fact give rise to a development leading to categorial totality. Once this be accomplished a complete account must follow of how categorial totality, with all its now unfolded content, freely releases itself into self-externality. Lastly, one must establish how the given determinacy of this result leads to a self-determination of reality that achieves totality with a final self-ordering element of its own.

Although Hegel has addressed all three of these tasks at great length, the results of his efforts have not been systematically evaluated. So long as that remains the case, and if no other attempts be made to fulfill these tasks, true knowledge of reality will be but a program for philosophy without foundations.

## Notes

1. See Willard Van Orman Quine's "Two Dogmas of Empiricism," in *From a Logical Point of View* (New York: Harper and Row, 1963), for a classic statement of this position.

2. In the Introduction to the *Phenomenology of Spirit* Hegel makes these arguments, without there taking up the other alternative notion of knowing as a structure of referring whose act generates its own referent.

3. This self-elimination of transcendental cognition is precisely what Hegel observes phenomenologically in the chapter entitled "Absolute Knowing" in his *Phenomenology of Spirit*. As I have tried to show in "The Route to Foundation-Free Systematic Philosophy" (*The Philosophical Forum*, Vol. 15, No. 3, [Spring 1984]), this final collapse of the foundational quest for knowledge of consciousness leads directly to the starting point of the *Science of Logic*.

4. See Hans Georg Gadamer, *Truth and Method*, translation ed. by G. Barden and J. Cumming (New York: Seabury Press, 1975); Alasdair MacIntyre. *After Virtue* (Notre Dame, IN: Notre Dame Press, 1981); Hilary Putnam. *Reason, Truth and History* (New York: Cambridge University Press, 1981); and Richard Rorty, *Philosphy and the Mirror of Nature* (Princeton, NJ: Princeton University Press, 1980).

5. Hegel attempts to document their internal collapse in his *Phenomenology of Spirit*. In "The Route to Foundation-Free Systematic Philosophy" (*op. cit.*). I have tried to show how Hegel can present this self-elimination of metaphysical and transcendental discourse without making truth claims of his own.

6. G. W. F. Hegel, *Science of Logic*, trans. by A. V. Miller (New York: Humanities Press, 1969), p. 83f.

7. *Ibid.*, p. 82.

8. *Ibid.*, pp. 82–83.

9. *Ibid.*, pp. 824–825.

10. *Ibid.*, p. 825.

11. *Ibid.*, p. 50.

12. *Ibid.*, p. 843.

13. *Ibid.* p. 843; G. W. F. Hegel, *Philosophy of Nature*, trans. by A. V. Miller (Oxford: Clarendon Press, 1970), paragraph 247.

14. Hegel, *Philosophy of Nature*, paragraph 254.

15. G. W. F. Hegel, *Philosophy of Spirit*, trans. by William Wallace and A. V. Miller (Oxford: Clarendon Press, 1971), paragraphs 574–577.

16. *Ibid.*, paragraphs 381, 575–577.

# 5

# On Individuality

For centuries, philosophers, to their common grief, have been compelled to regard the relation between the universal and the particular as perhaps *the* problem underlying all others. Informing all disputes regarding thought and reality, concept and intuition, form and matter, scheme and content, theory and practice, norm and behavior, necessity and contingency, and so forth, the controversy over how the universal and the particular should be thought has straggled on without resolve.

The inconclusiveness of the debate has been largely due to the prevailing assumptions that the universal and the particular could be conceived by themselves and that they could provide the resources for conceiving the concrete character of what is. With one great exception,[1] thinkers have failed to conceive the missing link for their endeavors. This missing link is individuality, whose distinction from particularity has been chronically ignored, to the despair of legions of philosophers. As we shall see, unless individuality is conceived in conjunction with universality and particularity, neither the universal nor the particular can be thought, nor can the character of what is be rendered intelligible.

### i) The Incoherences of Thinking the Universal and the Particular without the Individual

Following Robert Berman, let us distinguish the universal, the particular, and the individual in a simple and familiar fashion: the universal is a class, the particular is an undifferentiated member of a class, and the individual is a unique member of a class, distinguished from all other members. What now happens if, following virtually all major philosophers with the exception of Hegel, we leave the individual aside, as something either ignored or inconceivable, and attempt to make sense of the universal and the particular by themselves, and of the real by their means?

As a class, the universal owes its constitutive generality to the differentiation of members. The plurality of members is something on which the universal depends, for only if the universal is something shared by more than one exemplar can it stand suitably distinct from the particular belonging to its class.

It might be objected that this plurality of members is superfluous, since a class might be described to have one member. Yet, the moment this is done, the putative class ceases to have any universality and its putative member thereby ceases to belong to anything general. With commonality and membership eliminated, all that remains is a term which, lacking any universal or particular dimension, becomes virtually indescribable and indeterminate.

Yet, if the universal cannot be what it is without the plurality of members of its class, can particulars have their own identity on the basis of this simple class-member relation? If the particular is merely an *undifferentiated* member of a class, constituting an instance of the universal without any further qualification, there is nothing about it in virtue of its particularity or its relation to the universal that distinguishes it from other members. If to be particular, as opposed to being individual, is to be an undifferentiated member of a class, then each such member is, as such, utterly undistinguishable. For each, qua particular, is simply a member of a class and such membership provides no resources for distinguishing members from one another.

What, then, can sustain their plurality, keeping them at a distance from one another? If the universal is just a class of undifferentiated members and the particular is such a member, neither provides any basis for preventing the members from being indiscernible and collapsing into one. Yet, if these particulars cannot be held apart but are conceptually identical, where does their particularity reside? They can no longer be contrasted with one another by means of any difference.

Can they then retain their particularity through the only contrast remaining, that between member and class? Even this option becomes untenable. Since, as shown above, the universal depends upon the plurality of members to constitute itself as a class, once members are recognized to be indistinguishable in their capacity as particular, the needed plurality evaporates. Then, the putative universal can no longer be differentiated from the putative particular since each are one, having collapsed into the indeterminacy of a class with one member. With the universal losing the differentiation of plurality on which its generality depends, the particular loses the last contrast term in distinction from which it might retain its own identity.

Naturally, if the universal and the particular cannot sustain their own constitutive character by themselves, they can hardly provide the key categories for construing the concrete reality of what is. It thus can come as no surprise that those theories that attempt to conceive being exclusively in terms of the relation of the universal and the particular, such as the form-matter conception of substance or the theory of definite description, cannot account for the identifiability of their objects.

### ii) Individuality as Constitutive of Universality and Particularity

The solution to the quandary is already suggested by the chief dilemma afflicting the attempt to conceive the universal and the particular by means of themselves. As we have seen, what prevents the universal and the particular from retaining any distinction from each other, and thereby any distinction whatsoever, is the lack of any resource to sustain the plurality of members of the class. It is not enough for each particular to be an undifferentiated member of a class. If their plurality is to be determined, enabling the relation of the universal and the particular to subsist, then each particular must be further determined so as to stand distinguished from every other.

Yet could this still be accomplished without employing more than the particular and the universal? Why not follow the traditional path of maintaining that particulars stand distinguished by virtue of belonging to different classes in addition to whatever ones they share? Then every member of a class will constitutively have a unique set of class memberships setting it apart from every other particular.

This remedy begs the question on two complementary grounds. On the one hand, the requirement it imposes on every particular, that of belonging to a unique array of classes, may incorporate universality and particularity, but it still remains a characterization irreducible to either one. To belong to different classes than any other particular is not itself class membership nor universality. On the other hand, insofar as this characterization refers to distinct particular classes as well as to pluralities of members belonging to each one, it employs differentiated particulars, which are precisely what are in need of an account.

Once, however, the stubborn restriction to the universal and the particular is abandoned, a simple solution is available: in order for there to be universality and particularity, each particular must be individuated, bearing a discrete identity that adds to its character as member of a class the further feature of being a unique member, distinct from all others. For the particular and the universal to be what they are, individuality must be given in conjunction with them. To be a class, the universal must refer to a plurality of members that are each, not just particular, but individual as well. Conversely, to be a member of a class, the particular must be one among others, each of whom is individual.

### iii) Universality, Particularity, and Individuality as Codeterminative of One Another

But what of the individual itself? Although universality and particularity may depend upon individuality for their determination, is individuality dependent upon them? If individuality did require universality and particularity as ingredient aspects of its own determination, then it would follow that individuality always involves a relation among a plurality of individuals who belong as unique members to the same class. Then, to be an individual would constitutively entail being one among other individuals of the same kind, sharing the feature of being a particular of a common universal, augmented by a contrastive relation securing their mutual differentiation. If reason comprehends at least what is universal in what is, and what is must be individual, then existence cannot be opaque to thought.

Yet what if the individual involved neither universality nor particularity? What could it then comprise? Stripped of all membership in any classes, the individual might qualify as a mere something, contrastable with an equally indeterminate other. Or it could also perhaps figure as either side of a relation in which something is determined by something else, such as in essence and appearance, cause and effect, ground and grounded, or substance and accident.

Yet none of these relations would provide it with anything like a unique identity, since more than one entity could equally occupy the position of each such term. For example, to be the other of something does not serve to identify which entity it is that occupies that position of contrast any more than being something uniquely identifies any entity. Similarly, to be simply a cause or an effect by no means singles out an entity, since an indefinite plurality of factors may play those particular roles. Moreover, if these relations were viewed as classes in their own right, for example, the class of what is something and other, essence or appearance, cause or effect, and so forth, then the individual in question would revert to an empty indeterminacy because none of these characterizations could any longer be applied to it.

In contrast, by being a member in a class, incorporating universality and particularity as elements of its own character, the individual has the resources it requires to account for its own individuation. Since it is then a differentiated member of a kind yet not the kind itself nor a member in general, the individual has an exclusive determinacy setting it uniquely apart. In this way, the individual possesses a discrete identity through its contrast with both the universal and the particular, a contrast that equally entails its contrast with other individuals.

Consequently, just as the universal and the particular owe their character to the individual, so the individual has its own identity through the universal and the particular. Only by standing in contrastive relation to the other two terms can the universal, the particular, or the individual maintain itself. And this is but the first respect in which the universal and the particular are inextricably linked to the individual. For through the very relations by which the universal, the particular, and the individual owe their character to one another, each term is further qualified in terms of the other two.

The universal, as a class distinguished from its undifferentiated and unique members, is equally something particular and individual. The universal is particular as one of the three terms. The universal is individual insofar as it is a unique term, specifically different from the particular and the individual to which it is linked. Moreover, the universal is particular as one among other undifferentiated members of the class of universals, just as it is individual as a unique member of that class, distinct from all other universals.

For its part, the particular, as an undifferentiated member of a class, is equally universal and individual. The particular is universal insofar as the universal, in its capacity as particular, shares membership in particularity. The particular is individual to the extent that it is a unique member of the respective classes of particulars and universals.

Finally, the individual, as a unique member of a class, is universal and particular. The individual is universal insofar as the universal and particular are also unique terms, sharing in that capacity. The individual is particular insofar as it is a member of the class of universals.

These transfigurations, whereby each category takes on the character of the others, might appear to destroy all distinction between the universal, the particular, and the individual. Yet the opposite is the case. It is only in their distinction from one another, whereby they figure respectively as a class, undifferentiated member of a class, and unique member of a class, that the universal, the particular, and the individual can function so as to play simultaneously the roles of their counterparts. Because of this further linkage of the universal with the particular and the individual, the particular with the universal and the individual, and the individual with the universal and the particular, their categorization sets the stage for conceiving the forms of judgment, understood as relations between factors distinguishing the latter in terms of the universal, the particular, and the individual.[2]

### iv) Ramifications for Theory and Practice

Leaving aside this further categorial development, what ramifications follow for theory and practice from the interconnection of universality, particularity, and individuality?

To begin with, certain long-bewailed dilemmas evaporate. The perennial challenges of Platonism and nominalism lose their common basis. This consists in the assumption that the universal and the individual are given independently of one another. From this bogus dogma, the Platonist concludes that only the universal truly is, as a transcendent reality of intellectual form, while the nominalist conversely concludes that only the individual truly is, whereas universals are merely phantoms of subjective thought. Since, however, neither the universal nor the individual can have its determination apart from the other, it is just as wrong to banish the universal to a transcendent realm or subjective fiction as it is to deprive existing individuals of an indwelling universality.[3]

Accordingly, Kierkegaard's related lament that reason cannot address existence because existence is individual but thought universal also loses its bite. Since universality cannot be thought without thinking individuality as an element constitutive of the universal, and individuality cannot retain its specificity without incorporating the universal and the particular, the supposed incommensurability between existence and reason collapses.

Does this then mean that we are in a position to deduce Herr Krug's pen, that is, to determine a priori every feature of facticity? Reason would have this totally constitutive character of an intellectual intuition if the *category* of individuality included as part of its own specification every content pertaining to the individual. However, identifying a term as a unique member of a class, which is to say, comprehending it as an individual, is not equivalent to specifying all of its qualities nor all of the relationships in which it may be embroiled. It involves merely setting it in contrast to other unique members of the class, leaving otherwise unspecified what features serve as factors of their distinction, as well as what other features may pertain to each individual without contributing to its individuation. Consequently, conceiving the individuality of some entity is not equivalent to conceiving it in all its singular detail.

Nevertheless, what does seem entailed in conceiving something as an individual is construing it as one of a plurality of individuals belonging to the same class. This plural character of individuality removes one of the great stumbling blocks of practical philosophy, namely, the perennial problem of conceiving how the interest or autonomy of the individual can be harmonized with the interest of the community. This problem turns out to be a false one once it is recognized that the individual cannot be atomistically conceived, as if what it is in its own right were given independently of its relation to other individuals. On the contrary, the logical connection of individuality with universality and particularity underscores how the autonomy of the individual does not exist apart from community insofar as the relation between individuals is constitutive of their respective independent identities.

Once again, however, a question arises as to how far the connection between individuality and universality can be pushed. If we grant that to be individual involves relation to other individuals of the same class, does this preclude the very existence of such entities as the last survivor of a species or a single, world state? It is hard to see how the extermination of all humans but one would any more rob that survivor of individuality than the emergence of a world state by conquest or destruction of or by union with all other polities would deprive that body politic of its own unique being.

Similarly, if self-consciousness is self-awareness of one's own exclusive identity, and hence dependent for its individuality upon contrastive relations with other self-conscious individuals, must a person cease to be self-conscious when removed from the company of others, either temporarily or permanently? And if we are compelled to acknowledge that individuals do not lose self-consciousness nor the power of speech or other reputedly intersubjective capacities when deprived of others, does this contradict the characterization of individuality as being a unique member of a class?

Certainly, one cannot be a property owner, a moral subject, a family member, a bourgeois, or a citizen without engaging with other individuals in the specific modes of interaction in which such types of agency are constitutively embedded. One only has entitled possession in reference to other persons, just as one is morally responsible only in relation to other morally accountable subjects. And, needless to say, one can only enjoy the rights and duties of membership in the family, civil society, and the state in conjunction with other members of these same institutions. As each of these entitled roles makes manifest, rights and duties make no sense other than in the context of relations of a plurality.

However, the same cannot be said of self-consciousness or the unique nature of a last human or of an unopposed political regime. One can be self-conscious in isolation from others, just as one can well imagine a last surviving human being or a solitary state remaining unique. Yet that such isolated individuals could exist does not mean that the logic of individuality is violated. So long as they remain unique exemplars of a type for which other instances are both conceivable and actually possible, be it in the past or future or in completely isolated places, such entities are still contrastable with other possible members of the same class and hence retain individuality. Thus even if to be self-conscious one must differentiate one's awareness not only from what is not consciousness but from other selves, this could well be achieved in memory or imagination without an immediate and continual perception of another similarly self-conscious individual.

A more problematic case is the individuality of a monotheistic deity.[4] Unlike the last human or a world state, the monotheistic god cannot possibly be contrastable with any other being of its type. Indeed, the argument in behalf of monotheism advances the stronger claim that the divine cannot be plural insofar as polytheism undermines the infinitude of divinity by limiting its gods by one another. Given the logic of individuality, the divine then ceases to be a class with unique members and the monotheistic deity loses its individuality. Such a god may be contrasted with what is mortal, but this differentiation of opposites does not serve to individuate either. By itself, it provides no more than a contrast between mortality and divinity in general.

The same lack of individuality would equally apply to the universe or nature. The moment any possible counteruniverse became actual, it would have to be spatiotemporarally integrated within a single nature incorporating our own. Hence, the universe must be just as unindividuated as would be "any" monotheistic god.

Nevertheless, even in cases where the factor in question cannot be an individual in respect to all its content, individuality still enters in as long as the factor can be subsumed under a class. In this respect, a monotheistic god and the universe would each be unique members of the class of entities that are otherwise without peer. Since any determinable entity will fall within the class of determinate factors, it is unthinkable how any factor could escape being an individual in some regard.

The class of all classes is no exception. It might appear to be a universal under which all particulars and individuals are subsumed, without itself being subsumed under any universal in contrast with other particulars of that class. Yet, the class of all classes is still particular and individual because it is a unique member of itself, comprising one class among others with the distinction of being the only member containing itself and the rest.

This ubiquity of individuality should come as no surprise, given how the universal and the particular not only require individuality for their own determination but also determine themselves as individual in virtue of retaining their own unique character. To exclude the individual from thought is therefore as shortsighted as it is vain.

## Notes

1. Hegel is the one major exception among great thinkers of the past. This essay expands upon the formulations of Robert Bruce Berman (made both in conversation and in his *Categorial Justification: Normative Argumentation in Hegel's Practical Philosophy* [Ph.D. dissertation, New School for Social Research, NY, 1983]), who has clarified what lies obscure in Hegel's *Logic of the Concept*, namely, the basic arguments showing, first, how attempting to conceive the universal and the particular without the individual is hopelessly aporetic, and, secondly, how the universal, the particular, and the individual are determined in terms of their relation to one another.

2. This is what enables Hegel to make the transition from his categorization of the concept, whose elements are universality, particularity, and individuality, to the categorization of judgment.

3. Georg Lukács makes this point regarding the common pitfall of Platonism and nominalism in his *Über die Besonderheit als Kategorie der Ästhetik* (Neuwied and Berlin: Luchterhand, 1967), p. 8.

4. Robert Berman has raised this case in conversation.

# Part II

# Autonomous Action

# 6

# Morality without Community

## i) The Three Schools of Contemporary Ethics

In revolt against traditional conceptions of the good, three theories have come to dominate contemporary ethics: utilitarianism, deontology, and communitarianism. Each begins by denying reason's ability to prescribe directly authoritative ends and actions, and each claims exclusive validity for its own alternative. Although all three thereby absolutize a different determination of ethics, the diversity of their positions reflects a differentiation inherent in moral life. To see this, we must first think through their salient points and then address the alternative by which they may be reconciled.

Given how these three positions follow upon one another, utilitarianism deserves first consideration. It takes reason's failure to dictate immediately what goals and activities should be performed as leaving all claims of ethical validity ultimately matters of preference. Whatever ends and actions may be assigned moral significance have their privileged place, not because their content can be directly rationally legitimated or because they help maintain an institutional framework immediately sanctified by reason, but because they are objects of personal desire whose attainment, as such, provides pleasure. Just as empiricism had given sensibility a not just contributing but governing role in the formation of knowledge, so here feeling and desire are deemed not just evidence for practical judgments inaccessibly to reason alone but the only evidence by which conduct can be judged.[1] All things and actions are thereby deprived of intrinsic value, obtaining worth only by being of use in satisfying the extraneous end of given desire.[2] At the same time, reason's inability to rank ends prevents the content of desires from being rationally ordered. Hence, conduct can no longer be praised or blamed by the qualities of its motivation,[3] for all motivations are ultimately cases of desire and each desire of each and every agent stands on a par, counting simply by being held as a purpose whose fulfillment promises pleasure. Given this qualitative indifference of desires and corresponding satisfactions, if any goals and activities are to be assigned any primacy, it can only be on the quantitative grounds that their achievement likely offers greater aggregate pleasure. This provides the utility principle, whereby the good is nothing but the greatest satisfaction of the interests of the greatest number, moral freedom is the liberty of following desire that every individual enjoys by nature,[4] and reason is relegated to a slave of passion, calculating the best means for promoting this empirically determined end.[5]

In reaction, deontology takes reason's incapacity to prescribe ends and actions to signify, not that ethics is left to calculate aggregate satisfactions of desire, but that the formal character of intended action is the source of its validity. However this formal standard is defined, be it as the universalizability of intentions or as conformity to a privileged choice procedure certifying approval by all concerned, it offers a paradigm of rational willing distinguishing the moral from the immoral without making any prior commitment to particular goals and activities, nor to any institutional frameworks they might sustain, nor, for that matter, to the privileged authority of preference calculation.

The latter utilitarian principle is rejected as a dogmatic hypothesis, hopelessly unworkable because of the incommensurability and contingency of desires and their satisfactions, and blind to any alternate solution. In rendering all conduct instrumental to the maximization of pleasure, utilitarianism must face the question of why that goal can have exclusive legitimacy and not be itself instrumental to some further end.[6] The naturalistic answer that all action is in fact directed to the maximization of pleasure is of little help. Not only is the universal necessity of this rule open to question on either empirical or a priori grounds, but simply as a descriptive thesis it is of no use in justifying why a utility principle can have any, let alone an exclusive, normative role. Moreover, ethical conduct, as opposed to psychological behavior, can only occur if the utility principle is not universally effective and compliance with it is instead a matter of choice. Then, however one might agree that, all things being equal, satisfying desires is preferable to frustrating them, it remains questionable whether maximizing happiness deserves the autocracy utilitarians claim or whether other normative concerns should take precedence.[7] In any case, even if the utility principle were granted normative status, the uncertainty of any action's effect upon aggregate happiness and the inability to reduce qualitatively distinct and conflicting pleasures to a quantitative measure render the utilitarian calculus simply inoperable.

If, then, neither the content of ends and actions nor the pleasure that attends their achievement can provide legitimacy for conduct, what else can render action conformable to moral principle than the form of the willing that underlies it? So long as an agent's intention has a lawfulness satisfying the normative requirement of universality, the quality of conduct's motivation can give it a moral character independent of desires and consequences. In accepting this as the only abiding alternative, deontology may depart from the consequentialism of utilitarianism, but it still joins utilitarian thought in providing an ethic whose standard applies to agents irrespective of what community ties they have, to the exclusion of any other norms. In this respect, deontology, like utilitarianism, offers a vision of morality without community in which a self-defining, disengaged individual agency is the focus for determining ethical norms. Whereas utilitarianism construes this determining agency as the empirically given individual, whose entitled freedom consists in choosing among de facto desires and pursuing their satisfaction on an equal footing with others, denontology appeals to an agent defined abstractly in terms of formal features of its willing, where the moral self is given prior to both its ends and relationships.[8] The deontological person is ethically free, not by being at liberty to fulfill personal preferences, but insofar as it exercises the autonomy of willing independently of its given interests and attachments in conformity with the privileged form by which moral conduct is distinguished. In both cases, the detachment of the moral agent permits ethical questions to be decided without embracing substantive qualities of actions or institutions.[9]

Communitarianism, on the contrary, rejects all such notions of a morality without community. It regards reason's incapacity to dictate the goals and activities of the good life as rendering ethical standards internal to forms of community whose own character is historically given rather than rationally prescribed. The utilitarian and deontological options are dismissed on the grounds that the deontological formal criterion is as arbitrary as utilitarianism's appeal to aggregate pleasure and that its privileged form can no more unequivocally identify valid conduct than can the principle of utility. The universalizability of the intentions of an action may, for instance, be a necessary condition of its morality, but it is not a sufficient condition that allows for differentiating moral from immoral conduct. Instead, communitarianism maintains that ethical standards only have an identifiable validity for agents who belong to a community within which membership entails a pursuit of common ends and activities by which members reproduce the bonds that unite them and the roles they exercise. This means, not simply that moral agents are inherently in relation to one another, but that the form of their agency and the content of its ends are predicated upon an existing institutional framework to which they constitutively belong. Accordingly, what is and what ought to be are no longer separated by any gap, such as might underlie the inapplicability of moral principle. Whereas the utilitarian calculus and deontology each enjoin us to realize an ought that is not yet at hand, the communitarian vision of obligation binds agents to reproduce the very mode of community that determines their moral identity and common duties. The ethical is thus inherently actual, for ethical norms are now seen to operate only within a context where their pursuit both presupposes and sustains an existing community embodying their realization.[10]

Given communitarianism's acceptance of the assumption that reason cannot directly prescribe the good, the community in question is an historical given, which cannot be independently legitimated. Hence communitarianism must refrain from identifying any particular form of community as ethically privileged. Although its appeal to community is intended to counter the formalisms of utilitarianism and deontology, communitarianism thus ends up embracing the formalist assumption of metaethics, namely, that it is possible to differentiate the ethical and the nonethical without at the same time distinguishing the ethical from the unethical. This leaves communitarianism with two alternatives. It must either accept a Burkean affirmation of the historical tradition of our community as an unquestionable framework for our moral reflection[11] or opt for a nihilist relativism, recognizing that the norms of every community are irreducibly particular and conditioned by unjustifiable givens. In the former case, communitarianism abandons its metaethical standpoint by embracing a particular ethical theory, to whom its allegiance is purely accidental. In the latter case, communitarianism follows metaethics in contradicting the claim to objectivity that both acknowledge to be endemic to morality.[12]

We, however, have another option, which involves neither a retreat to the tradition from which contemporary ethics rebels nor an embrace of any one of the three theories prevailing today. Instead, we can recognize that utilitarianism, deontology, and communitarianism reflect essential aspects of ethics that are not mutually exclusive and that, subject to proper reformulation, each captures dimensions of a unitary ethic dictated by reason independently of any of the appeals to given foundations that have long been discredited. In particular, utilitarian and deontological thought, for all their well-known problems, encapsulate modes of a morality without community that is rationally justifiable, inescapable, and reconcilable with ethical community. For its part, ethical community is not captive to historical givenness but comprises institutional orders of freedom that reason can determine and legitimate. Exploring this option is nothing new, for Hegel has done just this with mixed success[13] in his *Philosophy of Right*, distinguishing morality from both property relations and the ethical community of family, civil society, and the state.

Leaving aside the particulars of his discussion,[14] let us examine the logic of such a morality without community, which challenges the claims of exclusivity of the competing schools of contemporary ethics by revealing their compatibility.

### ii) Morality without Community as a Structure of Interaction

To avoid the most common misconceptions, we must begin by observing how a morality distinguishable from an ethic of community is still a structure of interaction, wherein the moral agent is defined in its relations to others. The interactive character of moral agency has largely been ignored because of how utilitarianism and deontology have emphasized the institutionally disengaged nature of the moral individual and how communitarianism has distanced itself from their positions. Generally, communitarian thinkers reject utilitarianism and deontology for advancing an ethical atomism.[15] Although this rejection is duly provoked by the failure of utilitarian and deontological thought to make explicit the interactive character of moral subjectivity, it also reflects a failure in communitarianism to recognize normative structures of interaction that are not absorbed into ethical community.[16] The charge of atomism revolves around the argument that the very agency affirmed by utilitarianism and deontology actually presupposes certain forms of community, despite the fact that utilitarian and deontological thinkers describe moral agency as if it were self-sufficient apart from all associations. If, however, we turn to moral agency,[17] we discover that it is characterized independently of any membership in community, while still being interactively determined.

In contrast to ethical community, morality is defined by two coordinate features that underlie its various modalities. On the one hand, it obligates moral agents to bring into being a good that does not yet exist but can only arise through their independent individual initiative. On the other hand, morality imposes its obligations upon moral agents, not by virtue of their membership in any existing community, but solely in their capacity as agents called upon to act on the basis of their own responsibility for the content of their intentions and actions. As communitarians readily point out, these aspects go together, for if agents belong to a community that gives them their ethical identity and duties, their common life is invested with normative validity, making it a reality that is as it ought to be.[18]

However, that morality entails obligations holding irrespective of community membership and involving an ought opposed to existence does not mean that moral agency is a function of the individual will independent of its relation to others. The contrary is suggested by the very fact that utilitarianism and deontology treat their respective moral agents as counting equally and taking one another into equal consideration when acting, be it in regard to personal happiness or the dignity of moral willing. It indicates that, in either form, moral deliberation and action proceed in terms of a structure of plurality defined by each participant heeding the coordinate moral standing of the others.[19]

Even when a deontologist like Kant mandates "duties to oneself,"[20] as if to uphold the atomist nature of moral obligation, these all turn out to aim at maintaining or strengthening the moral fibre one needs to obey one's duties to others. Without this reference to other moral agents, Kant's perfect duties to oneself to refrain from suicide, wanton self-abuse, self-stupefaction, lying, avarice, and servility would have no more rationale than his imperfect duties to oneself to develop one's natural and moral capacities. Hence, Kant, who stubbornly ignores this reference to other, is compelled to internalize it within the moral agent, at times splitting conscience into two selves,[21] at other times introducing the idea of God as imagined source of obligation.[22]

The same anomaly applies to Kierkegaard's lament that the moral subject can be nothing but self-concerned. Kierkegaard maintains that the only ethical contemplation is solitary contemplation of self[23] insofar as morality is essentially concerned with the motivation of conduct and the only intentions to which one has actual access are one's own.[24] Kierkegaard may be right that moral intention, being internal, cannot be observed by an outsider but can only be known and realized by oneself.[25] Yet that we cannot obtain indubitable knowledge of the intentions of others, either directly or at second hand, does not reduce morality to a self-relation or preclude imputing responsibility to others and judging the morality of their conduct. The epistemological problem of knowing other minds and their intentions is of no bearing precisely because it is rooted in a view of self that presupposes the absence of any constitutive tie between individuals. Although this assumption may have some role in the epistemic relation between knowers, it is out of keeping for the practical relation of moral agents. The reason is that occupying a moral stance involves engaging in an interrelationship in which one acts in view of other individuals whose moral capacity, be it as bearer of interests or as self-legislating conscience, constitutively determines what we oblige ourselves to do. To the extent that this is so, one cannot even have access to one's own moral reality without acting in regard to that of others.

Nor could one engage in the self-affirmation of a will to power to which Nietzsche reduces all ethics. In taking the rational unjustifiability of all norms, including reason's own claim to privileged authority, to signify that asserting any content as a universal standard is equivalent to imposing one's own will as a form of rule over others, Nietzsche is equally blind to how any imposition of moral obligation entails recognizing the same moral standing of those one holds accountable. Contrary to the unilateral conquests building his genealogy of morals, a moral agent cannot begin to determine which motivations and actions to will without already taking into account the coordinate capacities of those to whom one can be obliged.

Hence, even though morality may involve acting to satisfy personal interests and willing with a formally correct motivation, the freedom of moral agency is not reducible to the liberty of a natural will whose purposes are set by given desires nor to the autonomy of action conforming to a rational rule of intention.[26] Because of the moral subject's constitutive relation to others, moral agency exercises a freedom that can only be defined in terms of interaction. The stumbling block of atomism, the problem of relating originally unrelated agents, therefore never arises.[27] Instead, moral agents only are what they are for themselves and for others by willing in regard to the correlative interests, right, and responsibility of other moral agents, whom they recognize to be participants in the same relationship. This requires that moral agency have a specific manifestation by which it is recognizable to others, allowing every moral subject to recognize the moral standing of those to whom it is morally obliged and be recognizable in its own right as equally accountable.

What distinguishes moral agency from other normative roles such as property owner, family member, market participant, and citizen is that the factor by which moral subjects interact is that aspect of their action that is held to reflect the aims motivating its pursuit. Whereas owners interrelate as such in terms of external embodiments of their wills in indifference to whatever purposes motivate their disposal of property, and whereas family members, market agents, and citizens interact in terms of goals whose pursuit is predicated upon the institutions in which they participate, moral subjects interact simply in respect to their own determination of the purposes and motives manifest in those corresponding features of their action for which they are deemed responsible. Although this characterization says nothing about utilitarian promotions of happiness and deontological volitions of lawful intentions, it provides the basic threshold on which these intelligibly emerge.

This threshold is defined by two parallel distinctions by which the action of moral agents can figure as the factor of their interaction. Insofar as moral conduct minimally involves individuals interrelating in respect to one another's intended conduct, each agency and each act makes itself manifest in a dual way. On the one hand, in acting, each agent exhibits the internal determination of giving itself a purpose in light of a prior understanding of its circumstances, as well as the external determination of undertaking the chosen action itself. On the other hand, the agent's action occurs in the world subject to all the external causalities this involves, yet without simply being an externally given event devoid of purposive determination by the agent. Accordingly, the action stands differentiated into its deed, taken as an event, and the act, comprising that aspect of the deed prefigured in the knowledge and purpose of the agent. On these terms, each agent is held responsible for its act as anticipated in its knowledge and purposes rather than for all aspects of the deed, just as each agent holds others similarly accountable.[28] Embedded in this mutual relationship, each agent exercises a freedom that can only be had in conjunction with others, that of enjoying the right of being held accountable only for what it has knowledgeably and purposely performed. Given the reciprocity of the relationship, this right goes hand in hand with observing the coordinate duties of taking responsibility for one's acts and holding others responsible only for theirs. It is this reciprocity of right and duty that gives the distinctions of act and deed and purpose and responsibility a morally specific character as elementary features of moral agency. It is also what makes moral agency a form of an objectively recognized self-determination, where the agent individuates itself by making its own freely determined purposes define the morally relevant reality of its deeds.

However, simply interacting in terms of purpose and responsibility is only part of the self-determination of moral agents. What makes their acts moral in character is not just that they are performed with an accountability limited by the freely chosen purpose of the agent, but that they purposely affect the aims and actions of other agents, irrespective of any bonds of community.[29] Otherwise the distinctions of act and deed and purpose and responsibility would equally apply to morally indifferent activities, such as purely technical manipulations of things by an agent. Granted this further qualification that moral purpose refers to other agents, it might still appear that little can be said if we ask what limits on the content of purpose are inherent in moral interaction. Yet, the right and duty of acting with purpose and responsibility already carries with it a consideration that brings us close to the utilitarian principle. If moral agents are entitled to be held accountable only for that side of their deeds reflecting their freely determined purposes and if the achievement of their purposes can be called their interest,[30] then their coordinate duty to respect this dimension of moral agency constrains the content of each moral agent's purposes so as to promote the interests of all. In this way, the principle that agents ought to act so as to permit all to satisfy their freely chosen purposes has its place without reliance upon any naturalistic assumptions about human nature or sceptical dogmas concerning reason's limits. It also defines the interests at stake as inherently self-defined, excluding all forms of paternalism, doing so, once again, on the basis of nothing but the rudimentary structure of moral interaction. However, contrary to the autocratic thinking of utilitarianism, the principle of limiting one's purposes so as to promote the interests of all does not have an exclusive place, for the structure of moral interaction equally entails a further dimension in which deontological concerns have their play.

What gives room for deontology is that the actions of moral agents entail consequences bearing the same dual character as act and deed. For just as the action, as an event, is distinguishable from those of its features prefigured in the knowledge and purpose of the agent, so the consequences of the action comprise events embroiled in external linkages of all kinds, which are distinguishable from those ramifications of the act that the moral agent intended, based on an understanding of the circumstances. This introduces a new level of moral responsibility, where agents exercise the further recognized freedom of being held responsible only for those consequences of their acts that are prefigured in the knowledge and intentions that underlie their choice of purpose. The focal point of moral judgment now shifts from the content of purpose, as realized in action, to the content of intention, as realized in the action's ramifications.[31] Once again, the nexus of right and duty by which moral interaction is defined places its own limit upon what content intentions should have. Just as the right to be held accountable for only one's acts, as prefigured in purpose, carried with it the duty to respect the right of others to be held responsible on the same terms, so the right to be responsible only for the consequences of one's act that are prefigured in one's intentions entails the coordinate duty of recognizing the same entitlement of others. Hence, to enjoy the moral freedom to be responsible for only the intended ramifications of one's conduct is tantamount to having one's intention conform to the rule of harmonizing with the intentions of others, which is to say, to have a motivation that can be a motivation of all.

Although this formal prescription for intentions arises independently of atomistic assumptions, it does fall prey to the same problems of application that are the oft-condemned banes of deontology, as well as of utilitarianism. In acting, each moral agent must choose a particular purpose for a particular motivating reason, yet the requirements that the purpose promote the interests of all and that its underlying motivation be one that all could have does not provide any unambiguous specifications. Indeed, this is a problem for moral agency itself, and, in interacting, each moral subject is embroiled with determining precisely what particular content should be given that unity of purpose and intention, or of the general welfare and right. The forms this determination can take are manifold, but they all have a common thread,[32] given that morality enjoins agents, irrespective of their membership in any community, to determine and realize a good that is not yet at hand. Generally speaking, moral agents here determine themselves as conscience, each deciding for itself the specific manner in which the welfare and right of all can be realized through the consequences of its act, yet doing so in a way that the decided course of action should hold valid for all moral agents. The problem is that conscience's self-determination of the good has the same reciprocal character as every dimension of moral interaction: that is, whereas each moral agent, as conscience, exercises the right of deciding and realizing the particular determination of the good that only individual initiative can bring to be, each agent must equally respect others' right to do the same. Then, unless by miraculous chance every agent has hit upon the same specification of the good, each conscience faces a dilemma. Either it holds fast to its own dictate of conscience to the exclusion of the conflicting claims of others, which is tantamount to denying them their respective moral authority, or else it acknowledges the competing validity of their conscience at the expense of relinquishing its own moral integrity.

This difficulty would be overcome only if the congruence of all agents' purposes and intentions could be assured.[33] Such congruence is, of course, what ethical community provides insofar as its modes of interaction all entail roles whose aims are given in common by the institutions they sustain. As family members, individuals interact in terms of a shared household good by which their family identity is defined, just as market participants pursue needs for commodities whose only satisfactions are tied to those of others, just as citizens exercise their political freedom only by engaging in constitutional conduct that reproduces the body politic to which they belong. The moral situation, by contrast, can boast of no such systemic congruence.

Does this then rob moral agency of all legitimacy? It might, save for one abiding feature of morality that its interactive structure sustains—that it consists in a discrete mode of self-determination. Even though at every level the morality of conduct remains a problem, moral agents still succeed in exercising an entitled freedom whereby they individuate themselves, determining both the content of their acts and the form of their agency. The very fact that the validity of their purposes and intentions becomes an issue signifies that their moral accountability is something real, sustained in the relations between agents in which each is recognized master of the objectivity of its deeds.

If self-determination commands a unique validity owing to its freedom from foundations, allowing what is normatively valid to be determined by nothing having any lesser warrant,[34] then moral agency will share in the legitimacy common to each and every structure of freedom. In that case, the preceding outline of morality can lose its assertoric, dogmatic character and achieve rational justification by being shown to be part of the theory of the reality of self-determination.

Even then, however, two points remain to be dealt with, first, the compatibility of morality with ethical community and, second, the inescapability of moral agency. If it can be shown that morality and ethical community are mutually compatible and that moral agency cannot be dispensed with, then utilitarianism, deontology, and communitarianism can all retain a circumscribed truth.

### iii) Morality and Ethical Community

From the point of view of morality, ethical community can be compatible provided that its bonds are such that the moral agent can recognize in them an authority binding upon moral reflection. On the one hand, ethical community can satisfy moral subjectivity's concern for promoting the satisfaction of interest when it provides a social sphere where individuals can exercise their liberty of desire so as to satisfy their self-selected needs in reciprocity with others to the benefit of the welfare of all. As I have argued in *The Just Economy*, this can be achieved by a publicly regulated market economy in which economic disadvantage is continually countervened. On the other hand, ethical community can satisfy moral subjectivity's deontological concern for the lawfulness of intended conduct by enforcing a system of law of which all citizens are coauthors and whose articles are as inherently reasonable as constitutional and positive law allow.[35]

From the point of view of ethical community, compatibility with moral agency may be a sine qua non to the degree that freedom of conscience and respect for the satisfaction of desire must be honored if the bonds of community are to be fulfilled in the voluntary acts of its members. In other words, the laws of the state must be susceptible of meeting the formal requirements of moral reflection while prescribing a social order that satisfies the interests that it regulates.[36] Otherwise, moral subjectivity will directly impede the form of willing that membership in ethical community involves. This does not mean, however, that moral agents should be given license to disregard the norms of the community whenever their conscience so decides. The state must maintain the rectitude of its citizens if it is to sustain itself. However, this need to curtail the activities of conscientious citizens is not equivalent to stamping out the right to moral responsibility. Given the internal dimension of moral self-determination, community initiative can never coerce the agent's choice of purpose and intention, nor does the community's survival require curtailing every activity dictated by conscience in opposition to institutional norms.

Here again, the importance of not absolutizing any one form of morality comes to the fore. Ethical life becomes truncated if, for instance, the utilitarian hegemony of sensibility in moral reflection is carried over in the form of the empiricist doctrine of the primacy of the economy within community. According to this theory and practice, the freedom of desire exercised in market activity becomes the paradigm of autonomy, relegating civil law and government to abetting instruments of free enterprise.[37] On the other hand, ethical life suffers a similar deformation if the deontological hegemony of formal universality in moral deliberation is extended to community. In that case, the administration of civil law is rendered the essence of ethical life, at the expense of the other forms of community.[38]

## iv) The Inescapability of Morality

Yet if ethical community escapes these truncations and instead realizes the full range of the institutions of freedom, satisfying the demands of utilitarian and deontological thought as well as providing family, social, and political institutions where self-determination realizes common goods at hand in the communities to which one belongs, what role is left for moral agency? In cases where legitimate institutions are lacking, that is, in a revolutionary situation, all conduct falls into the moral predicament. For then what exists is devoid of authority and the only good is an ought whose realization depends on personal initiative. So too, when the institutions of community are only partly legitimate and the roles that membership entails have a tarnished authority, the moral attitude must intervene to right their wrongs. But what of the ideal case, where each ethical institution realizes a distinct mode of self-determination and political association succeeds in uniting the different spheres into a self-ordered whole? Is any room left for moral interaction, or does the autocracy of communitarianism finally win the day?

Morality persists for two reasons. First, it remains a perennial option precisely because no institutional practice can preempt a form of self-determination that operates independently of community. The existence of ethical community cannot exclude the possibility of any of its members at any time and place interacting in terms of their responsibility for realizing a good that they perceive to be not yet at hand. Since morality involves no particular community life, the only resources required for its pursuit are a plurality of agents who choose to interact in moral terms. Their involvement in institutional roles may preclude their engaging in practices that entail conflicting structures of community, but not their undertaking forms of action that are essentially indifferent to such membership.

Second, the very roles that family members, civilians, and citizens occupy may prescribe shared goals and activities, but, in each case, room for discretion is always at hand, leaving the individual to determine what should be done without any unequivocal direction from institutional practice. In those interstices of our life in ethical community, there is no escaping the responsibility and travail of moral decision if action is to remain self-determined. Communitarianism may wish to brush aside moral agency, as Athens once sought to dispose of Socrates, but morality without community is still a structural element of ethical institutions.

For these reasons, utilitarianism, deontology, and communitarianism can make peace, as long as they finally recognize their limits and the corresponding diversity of ethical conduct.

## Notes

1. Michael B. Foster, *The Political Philosophies of Plato and Hegel* (Oxford: Oxford University Press, 1968), p. 78.

2. How this fits the world view of the Enlightenment is something Charles Taylor describes, following Hegel's understanding in Charles Taylor, *Hegel* (Cambridge: Cambridge University Press, 1975), p. 181.

3. Charles Taylor, *Philosophy and the Human Sciences: Philosophical Papers 2* (Cambridge University Press, 1985), p. 319.

4. See Foster, *op. cit.*, p. 88.

5. See David Hume, *An Enquiry Concerning the Principles of Morals* (Indianapolis: Hackett, 1983), p. 83ff.

6. Taylor, *Hegel*, p. 402.

7. Taylor, *Philosophy and the Human Sciences*, p. 241.

8. See Michael J. Sandel, *Liberalism and the Limits of Justice* (Cambridge: Cambridge University Press, 1982), p. 176ff., for an apt description of deontology's conception of moral agency.

9. See Charles Taylor, *Philosophy and the Human Sciences*, p. 231.

10. Taylor, *Hegel*, p. 376.

11. *Ibid.*, p. 423.

12. Robert Bruce Berman discusses the corresponding dilemma of metaethics in his *Categorial Justification: Normative Argumentation in Hegel's Practical Philosophy* (Ph.D. dissertation, New School for Social Research, NY, 1983), pp. 27–29.

13. For a critical discussion of Hegel's achievement, see Richard Dien Winfield, *Reason and Justice* (Albany, NY: SUNY Press, 1988), Part 4, and Richard Dien Winfield, *The Just Economy* (New York: Routledge, 1988), Part 2.

14. I have analyzed Hegel's conception of morality at length in "The Limits of Morality" in Richard Dien Winfield, *Overcoming Foundations: Studies in Systematic Philosophy* (New York: Columbia University Press, 1989), pp. 135–170.

15. A good example of this rejection is provided by Charles Taylor's "Atomism" in his *Philosophy and the Human Sciences*, pp. 187–210.

16. Although morality is the only such structure of interaction here discussed, property relations also comprise normative interactions defined independently of community. See Winfield, *Reason and Justice*, Chapter 8, for an analysis of how this is so.

17. For a discussion of how the turn to moral agency is achieved systematically only within an ethical theory that is already well under way, see Winfield, *Reason and Justice*, Chapter 8.

18. Taylor, *Hegel*, p. 376.

19. Taylor makes this observation in his *Philosophy and the Human Sciences*, p. 232, but he mistakenly describes the structure of plurality as one of community.

20. Immanuel Kant, *Metaphysical Principles of Virtue*, in Immanuel Kant, *Ethical Theory* (Indianapolis, IN: Hackett, 1983), pp. 82–111.

21. *Ibid.*, pp. 77–79.

22. *Ibid.*, pp. 100–102.

23. Soren Kierkegaard, *Concluding Unscientific Postscript* (Princeton, NJ: Princeton University Press, 1968), pp. 284, 287.

24. In support, Kierkegaard claims that reality exists for an individual only in his or her own ethical reality, that all knowledge pertains to the possible rather than the actual, and that every reality other than the individual's own can only be known by reducing it to a possibility, precluding any immediate ethical relation between subjects (*ibid.*, pp. 280–281, 285).

25. *Ibid.*, p. 285.

26. See Berman, *op. cit.*, p. 148.

27. *Ibid.*, p. 149.

28. See G. W. F. Hegel, *Philosophy of Right* (New York: Oxford University Press, 1967), paragraphs 115–117.

29. I have here been following Berman's exegesis of Hegel's discussion of act and deed and of purpose and responsibility in Berman, *op. cit.*, pp. 156–157. However, at this juncture Berman introduces intention in distinction from purpose, as if intentions were those purposes that, following the utilitarian mold, aim at the welfare of all. As I show in what follows, the endemic mutuality of the entitled purposes of moral agents already entails concern for the welfare of all. Intention, by contrast, is better distinguished from purpose as Hegel has done, namely, as that second-order aim consisting in the intended consequence of the act that is one's purpose. It provides the formal element of motivation for morality's deontological dimension.

30. It is worth noting that Hegel introduces ''interest'' in reference to the intentions of moral agents, whose attainment constitutes their morally specific ''welfare.'' See Hegel, *op. cit.*, paragraphs 122, 125.

31. *Ibid.*, paragraphs 119–124.

32. See Winfield, ''The Limits of Morality,'' in *Overcoming Foundations*, for an examination of Hegel's analysis of these forms in his discussion of ''The Good and Conscience'' in his *Philosophy of Right*.

33. Berman neatly describes this dilemma and how ethical life resolves it in his reconstruction of Hegel's argument in Berman, *op. cit.*, pp. 159–160.

34. The unique validity of self-determination is argued for in Winfield, *Reason and Justice*, Chapters 6 and 7.

45. Michael Foster describes these two forms of reconciliation as alternate definitions of ethical life in Foster, *op. cit.*, pp. 89–90.

36. Foster argues this in *ibid.*, p. 89.

37. Foster discusses this problem in *ibid.*, pp. 79, 148.

38. *Ibid.*, p. 149.

# 7

# The Injustice of Human Rights*

At a time when foreign policies draw increasing criticism for advancing national interest without regard for human rights, the sanctity of the appeal to human rights has itself gone unchallenged. Reinforced by constitutional preambles, United Nations declarations, Helsinki accords, and presidential pledges, the consensus has reached such proportions that when advocates of human rights are caught supporting social and political injustice, they are attacked for hypocrisy, as if the principle they fail to apply were a self-evident truth.

What has been ignored is that human rights are themselves a contradiction in terms. Their contradiction, however, is of much more than theoretical significance, for when human rights are elevated to a principle of public affairs, they both exclude all specifically social and political critique and debase political freedom by reducing it to nothing more than an exercise of civil rights.

These practical consequences emerge from the basic dilemma entailed in conceiving human rights in the first place. This dilemma touches the very heart of the natural right conception which provides the foundation for the liberal tradition. Although liberal theory has virtually come to prescribe what passes for legitimate political discourse in this country by being the unquestioned dogma of political education in the public schools, as well as the common credo of the two parties, the mass media, and all who have achieved recognition as responsible participants in political affairs, it founders upon a simple fallacy directly embodied in the notion of human rights. This is the basic confusion of what is determined through freedom with what is given by nature. Natural right theory falls into this confusion by first granting that rights involve what individuals can freely will without being legitimately constrained by others, while secondly deriving rights from nature, considered generally as the natural order whose law is given independently of men and women's will, and more specifically, as the given nature of the individual human subject.

The problem besetting natural right theory is that the very content of rights prohibits them from being either natural givens or products of any natural condition, or from being attributes of the self, given prior to and independently of individuals' relations to one another. Although natural right theory turns to these natural, unwilled factors in answer to the inability of existing convention to prescribe what ought to be, the most basic examination of rights reveals that their normativity can be established no more on natural than on conventional givens.

First of all, to the degree that rights consist in the modes of autonomous action by an individual which others are legitimately obligated to respect, rights contain a normative dimension tied to conscious willing. Consequently, rights cannot be reduced to relations of nature, for whether the latter proceed through causal necessity or a probabilistic quantum mechanics, the absence of willing within natural events signifies the exclusion of self-determination and all normative questions of what ought to be. Since rights therefore refer not to what happens according to nature, but to what voluntary actions individuals may legitimately undertake, no anthropological fact of human species being can prescribe what men and women have a right to do. The human condition may mandate what individuals are anthropologically capable of doing, but not which of their humanly possible actions should be performed.

Nevertheless, as natural right theory itself recognizes, the normative dimension of rights precludes their reduction to merely operative rules of behavior. Since rights draw a distinction between just and unjust action, they effectively involve recognition of a principle specifying what ought to be done regardless of what happens to be given practice. Might cannot make right, for the achievement of compliance with given rules only signifies that behavior is rule governed, and not that it involves an exercise of freedom which ought to be respected.

Thus, although rights are not natural, in the sense of being given independently of willing, they are not just products of convention, relative to any order to which a community conforms. Rights do indeed come into being only by convention, arising within history instead of in a state of nature, but in doing so they can neither be bound to nor justified by the particular conditions of their enactment. Rather, they are rights and not ordered behavior only by being unconditioned and universal, for otherwise they would be stamped with a relative character undermining their required normativity and rendering them no more justifiable than any other mode of conduct. The great task of the theory of rights thus consists in conceiving what are those relations among individuals which have unconditioned universality even though they must be willed into being by individuals, who, being unbeholden to natural necessity, can just as easily will something else. For this theoretical endeavor, neither a natural or a purely positive conception will do, since the determination of rights can derive no more from given practice than from given nature.

If this means that rights cannot be founded in nature or existing convention, it must also be recognized that they are not derivable from any structure of the single self. Because rights consist in an exercise of freedom whose legitimacy is respected by the wills of others, rights cannot be understood simply with reference to one individual's manner of willing. Although a choosing will may be ascribed to an individual, irrespective of that individual's relation to others, an individual's right to act in a certain way further involves the duty of others to respect that mode of action. Consequently, rights exist not as a function of the self, but only in virtue of specific voluntary relations among a plurality of individuals. The conjunction of right and duty comprising rights consists in these interrelations, which must always have the form of mutual recognition and respect since one only has obligations when one's own exercise of freedom is acknowledged. Therefore, to refer to rights is to refer to those modes of interaction which have normative validity.

What determines the specific relations of these interactions is not nature or convention, but the demand of normativity itself. Normative validity requires unconditioned universality, as much in matters of justice as in matters of truth. For an interaction to be a relation of right and not just a given practice, it must be something that ought to hold irrespective of whatever particular conditions there may be which are not themselves relations of right worthy of the same respect. If an interaction were relative to any particular prior conditions that were not themselves rightful, the interaction would be determined by what stands outside right and accordingly forfeit its status as something that ought to be.

In this sense, relations of right are universally valid, being justified in any situation whose particularity is not already a specific relation of right. As such, their universality is no less unconditioned, for what alone can legitimately limit a relation of right is another rightful relation.

Consequently, the content of right cannot be determined by any independently given factors. Instead of being caused or grounded by something else, rights must be their own ground and thus exist for their own sake and no other. For this to be the case, they must have their specific character in virtue of their own relationship and not from any separate end, procedure or consequence. In other words, the interactions of right must be self-determined, and owe their entire content to the very mode of freedom they realize. As rights testify by their characteristic content as some respected prerogative to act, only freedom can provide normative validity, for self-determination is precisely what has unconditioned universality by being determined by nothing other than itself.

Therefore, the interactions of right can have no necessary relation to the given particularities of species being or to any other prior ground. Rights rather have their legitimacy by being self-determined structures of interaction and for that very reason, *they do not have foundations*.

The problem with natural right theory is that it attempts to give rights foundations. Whether this be done by grounding them in natural laws or the nature of the self, as in traditional liberal theory, or by determining them with a privileged procedure of construction, as in Rawlsian models, the same foundational fallacy is committed. So long as rights are determined by something other than themselves, they are left relative to a content which is outside right, and therefore illegitimate. Any attempt to escape this dilemma by making convention the source of all right, as practical holism, for example, undertakes, only reengages the foundational fallacy by substituting convention for the other grounds it seeks to avoid.

In this respect, the different modes of foundationalism in the theory of right parallel the various metaphysical approaches in the theory of truth. Just as what is right cannot be founded upon what is not already normatively valid, so the justification of truth claims cannot be based on what is not already justified as true. For this reason, philosophy can no more proceed from immediate references to reality or transcendental conditions than right can be based on facts of nature or procedures of construction. The attempts of the late Wittgenstein, Gadamer, and Rorty to supplant epistemological foundationalism by grounding philosophy in the given convention of discourse is as much an assertion of a new foundation as is the ethical nihilism of conventionalism in rights. Just as rights must be self-determined, so philosophical discourse must be self-grounding, and this it can only be if it proceeds from no given foundations whatsoever.[1]

If all these considerations indicate how the question of rights is bound up with the determination of freedom, it should also be evident that freedom has reality only in the interactions of right. Where the mutually concording willing of rights is lacking, the reality of freedom is undermined by being subject to the contingent circumstance of whether or not individuals choose to act in ways which violate each other's autonomy. With interactions of right, on the other hand, individuals have the reality of their freedom unconditionally respected, for rights consist in just that conjunction of rights and duties where the self-determinations of individuals reinforce one another. In other words, right is unconditionally universal, *objective* freedom, without which individuals have only the *subjective* liberty of the self to choose arbitrary particular acts subject to the arbitrariness of others.

Accordingly, when it comes to determining who has rights, what alone warrants consideration is whether the candidates in question have minds and wills with which to recognize and be recognized by others. Here natural differences can come into play, but only in the subsidiary role of providing preconditions, rather than determining principles for the needed minds and wills. For example, in matters of environmental and medical ethics it is necessary to determine who can bear rights by judging which organisms, as well as which homo sapiens, have the natural potential to exercise rights, a potential consisting in the ability to act in a recognizably willful way towards others and to respond to their actions with understanding and respect. Nevertheless, judging that homo sapiens have a species being allowing for subjectivity in a way in which a snail darter does not, or that an irreversibly comatose human being no longer has the natural prerequisites to participate in the interactions of right does not establish what are the specific rights which knowing and willing individuals should enjoy.

Consequently, one can reject all natural right, and yet speak of property rights, moral rights, family rights, economic and civil rights, or finally political rights, for their content derives not from natural differences, but from the different normative modes of freedom specific to each of their interactions.

Property rights, for instance, refer to those relations that hold when individuals recognize and respect the exclusive embodiment of each other's will in different possessed objects. Simply forming, marking or taking hold of an object cannot establish entitlement to its ownership unless other property owners both recognize these actions as signs that an individual has embodied his will in the object and respect that embodiment by laying their own wills in something other than that object. Precisely because this enacted relation between wills can alone turn possession into ownership, no individual's right to property can be restricted in virtue of natural differences such as race and sex, which have nothing to do with the ability to will in reciprocity with others.

Family rights, by contrast, are determined with regard to the enacted institution of the household. It acquires the normative dimension constitutive of family rights only when it has shed all unity based on the natural features of sexual difference and species procreation, and instead becomes established on the basis of a free mutual consent, where household roles are defined exclusively through the shared recognition of the equal responsibilities and respect due each adult member. If this makes any sexist division of household duties a violation of family rights, it also prohibits the marriage bond from being restricted to individuals who can and do have offspring, who are of different sexes, or who are of a certain sexual orientation. Similarly, the rights and duties between parents and their children do not rest upon the natural relation of parents and offspring, but upon the willed enactment of the family. Accordingly, the rightful parents of children, duty-bound to raise them, need not be their natural father and mother, nor man and woman, nor heterosexual. Indeed, if homo sapiens ever encounter other species who are also endowed with minds and wills allowing them to bear rights, then it would be just as wrong to prohibit them from entering into marriage and parental relations with human beings as to support *apartheid* or ban homosexuals from marrying and rearing children.

Analogously, economic rights arise only within the social sphere of the economy, where they specify the valid recognition of each individual's need, goods, and labor within the mutually agreed upon commodity exchanges entailed in every market relation, regardless of whether the participants be private individuals, publically owned enterprises or worker self-managed cooperatives. Where individuals can satisfy their wants directly from nature without entering into voluntary relations with others outside their household, their work and consumption involves no social right, but simply comprises a natural metabolism, or at best, a form of housekeeping, relating the anthropological givenness of men and women with nature through causal technical relations. Only when their needs are needs for commodities and the activity securing their satisfaction is tied to the reciprocal satisfaction of others, does economic activity involve the mutual recognition and respect comprising rights. Then the economic welfare of each participant in the market becomes a matter of right, involving the satisfaction of not just the natural requirements of life, but also the artificial needs generated in the market which require not just naturally scarce resources, but commodities produced in an unnatural multitude and diversity. Accordingly, poverty comprises the wrong of a socially specific disadvantage depriving the poor of the opportunity to exercise their economic right to earn a conventional standard of living above and beyond a mere subsistence existence.

Although the economic right to satisfy one's freely chosen needs in reciprocity with others can only be exercised within the market institutions of the economy, it is not automatically secured by the relations of plurality making it possible any more than are property or family rights. Whereas property and household relations cannot alone preclude persons and family members from disputing what they are respectively entitled to or from consciously violating the rights of others, commodity relations themselves provide no guarantee that all individuals will find willing parties to exchange, allowing them to satisfy their needs in reciprocity with others through action of their own choosing.

For this reason, a further public regulation is required to enforce and guarantee these rights, a regulation comprising a public administration of civil law and welfare on the basis of which individuals first obtain and exercise their specifically civil rights to enjoy their property, family life, and economic livelihood under the guarantee of public authority. In pursuing their functions, however, civil institutions do not give themselves the law and authority under which they operate.

If these conditions of their own existence are not to be imposed upon society, then a further public sphere of right is necessary to ground the other relations of right in its own institution of freedom without resting itself upon any external ground. This is provided by the sovereign state to the degree that its political order frees rights of foundations by 1) enforcing all non-political relations of right through its own activity of self-government, and by 2) realizing its own political freedom not on the basis of any outside authority, but in virtue of the state's own politically actual constitution. On these terms, political rights consist in that exercise of freedom accorded the individual as a recognized participant in self-government, determining the self-ordered order under which all other relations of right are held together. This is the right of a citizen, a role to be had only within a duly constituted body politic.

Finally, even so seemingly inward a matter as moral right requires a relation of recognition between individuals. This is so not just because moral action can only be taken towards those whose autonomous worth is acknowledged, but because individuals actually enjoy the right to be morally accountable only if others recognize them to be responsible for their actions. Events in this century have made horrendously clear how revoking this recognition strips men and women of their rights as moral subjects, leaving them to be condemned not for what they have willfully done, but for their race or social background.

As all these examples indicate, rights are constituted through specific enacted structures of reciprocal recognition in which the members of a plurality of individuals can choose a certain mode of action towards one another and have its legitimacy mutually respected. Consequently, when rights are violated, it is no natural relation which comes under attack, but rather an exercise of freedom involving certain normative relations between individuals. To condemn such violations thus means criticizing specific institutional distortions in these interrelations. There can thus be no social or political neutrality in defending rights, for what lies at stake is instituting the actual social and political structures which themselves comprise the valid exercise of the rights under attack.

The notion of human rights, however, bases the exercise of freedom not upon any enacted relations between individuals, but upon human species being, given by birth. This, his/her anthropological identity, is something naturally defined just as the species being of any creature. Consequently, the appeal to human rights cannot help but be formal in character. With all men and women supposedly born free and equal, enjoying rights given by nature rather than issuing from specific non-natural, artificial interactions of individuals, all injustice becomes reduced to a violation of human species being, leaving aside any question of what positive institutional arrangements might be required for rights to exist. Thus, from a purely theoretical point of view, it is no accident that those who make human rights the principle of politics generally denounce individual cases of repression without focusing attention upon those systemic social and political features of existing regimes which block the exercise of freedom.

This itself gives some indication of how the notion of human rights does not simply cast rights in an improper natural form, but also distorts their content. One aspect of this distortion is the untenable particular limit that the human rights conception places upon the requisite universality of right.

On the one hand, it is evident that our species being does not automatically make us a bearer of rights. Insane, severely retarded and comatose people, not to mention infants and children, are all certainly human, but they are nevertheless unable to manifest to others a mind and will capable of recognizing and respecting the rights of others and of determining itself according to the legitimate modes of property, moral, family, social or political relations. Consequently, they cannot exercise full rights or fulfill the obligations that go along with them, and they are treated accordingly.

Conversely, although we have so far failed to encounter any other species in whom we recognize the capacity to enter into relations of right, the example of science fiction certainly indicates how it is possible to imagine beings who are not human, but have a mind and will with which they can interact and exercise the rights involved in disposing over property, engaging in moral action, and belonging to a family, a society, and a state. In this respect, grounding rights in human species being is categorially identical to limiting rights according to such other natural differences as race and sex. Such restrictions have been appropriately judged to be counter to right, precisely because all that individuals need in order to bear rights are a mind and will capable of recognizing and being recognized by others.

It is worth noting that just as rights cannot be founded on species being, so the right to political self-determination cannot be based upon the given racial or ethnic unity of a people. If this is done, the source of law and authority becomes invested not in a politically self-organized citizenry having rights and duties to one another, but in the pre-political, noninstitutional unity of a people to whom the fiction of a unitary will is ascribed. On this basis, political life stands subordinated to a single power which is above all law and institutions precisely because it does not originate in any enacted relations among the plurality of citizens. Not only do political rights then get restricted to those who are nationals by birth, but politics becomes subject to the unrestricted dictatorship of whoever claims to represent the undivided people's will. The French Revolution fell prey to this destructive path, which has since been followed by many national liberation movements. It is the Nazis, however, who brought the appeal to the right of the people to its logical extreme by resolutely grounding their state in the natural unity of the German people, and consistently erecting the absolute rule of Hitler as the immediate and unique expression of the indivisible will of a master race unbeholden to any enacted rights or obligations.[2]

In this catastrophic form, the reduction of the rights of citizens to the rights of a people parallels the natural reduction at issue in human rights. The fatal problem for both is conceiving how rights can possibly be given by nature, independently of any structures of mutually willed interaction. Although the affirmative resolution of this question is taken for granted by human rights advocates and natural right theorists in general, there is an open contradiction between any determination of right by nature and the reciprocally recognized self-determination of freedom in which rights consist.

In effect, liberal theory admits this difficulty, by recognizing that in a state of nature where no enacted institutions exist, there is nothing to guarantee that the freedom all men and women are born with will enjoy any mutual respect and not turn into the general license where what one individual wills violates the person of another. No natural laws can secure such rights, for law can only command voluntary obedience if it is enacted and publicly proclaimed by a will whose legitimate authority is already universally recognized. In that situation, one has an instituted common will whose decree all have given their consent to obey, thereby allowing themselves to be determined by a universal law they have actually imposed upon themselves.

This mutually respected self-determination of a plurality of individuals is, however, precisely what is lacking in a natural condition. There what is clear to reason may have binding force in rational argument, but not upon the will all possess by birth. It can always defy what reason ordains, let alone what others will, exactly because, as an individual will beholden to no established agreements, it has the freedom to choose its own particular ends by itself. Consequently, the state of nature is endemically a state of war in which human rights have no secured existence at all.

It is for this reason that the liberal tradition recognizes the necessity for a social contract where all agree voluntarily to establish a common authority whose constitutive function is to secure the exercise of freedom defined by everyone's human rights, but left unenforced in nature. What the tradition fails to recognize, however, is that the social contract establishing such a government requires the very same unanimous respect for right that is lacking in the state of nature and whose absence requires the founding of a public authority in the first place. Namely, by its very definition, the social contract can only come into being when the prospective members of society are already all resolved to honor each other's rights by taking the common measure of entering into agreement to institute civil government. Without this prior unanimous commitment, the social contract not only has no binding force, but cannot even be entered into, whereas only without such shared commitment, under a state of war where the common recognition of rights is lacking, does the need for a social contract arise.

Be this as it may, it is important to note the character of the body politic which would get erected on the basis of human rights, both because it presents what liberal theory takes to be the proper form of government and because it reveals the prime injustice that any political pursuit of human rights involves.

First of all, since the principle of human rights defines the exercise of freedom independently of any social or political relations, the government contractually instituted to guarantee these rights does not exist to realize political freedoms specific to its own governing activity. It rather exists for the sole sake of securing rights given prior to and separately from it. So long as the government protects these human rights and has the original consent of all it governs, it can take any form whatsoever. This is why Locke in Chapter X of *The Second Treatise of Government*, to take a classic example, sees fit to allow civil government to be either a democracy, an oligarchy, or a monarchy and still be true to itself.

Accordingly, when persons enter a social contract to secure their human rights, the exercise of freedom they achieve does not consist in any specific participation in government, but merely involves those actions that can be pursued as private individuals, following particular ends of their own personal choice which do not trample upon the natural liberty of others. In effect, they give their consent to a public authority to which they hand over the monopoly of political action, so long as it serves their natural rights. In this way, the pursuit of human rights entails a system of government where the citizen is free not to participate actively in self-government, but to exercise a pre-political liberty.

Instead of comprising the self-determined engagement in the sovereign affairs of state, political freedom here gets reduced to civil rights, that is, freedom to pursue one's particular aims and interests under the protection of public law and authority. At the same time, these civil rights themselves here lose their specificity as enacted relations of a civil society, and get reduced to functions deriving their content from human species being.

What results from this double reduction is a public domain in which the autonomy of political action has given way to an administration of government over a citizenry that has voluntarily relinquished political participation for the sake of pursuing its private concerns in security. It is this debasement of political freedom that comprises the fundamental injustice in making human rights the principle of public affairs.

As recent presidential campaigns demonstrate, these consequences of natural right philosophy are not matters of theory alone. They are all too well reflected in the system of political practice which pays its continual and hardly rhetorical homage to human rights.

The spectacle is a familiar one. While citizens exercise their modicum of civil rights, actual governing has fallen to the parties, under whom political activity has become the private vocation of professional politicians. All that is left to the citizen at large is either infrequent and less and less attended trips to the ballot box to reestablish the same gulf between voter and government, or the option of taking to the streets, an option involving no actual exercise of political power, but only an attempt to influence those who govern.

Accordingly, the politicians appeal to their constituencies not as participants in self-government, but as private individuals, taxpayers rather than citizens, bearers of class, ethnic and other particular interests rather than as subjects of political action and principles that lay hold of the entire politic. Under these conditions, that constituency can answer back only with the voice of public opinion, where it appears in the capacity of a passive, atomized mass of individuals expressing their personal preference, instead of as a citizenry engaging in an organized exercise of political power. Not surprisingly, the talk on either side is not of realizing self-government through political program, but of leadership, where what counts are the personal qualities of the competing party professionals. If this leaves the individuals holding no public office without opportunity to pursue anything but their private aims, it equally leaves government a besieged instrument of particular interests, be they those of the party oligarchies or of the various social groups vying for influence. In this, as in all the other respects, human rights are here the order of the day.

If their debasement of political freedom is to be challenged, then the critique of human rights must be complemented by a theory of the just state which conceives political sovereignty so that it provides the system of rights with a self-ordered whole free of foundations. Instead of deriving political rights either from what is given by nature or from the structure of the single self, this theory must account for them without losing sight of the constitutive factor of an interacting plurality of individuals required for the mutual respect underlying all rightful obligation.

This entails conceiving the rightful exercise of political freedom exclusively in terms of those enacted relations of concomitant self-determinations which could constitute the activity of self-government, an activity free from domination by particular interests, yet bound to secure the other institutions of right (including those in which private interests are properly at play) in conformity with the exercise of political freedom. If there be such a structure of interaction in which individuals can practice a mutually respected self-rule undertaken for its own sake rather than for independently determined ends, then political rights would be granted an autonomous life of their own consisting in a real freedom to participate in governing. In that case, the rights of political freedom would be both irreducible to the properly social concerns of civil rights and free from the dilemmas of natural right.

So long, however, as this problem of political justice remains ignored and unattended, the injustice of human rights will well outlive the piety of its defenders.

## Notes

* This essay is a revised and expanded version of a paper of the same title delivered at the Tenth Interamerican Congress of Philosophy in Tallahassee on October 21, 1981.

1. For a detailed discussion of how this is possible, see Richard Dien Winfield, "The Route to Foundation-Free Systematic Philosophy," *The Philosophical Forum* (Spring 1984), Vol. 15, No. 3, and republished in Richard Dien Winfield, *Overcoming Foundations: Studies In Systematic Philosophy* (New York: Columbia University Press, 1989), pp. 13–33.

2. Hannah Arendt has developed these points at length in *On Revolution* (New York: Viking Press, 1976) and *The Origins of Totalitarianism* (New York: Harcourt Brace Jovanovich, 1973).

# 8

# Freedom as Interaction: Hegel's Resolution to the Dilemma of Liberal Theory

The problem of making freedom the principle of right has dominated practical philosophy ever since the legitimacy of prescribed forms of justice was called into question by the demand that individuals be beholden only to what issues from their own consent. The authority of set virtues, given means of conduct, and any fixed essence of goodness has crumbled before this standpoint of the autonomous will. It has set aside those theories conceiving justice as *praxis*, that is, as conduct that is valid in virtue of embodying predetermined universal modes of action. In their place, it has introduced the problem of establishing what justice is, not by contemplating those given forms that action ought to realize, but by considering what relations emerge from the determining of the will itself. Modern practical philosophy has adopted this framework, where the will stands as the privileged determiner out of which all right is to be derived, and has accordingly set itself the task of working out a theory of justice whose principle is freedom.

Paradoxically, this very attempt to make freedom the principle of valid practical affairs has foundered precisely because taking freedom as a principle contradicts the basic structure of freedom itself.

It does so simply because making the free will a principle from which justice is derived turns it into something that determines what is other than itself. To be self-determining, however, the free will must determine its own self and not what is its other. When the will gets treated as a principle, it is rendered a determiner whose character is given prior to its act of determination, and whose act determines something else that is therefore not self-determined, but determined by what is prior to and other than it. By contrast, if the will is to be self-determining, then its own character can not be given prior to its act, but must be determined through it. Consequently, what it determines will be self-determined, for it is nothing other than its own act, that is, itself.

The importance of these elusive contrasts between positing and self-determination is brought into focus when one grasps the universal, particular and individual dimensions of autonomous willing, which together comprise the structure of individuality basic to freedom.[1]

To begin with, the will possesses a dimension of universality to the degree that it is never bound to any particular content, but is always free to will something else and then withdraw itself from that content to give itself another. Instead of being limited to any specific set of aims, the will rather defines itself by always exhibiting but one particular *instance* of its self-determination in whatever content it wills. If, on the contrary, the will's character were defined by any specific set of ends, then it would no longer be a self-determining, free agency, but a capacity externally determined by a content other than itself.

Although the quality of universality, of being unrestricted to any particular determination, thus underlies each and every example of willing, it forms only a single component of the will's structure. By itself, this universal dimension comprises a purely negative freedom to which the will cannot be reduced without contradicting its self-determining character. For if the will be defined only in terms of its universality, as a mere capacity to be unbeholden to all given content, then it has no particular content of its own whereby it could actually be self-*determining*.

To be a will, agency cannot just remain unbound to any given determination; it must will *something* and thereby bring a dimension of particularity to its universality. Accordingly, the will has the further aspect of particularity in that, in order to determine itself, it must go beyond its negative freedom and actually give itself a specific content. In so doing, the will does not lose its universal character and become something other than itself. Rather, because the will must will to be what it is, and to will it must will something, the willing of a specific content does not cancel the will's autonomy, but realizes it instead. It does so by providing the will not just with determination, but with its own *particularity*, in as much as in willing something the will determines itself in one instance of its general free agency.

In virtue of this component of particularity, it is evident that the will cannot be conceived as a mere faculty or capacity that can be defined prior to and independently of its actual willing of something. Simply to be self-determining agency, the will must have particular determination as part of its essence, and thus must be conceived as actuality.

Its actuality is of a special kind, however, for it integrates both universality and particularity. On the one hand, as much as the will is unbeholden to any given content, it must no less will a particular end in order to be self-determining. On the other hand, although the will necessarily restricts itself to a particular content in willing something, it thereby remains *self*-determined rather than determined by something else precisely because what it has determined is an agency that is never bound to the particular content it has given itself, but can always cast it aside and will another. In these respects, the will combines universality and particularity in its self-determination, and thereby exhibits the further dimension of individuality that contains within it the two others.

The will is individual in this sense, that what it is is not reducible to any prior universal form or capacity, but is only to be had in its actual particularization. Only in giving itself a particular content does the will stand at one with itself, for it has its defining identity as a self-determining agency precisely by determining itself in particular fashion. Consequently, the will is concretely universal, having its general character only in the activity of giving itself a particular content that builds its own free development. As such, the free will thus wills nothing other than itself, for in its individual act, at once universal and particular, what it determines is its own self-determination.

These most rudimentary features of the free will say nothing by themselves of how its agency is actually realized.

However, they do indicate that its own self-determination will be undermined if it be made a principle out of which the forms of justice are derived. In that case, the free will is rendered a merely universal determiner, in that its character is given prior to the form of justice it determines. Since its particular act of determination here falls outside its essence, as a derivative function that adds nothing to its character, the will is stripped of the particular and individual dimensions allowing for any real self-determination. The very freedom whose primacy is here asserted thus loses all actuality precisely by being the prior principle of what it determines. Conversely, the derivative forms of justice cannot be actual realizations of freedom themselves, for they are not self-determined structures, whose essence belongs to their particular existence, but relations dependent upon the prior principle of the will for both their form and content. On both sides, the individuality of freedom is unrealized.

Despite these basic problems, the overwhelming majority of modern thinkers of freedom have ignored its individual character and fallen into the trap of treating the free will as a principle of justice.

There is, however, an alternative conception of freedom, first developed by Hegel, which gives due respect to the individual structure of the will. Although it has fallen into general disregard by both practical philosophers at large and interpreters of Hegel, this conception is well worth reconsidering for the basis it affords for developing the theory of justice today.

Not surprisingly, the importance and necessity of Hegel's concept of freedom are brought to light precisely through following what actually happens when one does attempt to make the free will the principle of valid practical relations. This, of course, is the path of traditional liberal theory, which develops its theory of justice from the postulate of the free will. By tracing the immanent logic of its inquiry, one not only sees what is wrong with the liberal tradition's conception of freedom, but what is required to conceive freedom properly. It is this examination that leads to the concept of freedom as interaction first clearly formulated by Hegel.

### i) The Logic and Illogic of the Theory of Liberty

However misbegotten be the problem of making freedom the principle of justice, the problem both motivating and defining liberal theory, it is neither fortuitous nor arbitrary. It must be confronted once it is recognized that valid conduct cannot proceed from prescribed virtues, but must be self-determined, that just public authority cannot be based on a division of ruler and ruled, but must realize self-rule, that in all spheres of practical life what is valid must accord with and realize the autonomy of the will.

From this perspective, freedom must face the given reality of ethical affairs as the one unconditional principle in terms of which that reality must be structured and reconstituted in order to be just. This critical opposition, faced historically by the originators of liberal theory, immediately places self-determination in the position of a given form, out of which the valid relations of practical life are to be determined, rather than a freedom already situated in a world of its own. Although self-determination is properly at one with what it determines, here it is cast in the role of a positor, having both its specific character and existence prior to what it posits.

The ethical problem of freedom arises in terms of this conflation of self-determination and positing,[2] and in this form, it provides liberal theory with its starting point: the will conceived as a given structure, whose character stands defined prior to any actual self-determination, and whose right is to be realized as the first principle of justice.

As something given, the will is here a natural will, whose agency does not arise within any enacted practical relations, but rather precedes them all as an irreducible postulate. In other words, its autonomy exists not in virtue of any agreements or institutions, but in a state of nature that is a ''natural'' condition precisely by existing independently of the will's self-determination. Since the will itself exists in such a state of nature, being given rather than determined and brought into existence through willing's own act, the state of nature is logically prior to any instituted relations that could be in accord with the freedom of the will.

Further, since this natural will has its own form prior to any particular self-determination, simply by being primordially given, it is merely universal in form. Lacking particular self-determination as part of its essence, it is not an individual structure, which is inherently actual in so far as it cannot be defined apart from its particular existence. In its given universality, the will is rather a natural *capacity* common to all individuals. As here conceived, the will is a universal faculty which all are born with and naturally possess in equal form. So it provides the canonical first proposition of liberal theory: that all men are free and equal in the state of nature.

The freedom of such a will is accordingly natural *liberty*, the mere capacity of unfettered choice that all enjoy by birth. Because the will is a given universal structure, with no element of particularity within itself, it is not only a mere faculty, but one that must choose from independently given alternatives that can alone supply it with a particular content to will. These alternatives may thus be given either by what exists externally in nature, or by separate subjective faculties, such as reason or desire. However it be supplied, the particular content that the will chooses is independently derived, rather than actually determined by the will itself.

Consequently, although the natural will has the liberty to choose whatever alternatives it wants, it is still always bound to choices that are given to it rather than determined through freedom. From the vary start, then, the natural will bears the taint that it can never act with the unconditioned universality required for normativity, since its liberty is relative to the independent alternatives before it. This means at the same time that the natural will can never give itself a particular content at one with its universal form, and thereby attain the individuality of actual self-determination.

On this basis, what alone can provide the real existence of such a will is an embodiment that is external and given, yet stands as the express objectification of a will that must seek its particular content entirely outside itself. This generic realization of the natural will is accordingly a naturally appropriable property, which alone comprises the objectification of that merely universal will that can claim for its own existing self-determination nothing more than some externally given thing. Thus, the liberty all men are born with has its corresponding embodiment in a natural right to property.

This reality of liberty is as much a problem as the general predicament of choice, however, in so far as the individual identity of each natural will is something given. Because the will, as the universal natural faculty of liberty, is a capacity common to all, what individuates one agent from another must be particular desiderata extraneous to the structure of the will itself. This means that individual wills stand differentiated from one another by nature, with their universal form given particular embodiment in different subjects who face one another not through willing and in accord with its common liberty, but in a given condition where what makes each particular is unmediated by freedom. In this way, individuals, born free and equal, immediately oppose one another as independent agents, ready to exercise their separate liberty without any agreements, laws, or other acts of will concomitantly determining their interrelation. Rather, precisely because their respective particularity is something given, their immediate plurality excludes all preestablished harmony. Since each will has its particular identity not in function and in realization of the common form of willing, but as part of a given condition, the distinct individualities from which liberty gets naturally exercised are not already integrated into any system of mutual respect and peaceful coexistence.

Furthermore, because what each individual shall choose to will is a particular content supplied independently of liberty, there is nothing to prevent an unrestrained conflict between the separate volitions of the different agents. Be it given by outer circumstance, inner desire, or rational reflection, whatever content one individual wills can just as much contradict the choice of another. Even if the external alternatives, structure of desire, and reason were to offer the same options to all, the very liberty of each individual to will a given content would rule out any guarantee of harmony.

Consequently, the state of nature necessarily suffers from an endemic lack of concurrence between wills, which leaves in question individuals' ability actually to exercise their liberty and embody it in property without restraint and interference from others. As much as individuals are born free and equal with a faculty of choice generically embodied in property, the state of nature of their liberty is no less a state of war where no will or property is secure from the license of others. Therefore, the will all are born with is not only just a *faculty* of choice bound to given alternatives, but one which enjoys merely the *right* to its own liberty and property. Given the endemic war of all against all, this natural right is not a natural reality, but an imperative, lacking the force of mutual agreement that can supply right with the duty ensuring its respect.

Under these conditions, no "natural law" evident to "right reason" can overcome the insecurity of liberty by mandating rules of respect for right. For any law to command and oblige obedience, it cannot just be revealed by reason, but must issue from a will whose authority each individual has chosen to respect. A "natural" law, however, has no such author, precisely because in a state of nature there is no legitimate lawmaker, but only a plurality of individuals born free and equal. Any attempt to bestow validity upon natural law by ascribing it to a transcendent will of God can only fail, for liberty cannot be made to conform to divine commands, without relinquishing its constitutive character of being unbeholden to any content it has not chosen for itself.

Instead, the predicament of the merely universal will, of freedom taken as a principle, entails a very different course to salvage the reality of freedom and make it the basis of existing justice. This course is mandated in a twofold way:

First of all, because the externally determined particularity of each will in no way resolves itself into the common realization of liberty, the inherently individual structure of the will lacks the individual reality that could secure it actual freedom. Since, however, the given form of willing cannot provide by itself the integration of its particular content with its universal form, it requires some further agency to make the particular act of each will accord with the universal realization of willing.

To overcome the state of war natural to liberty, there must be a higher authority empowered to protect each will and its property by legislating and enforcing the unimpeached coexistence of all individual persons.

On the other hand, given the natural existence of wills and their natural right to exercise their liberty, the agency mediating their plurality must issue from the consent of all, if it is not to violate the very autonomy it is called upon to protect. Thus, if the new authority is to serve the liberty that cannot actually exist without it, then all individuals in the state of nature must will it upon themselves and agree to recognize and respect its validity. Consequently, the new order, required to secure natural liberty by suppressing the license of the state of nature, can arise only through a "social contract" in which all agree to join as members of a civil society and institute a public authority ruling over it to whom they give their consent so long as it restricts itself to realizing their liberty and property.

On this basis, however, the social contract has a dual character,[3] which ultimately leaves liberal theory unable to secure freedom an institutional reality in general, as well as to distinguish between civil society and state in particular.

Because the right of person and property requiring security is itself something natural, the public authority that is contractually instituted is external and ex post facto to the structure of liberty. Its governing activity does not constitute liberty, but merely preserves person and property as already given in the state of nature.

Consequently, the social contract is not just a mutual covenant between equals, securing each the power to exercise their liberty by accepting the duty of respecting that of others. In so far as the freedom herein realized is neither created by the new authority, nor specific to its institutional practice, but a liberty constituted prior to and separate from it, freedom here does not involve any participation in government. Therefore, at the same time that individuals mutually agree to join together in civil society, they each enter into an equal, nonreciprocal relation to the new authority, a relation between ruler and ruled consisting in their consent to abide by its law and government, so long as it lets them enjoy their personal liberty and private property. Here they agree to hand over the monopoly of public action to the government itself, in exchange for "civil" rights involving no more than the right to exercise their natural rights to liberty and property under the protection of public law and authority.

With legitimate public authority accordingly exercising a power distinct from the liberty of individuals, there is no political freedom to participate in self-government, but only the freedom to institute or replace the ruling regime and then retreat to those essentially prepolitical activities that the public authority allows to be pursued.

As a result, not only is freedom deprived of any political realization, but government itself is merely civil in character, and thereby indistinguishable from civil society. Instead of being a *sovereign* body *politic*, existing for the sake of its own ruling activity and thereby exercising true political self-determination, the instituted government has as its aim the liberty of person and property given to it by nature. Consequently, its rule is relative, receiving its fundamental law from elsewhere—namely, the prepolitical sphere of the state of nature. Like liberty itself, the will of public authority thus has only a formal freedom. It can not determine its own ends, like a truly sovereign state, but can only choose the given means for realizing natural right. In other words, the regime arising from social contract is not a state standing over civil society with aims of its own, but a *civil* goverment, administering the harmony of civil society against which it has no autonomy.

Nevertheless, as the final arbiter among persons, civil government has a will of its own no less than they do. Accordingly, its first and foremost function is legislative, determining what is publicly valid, not as an embodiment of the good or of given means of conduct, but in virtue of being willed by legitimate authority as a law to be obeyed voluntarily by the consenting members of civil society. As such, the laws of justice do issue from a structure of the will, and must also be publicly proclamated since they address persons who follow them only in conscious and willful recognition of their authority.

Although this seems finally to make the free will the real principle of justice, the legislation in question is only a formal lawmaking, suffering from the same falling asunder of particular and universal that afflicts liberty in general. Instead of determining the particular statutes of law from out of its own universally valid will, civil government legitimately enacts only what is given by the "law" of nature, namely, the lawful preservation of person and property. Since its legislation is thereby limited to a merely *civil* law, whose content derives from the character of liberty found in the state of nature, the rule of civil government cannot break the will's bondage to particular determinations that are not its own.

Indeed, it is precisely this dependence upon externally given content that undermines the very power of civil government itself. In virtue of the constitutive conditions of the social contract, the standard of just rule here lies outside the positive institutions of government, in the implicit principles of natural right. As a result, there is no seat of authority within civil government that can certify the legitimacy of its measures in the binding way in which, for instance, the judicial branch of a state exercises its own politically mandated role by interpreting the enacted constitution and thereby determining the legality of government policy on grounds that are political in origin and objectively valid for all citizens. Where freedom is a given principle and justice is no more than the realization of liberty, it must simply be left to personal judgment to decide whether government is properly enacting natural law. With no institutional seat of authority available, individuals have the prerogative to withdraw their recognition of the legitimacy of civil government as soon as they judge it to have transgressed its natural mandate. Their original consent agreement gives them the right to do so, in default of any other nonnatural source of authority. What this means is that the members of civil society are completely at liberty to throw off the obligations of the social contract and revert to a state-of-nature relation to civil authority where no laws or agreements have any binding force upon them.

Consequently, the authority of civil government is itself no more secure than person and property in a state of nature, in so far as respect for both is but a matter of personal choice. Although civil government is instituted to guarantee the exercise of liberty, its very character makes it just as inherently unstable as the right it is meant to realize.

Indeed, the ultimate inability of civil government to have a recognized reality any less contingent than that of harmony in the state of nature, reflects a basic dilemma casting in doubt the very possibility of social contract itself. Namely, just as the authority of civil government depends upon unanimous respect by the members of society, so social contract requires a similar unanimity of willing simply to be entered into. By its very definition, the social contract can only come into being when the prospective members of civil society are already resolved to honor each others' natural rights by taking the common measure of contracting with one another to institute civil government. Such unanimous respect for right, however, is precisely what is lacking in the state of nature, and whose absence requires the founding of public authority in the first place. Without it, the social contract not only has no binding force, but can not even be initiated, whereas only without such prior shared committment, under a state of war, where there is no common recognition of rights, does the need for a social contract arise.

Driven by its own internal logic, the attempt to make freedom the principle of justice here comes to an impasse in these final aporias. Freedom, postulated as liberty, the universal capacity of choice whose particular alternatives are given to it, must be sustained through a social contract precisely because the unmediated plurality of the state of nature precludes the general recognition of right. However, because social contract issues from the given liberty of persons, it lacks the preexisting agreement that alone allows it to be convened and binding. Since all higher authority derives from this contract, not only can such authority not be relied upon to enforce the original covenant, but its civil government has no more respected reality than the given wills whose harmony it is designed to ensure. With the authority of civil government necessarily problematic, the realization of the individual will is itself thrown into question, in the absence of any secured recognition by others. As a result, instead of freedom determining an existing system of justice, all that is left is an unrealizable right at both levels of natural liberty and civil society. The quest of liberal theory here grinds to a halt before a hopelessly hypothetical civil government, wherein willing remains a formal imperative of only universal character, facing both the indifferent particularity of its alternative contents and the immediate conflicting particularity of the given plurality of wills.

### ii) The Indicated Requirements for Conceiving the Reality of Freedom

If this outcome presents a dead end, it no less lays bare the problems that must be overcome to conceive freedom as the reality of justice.

As might be expected, these problems all revolve around the dilemma of securing individuality for the will's action. At every turn, the course of liberty has set in relief this central difficulty in a dual manner. On the one hand, it has demonstrated how freedom is deprived of reality so long as the particular content of the will and its relation to others is not determined through the will's own universal form. Conversely, it has shown that when the will is reduced to a determiner and the content of justice has the corresponding form of determined, rather than self-determined determinacies, the will can neither achieve any objective existence for itself, nor establish a real community in which freedom is actual.

In terms of the unfolded logic of liberal theory, these insights provide the following lessons:

First, the free will cannot be a natural will, whose defining character is given prior to its actual self-determination. In other words, freedom must not be reduced to liberty, for the autonomous will cannot be conceived as a merely universal faculty of choice, whose particular content and relation to other wills is extraneously given.

By the same token, the free will cannot be a monological structure, that is, a structure of the self, determined independently of the plurality of particular persons in whose context individual identities are distinguishable. Monologically defined, the will is a capacity all selves bear *per se*, and thus cannot serve to differentiate one another. So conceived, the will is automatically reduced to a merely universal faculty with no element of particularity within itself that could individuate one will from another in virtue of self-determination rather than through independently given factors. On this basis, the aspect of particularity, giving freedom the determinacy required for actual self-*determination*, cannot be referred back to the will as a determinacy *of* its own *self*, but remains irreducibly a determination of something other. Consequently, any monological conception of the will, be it conceived as a faculty of liberty or an agency determined by practical reason, leaves freedom without reality, and therefore fails to grasp what *is* the free will and the system of justice consisting in its exercise.

These two lessons, that the free will is neither a natural will nor a monological structure, entail a third: Namely, the will is free only by actually giving itself a particular content that derives from willing and willing alone. The free will must will itself and nothing else, but not do so in an empty solipsism of noncontradiction, as in the inner application of a categorical imperative. Rather, it must will its own *particularization*, such that its act of will stands in relation to other wills as an individual one, bearing a particular content specific to itself, yet exhibiting a universal form common to them all.

However, as the aporias of liberal theory have indicated, the free will cannot stand in any immediate, given relation to other wills, for then their particular differentiation from one another is not determined by willing. Consequently, the free will, in willing its own particularization, must also will its relation to others. These others must themselves be free wills as well, for otherwise, the first will, willing its relation to them, will not be able to stand individuated against them, as a particular instance of free willing in general. To be free wills, however, they too must not stand in a relation to others imposed independently of their own willing. Consequently, the free will can will its relation to other free wills only if they concomitantly will that same relation to one another as their own self-determination.

This means that free willing is not the action of a single will alone, but rather a self-determination by one will bound up with the self-determination of another. In order to will itself in a particular manner, the free will must engage in a reciprocal relation to other wills, a relation in which each determines itself as an individual by willing its relation to others in virtue of these others simultaneously willing their own particularization and having it voluntarily establish the same interrelationship. Thus the very exercise of freedom is directly accompanied by the objective recognition of right, since each self-determination is bound up with respect by other wills of its particular realization, as well as with respect for the particular self-determination of these other individuals themselves. Accordingly, freedom is not a natural or monological potential, but an actual structure of interaction consisting in the interdirected and mutually respected actions of a plurality of wills.

As such, freedom is not a principle from which the relations of justice are to be derived; rather, freedom is itself an existing relation of right, that is, justice is the very reality of self-determination.

### iii) Hegel's Conception of Freedom as Interaction

This insight, which by itself says nothing of how such interaction concretely proceeds, has been furthest developed by Hegel, who makes it the very foundation of his entire *Philosophy of Right*. Whether or not he has properly conceived freedom in the full range of its constitutive structures of interaction, he has at the very least supplied the terms for understanding how freedom can be thought as interaction, and of what interaction consists in the most basic sense.

The key Hegel provides is the notion that freedom is neither a natural given, nor an attribute of the self, but rather an intersubjective process of reciprocal recognition, whose interaction constitutes right.

The individuals involved in this interaction indeed have natural endowments and subjective faculties of knowing and choice, which Hegel himself specifically addresses in his theory of Subjective Spirit. In fact, for the interaction of freedom to proceed, the individuals involved must have a natural corporeal existence in order to act in the world of others and make themselves and their actions recognizable, as well as the ability to choose what they will do and the mental capacities required to recognize the actions of others. Although these are prerequisites for the reciprocal self-determination of free wills, and indeed provide all that is necessary for them to proceed, it is nevertheless the nonnatural, nonmonological relation between selves that allows their action to take on the additional character of free and rightful action.

How this actually occurs is the problem that Hegel addresses in his development of Objective Spirit, which comprises the subject matter of the *Philosophy of Right* by being at one and the same time the reality of right and freedom in virtue of the interaction determination of the free will.

Logically enough, Hegel's first concern is establishing the minimal determination of the interaction of freedom, which is to say, the most indeterminate, abstract right of all.

The basic individuality of self-determination and the lessons of liberal theory already point to a notion of reciprocal recognition, but how this realizes itself as the element of freedom must be spelled out.

Hegel provides the required account by simply thinking what interaction must entail to grant the free will its individual reality, in face of the demonstrated limits of natural liberty and its monological willing.

The basic features are already at hand. To begin with, each free will must will its own particularization, not what desire urges or reason compels, but simply an objectification of itself that has a particular content distinct from the objectifications of other wills. This external realization not only must derive its constitutive character from the will itself, but be nothing other than the will's own self-determination, individuating it from other free wills by being a particular sheer embodiment of that will excluding all others from the same domain.

For this to be the case, the respective embodiments of each will cannot stand differentiated from one another as immediately given, indifferent monads in want of a preestablished harmony. Rather, there is actual unimpeded self-determination only when each will establishes its own particular domain in recognition and respect of the objectifications of others, whose correlatively limited embodiments grant it a recognized objective existence on its part. Thus, each will particularizes itself by giving itself an embodiment limited in accord with those of others, who likewise recognize it by determining their own distinct domains in an unconflicting manner. Self-determination *is* thereby a relation to other, comprising an intersubjective process of reciprocal recognition, where the recognition in question consists both in a theoretical awareness of the objectifications of other wills, and in the practical act of embodying one's own will in such a way that it does not conflict with theirs.

The only matters that need be further specified to complete the actual engagement of this process are the respective characters of the wills involved and the factors providing their objectifications. They, of course, are intimately connected, given the nature of freedom's individuality.

On the one hand, since each will here freely determines itself only in a recognized and recognizing objectification, what gives it its sole recognizable character as a particular free will is the external embodiment others respect as its own. This means that each will has no specific character in itself, but only distinguishes itself in the external domain comprising its respected embodiment. Thus, even though the will is free in this most basic interaction, it is an abstractly individual will, whose self-determined particularity lies outside it in a separate entity.

On the other hand, this external entity, which every such will needs to supply it with the recognizable and recognized medium of its self-determination, has no other status than that of a receptacle for the particularization of the will. Whatever independent characteristics it may have are here a matter of indifference, for the free will has willed itself through it, not by choosing its medium's given determinations, but by rendering them subordinate accidents of its own particular embodiment. Consequently, the basic relation between free wills is mediated through factors that are simply some thing or other in which these wills lay themselves for the sake of their own mutually limited embodiment.

Hegel has drawn all these conclusions,[4] and further recognized that on their basis, the minimal structure of freedom consists in the interaction of persons through property. In contrast to liberal theory, which conceives both person and property as monological relations given within the state of nature, Hegel understands them to be the specific terms of the most elementary interaction of freedom. As such, they cannot be thought apart from an intersubjective process of reciprocal recognition, and therefore, comprise a non-natural right that actually exists in the constitutive property relations between persons.

This right is what Hegel appropriately calls Abstract Right, and in his development of its relations, he makes clear the elemental character of person and property in their roles within the most indeterminate interaction of self-determination.

As Hegel argues, the person is precisely the free agent who simply wills his own particularization in an external embodiment in virtue of other persons recognizing it to be the domain of his will and not their own. They can afford it the objective respect allowing its owner to be an individuated person only, however, by willing their own property ownership in such a way that it does not conflict with the domain of other persons. This recognizable objectification of the person is property, in so far as it is an external entity whose only relevant feature vis a vis personhood is that it does embody the person's will in a particular object from which all other persons have excluded their self-determination. The taking of property by one person is thus bound up with the taking of other property by other persons. Indeed, only with reference to the intersubjective aspect of recognition, can one distinguish between mere possession and property, for rightful ownership is not a matter of physical grasp, but of respected possession.[5]

Unlike liberal theorists, Hegel takes full account of this in his consideration of how a person takes possession of property in the first place. This act of self-determination is, of course, the starting point of any development of Abstract Right, since all further relations between persons, such as contract and the committing of wrong, involve individuals who have already given their wills a recognized particular embodiment in some previously established property.

Hegel realizes that taking possession of property cannot be understood simply as a relation between a person and a rightless world of things waiting to be appropriated from nature. Rather, the person stands opposite the external factors in which he can objectify his will only in reference to other persons who are themselves in the process of recognizing those factors as his property by correlatively laying their wills in other analogously rightless factors. For this to occur, each person must take posession of property in such a way that his appropriation of the external factor involved is immediately recognizable to others. Consequently, as Hegel makes clear,[6] taking ownership of a factor necessarily involves either some perceivable physical contact with it, a working upon it to alter its outward form, or a marking of it, not because any of these single acts themselves establish rightful ownership, but because they can designate to others that the person has embodied his will in the factor in question.

Since, however, the actual establishment of ownership depends upon how other persons choose to recognize these actions through their own self-determinations, what one individual does to a factor does not have any rightful status unless others are engaged in physically grasping, forming, or marking their own factors in corroboration of a mutual respect for each other's domains. Only within the reciprocity of this interaction do individuals leave behind the unmediated giveness of mere possession and instead take rightful ownership of property, facing one another as free persons, whose distinct particularities are not independently given, but established through their own interrelated willing.

On this basis, a right to property comes into existence in conjunction with the exercise of the duty to respect it. The freedom of the person here manifests its inherent individual actuality, for only through the contrastive recognition process securing it its objective embodiment can it even be exercised.

Nevertheless, the interaction of persons through property is subject to conflicts that cannot be resolved on the basis of its abstract right alone. Hegel is well aware of this, and understands that property relations, as actual as they are, cannot comprise the exclusive reality of freedom, but point instead to further structures of interaction constituting more concrete spheres of right.

What shows the limited character of Abstract Right, and thereby points beyond it to other forms of self-determination, is nothing other than the immediate arbitrariness of all the components in its interaction. Simply because the recognition process of personhood proceeds through individuals choosing which factor to make their own and which to honor as someone else's, it is always possible for a nonmalicious wrong to occur where persons disagree over which factor has been rightfully recognized as the property of a certain person. Since, however, the interaction of persons contains no higher authority than that of the mutual respect in which they stand, such nonmalicious wrong cannot be adjudicated if the persons involved do not themselves give up their conflicting interpretations.[7] Similarly, as Hegel explicitly argues,[8] the role of choice within property relations allows both for fraud, where one person intentionally misrepresents his property within a contract in order to use its rightful form of mutual recognition to sanction an improper exchange, and for outright crime, where a person chooses to violate the property rights of others, despite his own need of their recognition to possess rightfully what he himself has. In either case, all persons can do to right the wrong is take an action that may itself stand as a vengeful wrong if others happen not to recognize it as a rightful retribution.[9]

Consequently, although the interaction of persons realizes freedom in an existing right of property relations, these relations stand in need of some further form of interaction to right wrong in an objectively recognized and abiding way.

This does not mean that the elementary interaction of personhood leaves freedom with an insecure reality leading back into the quandaries of social contract theory. Indeed, Hegel does go on to conceive a civil administration of justice that adjudicates disputes among persons through a lawful enforcement of their abstract right. This public authority, however, neither issues from a social contract, nor secures natural rights, nor gets identified with the state. Rather, in Hegel's conception, the civil administration of justice exists as a specific institution of civil society, which regulates the nonnatural personhood and property of its members on the basis of laws it receives from a sovereign state standing over society with political ends of its own. Although Hegel does at times collapse the distinction between civil society and state, most notably in his estatelike characterizations of the three social classes[10] and in his introjection of class distinctions into the structures of the state,[11] his theory of interaction allows him to radically demarcate the two spheres.

The framework of interaction makes this possible because it establishes right as something first determined within the specific structures of reciprocal recognition comprising a certain form of self-determination. Accordingly, the particular components of a sphere of interaction, which could distinguish it from others, have their relevant features not in virtue of any predetermined principle, but through the individual character of the interrelated self-determinations comprising it. Just as the minimal right to objectify one's will in a particular embodiment involves the agency of personhood and the medium of property, which themselves stand determined only within the relations of Abstract Right, so the interactions that could comprise social and political realms of freedom would also have distinct agencies and mediums for their respective rights, which could not be reduced to one another or derived from any prior relation.

In the *Philosophy of Right*, Hegel attempts to develop the specific interactions that do comprise separate spheres of society and state, and does so in terms of components that are irreducible. Civil society is described as the realm in which individuals exercise the specific agency of the civilian or bourgeois, by entering into relationships with others where each individual pursues a particular interest of his or her own that can only be realized in conjunction with the realization of that of others. On this basis, civil society involves, in the first instance, a system of interdependent needs, whose members exercise the social freedom of pursuing the satisfaction of needs of their own choosing, which can only be satisfied by what others have. Accordingly, the agency of the civilian is immediately bound up with the specific reciprocal self-determination comprising the commodity relations of economic interaction.[12]

By contrast, the state entails an entirely different right, for Hegel, involving its own agency and medium. Instead of comprising a civil government in the service of natural right or any other predetermined principle, it consists in the interactions of individuals through institutions allowing them to relate to one another not on the basis pf property relations or their interdependent interests, but through self-determinations that have as their end the policy of government. Here, the freedom at issue is one of participating in self-government, and only in its exercise, which requires specific political institutions, is the person not just a civilian, but a citizen as well.

If nothing else, these brief indications at least suggest how the theory of interaction could address civil society and state without conflating them.

Whether or not Hegel has correctly determined society and state, let alone the other spheres of right, is itself an open question in the absence of any systematic critique of the entire *Philosophy of Right*. Nevertheless, his conception of freedom as interaction has established a new terrain for practical philosophy, where justice can be conceived as the existing reality of self-determination, and where distinct social and political spheres of right need not be excluded.

In face of the challenge to renew practical philosophy on its basis, it must not be forgotten that if interaction is itself made an abstract principle, a criterion of justice, or a standard of legitimation from which further institutional structures are derived, then the individuality of freedom is once again forsaken for the dilemmas of liberty.[13]

## Notes

1. Hegel has sketched out these three constitutive aspects of the self-determining will in paragraph 5 through 7 in the *Philosophy of Right*, trans. by T. M. Knox (New York: Oxford University Press, 1967), providing the basis for what here follows.

2. For the most complete account of the logical distinction between positing and self-determination, see Hegel's *Science of Logic*, trans. by A. V. Miller (New York: Humanities Press, 1969), where he attempts to present in succession the exhaustive development of the relations of positing (as the Logic of Essence) and self-determination per se (as the Logic of the Concept.).

3. Hannah Arendt has discussed at length the importance of the two aspects of mutual covenant within the social contract in *On Revolution*, (New York: Viking Press, 1976), p. 169ff.

4. See in particular paragraphs 41–45 of the *Philosophy of Right*.

5. See *ibid.*, paragraphs 45–51.

6. See *ibid.*, paragraphs 54–58.

7. See *ibid.*, paragraphs 84–86.

8. See *ibid.*, paragraphs 87–90.

9. See *ibid.*, paragraph 102.

10. For a detailed critique of Hegel's class conception, see Richard Dien Winfield, *The Social Determination of Production: The Critique of Hegel's System of Needs and Marx' Concept of Capital*, (Ph.D. dissertation, Yale University, 1977), pp. 140–158.

11. See paragraphs 303–308 in the *Philosophy of Right*.

12. See Winfield, *Social Determination of Production*, pp. 74–162, for a detailed critique of Hegel's account of the System of Needs.

13. Such appears to be the mistaken course of Hannah Arendt, Jürgen Habermas, and others who have taken the reciprocal recognition of a plurality of individuals in an uninstitutionalized form and made it the ideal of all institutional life, rather than following Hegel in conceiving interaction as a system of distinct individual structures of reciprocal recognition, each comprising a separate *existing* right with its own agency, medium, and institutions.

# 9

# Hegel and the Legitimation of Modernity

Ever since Hegel's death, his philosophy of right has been the object of an incessant, often vehement debate, impelled by an awareness that at issue are the problems most central to modernity. Unfortunately, the ensuing discussion has generally been restricted to establishing whether Hegel's theory of right provides insight into the structure of the modern world, in order then to celebrate or condemn his thought as progressive or reactionary.

For all the literature it has generated, this prevailing interpretative approach has rested on an unexamined premise that has made it blind to Hegel's own fundamental concerns. Unlike the work it criticizes, it assumes that one can directly refer to our own age as a criterion by which to judge conceptions of right, and so speak of what is "progressive" and just in one and the same breath. It fails to recognize that whether or not Hegel's philosophy of right corresponds with modern reality has no normative theoretical or practical significance unless it has already been established that modern relations are intrinsically just. They are not given facts of nature subject to laws independent of our wills, but historically emergent structures susceptible of practical critique and alteration. Consequently, a discrepancy between a theory of right and existing institutions may require, not a revolution in science, but one in reality.

Hegel is aware of this in the most uncompromising way. He not only rejects any prescriptive role for historically given institutions, but he demands that the structures of right be conceived without any constitutive reference to what one already "finds" in reality.[1] He recognizes that if the theory of justice were to rely upon such immediate givens for its content, it would be doubly at fault: both for claiming normative validity for what is only relative to it as a particular circumstance, and for committing the basic metaphysical error of assuming the correspondence of its thought with reality by directly asserting the truth of what it finds given.

Accordingly, for Hegel, the legitimacy of modernity cannot be taken for granted but is rather a very real problem that must be addressed *within* philosophical science from the vantage point of the theory of justice. Few interpreters have heeded this point, and consequently there has been little attempt to come to grips with the actual arguments that give Hegel's philosophy of right its seminal role in the evaluation of modernity.[2]

At the heart of the matter is Hegel's concept of freedom, for, Hegel's theory of justice is more radically a theory of freedom than any other. What immediately sets Hegel's philosophy of right apart is that it devotes itself to establishing and determining justice as freedom, not by postulating freedom as the prior principle of justice, but by developing the structures of justice themselves as the constitutive reality of freedom.

In contrast to liberal theory, Hegel does not proceed from any predetermined notion of freedom which then is employed as a principle to determine and legitimate the various relations of right. Hegel recognizes that such an endeavor is inherently aporetic for the simple reason that taking freedom as a principle robs it and the justice derived from it of all self-determined reality. The moment one treats freedom as a principle, it gets reduced to something, whose character is given prior to what it determines. Consequently, freedom does not exercise any *self*-determination in the structures of justice derived from it, for it does not give itself any further determination in them but rather determines, as a principle, what is secondary to and other than it. Conversely, the derivative relations of right are not self-determined structures themselves, for they are determined by what is given prior to and separately from them. What results is a freedom with no objective reality and a system of justice unable to exhibit the very principle that can alone legitimate it.

Hegel avoids this dilemma from the very start by conceiving right as the Idea of freedom, that is, as the system of justice consisting in the relations in which the free will determines itself in all its possible modes and thereby achieves its full realization. Hegel expressly declares that the philosophy of right can have no other task than following out the self-determination of the Idea of freedom, and it is on this basis and this basis alone that Hegel confronts the legitimacy of modernity.

That such a course by taken, and that it lead to a questioning of the modern age, are matters that Hegel does not take for granted. His development of right as the reality of freedom deals with these issues directly precisely through what it establishes freedom to be.

Three major arguments are here entailed. These can be briefly indicated in the form of three theses concerning the character of freedom.

### i) Hegel's Three Basic Theses on Freedom

1) First of all, freedom is the sole substance and content of justice. Nothing else can provide normative validity for action. Hegel seeks to establish this with a twofold argument that is both negative and positive in character.

On the one hand, he attempts to show that conduct which is not self-determined, but is given its character independently of free willing, can have no unconditioned universality. In contrast to freedom, such action is, as Hegel generically describes it, *naturally* determined, and insofar as it depends on something other for its essence, it cannot be an end in itself, as would be required for normative validity. In Hegel's view, the ethics and politics of Plato and Aristotle present the classic examples of a theory of justice based on natural determination, where conduct is valid, not by being self-determined, but by embodying prescribed universal virtues, given means of conduct, and a fixed essence of goodness. In scattered critical remarks in the *Philosophy of Right*, Hegel effectively argues that such a theory cannot establish normative validity for its given standards of conduct without introducing an unconditioned agent to determine and impose them, a figure such as Aristotle's absolutely good man[3] or Plato's philosopher king,[4] whose autonomous rule contradicts the very framework of natural determination that it seeks to sanction.

On the other hand, Hegel goes beyond this critique to present a positive proof that justice cannot be anything but the realization of freedom. This proof effectively consumes his entire development of right. It consists, first, in the demonstration that freedom is itself a structure of justice, irreducibly entailing rights and duties which are for their own sake, and then, second, in the comprehensive demonstration that every normative sphere of action has its valid universality by comprising a specific structure of freedom. What provides these demonstrations are the arguments supporting the second and third major theses on freedom that distinguish Hegel's theory.

The decisive second thesis, which sets Hegel apart from all preceding thinkers of freedom, can be stated as follows:

2) Freedom is neither a faculty given by nature nor a capacity of the self, but a structure of interaction between individuals wherein the self-determination of each is constitutively related to that of others through mutual recognition and respect.

According to this claim, freedom can only be understood as an intersubjective process, where the self-determinations of individuals stand indissolubly linked together in a reciprocal relation where each will autonomously determines itself in accord with the realization of others. On this basis, freedom is itself an existing right, whose respect is ensured by its very exercise. As such, freedom in not a principle of justice but rather an actual structure of justice itself, for it consists in a real exercise of freedom among individuals that goes hand in hand with the honored duty to respect it.

By itself, of course, this thesis says nothing concerning what is the specific content of freedom's interaction, what are the particular rights and duties it involves, or what institutional forms are entailed in its process. Nevertheless, the thesis sets the stage for an ethical evaluation of modernity by characterizing freedom, the substance of justice according to Hegel's first thesis, as something that exists, not by nature or in virtue of the single self, but only through commonly enacted structures of interaction that may or may not arise depending upon what relations individuals establish with one another.

This means that one should neither automatically recognize the authority of historically given institutions nor be indifferent to them. If freedom is a structure of interaction, then it can come into existence and bring justice to the light of day only within history through the establishment of certain forms of interrelated self-determinations. If, however, its universally valid structures of justice are to arise within history, there must emerge within history a point from which an unconditioned, free institution of practical relations can occur. Such a moment would first have to liberate itself from the hold of all natural determination, as it is embodied in whatever past traditions and given authority contravene the interaction of freedom. Then, a new foundation of practical relations would have to be undertaken realizing the constitutive structures of freedom. These two aspects of liberation and constitution are precisely the negative and positive developments that together constitute revolution in the true sense of the word.[5] Consequently, the history in which freedom's interaction can emerge must be such as to arrive at revolution, not in the orthodox Marxist sense of a necessary, socially conditioned seizure of state power, but in the preeminently political sense of an unconditioned transformation of all practical bonds into relations of free interaction.

By conceiving justice as freedom, and freedom as interaction, Hegel is inexorably led to consider history as the domain in which freedom comes into being. He thereby not only finds himself forced to evaluate modernity with regard to the historical emergency of freedom, but to do so in light of the problem of conceiving how history can bring forth revolution that establishes freedom as an existing world.

For these reasons, one can rightly claim that Hegel is not only a philosopher of freedom but the philosopher of revolution par excellence. However, both *freedom* and *revolution* are empty words unless one confronts the de jure question of what are the constitutive structures of freedom that give revolution its content and legitimacy. This de jure question is what Hegel primarily addresses in the *Philosophy of Right*, and his answer can be schematically expressed as his third thesis on freedom:

3) The interaction of freedom is not a single interrelationship leaving beside it institutions that are naturally determined, but a system of right that attains unconditioned universality by incorporating all practical relations as determinations of freedom. This system does so by having as its necessary and exhaustive reality the distinct structures of interaction comprising the just spheres of person and property, morality, the family, civil society, and the

state, all of which owe their existence to a world history that has its own developmental, universal character by bringing them into being.

The arguments supporting this final encompassing thesis are what alone provide the relevant yardstick with which Hegel evalutes the legitimacy of modernity, and it is to them that one must turn to judge his own theory, not as progressive or reactionary, but as a true or false account of what justice is.

This is not contravened by the fact that Hegel's own working out of the structures of right was accompanied, and often inspired, by his intent following of the events of his day and his own journalistic attempts to intervene in them. Indeed, Hegel was deeply stirred by the French Revolution's call to make politics a sphere of freedom, and then equally dismayed by its eventual failure to institutionalize political freedom in actual organs of self-government. He was struck by the development of capitalism in England, threw himself into a study of political economy, and closely watched the social struggles gripping the land where he saw an unprecedented civil society being born. Once again, he felt deeply ambiguous about these modern developments. On the one hand, he perceived a liberation from the hold of natural needs and traditional privilege and inequality, a liberation consisting in the welcome establishment of a new realm of freedom where individuals had the right to pursue their own particular interests, determine their own needs, choose their livelihood, and thereby relate to others through freely entered commodity relations. On the other hand, however, he saw growing extremes of luxury and poverty, increasing class antagonisms, and the alarming tendency of the new society to overwhelm all other spheres of life and to subordinate them to its limitless accumulation of wealth. So too, he celebrated the Reformation's liberation of religious conscience from the shackles of external authority, yet recoiled both from the Enlightenment's elevation of the understanding to an absolute for which all else is a mere thing, and from the subjectivity of Romanticism, which had withdrawn from the world back into itself in a vain solipsism. All three modern phenomena drew Hegel's attention and elicited a train of thought.

Nevertheless, what set Hegel on the path of his theory of interaction was not so much the upheavals of the age as the philosophical problems he found in the leading theory of justice of his day, the practical philosophy of Kant.[6]

### ii) Hegel's Critique of Kantian Practical Philosophy

Hegel comes to conceive freedom as interaction by thinking through the problems of Kant's practical reason, and he then develops the resulting concept of right such that the spheres of morality and legality, into which Kant collapsed all practical relations, become reformulated as the particular interactions of abstract right and morality, to which are added the separate ethical spheres of the family, civil society, and the state. Consequently, it is important to understand the critical encounter with Kant that makes possible and compelling Hegel's own contribution.

To begin with, that Kant's theory can play so important a role for Hegel's philosophy of right is due to Kant's theoretical advance beyond the conception of freedom put forward by the classic representatives of the liberal tradition Hobbes, Locke, and Rousseau. This advance consists in Kant's recognition that freedom cannot be conceived as liberty, that is, as a faculty of choice, free to choose among ends given independently to it. Although such liberty allows the will to be unbeholden to any particular content, since it can always choose another, it leaves the will bound in general to ends which it has not determined itself, but rather found before it. Consequently, liberty cannot afford the will the *self*-determination constitutive freedom, for no matter what it chooses, the particular content it wills does not derive from itself but from something other. On the basis of liberty, action thus stands conditioned by whatever array of alternatives lies given before it, and therefore can never have any universal, normative validity.

Kant's entire theory of practical reason is motivated by the need to overcome this heteronomy of liberty and to establish a basis for universally valid relations of justice by conceiving instead how the will can give itself an end that owes its content to the will itself. For Hegel, the problem Kant here addresses must be resolved if there is to be any philosophy of right at all. Autonomy rather than liberty must be recognized as the substance of justice, which is to say that freedom must be thought in its actual self-determination.

Kant's raising of the issue is itself an achievement that Hegel never tires of commending, all the more so since it leads him to the insight that opens the door to his theory of interaction. This insight is the notion that the will is free only insofar as it is individual in character, manifesting dimensions of universality, particularity, and individuality in its determination. In paragraphs 5 though 7 of the *Philosophy of Right*, Hegel briefly outlines this basic tenet, which is as decisive for his critique of Kant as it is for his own theory of freedom.

To begin with, Hegel observes that the free will has universality insofar as whenever it acts it exhibits only one instance of its general capacity to determine itself. It is not bound to the particular content it wills, for it is always free to set it aside and will another. The will's autonomy has no reality, however, if it is limited to this universal quality of being unrestricted to any particular end. By itself, this universality comprises merely the negative freedom of liberty, whose unbeholdenness to any given content leaves out of account the *determination* self-determination requires.

This must not be lost sight of, for the will can only determine itself if it actually wills something, and so adds a dimension of particularity to its universal character. As Hegel notes, in doing this the free will gives itself new determination, but it does not thereby cancel its universality and turn into something else. Rather, it remains at one with itself in its specific act, for it has here determined its own self, which has its general character of being unbeholden to any specific content, only in actually willing something as a particular instance of itself. In other words, in being self-determining, the will *determines* itself in such a way that its determination is of its self and therefore is its *own* particularity.

As a result, the free will is not simply universal or particular but individual as well, in that its self-determination gives it an identity bound up with its particular act. Since the free will is at once universal and particular, having its unrestricted autonomy in giving itself a specific content, it is not a universal capacity, definable prior to its actual willing, such as the liberty all men are said to be born with. Rather, the free will, Hegel argues, is an individual structure, whose character is first constituted in the particular self-determination building its unique development.

In Hegel's eyes, what are of positive significance in Kant's theory of justice are those aspects that give expression to the constitutive individuality of freedom. Kant's positive characterization of the free will in terms of practical reason, and not practical understanding,[7] makes this more explicit, for Kant's differentiation between the two first make possible a concept of autonomy that is not reducible to liberty. This is evident to Hegel for the very reasons that lead him to consider Kant's introduction of distinct faculties of the understanding and reason a major advance in thought. In Hegel's view, Kant's demarcation of reason from the understanding is of fundamental importance, because it lays the groundwork for thinking individuality, which is necessary not only for freedom but for the concept that Hegel considers the element of systematic philosophy.

The basic formulations in Kant's *Critique of Pure Reason* suggest as much when they are examined in light of the relations of universal and particular that hold in each faculty. On the one hand, Kant characterizes the understanding as the faculty of rules, which comprehends appearances as objects by unifying the sensible representations given in intuition under concepts through an act of judgment. Although the understanding here exercises spontaneity in bringing the manifold content of intuition under rules and thereby uniting them in one consciousness as objects of knowledge, its judgment refers a concept to sensible particulars given independently of it. The concept in question is itself a representation of a given representation, so that, although it is something general,its universality is not concrete, as in individuality, but formal, having reference to particulars that are not immanent to it. Accordingly, the understanding cannot know anything particular by concepts alone, nor can it know anything free and individual, for its unifying law is a law of necessity that subsumes the given particulars of sensible representation under universals extraneous to them as well.

By contrast, Kant defines reason as the faculty of principles, which thinks by syllogism, concluding something particular from a general premise. Instead of understanding perceptions through judgment, where concepts are applied to given particulars, reason conceives ideas by determining the particular out of the universal in terms of concepts alone. This effectively makes reason a faculty for thinking individuality, and Kant accordingly grants it the capacity to think the idea of freedom, which the understanding can never know.

What, however, seals the ethical relevance of reason is the further feature that reason's determination of the particular from the universal directs it upon what is unconditioned. By concluding the particular from the universal, reason no less determines the universal ground of its conditioned conclusion. Accordingly, the ideas reason thinks as principles determining the particular, that is, as concrete universals, are ultimately the totality of the conditions to a given conditioned.

Already in the *Critique of Pure Reason*, Kant draws the practical consequences that Hegel considers decisive: one cannot use the understanding to determine justice, for taking the standard of right from experience amounts to deriving what should be universally valid from what is conditioned by the causal necessity of particular circumstance. Because valid conduct must rather be *unconditioned* and *for its own sake*, right has to be determined from a principle of reason, whose ideas alone are unconditioned by virtue of their incipient individuality.[8] With this argument, the needed distinction of practical reason from practical understanding lies at hand, indicating the positive alternative to liberty that gives Hegel the impetus for conceiving freedom as interaction.

Kant has shown that, if willing is to be just, it must not simply choose among ends given to it in experience by the understanding. By itself, a practical understanding offers no more than causal rules relating the given end of choice with the action bringing it into being. Its essentially technical, means-end calculus cannot have normative validity, as Utilitarianism falsely claims, because its empirical end is itself always conditioned and contingent, and therefore neither an end in itself nor something that an individual will necessarily choose in the first place.

For there to be right, Kant counters, reason must be practical, which is to say that the will must give itself its end through an unconditioned principle and thereby achieve an implicitly individual determination. However, that reason be practical requires further that the will be free, not just to exercise its liberty to choose among given alternatives, but to exercise the distinct autonomy of determining itself independently of all extraneous particulars of experience, and solely in virtue of the unconditioned, individual determination of reason. Consequently, practical reason directly presents a new positive determination of freedom at one with the normative validity of action.

In these elements of Kant's characterization of practical reason, Hegel finds expressed the most essential feature of right: that justice consists in the determination of the free will, whose freedom is unconditioned and individual in character, in contrast to the conditioned choice of liberty. Nevertheless, Hegel rejects the entire Kantian framework because, in thinking it through, he finds practical reason unable to realize the individuality of free willing that it itself first poses as the genuine content of right. This critical judgment constitutes the negative side of Hegel's "sublation" of Kantian ethics, and it immediately introduces the positive side on which hangs Hegel's evaluation of modernity.

The basic problem Hegel uncovers is that, despite Kant's introduction of syllogizing reason and autonomy, the determination of the particular is still ultimately given to the universal in each, such that Kantian reason remains bound to the understanding while freedom fails to rise beyond the liberty of choice. Hegel sees the core of the difficulty in Kant's conception of reason. Although reason for Kant generically seeks the unconditioned universal that determines the particular, the particular in question is actually provided independently by the understanding in the form of a given rule of experience that supplies the minor premise of the syllogism.[9] Furthermore, since the understanding alone has knowledge of objectivity, whose reality is grasped not from universal concepts but from the given particulars of intuition, the ideas of reason are not real, but irreducibly transcendent. Consequently, reason can here prescribe no law to reality nor contain any grounds for either knowing it or determining anything real and particular. All such reason can do is provide a subjective regulation for the understanding, bringing its rules into consistent harmony, achieving the formal identity of noncontradiction that is indifferent to the particular content involved.

Whereas Kant sees this as the fate of thought, Hegel regards it as an abandonment of reason that reduces the unconditioned, individual determination of rational principle to the formal lawfulness of the understanding. The example of Kant indicates that unless the concepts of reason are individual in character, determining the particular through the universal rather than letting particular existence fall outside it, neither can the real be rational nor reason be actual. For Hegel, the ethical import of Kant's conception is clear: with individuality barred from objective existence and reason relegated to an external ordering of given particulars, practical reason cannot possibly provide freedom the self-determined reality it requires.

Hegel views Kant's development of the categorical imperative as a revelation of this itself. From the start, Kant binds himself to the structure of choice by having practical understanding follow the lead of theoretical understanding in its relation to reason, by supplying practical reason with the particular content of willing it is supposed to determine through a principle. This content is the maxim of the will, which is nothing more than the familiar causal rule of the understanding connecting a given end with the action bringing it into being. In line with his treatment of reason, Kant accepts the framework of the maxim as the source of the particular end of willing, and he then asks what can be the unconditioned principle of its choice. The answer is predictable enough. Given the structure of choice, where action proceeds through rules of the understanding, the only thing that is not relative and conditioned, but necessary and dependent upon choice alone, is the form of choosing, namely, the lawfulness of the maxim of the will, which is nothing but the same universal aspect of willing that liberal theory had previously isolated and made its principle. Consequently, the principle of practical reason becomes the categorical imperative to act so that the maxim of one's will is a universal law. In effect, what Kant has here done to eliminate the heteronomy of liberty is to have choice will its own empty form, which remains incapable of generating particular ends of its own.

Because of the prior specification of the maxim, this categorical imperative does not determine the will by *concluding* its particular end from a universal principle; rather, the categorical imperative can only operate as a rule of the understanding, a moral law for *judging* whether the given choice contradicts the general form of choosing. However, as Hegel argues in his famous discussion of Kant's example of the depositum, the formal universality of the categorical imperative provides no particular criteria for determining which particular maxims can or cannot be a universal law. In effect, practical reason not only restricts autonomy to an internal judgment of maxims, but it cannot even arrive at a determination concerning them. Consequently, autonomy, mandated to overcome the heteronomy of liberty by inwardly obeying the categorical imperative, cannot thereby give itself a particular end actually specific to the universality of the will. Its freedom simply has no reality, for the individuality of self-determination is nowhere achieved.

In lieu of an applicable moral law, the real relations between individuals thus remain governed by choice. Accordingly, when Kant considers the external reality of free selves, he cannot help but revert to the path of the theorists of liberty and conceive legality as a hypothetical civil order, issuing from the consent of individuals with the single purpose of insuring the lawful coexistence of their choosing wills. Because personal autonomy still provides the sole unconditioned principle of justice, even though it can have no reality of its own, the derivative public order is restricted to maintaining the harmony of individual willing, and its civil authority thus only restates the formal universality of practical reason, willing the noncontradiction of choice.

In Hegel's view, this means that public action is itself robbed of freedom, for it cannot determine its own particular ends but must accept them from the independently given structure of practical reason. Furthermore, the entailed reduction of public life to a function of autonomy precludes its differentiation into separate spheres of freedom, such as the family, society, and state, each with their own specific institutions and aims.

Nevertheless, what seals the failure of Kant's conception of legality in Hegel's eyes is the endemic inability of its civil order to come into existence and secure its own authority. Because it can arise only if all individuals actually choose to unite to realize their respective autonomy and honor their mutual agreement, the civil order really presupposes that all individuals do will in accord with practical reason. That, however, is just what cannot be guaranteed, let alone be done at all, which is what provides the rationale for establishing a civil order in the first place. Therefore, the justice of legality is here no more realizable than the moral law from which it proceeds.

### iii) Hegel's Resulting Move to Interaction

For Hegel, the ultimate irreality of Kantian justice presents an unequivocal lesson. It demonstrates that the unconditioned freedom providing normative validity for action can only be realized if the will overcomes the heteronomy of liberty by willing, not the mere lawfulness of its maxims, but an actual particular determination of itself. The example of practical reason shows that the free will cannot escape the hold of natural determination by willing itself as the form of choice, for this form's abstract universality leaves the particular content of action undetermined by freedom, as manifest by the fact that the lawfulness of the will's maxims neither gives it a specific end nor differentiates it from others. Accordingly, the free will must instead will itself as actual self-determination by particularizing itself in an act whose specific content is immanent to its general form. This involves not only determining the content of willing independently of both inner desire and reason as well as outer circumstance, but having it be the positive individuation of the will itself.

What leads Hegel beyond practical reason to interaction is his realization that the will can particularize itself only in relation to other wills, and indeed, only by willing that relation as well. On the one hand, in order for willing to have a particularity specific to freedom, its determination must exhibit both a form common to the will in general and a content exclusively its own. A solitary will, or one dealing only with nature, cannot have this individuality of freedom, for its act refers only to what is not a will, against which it cannot individuate itself as a particular instance of a commonly existing structure of willing. To do so, the willing in question must rather stand in a contrastive relation to other willings, in which their dual identity and difference are a reality.

On the other hand, Hegel recognizes that this relation to other wills cannot be imposed upon willing, as something independently given. If that were the case, the particularity of the will would not be self-determined but determined in virtue of a contrastive differentiation beyond the bounds of its volition. Consequently, if the will is to be free, it must particularize itself by no less willing its relation to other wills.

These other wills, however, cannot be self-determined themselves, and so afford the necessary contrast term for the first will's individuation, unless their relation to it and other wills is also voluntarily established through their own particular self-determination. Hegel, led to this point by thinking through the problem of freedom's individuality bequeathed by Kant, now comes to the conclusion that marks his positive step beyond the quandaries of practical reason.

In order for wills to particularize themselves, he reasons, their self—determination must be a reciprocal interaction in which each wills its own objectification and relation to other by virtue of honoring the particular self-determination and relation to other that these wills simultaneously give themselves through the same act of mutual recognition and respect. Only through this intersubjective process can the requisite contrast of self-determinations be one that all have agreed to and voluntarily established through the very content they have each willed.

Consequently, Hegel concludes, freedom is not a natural endowment or a structure of the self but an interaction of a plurality of individuals, consisting in a reciprocal recognition process whereby each determines himself in an objectively respected act of willing by recognizing and being recognized by analogously self-determining individuals.

Hegel is well aware that the interaction of freedom can only proceed if the individuals involved already possess a natural corporeal being and the subjective capacities of mind and choice, all of which Hegel attempts to account for in his theory of Subjective Spirit. Without these presuppositions, individuals would be unable to recognize how others have willed, choose a particular objectification to will in respect of that of others, or finally give their self-determination a recognizable presence in the world. Nevertheless, it is only through the enacted plural relations of their reciprocal recognition that their willing acquires the further qualities of free action and normative validity as well.

These latter aspects go together, Hegel realizes, because freedom irreducibly involves mutual respect for the contrasted self-determinations constituting its individual structure. Therefore freedom is not a principle of justice, out of which relations of right are to be derived, but an actual structure of right, whose exercise is immediately bound up with respect ensuring it objective reality.

Hegel takes in earnest this positive result of his Kant critique, and accordingly he does not fall into the trap of such subsequent thinkers as Hannah Arendt and Jürgen Habermas, who have reinstated the dilemmas of liberty by taking freedom's reciprocal recognition as a noninstitutionalized ideal with which to legitimate derivative structures of justice.

Hegel instead realizes that the basic concept of interaction is itself a specific relation of right, whose justice is the most indeterminate and abstract of all. Freedom is without further qualification the interrelationship of individuals in which each objectifies his or her will in a particular embodiment whose limits accord with those that others give their own wills by respecting one another's self-determinations. In this minimal interaction, the objectification of each will has no other character than that of being its own particularization, respected by others who have willed similar domains of their own. Conversely, the will of each has no other individuating feature than that of the particular embodiment it has given itself. Through it, each will is objectively free, but in an abstract manner, for although its particularity is determined by it itself, it lies immediately outside the will in its willed embodiment. On its part, this embodiment is equally indeterminate, for it is simply some external thing, figuring within the interaction as but a medium for the will's recognized self-determination. The specific natural features of this factor have no constitutive significance with respect to the will's particularization, for the will here wills not them, but its own objectification. Providing a receptacle for objective freedom, they are rendered mere accidents of what here stands recognized as the will's own particular domain.

What is thus entailed in the immediate concept of interaction is no universal ideal of freedom, awaiting embodiment, but rather the real relationship of persons through property, which Hegel recognizes to be the specifically abstract right of interaction's minimal reality. It accordingly builds the starting point of Hegel's theory of justice, presenting the identity of freedom and right in its most basic form. Here begins the positive sublation of the Kantian position, which finally gives Hegel the conceptual means for confronting modernity.[10]

### iv) Person and Property and the Problem of Morality

Property relations are the most elementary structure of self-determination, contrary to the claims of Marx and others, who have argued that person and property are themselves derivative of economic relations. Hegel's concept of abstract right shows that one has no particular needs or other properties within oneself that enter into one's self-determination as property owner. Rather, what alone individuates one as a particular *person* distinct from others is the specific factor in which one's will has a recognized objectification. Conversely, a factor is *property* not because of its useful properties or any other particular feature, but solely by virtue of being the recognized receptacle of a person's will. Consequently, Hegel turns aside the Jacobin demand for ownership of equal amounts of property, recognizing that the question of what or how much one owns may have relevance for other more concrete spheres of right but not for property relations themselves. Abstract right mandates only that persons must have property of their own, since otherwise they have no objective self-determination. It cannot prescribe what or how much they own.

As for the doctrines of economic determinism and base and superstructure, Hegel well recognizes that the commodity, contained in all economic relations as their most basic element, itself presupposes abstract right. This is so simply because without goods being possessed by different wills there could be no exchange relations in which objects could bear value and figure as commodities.

What abstract right does presuppose, however, is, first, that nature and natural determination in general have lost all independent power over the will of individuals. For things to be appropriated as property, Hegel realizes, they must face the individual as rightless *factors*, with no recognized independent spirit standing in the way of the objectification of his or her will. This means, that the desacralization of nature is a precondition of abstract right. In other words, the freedom of the person exists not in a state of nature but only *historically*, where individuals have liberated themselves from the hold of nature.

Because of the interactive reality of property, however, more is required of nature for it to be an embodiment of the person's self-determination. As Hegel argues, a rightless thing can be a factor only if individuals can also objectify their will in it in a *recognizable*, particular manner, either through direct physical contact, by acting upon it to alter its form, or through marking it.[11] Therefore, certain things, such as distant galaxies or the air we breathe, are not factors for a person's will, even though they be devoid of any recognized will of their own. For this reason, Hegel terminologically distinguishes between the thing (*Ding*) and the factor (*Sache*) of property.

All these aspects of the factor through which persons interact provide but one side of the freedom of abstract right. Hegel conversely recognizes that individuals can only be persons if their right to determine themselves through property is not tied to any limiting conditions separate from their recognizable ability to make their will known. Although it is possible to withdraw one's recognition of the personhood of a comatose individual without violating abstract right, it is not possible to limit personhood by sex, race, class, national origin, or any other matter extraneous to the will's operation. Hegel accordingly condemns Roman right despite its introduction of free property, because it allows only the select few to qualify as persons.

Of course, the non-natural universality of the person ultimately means that personhood cannot be restricted to homo sapiens either. However, insofar as man has yet to meet another natural species in whom he can recognize an autonomous will, this natural limit has yet to appear in any other realm than that of science fiction.

In any case, the reality of abstract right presupposes, not just that nature is desacralized, but also that individuals come to be recognized as bearers of a free will, irrespective of any natural determinations unrelated to the will's recognizable expression. Hegel notes that only in modern times has this precondition begun to be realized, establishing the most elemental of rights, the right to property, as a universal aspect of the life of willing individuals.

Although these preconditions render the existence of abstract right a result of specific historical developments, they are not themselves structures of justice. Accordingly, they do not displace abstract right as the starting point of the theory of right. Nevertheless, as much as property relations constitute the most basic interaction of freedom, Hegel recognizes that abstract right entails conflicts and wrongs that cannot be resolved and righted through its own means alone. By its very character, the reciprocal recognition determining property relations leaves it a matter of contingency what individuals happen to choose as the factor of their will and what they thereby decide to acknowledge as the domain of others. Therefore, it is always possible for persons to enter into conflicts of nonmalicious wrong when they disagree over what factors are the rightful property they have recognized, to befraud one another by using the contractual form of reciprocal recognition to acquire property through misrepresentation, and finally to commit crimes by simply choosing to violate openly the property rights of others. As Hegel argues, the interaction of persons provides no higher authority to adjudicate conflicts of entitlement or to punish fraud and crime with an objectively recognized use of force. All it offers are persons on an equal footing. Consequently, any attempt by a person to right wrong is always subject to being a further wrong, for so long as the parties involved choose not to recognize the attempt as rightful retribution, it remains an illegitimate act of revenge.[12]

This means that the reality of abstract right not only has certain historical preconditions but also requires the coexistence of additional structures of justice to resolve the internal dilemmas of property relations. Hegel understands that abstract right does not thereby become the *principle* of derivative relations of justice, reinstating the aporias of liberty. Rather, abstract right becomes the most rudimentary component of a more encompassing reality of freedom, whose other forms of right all presuppose and refer to personhood as an *element* of their own specific interaction.

Logically enough, Hegel concludes that, in the first instance, the deficient abstractness of personhood calls into play a mode of self-determination in which individuals recognize that only through their own action towards others will right be brought into existence and that only in realizing it will their own conduct have normative validity. On this basis individuals interact not simply as persons, giving their wills a particular embodiment in property, but as moral subjects who make it their own intention to do right in general, and to that extent recognize one another as rightfully responsible for their own actions.

In effect, Hegel's positive sublation of Kantian practical reason here reaches the point of incorporating its moral standpoint into the interaction of freedom. However, this incorporation involves a fundamental recasting of Kantian morality.

Although Hegel here grants moral subjectivity its valid right, he does not conceive it as an inner determination of the self. Instead, he develops it as an intersubjective structure consisting in action towards others which is recognizably related to the inner intention of its author. Hegel realizes that an individual can actually determine him or herself morally only by taking action both affecting other subjects and prefigured in a conscious purpose positively relating to their right and welfare. Such action is indeed of interest for the right and welfare of the doer himself, but only within the context of the plurality of moral subjects. That plural context affords the sphere for the realization of what is morally right, and thus the constitutive framework for moral action itself. Accordingly, throughout Hegel's discussion of purpose and responsibility, intention and welfare, and good and conscience, moral subjects always stand in relation to one another through actions they have respectively intended. Without acting towards others they have not determined themselves morally, whereas without intending what they do, their behavior has no morally accountable character.

Hegel here pays due regard to the role of inner intention in morality which Kant so emphasizes, without neglecting the equally critical side of action which Kant ignores. Hegel's negative critique of practical reason already indicated that both sides must be present if there is to be any moral willing at all. In his reformulation of the moral standpoint, Hegel now provides the positive lesson: moral actions are only those deeds that are prefigured in conscious purpose, whereas the moral intention of purpose concerns only those consequences of a real action that are relevant to the realization of right and welfare.[13]

Significant though these internal transformations are, what most radically manifests Hegel's departure from the Kantian moral standpoint is the status morality is given as a particular mode of interaction. Whereas Kant makes morality the one firm basis of normative validity, from which only legality can be distinguished as a derivative sphere, Hegel recognizes morality to be a form of self-determination that not only presupposes abstract right but serves as a bridge to independent structures of ethical community of which Kant cannot conceive.

Hegel realizes that, as much as abstract right calls for moral action, the required relations of morality are themselves inherently problematic. On the one hand, moral subjectivity has its own valid self-determination only insofar as it realizes the universal good encompassing right and welfare as the objective unconditioned end of action. On the other hand, this moral good lacks all particular determination within itself precisely becaue it is an unrealized ought that can only be brought into existence through the self-determination of the moral subject. Therefore, although the moral subject should have good intentions and bring into being what is objectively valid, the good in question is itself utterly abstract and can only be determined by the particular subjectivity of conscience. Conscience, however, cannot arrive at determinations that are objectively valid because all it has to rely on is its own subjective choice as to what is good. Consequently, the structure conscience provides for determining the good is just as empty and abstract as the good itself.[14]

Although this implicit identity of the good and conscience seals the uncertainty and anguish in which morality must proceed, it provides the basis for the interaction of ethical community, to which Hegel moves by virtue of thinking through the structure of moral action. This transition from morality to ethical community relegates moral subjectivity to a subordinate position within the total structure of justice while no less preserving it as a valid, if troubled, component. In this regard, Hegel's move entails a clear break with the tradition of Kantian and classical Greek theories of justice. Whereas Kant collapsed all right into morality and legality, Plato and Aristotle excluded the subjective reflection of moral conscience from their concept of ethical institutions. By contrast, Hegel here introduces an ethical life irreducible to abstract right and morality, which nevertheless incorporates their respective freedoms in its ethical order.

What makes this especially significant for the evaluation of modernity is that Hegel's ensuing development of ethical community brings to a head the de jure question of what justice is by providing the structures of interaction affording freedom its totality. Indeed, the determinations of abstract right and morality already make certain judgments possible. Hegel himself considers the correlative desacralization of nature and universalization of personhood to be works in progress of the modern era and he recognizes moral subjectivity to have begun to win its due as a valid mode of freedom only in modernity. On both counts, modern relations would seem to exhibit intrinsically just forms of self-determination.

Nevertheless, the presence of abstract right and morality can hardly sanctify modern times by itself if the reality of freedom is crowned by ethical community. Ethical community's encompassing institutions have to be present as well, for only then can modernity be a world of justice where the philosophy of right can be the age grasped in thought because the Idea of freedom is actually at hand.

v) The Unprecedented Ethical Community of Civil Society and State

At first glance, what Hegel develops as ethical community are institutions familiar enough in modern times: namely, the family, society, and the state. What is not so mundane is that these three spheres are conceived to be structures of interaction that are ethical in character. As interactions, they are, like personhood and morality, normatively valid relations between individuals, consisting in specific modes of reciprocal self-determination.

What distinguishes them as spheres of ethical community is that they are institutions of freedom in which the particular self-determination of their members has its realization in none other than the common structures of the ethical community to which they belong and through which they act. Whereas Kant left autonomy without reality by restricting ethics to the inner legislation of moral duty while relegating all external relations (including property, family, civil government, and world law) to the nonethical sphere of legality, Hegel here conceives the family, civil society, and the state as ethical interactions precisely insofar as they give subjective freedom actuality by being the existing framework of its realization. In contrast to morality, where the universal good is an ought to be, ever opposed to the particular willing of conscience, ethical community comprises an interpenetration of universal and particular, where one has free reality because the family, society, and state in which one acts have the realization of one's freedom as their substance.

Hegel recognizes that it is no more self-evident how the special unity of ethical community works itself out than how the family, society, and the state can provide the modes of its existence. Accordingly, in the *Philosophy of Right*, Hegel attempts to show that the minimal determination of ethical community comprises the unity of the family, that this unity entails the further ethical order of civil society into which the family is incorporated, and finally, that civil society both requires and provides the prerequisites for the state, whose political bonds of recognition bring ethical community to an encompassing whole.

In terms of this sequence, what is of preeminent importance is the relationship of civil society and state, for on it depends the total structure of ethical life. To a certain extent, the whole relation is a novel one, for although Hegel is not the first to coin the term *civil society*, he is generally recognized to be the first to conceive civil society in radical distinction from the state. Previously politics was conceived either in the classical Greek fashion, as the exclusive domain of public life in contrast to the household, or, in the manner of the liberal tradition, as a *civil* government, whose duties were a function of a civil society that itself derived from a naturally determined liberty. By comparison, Hegel demarcates civil society from the state by having the economy, social interest groups, and the public administrations of civil law and welfare all fall within civil society as necessary components of social freedom, while making the independent concern of self-government be the specific activity and raison d'etre of the state. On this basis, Hegel gives an entirely new mandate to public life.

To begin with, by conceiving civil society as a separate sphere of ethical life, he bestows normative validity upon a community of interest whose institutions allow individuals to relate to one another solely by pursuing particular ends of their own choosing which can be realized only in conjunction with the similar pursuits of others. This basic interaction of civil society extricates its members from all traditional custom and hierarchy and sets them on the equal footing of their caprice and desire, free to exercise the right of acting in public for their own interest to the degree that the interests of others are thereby advanced. In this regard, civil society becomes a power of division and dichotomy, separating individuals from the given bonds of the historical past and setting them against one another as bearers of particular ends, whose only positive relation is that of mutual dependence.

Nevertheless, Hegel recognizes this very disunion to be an *ethical* unity because it not only liberates individuals from externally imposed ties but also establishes the series of institutions in which the freedom of particularity achieves a normatively valid realization. Civil society is therefore indispensable, for without its social right public life becomes a constraint upon its members, neither embodying their chosen interests nor allowing them the free reign to relate to others for particular ends of their own.

Significantly, Hegel conceives economic relations to be the basic institutional structure of civil society. Most interpreters have taken this to mean that Hegel follows the path of the classical political economy of Steuart, Smith, and Ricardo, since they also developed the economy within what they too called civil society. What these interpreters ignore is that the "civil society" of the political economists is distinguished, not from an independent political sphere, but from a "civil government" devoted to the same civil rights, deriving from liberty, which are supposedly operative in the market place. Accordingly, its economy can be called a "political" economy insofar as the ends ascribed to politics are ultimately indistinguishable from those of society.

Nothing could be farther from Hegel's approach. Because he radically demarcates civil society from the state and conceives both as structures of interaction independent of natural determination, what he develops is not a political but a thoroughly *social* economy. In so doing, Hegel initiates a critique of political economy that not only outstrips that of Marx and his followers but also makes them its victim.[15]

They, of course, have striven to eliminate the natural reductions of political economy and to determine all economic relations as social in character. In working out their theory, however, Marxists have generally continued to conceive need, utility, and use-value production as natural givens of the human condition.[16] Furthermore, they have judged the state to be an instrument of class interest, better done away with, thereby advancing a position that takes the liberal conflation of civil society and state to its logical extreme.

Hegel, on the contrary, first shows that economic need, utility, and use-value production owe their character to social interaction. Although civil society does relate its members to one another through their needs, it does not do so as a natural condition. It rather builds an historically emergent framework in which individuals act to satisfy, not their physical requirements or psychological desires, but those freely chosen needs whose means of satisfaction can only be had through other analogously needy individuals. Although the particular content of these *economic* needs remains a matter of personal preference, it is no less predicated upon the relations between the individuals bearing them. If these relations are such that individuals can satisfy their biological needs without entering into interaction with one another, then these needs have no economic character and reality. Thus, the need at play in economic interaction is socially determined from the outset and does not involve wants whose objects either lie already in the private domain of the individual or are freely available from nature.

Hegel accordingly recognizes that economic need is not satisfied with mere natural or psychological things, such as the air we must breathe or the affections we desire, but with *commodities*, goods expressly owned by other members of civil society who are willing to exchange them to satisfy their own social wants. As he further points out, in opposition to political economists and Marxists alike, these commodities bear utility that is social and not natural in character, for they satisfy the specifically social needs of those interested individuals facing their owners, rather than the wants of human nature. Consequently, the production of goods bearing utility is equally a social matter, predicated upon civil society's system of interdependent needs. As Hegel duly recognizes, a product can have economic use-value only by being fashioned as a commodity for the needs of other individuals.[17] By contrast, all natural, subsistence production has no economic reality of its own, for the wants, work, and products it involves relate man and nature instead of relating individuals to one another in the civil interaction of the economy.

What all this entails is that economic relations proceed through acts of commodity exchange, where individuals acquire what they need from someone else by voluntarily giving in return some good of their own which that other individual correlatively seeks to have. In this way, the basic relations between the members of civil society are mediated by commodities.

Needless to say, the justice of this mediation has been called into question most notably by Marx, who argues that commodity exchange gives rise to the reification of commodity fetishism, where the social relations between individuals figure as relations between things ruling over men's lives. However, Hegel's conception of economic interaction shows how the exact opposite is the case.

First of all, in commodity exchange, the goods through which individuals interact are not things but social factors bearing value by virtue of the interdependent self-determinations of their owners. Secondly, commodity exchange takes place only insofar as the participating individuals recognize one another both as free persons, objectively owning their respective goods, and as free members of civil society, exercising the common right of satisfying needs of their own choosing. Instead of facing one another as subjects of things, they lord over their commodities, using them as means to interact as independent bearers of need, enjoying the recognized freedom to pursue their particular ends in public. Accordingly, engaging in commodity exchange is an ethical right, for it realizes the particular self-determination of the individual in unity with the existing system of the economy.

Nevertheless, Hegel recognizes that civil society can neither restrict itself to economic relations nor let them have free sway. The rudimentary reason for this is that the economy cannot guarantee the realization of the very needs its interaction generates. Precisely because the economy consists in commodity relations resting on mutual agreements of exchange, it is a matter of contingency whether its members encounter other willing parties whose respective needs and goods correlate with their own. Hegel draws the unavoidable conclusion: so long as the economy is left to its own logic of interdependent self-determinations, there is nothing to prevent economic relations from resulting in crises, overproduction, unemployment, and an amassing of riches by some and a growing poverty of others.

This is a matter of injustice because of civil society's own ethical relations. Unemployment and poverty may not be violations of abstract right, but they are social wrongs once economic interaction has established the civil right of individuals to pursue and satisfy their chosen needs for commodities. The important point is that, although Hegel is certainly struck by the glaring disparities of wealth in the economies of his day, he does not view this as an historical disease afflicting a certain stage of economic development. Rather, he considers it a problem endemic to economic relations which reveals their limited justice.

As a result, Hegel recognizes that civil society cannot reduce itself to an economy. On the one hand, it must allow its members to organize into social interest groups to press for what the economy does not deliver on its own. On the other hand, it must also contain an administration of civil law and a public administration of welfare to guarantee and enforce the personhood of its members and their right to satisfy their needs through their own free action. Since all these public institutions operate on the basis of the economy, they do not annul or replace commodity relations but rather regulate them so that the ethical right of economic action has its intrinsic contingency externally resolved. Although the economy thereby remains the basic structure of civil society to which public administration refers, its own justice mandates that it be a subordinate and not a determining base of society. In arriving at this differentiation of social institutions, Hegel's development of civil society thus effectively demonstrates how the economy must have a subordinate position within society if social freedom is to be realized.

There is, however, another side to Hegel's subordination of economic relations that is even more decisive. It consists in the fact that the public administrations of civil law and welfare that rule over the economy are themselves *social* institutions falling within the community of interest of civil society. In contrast to liberals and Marxists alike, Hegel does not identify them with the state but explicitly characterizes them as civil, as opposed to political, institutions. Hegel recognizes that the public enforcement of civil law and welfare is relative to the pursuit of particular ends constitutive of civil society. What these institutions realize are not any political rights to participate in self-government, but the civil rights to enjoy one's person and property under the protection of public law and authority and to have the publicly guaranteed opportunity to satisfy one's own needs through action of one's own choosing. The activities of these institutions are thus not for their own sake but for the sake of advancing the particular interests of the members of society. Even when this is so broadly defined as the public welfare, it is still an end which is separate from the administration of society. In other words, the institutions of civil law and public welfare neither provide the members of society with political freedom nor constitute a self-determining government whose ruling activity is an end in itself, and thereby politically sovereign.

Hegel realizes the dual consequences of this limitation. On the one hand, the public administrations of civil society cannot be the crowning order of ethical community, for they leave the structures of interaction without an institution of freedom that holds them all together in a self-determined whole. On the other hand, any "liberalism" or "socialism" that reduces government to an administration of civil law and/or public welfare undermines political freedom and must be rejected. Hegel explicitly attacks the "welfare state" in this regard for making government an instrument of civil society with no political ends of its own.

Accordingly, what civil society calls for is not civil government, a welfare state, or any political order based on class or other social interests. Rather, concludes Hegel in an unprecedented move, civil society demands a free political domain radically distinct from itself. The very limits of social freedom make necessary a sovereign state whose body politic gives freedom totality by integrating all interaction into its realm and by determining that realm through its own self-governing activity as a self-determining whole.

Admittedly Hegel's treatment of political institutions has received no sustained critique since Marx's early attempt,[18] which itself survives in only a very fragmented form. Nevertheless, it is the basic character of the state as an ethical institution incorporating all other relations of right within itself that sets the highest general bounds of the interaction of freedom and thus provides the ultimate measure for Hegel's judgment of modernity.

Hegel's move beyond civil society gives politics a twofold mandate. On the one hand, the state must be an ethical association whose members interact, not as civilians pursuing separate particular interests, but as citizens willing government policy as the end of their own free action insofar as the state in which they act is itself the existing structure of their political freedom to govern themselves. In this ethical unity of universal and particular, individuals exercise their respected rights as citizens by willing the universal determination of the state, while the state has its sovereign validity for them by being the actuality of their particular political autonomy. Contracy to the "politics" of civil government, class rule, or the welfare state, the self-determination of the citizen is here participation in self-government because the body politic in which the individual can exercise that right has as its end, not particular interests or public welfare, but the realization of self-rule.

On the other hand, for the state to be this sovereign sphere of self-government, it cannot cancel the social freedom of interest or any of the other modes of recognized self-determination. This would set it against its own members and thereby destroy its constitutive ethical unity. Instead, the state must contain all these freedoms within itself, preserving their rights through its own rule while maintaining its own sovereignty by preventing any of these component spheres from subordinating politics to their specific concerns.

The state must thus insure that its citizens enjoy their freedoms of personhood, moral subjectivity, family life, and social action without allowing these to undermine their political freedom. In this regard, the state has the right to counter the arbitrariness of conscience when its acts violate the laws of the state, and even demand the lives of its members when needed to defend the political freedom of national sovereignty.

With respect to society, Hegel realizes, the state has a similarly dual relation. On the one hand, it must provide the administrations of civil law and public welfare with the adequate legislated means to carry out their *social* regulation of the economy. On the other hand, the state must intervene in society on purely political grounds to insure that class struggles, economic power, and other social factors do not take hold of politics, preventing citizens from exercising self-rule and subordinating government policy to some social interest. Only by keeping civil society in its subordinate position can the state preserve its own freedom.

In this dual capacity, politics gives freedom totality by establishing the integral reality of all other modes of interaction through its own self-governing activity. As citizens of the just state, individuals thus attain on their part the freedom to determine the totality of practical life through their own willing.

Given this achievement of the state, the only remaining matter of right, besides the relations between states, is the question of the historical process whereby such a totality of freedom can come into existence. Hegel concludes his philosophy of right with this problem, and it is here that he finally judges modernity by asking whether the modern age is the historical epoch in which all the structures of interaction come to the light of day.

## vi) Hegel's Judgment of Modernity

The importance of this judgment has been established as it must be done, by laying out the basic outline of personhood, morality, and the ethical life of society and state in Hegel's conception of freedom. Now the judgment itself can be introduced by indicating what the historical developments are that Hegel considers constitutive of modernity. Hegel sees the modern age determined by three unprecedented developments: the Reformation, the rise of capitalism in England, and the French Revolution.[19] Hegel understands the first of these, the Reformation, to have effected a liberation of religious conscience from external authority that grants subjectivity the right to rely upon its own certainty in determining what holds valid for it. Accordingly, the Reformation has a just ethical dimension, for it carries with it the standpoint of morality, giving its independent conscience a respected existence. Hegel recognizes that this moral aspect of the Reformation has an intrinsic validity and that its worldly presence does not preclude any other structures of interaction. Nevertheless, the Reformation does not itself establish a secular order in which subjective freedom has its existing realization, even if it frees conscience from the rule of the church. Consequently, Hegel concludes, modernity must involve more than a Reformation if it is to bring justice into being.

Hegel considers the rise of capitalism in England to provide a certain measure of the required complement to the Reformation—but not only that. On the one hand, the economic development beginning in England has stamped the modern age with the most basic features of civil society. Capitalism has emancipated individuals from the hierarchy and natural determination of past tradition, desacralizing nature by subsuming it under the universal hold of commodity relations, and setting individuals against one another in the social equality of their interdependent need. It has put in motion the commodity circulation in which individuals can exercise their civil right to decide what they want and to satisfy their needs through freely chosen action. In these respects, Hegel acknowledges, the capitalist development of modernity has established certain just relations of civil society.

However, Hegel observes that the rise of capitalism has on the other hand left necessary structures of civil society unrealized, and thereby distorted those relations that it has brought into being. Capitalism has certainly set loose the free activity of economic interaction, but it has not engendered the adequate social administration of the economy that must secure the public welfare. In England, Hegel sees before him the full spectacle of the contingency of satisfaction endemic to economic relations: unprecedented wealth and poverty side by side, unemployment and overproduction, growing class antagonisms, and everywhere the spread of these troubled market relations beyond all given limit. Indeed, Hegel does witness attempts to remove the social injustice, but they either fail to curtail the unrelieved want or substitute a public dole for the guaranteed opportunity to satisfy one's needs through activity of one's own choosing.

In effect, what capitalism presents Hegel is a society that is not fully civil because the economy is its determining base rather than a subordinate sphere lorded over by the civil administrations of justice and welfare. Modernity may have here introduced the basic economic structure of civil society, but it has not thereby realized social freedom in full. Rather, it has left that as unfinished business, which, Hegel notes, already confronts England with the threat of an uprising to transform its society.

The problem with capitalism, however, cannot be merely social in character. Given the dual relation of the state to civil society, the distorted character of modern society would have to be reflected in a corresponding failure of its political institutions. Hegel is cognizant of this, and in turning finally to the French Revolution as modernity's third determining development, he finds the expected problem.

Hegel's political diagnosis has two sides. On the one hand, Hegel grants, the French Revolution has introduced the valid ethical notion that freedom is the legitimate substance of politics and that all members of the state have the right to be citizens and participate in self-government. Through the revolution's own act, modernity has brought history to the point of sweeping aside all given authority and tradition and replacing them with institutions of freedom determined through the sovereign rule of a free state.

On the other hand, Hegel observes, the revolution has failed to carry out the actual constitution of freedom which it has made the order of the day. Instead of erecting political institutions with ethical community's concrete unity of universal and particular, it has offered the spectacle of ruling factions devouring one another in the name of the will of the people. The volition of that abstraction is not only prepolitical in origin, but a will whose solitary oneness excludes the plurality of interaction that can alone bring freedom, rather than arbitrary domination, into politics. By failing to establish organs of self-government, the revolution has put state power in the hands of particular usurpers whose claims of universality cannot mask their inability to raise the body politic above the play of interests.

As for the concurrent attempts at restoration, Hegel recognizes that they can offer no way out of the dilemma either. Because they only reestablish traditional authority, the state remains without the legitimate sovereignty that political institutions of freedom can alone provide. As a result, politics in modernity stands unable to assert its proper hegemony over social interest and so realize the just relation between state and civil society.

Hegel realizes that this political failure does not just mean that society is left at bay before the free play of its economy. Rather, Hegel here sees modernity facing the critical danger of society overwhelming politics and all other spheres of interaction, making its own distorted relations the real determining base of practical life.

Consequently, Hegel must finally conclude that modernity cannot be granted legitimacy. Although it has introduced fundamental elements of personhood, morality, civil society, and the state, it has not brought into being the totality of ethical community. Therefore, modernity stands as a yet open chapter in the unfinished history of freedom's emergence. Hegel has no predictions to offer, but only the observation that in the years to come the fate of justice will hinge upon the unresolved problems of civil society and the state.

### vii) The Question of Justice Today

A century and a half has passed since Hegel made his judgment of modernity. Other revolutions and restorations have come and gone, although this time their protagonists have defined themselves, as much in reference to Hegel as to anything else. Nevertheless, the briefest survey of recent regimes invites the question of whether our own day has confronted the lessons of the philosophy of right and in any way advanced towards the realization of social and political freedom that could grant it legitimacy.

In our liberal democracies, the spectacle certainly seems to suggest the economic domination of society and the social subordination of politics that Hegel feared. Most criticism has fallen on the condition of public welfare as it lies under the relatively free sway of commodity relations, but the condition of politics appears most in jeopardy. While citizens exercise their modicum of civil rights, actual governing has fallen to the parties under whom political activity has become the private vocation of professional politicians. They accordingly appeal to their constituencies not as participants in self-government but as private members of society, taxpayers rather than citizens, bearers of class, ethnic, or other particular interests rather than as subjects of political interaction. Under these conditions, that constituency can only answer back by taking infrequent and ill-attended trips to the ballot box to reestablish the same gulf between citizen and government; by taking to the streets, which involves no wielding of political power but only an attempt to influence those who govern; or by responding with the voice of public opinion wherein a passive, atomized mass of individuals express their personal preference instead of engaging in governing themselves.

If, further, the society of such liberal states remains victim to the contingencies of economic relations, today's social democratic regimes perhaps realize the public administration of welfare more thoroughly. However, their professed subordination of government to that end seems to effect the characteristic distortion of the welfare state, which Hegel attacked for reducing politics to a civil management of the public welfare.

As for contemporary communist regimes, they would appear to bring this social reduction to a greater extreme, while striking at civil freedom as well. In erecting their one-party worker states, they have explicitly subordinated political power to a particular class interest. At the same time, however, they have restricted the interaction of social groups such that the working class is itself unable to express and advance the interest on which the state is supposedly founded. As a result, the interaction of politics is supplanted by the single will of a party, whose domination of society leaves its own interest the sole arbiter of public affairs.

Finally, the experience of Nazi rule seems to present a complete destruction of political and social interaction, for here the natural determination of a people replaces freedom as the basis of state and society, and political power is concentrated in the natural will of a leader who stands above all reciprocal relations as the immediate expression of a master race.

If these are the regimes that modernity has left at our door, the challenge of Hegel's philosophy of right has only grown stronger with the passage of time. This challenge is at once theoretical and practical. In face of the open history of freedom, it is now our affair whether the theory of interaction will remain ignored or whether thinkers will pursue its arguments further while citizens choose to make them the basis of political action.

## Notes

1. See paragraph 2 and the note to paragraph 3 in Hegel's *Philosophy of Right*, by T. M. Knox (New York: Oxford University Press, 1967).

2. Joachim Ritter is an exception to the rule, and in his essays on Hegel's practical philosophy, (Joachim Ritter, *Hegel and the French Revolution: Essays on the Philosophy of Right*, trans. by Richard Dien Winfield [Cambridge, MA: the MIT Press, 1984]) calls attention to Hegel's understanding of modernity by focusing upon the central problems of right with which Hegel is concerned.

3. See 1113a33–35, 1176a13–16, 1176b25, 1284a3–34, 1288a27–28, and 1288a32–b4 in Aristotle's *Nicomachean Ethics* (1094a–1181b) and *Politics* (1252a–1342b).

4. M. B. Foster has discussed this point at length with reference to Hegel's critique of Plato's *Republic* in his neglected work, *The Political Philosophies of Plato and Hegel* (New York: Oxford Univerity Press, 1968).

5. Hannah Arendt has emphasized this in her important critique of modern revolutions, which applies Hegel's distinction of society and state, without, however, recognizing the legitimacy of civil society's subordinate structure of freedom. See Hannah Arendt, *On Revolution* (New York: Viking Press, 1976).

6. The seminal importance of Hegel's critical encounter with Kant's practical philosophy is laid bare by Ritter in his essay, "Morality and Ethical Life." (*Hegel and The French Revolution*, pp. 151-142). Ritter goes so far as to suggest that Hegel's philosophy of right can be understood as a sublation of Kant's theory in the dual sense of having its own framework immanently emerge from the inherent dilemmas of the Kantian position and of superceding it by incorporating its standpoint as a subordinate element within the developed reality of freedom.

7. The importance of the distinction between practical reason and practical understanding has been largely ignored by John Rawls, among others, who tends to reduce practical reason to practical understanding in his *A Theory of Justice* (Cambridge: Harvard University Press, 1973). Consequently, he is unable to leave behind the empirically conditioned framework of Utilitarianism, which makes practical understanding the principle of justice. This is evident in his conception of the so-called original position, where the given alternatives of choice are merely rendered indeterminate through a postulated veil of ignorance, instead of being replaced by a positive principle of self-determination that can grant the will a content deriving from itself.

8. See Kant, *Critique of Pure Reason*, B372/A316ff.

9. To take the classic example of syllogism—All men are mortal, Socrates is a man, therefore Socrates is a mortal—the universal principal (All men are mortal) determines the particular (Socrates) only by virtue of being supplied with the minor premise (Socrates is a man), whose particular content can only be known by the understanding in the Kantian framework.

10. Ritter is one of the few interpreters who appropriately emphasizes the significance of Hegel's concept of abstract right and how it is the basic structure of interaction, irreducible to no other. In his essay "Person and Property," (*Hegel and The French Revolution*, pp. 124-150), Ritter dissects the elemental character of the relations of persons through property in Hegel's theory and at the same time points to the deficient abstractness that leads Hegel to develop further spheres of right as necessary components of freedom's full realization.

11. See paragraphs 54–58 in Hegel's *Philosophy of Right*.

12. See *ibid.*, paragraphs 82ff and 102.

13. See *ibid.*, paragraphs 117 and 125.

14. See *ibid.*, paragraph 141.

15. For examples of current attempts to pursue this critique further, see David P. Levine, *Economic Theory* (London: Routledge and Kegan Paul, 1978), and Richard Dien Winfield, *The Social Determination of Production: The Critique of Hegel's System of Needs and Marx's Concept of Capital (Ph.D. dissertation, Yale University, 1977)*, and Richard Dien Winfield, *The Just Economy* (New York: Routledge, 1988).

16. For a critique of these natural reductions, see Winfield, *The Social Determination of Production*, pp. 164–188, and Richard Dien Winfield, "The Social Determination of the Labor Process from Hegel to Marx," *The Philosophical Forum*, Vol 11, No. 3 (Spring 1980), pp. 250–272, Chapter 13 in this volume.

17. See Hegel, *op. cit.*, paragraphs 192 and 196.

18. See Karl Marx, *Critique of Hegel's 'Philosophy of Right'* (Cambridge University Press, 1970). In what remains of this text, Marx makes two important observations. He shows that Hegel's characterization of the head of state as a monarch involves a natural determination of royal birth that violates the proper freedom of political interaction. Second, Marx rightly points out that Hegel's insertion of estates as institutional elements of the legislature (paragraph 301ff.) makes class interest a determining factor in politics, contrary to the basic separation of civil society and state. Both of these inconsistent features must be removed if political interaction is to be properly conceived in its ethical universality. Marx, however, never made the proper revisions, but instead finally accepted the originally liberal notion that politics can never rise above particular interests. Accordingly he made his call for the withering away of the state

and the erection of a communist society where public freedom is eliminated in favor of a technical domination of nature setting men ''free'' to engage in the purely private activities of their natural species being.

19. Ritter discusses this in his essays, ''Hegel and the Reformation'' and ''Hegel and the French Revolution'' (*Hegel and the French Revolution*, pp. 183-191 and 35-89).

# 10

# The Dilemma of Labor

> The direct relationship of labor to its products is the relationship of the worker to the objects of his production... When we ask, then, what is the essential relationship of labor, we are asking about the relationship of the worker to production.[1]

With these words from 1844 the young Marx posed the thematization of Civil Society in terms of the reflective structure of consciousness that has been the inadvertent strait-jacket of Marxist discussion ever since. While the specific program of the *Grundrisse* and *Das Kapital* has lain forgotten, egological categories of need and interest, of alienation and defiance have been thrown upon a contradiction of *forces of production* and *relations of production* to give the living proof that quantity turns into quality, just as ice turns to water. *Labor* has become the object of adoration and apology, as that original relation that can never seem to cut through the facticity of history.

All this casuistry and accommodation finds its source in none other than the false problematic that Marx first presents in the *1844 Manuscripts:* the attempt to formulate the concept of *social* production by means of a notion of laboring activity that is itself specified through the reflection of an ultimately presupposed subject.

"The direct relationship of labor to its products is the relationship of the worker to the objects of his production." The negative process of labor *is* identified with the negative process of the laborer; the specification of the product in and through labor *is* a determining grounded in the structure of the laboring individual as a self-conscious subject.

"When we ask, then, what is the essential relationship of labor we are asking about the relationship of the *worker* to production." Not only is the laboring act to be understood as a self-relating of a presupposed individual, but *labor* as a *social* category, constitutive of a system of production, is to be conceived from the absolute starting point of the worker's independent reflection upon his circumstance.

*Labor* as *alienated, labor* as epistemological category, *labor* as irreducible factor beside *interaction, labor* as source of Abstract Right, as germ to the opposition of *forces of production* and *relations of production* and of *base* and *superstructure*—these are nothing other than the changing faces of the *aporie* that lies in this program of 1844.

Economics, in the form it has taken as a modern social science, has of course avoided *this* dilemma by simply not facing the problem that lies at the bottom of all of Marx's considerations of labor. Instead of investigating labor in the constitution of modern society, economics has taken work as informed by reflection and carried through this formalism to its limited end. For in modern economics production has been excluded from social theory in the true sense of the word, and been reduced to a sphere of technique, manipulated by the *ratio* of the self-determining individual who *finds* him or herself with others beset by need and given relationships. Here Capital can be nothing more than the instrument ruled by the entrepeneur and serviced by the worker. The process of production is a calculable, rational one, where objects are subdued in a causal procedure.

Kant has provided the framework for this conception. He writes that economics, whether of the household, agriculture, or the state, cannot "be reckoned as practical philosophy. . . For all these contain only rules of skill (and are consequently only technically practical) for bringing about an effect that is possible according to the natural concepts of causes and effects, which, since they belong to theoretical philosophy, are subject to those precepts as mere corollaries from it (viz. natural science) and can therefore claim no place in a special philosophy called practical."[2] He has had the consequence to recognize that when the *Faktum* of Freedom is taken as the basis of human praxis, any occupation with the satisfaction of need through labor must stand outside the relation of individuals to each other as free selves, and merely express a response to the bond of the empirically conditioned side of agents with the mechanism of external Nature. Because the social objectivity of self-determination is here deprived of any concrete content beyond the formal regulation of the categorical imperative and a civil order hypothetically posited on contractarian lines, the assumed autonomy of Practical Reason must exclude from its domain all reference to the heterogeneous particularity of both needs and the activity securing their satisfaction. From this standpoint labor can only be a means for an individual, completely external to one's existence as a free being, and to one's *social (sittliche)* relations with others.[3]

As a result the whole sphere of economic life can be nothing but a factual collection of technical procedures whose animating source is to be found in the arbitrarity of the self-determining, and therefore indeterminate, individual. In place of a concept of Civil Society, we are left with an empty formula. Max Weber gives it its classic, most bare and honest form: "We shall speak of economic action only if the satisfaction of a need depends, in the actor's judgment, upon relatively *scarce* resources and a *limited* number of possible actions, and if this state of affairs evokes specific reactions."[4]

The entire Marxist discussion begins by rejecting this reduction of production to the conscious application of technologies in relation to need. The task now becomes one of realizing labor as a social process. And in the *Grundrisse* and *Das Kapital* this general program takes its *final* determinate form as a concept of the System of Needs of Civil Society,[5] that specifically modern reality in which for the first time the process of production is freed from the household and natural conditions, to emerge as an independent sphere of social interaction in which the private self-seeking individual as such becomes. This is a realm where labor has its determination and actuality in the self-distinguishing *of capital*, instead of in relation either to anthropological assumptions of humans' relation to nature, or to some presupposed notion of self-consciousness. For the *Grundrisse* and *Das Kapital* reveal precisely how production is socially determined as a reality constituted by nothing other than capital's self-developing *intersubjective* process.

Yet before this *solution* is reached, Marx gives us that attempt which remains caught in the standpoint of reflection at the same time that it reaches for a concrete social theory. The predicament of Marxism has been defined by the apologetic acceptance of that inconsequent problematic and by the complete ignoring of *how* Marx has specified labor as a social reality in the *Grundrisse* and *Das Kapital*.

In order to come to the real achievement of Marx, it is first necessary to clear away the false notions of labor that have dominated Marxist discussion, beginning with the original formulation of 1844. On this basis it is then possible to recognize the fundamentally intersubjective framework from which Marx is finally able to determine the concept of Capital.

The *1844 Manuscripts'* concept of alienated labor serves as a point of departure for the subsequent Marxist discussion that has been unable to actually grasp the labor process as a social reality. This is due not so much to its early origin, as to the radicality with which it demonstrates how the attempt to understand the system of production upon the basis of the determining of a presupposed self-consciousness directly leads to the actual annulling of any notion of society or of the individual.

The drama of alienated labor is this open contradiction that falls victim to its own inability to coherently unite the opposition from which it begins. This is the factually discovered opposition of labor as *objectification* to labor as *alienation*.[6] Here we have exposed the fatal dichotomy of an act of labor determined in complete indifference to any social context whatsoever and the social fact of the private appropriation of the product of labor.

The first moment is *labor* as such, that original *praxis* in which self-consciousness achieves its concrete reality independent of a system of social relations. The standpoint of reflection is constituted in this practical creating of an objective world[7] whereby "Man makes his life activity itself the object of his will and of his consciousness. . . . Through and because of this production, nature appears as *his* work and his reality. The object of labor is, therefore, the *objectification of man's species life:* for he. . . contemplates himself in a world that he has created."[8]

That such an absolute self-positing can be realized in this way is problematic enough. For on the one hand, the laboring act would seem to already depend upon the *existence* of the subject and an objective world. And on the other hand, the product of labor can neither constitute the totality of objectivity (for even the laborer in his or her own *existence* stands beside it) nor contain within its own determinateness the negative process of its creator.[9]

Yet even accepting Marx's claim that *labor as objectification* is constitutive of self-conscious freedom, the insolvable problem remains of how this autonomy is to be limited by the social form of appropriation and transformed into a state of *alienation*. This second moment demands that the *fact* of capitalist property relations somehow negate this unlimited self-affirmation in the labor process at the same time that it maintains the worker's standpoint of reflection within his productive act. For *alienated labor* is based upon the individual's *recognition* of himself as alienated.

The way in which Marx attempts to make these contradictory moments coincide is by simply annulling all social relations within the capitalist form of production and substituting relations of force and domination that still must leave the autonomous individual somewhere to be found.[10]

Here the worker has no subjective relation *to* the capitalist, but rather 'The worker exists as a worker only when he exists *for himself* as capital."[11] The laborer is in his self-affirming praxis only when he is already a dependent moment, the property of the capitalist.

On the other hand, the capitalist has no relation to the laborer as a person, for he is "the *governing power* over labor."[12] The labor of the worker is thus "forced labor."[13] "The *estrangement of man* from man"[14] is here so complete that it seems foolish to speak of any *social relations* or of any *society* whatsoever, for even the presupposed mediations of property and exchange are themselves immediately annulled when the *Person* is treated as a *Thing (Sache)*.[15]

The worker's very entrance into the labor process contradicts these foundations of his ruling master. In order for the subjective reflection of the individual to still be tied to his laboring activity, he must give himself up as a Person when he gives his labor up to Capital. Marx describes this impossible situation when he says that "the worker has become a commodity."[16]

Somehow the entire subject of the laborer is supposed to be bought, and yet he is the one to sell himself! And even though the worker here exists for others as a mere object (which contradicts the form of contract through which he becomes capital's property), he still somehow maintains his independent perspective within the labor process, so that "the object which labor produces—labor's product—confronts it as *something alien*, as a *power independent* of the producer. . . his labor. . . exists *outside him*. . . and. . . becomes a power on its own confronting him."[17] How this conscious awareness over and against the product can be is mystery enough, for this arrangement of production would seem to exclude the very *objectification* by the worker himself which in principle constitutes the coming to be of his own reflective standpoint. The product stands as the property of the capitalist, and the laboring act serves capital instead of positing the autonomy of the worker. This entire relation of alienated labor presupposes the self-consciousness of the worker at the same time that his situation should be annulling it! Yet if the worker does have the intuition of himself in the objectivity of the product to begin with (through the moment of *objectification*) how can this be limited by *anything* external?

Marx would like to say that this whole construct nevertheless holds itself together as a system of production which exists in the form of a contradiction. He writes that "Labor, the subjective essence of private property as exclusion of property, and capital, objective labor as exclusion of labor, constitute *private property* as its developed state of contradiction."[18] It should be seen, however, that little subsists at all when the subjectivity of the worker and his relation to the given form of private appropriation cannot in themselves be coherently formulated. As long as the act of labor is unable to unite both these moments in its own specification, social production is an empty phrase. The "developed state of contradiction" contains little more than the affirmation that the *objectification* in the labor process is fundamentally indifferent to the capitalist relationship within which it should emerge. The problem is that Marx has here stood firmly by the standpoint of an irreducible reflection and nonetheless attempted to elevate the labor process above technique to the level of the becoming of freedom.

Only when he leaves behind the conception of *externalized society* and *alienated labor* is Marx able to approach the problem of Civil Society. This he does in the *1844 Manuscripts* in describing none other than his ideal of *communist* society. There "the individual *is the social being*.[19] . . . Man, much as he may therefore be a *particular* individual. . . is just as much the *totality*—the ideal totality—the subjective existence of thought and experienced society for itself.[20] . . . They relate themselves to the *thing* for the sake of the thing, but the thing itself is an *objective human* relation to itself and to man[21] . . . Indeed, his own sensuousness first exists as human sensuousness for himself through the *other* man."[22] What is loosely described is that System of Needs within which the labor process *is* a social relation constitutive of what Marx here calls the species being and what Hegel calls the private individual of Civil Society. It must remain a beyond for Marx as long as he remains unable to determine the process of production as an intersubjective, fundamentally social relation, and not as an egological fact of life subjugated to a particular set of 'social' circumstances.

The extreme form of the failure to conceive social production that is expressed in the *1844 Manuscripts'* concept of *alienated labor* should not obscure the perseverance of this dilemma in the would-be "historical" discourse of the developing contradiction of the forces of production and the relations of production that appears to have replaced Alienation as a central theme in Marx's later works.

One of the earlier statements of this problematic is found in the 1848 writing *Wage-Labor and Capital*. Here it does seem that the very starting point of the analysis is the recognition of the unsolved task of the *1844 Manuscripts*. Marx writes: "In the process of production, human beings work not only upon nature. . .In order to produce, they enter into definite connections and relations to one another, and only within these social connections and relations. . .does production take place."[23]

Yet the generality of this principle, its indifference to the historical emergence of the private individual and to the specific task of the thematization of Civil Society indicates its weakness. This becomes clear in its unfolding in the classic doctrine which Marx here expresses in these words: "the *social relations within which individuals produce, the social relations of production, are altered, transformed, with the change and development of the material means of production, of the forces of production. The relations of production in their totality constitute what is called the social relations, society, and moreover, a society at a definite stage of historic development, a* society, with peculiar, distinctive character."[24]

Although the stated distinction of *relations of production* from *forces of production* avoids all explicit reference to the role of the individual laborer, Marx has here reproduced the reduction of the laboring act to a determination of technique that nonetheless must of itself affect the structure of social relations within which it *is*.

The forces of production are dead objects whose process is entirely external to them. They are determined as productive instruments only in and through the so-called relations of production that in turn are themselves relations *of production* only by containing these forces as a mere object. The *development* of these forces can take place only from outside of them, through none other than the agency of the so-called relations of prodution. Yet Marx has separated one from the other, reducing both to things essentially specified from without. Only a presupposed self-consciousness existing beyond both of these "things" can provide the unity that allows *forces of production* and *relations of production* to stand side by side in relation with each other and together constitute the foundation of society. Because neither moment contains within its own determination the *emergence* of the other and their opposition, which would allow both to exist as distinguished moments of a whole, the system of social production *is* only through the subjective act of our investigator—Deus ex machina Karl Marx. In themselves neither the *forces of production* nor the *relations of production* can specify a *social* form of production, for the one is a mere instrument, a technique devoid of a social reality in its isolation and difference from relations of production, and the other is a formal set of relations that are somehow unable themselves to specify the material act of production. The social unity which should be differentiating itself into these two opposed moments is simply not to be found.

Inevitably, when it comes time to transform the empty quantitative change in the forces of production into a *determining* of a set of relations of production, Marx must pull consciousness out of a hat to break through the indifference of number.[25] The contradiction of *forces of production* and *relations of production* becomes a threesome. For if a social process is now to be salvaged, then "three moments, the forces of production, the state of society, and consciousness, can and must come into contradiction with one another."[26] Of course it is only the latter, consciousness, that is able to "solve" the contradiction.

The dilemma is just as great when the relations of production are themselves opposed to a legal and political Superstructure whose Ground they are supposed to be. The '"Preface" to *A Contribution To The Critique of Political Economy* gives the most famous expression to this theory. Marx here explains that "The totality of these relations of production constitutes the economic structure of society, the real foundation, on which correspond definite forms of social consciousness. The mode of production of material life conditions the general proces of social, political and intellectual life,"[27] and when the forces of production transform the relations of production, so has an entire world been born.

Yet because the "totality of these relations of production. . . the real foundation" does not contain in its own determination the emergency of the opposition of itself to its *superstructure*, the correspondence between the two is an empty external accommodation that has nothing to say about the necessity of their interrelation or what they may be in themselves. With every social phenomenon the mere *expression* of the *relations of production*, neither the limits of the totality of society, nor the determinate and necessary differentiation of this whole into its distinct elements can be grasped. Once again an independent consciousness must introduce itself to claim that the given *is* a relation of *base* and *superstructure*. As Hegel writes, "it is a dead halt, which does not of itself go beyond itself, and proceed to a new content; it has to get hold of something else from somewhere or other in order to have once more a content. . . In that this reflection does not even have its own negativity as its content, it is not inside actual fact at all, but for ever away outside it."[28]

The oppositions *forces of production—relations of production, base—superstructure* are both empty schemas unable to give themselves a content.[29] Each presents a pair of determinations indifferent to each other within their opposition. The conditioning of one element by the other can offer nothing as to the nature of each in itself.[30]

Historical process becomes a mysterious sequence in which the relations of production commune with the *superstructure* in an unspeakable way. And the system of *social* production is itself just as much an enigma, for here *no* concept can be given to constitute the labor process in its own determinateness *as* a social relation.[31] Technique has fallen outside of intersubjectivity, and Marx's political economy has become its own annihilation, a fate that Kant, for one, would call well-earned.

Although *alienated labor* is no longer the specific form in which the labor process is determined through an individual self, the distinction of *forces of production* from *relations of production* has maintained the same self-defeating dependence upon an external consciousness in order to bring together the transforming of Nature and human interaction *as* a social process.

To break through this problematic bondage to a presupposed standpoint of Reflection,[32] Habermas has tried to lead the Marxist discussion of production to the level of Hegel's *Jenaer Realphilosophie,* where labor, language and reciprocal recognition are factors in which self-consciousness can first become thematized and through which a self-differentiating structure of society is able to constitute itself.[33]

However, in opposition to Hegel, Habermas is unable to conceive any immanent relation between the dialectic of Representation and labor and that of Reciprocal Recognition. As a result, both are set indifferently beside each other as irreducible principles.[34] On the one side stand language and labor as self-objectifications of an individual who is independent of any context other than the subject-object relatedness of consciousness.[35] And on the other side stands Interaction, conceived without any relation to a social world, and merely representing the reciprocal recognition of two individuals as constituted from out of the dialogical self-reflecting of each individual upon the other.[36]

Habermas takes these two elemental relationships as those factors from which Hegel has been able to determine the *Ich* as the identity of the universal and the particular, and further recognizes that the possibility of a theory of social production rests on the grounding of these factors within a self-determining unity that is not the self-consciousness which they are to thematize, but rather that unity which Hegel has called *Spirit (Geist)*.[37]

It is this relation that Habermas seeks to formulate by specifying a social structure that unites labor and interaction without subjugating one to the other. Characteristically, however, Habermas cannot determine the system of production as the sought after structure of mediation.[38] He instead opposes the dialectic of *social production* to that of the *class antagonism* just as he had set *labor* against *interaction*, thereby reproducing the same dichotomy at another level.[39]

When finally Habermas does come to formulate the mediating unity of *labor* and *interaction*,[40] he is unable to determine it without identifying it with interaction itself.

One of the most obvious examples is when Habermas claims that Hegel later preserves the unifying structure of *labor* and *interaction* that is first developed in the *Jenaer Realphilosophie* only in the *Phenomenology of Spirit*'s relation of *Lordship* and *Bondage*. This relationship, which should integrate the two irreducible factors of labor and reciprocal recognition in an identity constitutive of *Spirit*, is *as a whole* nothing other than the structure of *interaction* which constitutes *itself* in and through the *moment* of *labor* that is here introduced only as a result of the ensuing confrontation of *Lord* and *Bondsman*. Hegel openly contradicts Habermas's notion of the absolute indifference of *labor* and *interaction*, and also explicitly states that the process of *Lordship* and *Bondage* is still an abstraction from *Spirit*, and in no way constitutes a *society* within which the person is individuated.[41]

Outside of this unfortunate reference, Habermas offers only two other suggestions for the social reality that must accomplish the unifying task of *Spirit*: Cooperation *within* the labor process and, above all, Abstract Right.

Cooperation, however, as *distinct* from the system of production, cannot itself contain the determining of the act of labor, but merely state an external application of *interaction* upon *labor*.[42]

Abstract Right, on the other hand, is treated as a *social* reality that still falls outside the constitution of the system of production. Habermas wants to show that Abstract Right is the existing bond of *labor* and *interaction* that nonetheless emerges from out of the production process. "Possession as the substrate of legal recognition arises from the labor process. Thus instrumental action and interaction are linked in the recognized product of labor."[43] However, when Habermas attempts to describe the *positing* of Abstract Right, and the uniting of *labor* and *interaction* within it, he is forced to retreat from all notions of a system pf production, and ends up having *labor* create Abstract Right, which itself exists as a form of interaction alone.[44] For when he uses the term *social production* (*gesellschaftliche Arbeit*) to designate the creator of Abstract Right, it is still nothing other than the *objectification* of *labor* that is to account for this *social* relation![45]

Yet *how* the determination of *property* and the *Person*, the immediate forms of Abstract Right, in any way depends upon the worker's self-objectification within the labor act, or even upon an existing *social* process of production, must remain a mystery. Habermas can only make the familiar claim that through some sort of *institutionalization* the repeated exchange of produced commodities gives birth to the *Person*. Such *normatization (Normierung)*, however, would indicate an introduction of some Deus ex machina in order to prop up an Abstract Right that is deficient because it does not contain its own *administration* and *is* merely *abstract*.[46]

The real problem here concerns the very possibility of discussing relations of *property, Person,* and *contract* at the level of *actual Spirit (wirklicher Geist)*, and not alongside, or even including, the "irreducible" principles of *subjective Spirit (subjektiver Geist): labor* and *interaction*.[47] Even accepting that Habermas has somehow made clear a distinction between *labor* and *social production*, the question remains of how the system of production can maintain its own structural claims when within its sphere Abstract Right is born. For the standpoint of the *Person* presupposes the abstraction from commodity relations as such, which in this case would mean the dissolution of the world whose living process would contain Abstract Right, as well as signify the return to the relatedness where Nature is a mere *Thing (Sache)* and the individual a mere independent will.

Habermas comes to this quandary because he is unable to make the pre-social relation of *labor* and *interaction* moments in a process that brings itself to the level of Civil Society. Although he recognizes the necessity of overcoming all reference to a presupposed knowing self in the construction of a genuine theory of social production, Habermas's initial exclusion of *interaction* from *labor* leaves him in that tradition that has kept the process of *Das Kapital* outside of Marxist discussion. Because he is unable to systematize social production without reference to the "principles" of *subjective Spirit*, Habermas is equally unable to distinguish commodity relations from those of Abstract Right. The attempt to pose the *Person* as the immediate result of the productive process only expresses the failure to conceive that individuation which is in and through Civil Society.

Nevertheless, for all its inadequacy, Habermas's discussion of *labor* and *interaction* does have the virtually unique distinction of at least having posed the problem of specifying social production in terms of intersubjective relations. If Marxist discussion is to raise itself above the prevailing false notions of labor, it must come to the *Grundrisse* and *Das Kapital* with this problem before it. For when Marx's determination of capital can be grasped as the specification of a self-informing sphere of interaction, whose every aspect owes its determinateness to capital's intersubjective distinguishing and not to any external pre-social reflective standpoint, then and only then will production be secured a truly *social* determining.

## Notes

1. Marx, *Economic and Philosophic Manuscripts of 1844*, trans. by Martin Milligan (New York: International Publishers, 1964), p. 110.

2. Kant, *Critique of Judgment*, trans. by J.H. Bernard (New York: Hafner, 1951), p. 9.

3. Thus Kant describes "work, i.e., as occupation which is unpleasant (a trouble) in itself and which is only attractive on account of its effect (e.g., the wage)," *ibid.*, p. 46, and that "In *work* the occupation is not pleasant in itself, but is undertaken for the sake of the end in view." Kant, *Education*, trans. by Annette Churton (Ann Arbor, Ann Arbor Paperback, 1960), p. 68.

4. Max Weber, *Economy and Society*, ed. by Roth and Wittich (New York, Bedminster Press, 1968), Vol. 1, p. 339.

5. This, capital's sphere of social interaction, is first thematized, in Hegel's *Philosophy of Right* under the heading, "The System of Needs" (paragraphs 189–208).

6. Marx writes "We have accepted the *estrangement of labor*, its *alienation*, as a fact, and we have analyzed this fact." *Op.cit.*, p. 118.

7. *Ibid.*, p. 113.

8. *Ibid.*, pp. 113–114.

9. Lukács claims to find in Hegel the precursor of such a concept of *labor*. Referring to both the *Jenaer Realphilosophie* and the *Science of Logic*, he writes that "With Hegel, the concrete analysis of the dialectic of human labor sublates the antinomy of causality and teleology, i.e., it reveals what concrete position consciously purposive human action occupies within the entire sphere of causality, without bursting this sphere apart." *Der Junge Hegel* (Neuwied and Berlin: Luchterhand Verlag, 1967), p. 428. And further, "In this way the mechanistic separation of theory and practice, which Kant's and Fichte's subjective idealism had worked out, was sublated, and an objective connection between human practice and objective reality was established." *Ibid.*, p. 437. What Lukács fails to recognize (as is also the case with Habermas in "Labor and Interaction") is that in Hegel's discussion the negative process of the laboring individual is itself a *moment* in the self-development of the intersubjective structure of *Spirit*. Lukács turns this relation around, and falsely claims that "The laboring human being is precisely. . .the primordial phenomenon of the identical Subject-Object, of Substance becoming Subject." *Ibid.*, p. 589.

Habermas, on the other hand, attempts to formalize Marx's theory of social production according to the schema of the objectification of labor that appears here in the *1844 Manuscripts*. Making reference to Fichte's absolute Ego, Habermas claims that "only in its process of production does the species first *posit* itself *as* a social subject." *Knowledge and Human Interests,* trans. by Jeremy J. Shapiro (Boston: Beacon Press, 1971), p. 39. At the same time, however, he affirms that not only is the system of social labor "always the result of the labor of past generations" (p. 39), but that "the absolute ego of social production is founded in a history of nature that brings about the tool-making animal as its result" (p. 41). These *conditions* naturally destroy the absolute autonomy at the basis of any authentic self-positing.

10. This reduction of capitalist social relations to forms of external violence is immediately based on an inability to understand that the laborer is the free owner of his labor power, which he sells to the capitalist as any other commodity. The individual of Civil Society is in principle *not* propertyless, if only on the basis of his absolute right to distinguish his capacity to work as *his* commodity. The *Grundrisse* and *Capital* systematically develop this point, thereby refuting the theory of proletarian revolution basing itself on the propertylessness of the worker that Marx first states in the *Introduction to a Contribution to the Critique of Hegel's "Philosophy of Right."*

11. Marx, *op.cit.*, p. 120.

12. *Ibid.*, p. 78.

13. *Ibid.*, p. 111.

14. *Ibid.*, p. 114.

15. Habermas is one among many who take this conceptual confusion as proof that bourgeois society contradicts its own presuppositions. In *Strukturwandel der Oeffentlichkeit* he claims that "the maintenance of the sphere of commodity circulation and social labor . . . [is possible] only through the exercise of force" (Neuwied and Berlin: Luchterhand Veriag, 1971), p. 152, because, as Marx is alleged to have discovered, modern society is "a class society, in which the chances of the social ascent from wage-laborer to property-owner become ever slimmer . . . First of all, what are obviously lacking are the social presuppositions for the equality of opportunity, that everyone with ability and 'good luck' be allowed the status of property-owner and thereby qualify to become the private individual of public life. This public life, which Marx sees himself confronting, contradicts its own principle of universal accessibility" (pp. 151–152). What Habermas has done is to once again forget that the wage laborer is a member of Civil Society, an individual of recognized need and will, and owner of at least the commodity that is his labor power. Habermas has also confused the principles of self-determination within the System of Needs and the sphere of Abstract Right by not distinguishing between property and commodity relations, something that Hegel first systematically does in the *Philosophy of Right.*

Shlomo Avineri is entirely incorrect when he claims that Hegel shares the viewpoint that Habermas here advocates. Hegel does not in principle affirm that poverty is the dissolution of Abstract Right. Avineri says as much when he writes that ''since poverty is basic to Hegel's view of the person, Poverty becomes for him not merely the plight of people deprived of their physical needs, but of human beings deprived of their personality and humanity as well.'' Cf. his *Hegel's Theory of the Modern State* (Cambridge: Cambridge University Press, 1972), p. 136.

16. Marx. *op,cit.*, p. 65.

17. *Ibid.*, pp. 107–108.

18. *Ibid.*, p. 132.

19. *Ibid.*, p. 138.

20. *Ibid.*, p. 138.

21. *Ibid.*, p. 139.

22. *Ibid.*, p. 143.

23. Marx, *Wage-Labor and Capital*, trans. by Harriet E. Lothrop (New York, Labor News Company, 1902), p. 35.

24. *Ibid.*, p.36.

25. The ''dialectical'' use of the transformation of quantitative into qualitative change in Marxist discussion is well refuted by Lukács, quoting from the section ''Nodal Line of Measure Relations'' of Hegel's *Science of Logic*: ''. . .the reduction to quantitative terms must affect not only the basic elements of the process but also its individual stages, and the fact that this procedure makes it appear as if a gradual transition were taking place, goes unobserved. But this gradualness only applies to the externals of change, not to their quality; the preceding quantitative situation, infinitely close to the succeeding one yet possesses a different existence qualitatively . . . One would like to employ gradual transitions in order to make a change *comprehensible* to oneself; but the gradual change is precisely the trivial one, it is the reverse of the true qualitative change. In this gradualness the connection between the two realities is abolished—this is true whether they are conceived of as states or as independent object; it is assumed that. . .one is simply external to the other; in this way the very thing necessary to *comprehension* is removed . . . With this growth and decay are altogether abolished, or else the In Itself, the inner state of a thing prior to its existence, is transformed into *a small amount of external existence* and the essential or conceptual distinction is changed into a simple, external difference of magnitude.' '' *History and Class Consciousness*, trans. by Rodney Livingstone (Cambridge, MA: The MIT Press, 1971), p. 162.

26. Marx and Engels, *The German Ideology*, ed. by P.J. Arthur (New York, International Publishers, 1970). p. 52.

27. Marx, *A Contribution to the Critique of Political Economy* (New York, International Publishers, 1970), pp. 20–21.

28. Hegel, *The Phenomenology of Mind*, trans. by J.B. Baillie (New York, Harper and Row, 1966), pp. 117–118.

29. "A table of contents is all that undertanding gives, the content itself it does not furnish at all." *Ibid.*, p. 112.

30. For this reason, Marx is never able to actually spell out how forces of production and relations of production are to be distinguished from one another. It often appears that the former may be the production process itself (including the organization of labor) and that the latter is the set of "property" relations corresponding to this arrangement. Yet such a distinction can hardly maintain itself when the organization of production is constituted in and through the intersubjective relations embodied in commodity ownership, exchange, and so on. In the *German Ideology* Marx gives model statements on this hesitating tautology. At one point he writes: "The various stages of development in the division of labor are just so many different forms of ownership, i.e., the existing stage in the division of labor determines also the relations of individuals to one another with reference to the material, instrument, and product of labor." *German Ideology*, p. 43. At another time: "Division of labor and private property are, moreover, identical expressions: in the one the same thing is affirmed with reference to activity as is affirmed in the other with reference to the product of the activity." *Ibid.*, p. 53. However, as the capitalist system so clearly demonstrates, the division of labor just as much specifies the relation to the product as the relation of commodity ownership lays hold of the laboring activity itself.

31. Hegel describes the general methodological problem of this construction as follows: "according to this way of working each determination, each mode, can be applied as a form or schematic element in the case of every other, and each will thankfully perform the same service for any other. With a circle of reciprocities of this sort it is impossible to make out what the real fact in question is, or what the one or the other is. We find there sometimes constituents of sense picked up from ordinary intuition, determinate elements which to be sure should mean something else than they say; at other times, what is inherently significant, viz. pure determinations of thought—like subject, object, substance, cause, universality, etc.—these are applied just as uncritically and unreflectingly as in everyday life." *Phenomenology of Mind*, p. 108.

32. Although such an attempt would seem to abandon epistemology as such, Habermas still feels ready to discuss labor as an historically mediating epistemological category alongside the instrumentarium of *labor* and *interaction*. In *Knowledge and Human Interests* he suggests a transcendental structure of experience where the "forms are categories not primarily of the understanding but of objective activity; and the unity

of the objectivity of possible objects of experience is formed not in transcendental consciousness but in the behavioral system of the cognitive process'' (p. 34). It is really only the latter phrase that maintains any sense through Habermas' argument—that *labor* merely offers a given stuff to thought, without itself being a moment in the constitution of knowing. For we hear that ''The system of objective activities creates. . .the transcendental conditions of the possible objectivity of the objects of experience'' (p. 28), or better still, that ''what provides the material that reflection is to deal with in order to make conscious basic synthetic accomplishments is not the correct combination of symbols according to rules, but social life processes, the material production and appropriation of products'' (p. 31). It should be clear that the process of reflection itself remains entirely independent of the supposedly historical mediation of *labor.* Indeed the content of the ensuing knowledge may depend upon the particular facticity of the material offered by this or that labor process, but the formal nature of this epistemological knowing (where the reflective relation of Subject-Object is still the absolute starting point) remains necessarily ahistorical and independent of *labor* itself.

When Habermas claims that ''the objectivity of the possible objects of experience. . .is equally binding on all subjects that keep alive through labor'' (*ibid.*, p. 35), he is offering no more than a customary consensus and not a transcendental structure of knowing. Furthermore, the labor in question is a completely ahistorical form. He admits this, calling *labor* ''the invariant relation of the species to its natural environment, which is established by the behavioral system of the instrumental action'' (p. 35).

33. Habermas does this most explicitly in the essay ''Labor and Interaction'' (in Habermas, *Theory and Practice [Boston, Beacon Press, 1973]).*

34. *Ibid.*, pp. 161–162. It is true that Habermas does speak of *language* as the presupposition of both labor and interaction (*Ibid.*, p. 158). However, he does not take any notice of the successive emergence of labor and interaction in the *Jenaer Realphilosophie* itself, and progressively allows the acknowledged priority of language to drop from sight.

35. ''The dialectic of representation and of labor develops as a relation between a knowing or an acting subject on the one hand, and an object as the epitome of what does not belong to the subject on the other. The mediation between the two, passing through the medium of symbols or of tools is conceived as a process of externalization of the subject—a process of externalization (objectification) and appropriation.'' *Ibid.*, pp. 163–164.

36. ''In contrast to this, the dialectic of love and conflict is a movement on the level of intersubjectivity. The place of the model of *externalization* is therefore taken by that of *separation* and alienation, and the result of the movement is not the *appropriation* of what has been objectified, but instead the *reconciliation*, the restoration of the friendliness which has been destroyed.'' *Ibid.*, p. 164.

37. Habermas claims that "it is the dialectical interconnections between the linguistic symbolization, labor, and interaction which determine the concept of spirit." *Ibid.*, p. 143.

38. Nonetheless, he *still* writes that "Marx. . .sees their connection effected in the system of social labor. That is why 'production' seems to him the movement in which instrumental action and the institutional framework, or 'productive activity' and 'relations of production,' appear merely as different aspects of the same process. . . Marx starts with the premise that work always takes the form of social labor." Habermas, *Knowledge and Human Interests*, pp. 53, 326.

39. Habermas writes: "Unlike synthesis through social labor, the dialectic of class antagonism is a movement of reflection. For the dialogic relation of the complementary unification of opposed subjects, the re-establishment of morality, is a relation of *logic* and of *life conduct* at once." *Ibid.*, p. 58. The uniting structure for these two elements turns out to be nothing other than conscious experience! For several pages later, Habermas declares that "social theory, from the viewpoint of the self-constitution of the species in the medium of social labor and class struggle, is possible only as the self-reflecting of the knowing subject." *Ibid.*, p. 63.

40. Without any explanation Habermas stops mentioning the independent role of *language* and discusses labor as if its *externalization* would comprehend that of language. And later he seems to combine interaction and language by reformulating the relation of labor and interaction as one of instrumental and communicative action.

41. See the introduction to Chapter VI—"Spirit"—of the *Phenomenology of Mind*. It is also to be noted that when Habermas describes the emergence of the system of production in the *Jenaer Realphilosophie*, the immediate source is a form of interaction alone. He observes that "subjective spirit goes over into the sphere of actual spirit only after the struggle for recognition has led to a system of social labor and to emancipation from the state of nature." Cf. *Theory and Practice*, p. 187.

42. Habermas, *Knowledge and Human Interests*, p. 326. It is to be noted that in *Das Kapital* cooperation appears as a specific *moment* in the self-development of the concept of capital.

43. Habermas, *Theory and Practice*, p. 159.

44. And it is on this basis that Habermas intends to criticize Hegel's distinction of Abstract Right and Civil Society, writing that "although right determines the form of social intercourse, it is introduced from the *outside* under the title of jurisprudence. It constitutes itself independently of the categories of social labor, and only *after the fact* enters into its relationship with the process to which, in the Jena lectures, it still owed the moment of freedom, as a result of liberation through social labor." *Ibid.*, p. 167.

45. "Abstract Right documents a concrete liberation: for social labor is that process in which consciousness makes itself into a thing, in order thereby to form itself into its own proper form..." *Ibid.*, p. 128.

46. "Thus the relation of reciprocal recognition, on which interaction is based, is brought under norms by way of the institutionalization of the reciprocity established as such in the exchange of the products of labor." *Ibid.*, p. 160.

47. "Subjective Spirit and "Actual Spirit" here refer to divisions within the *Jenaer Realphilosophie* that do not correspond to the levels of subjective and objective Spirit in the *Encyclopedia*, but rather represent early formulations approximating Hegel's discussion of Abstract Right and Ethical Life in the *Philosophy of Right.*

# 11

# The Young Hegel and the Dialectic of Social Production

When dialectical and historical materialism is shorn of the Diamat and confronted with the incommensurably more systematic argument within the *Grundrisse* and *Capital*, a certain spectre comes out of its neglected corner to haunt all who speak in the name of the classics. This chimera is the great secret of Marxist discussion, holding the unspoken truth that Marx's determination of capital is but the thematization of a *particular* sphere of interaction, a thematization which by itself can neither ground its own method nor establish the immediate access of its starting point nor pose itself as the accomplished grasp of the totality of social reality.

It is a rare moment when such necessary admission is not passed over in silence. Even among all the literature addressed to the seminal relation of Hegel and Marx, one hardly finds any serious recognition of the pressing need to finally specify that philosophical program which can give determinateness to the dialectical method, realize that method's immanent unity with the concept of capital, and abolish the fragmentary status of the *Grundrisse's* and *Capital's* essential argument.

One of the few exceptions to this conspiracy of indifference is Lukács' *The Young Hegel*. Whatever be the merits of this work's actual conclusions, it has at least brought the focus of Hegel and Marx interpretation to the point of examining the relationship between the emergence of dialectical presuppositionless determination and the problem of thematizing that sphere of social interaction developed by Marx in the concept of capital and by Hegel in the System of Needs. For here Lukács has attempted to establish the continuity of Hegel and Marx by demonstrating how the young Hegel rises to overcome the last remnants of egological discourse in resolutely confronting the methodological requirements of the social determination of production to which Marx will later devote the investigations of his mature writings. And because it is bourgeois society that constitutes itself so that need and labor achieve their determination wholly through the pure intersubjective self-activity of capital, and without reference to any natural or reflective determinations, Lukács is also able to world-historically situate Hegel's encounter with the problem of determining production in and through interaction. On this dual basis *The Young Hegel* goes beyond mere Hegel interpretation to instead attempt an elucidation of the theoretical framework where the very task of *Capital* can have its *grounded* solution.

If such a work were of solely historiographic interest, it might suffice to remark that here Lukács has once again revealed the sham of his own self-purported departure from the Hegelianism of his early writing. For in simply drawing a compass wide enough to indicate an immanent relation between the concept of capital and the kind of philosophical considerations first developed by Hegel, Lukács has reaffirmed a most serious respect both for Hegel's own program and for the fundamentally philosophical status of Marx's principal systematic writings, the *Grundrisse* and *Capital*.

Yet, the very scope of Lukács' expressed intention in *The Young Hegel* demands a response that rises above the gossip of a sociology of knowledge.

Certainly, the critical reception greeting *The Young Hegel* since its appearance in 1948 has failed to meet this challenge and come to grips with the stated problem and the exigency of its resolution.

In Eastern Europe the little attention paid the work[1] has dwelt upon the formal consideration of whether or not Lukács has slighted the unquestionable theoretical leadership of Marx and Engels by emphasizing the progressive strain in Hegel's thought and thereby obscuring the eternal struggle of materialism and idealism in the annals of philosophical development. On the one hand, we have the likes of Bela Fogarasi seeing fit to defend Lukács' favorable portrayal of Hegel in so far as *The Young Hegel* does not pretend to judge the entirety of Hegelian philosophy, but only to consider its positive, and most rational moments.[2] On the other hand, there is the sharp criticism such as Rugard Otto Gropp delivers, where Lukács is taken to task for having obliterated that epochal distinction between Hegel's objective idealist dialectic and the materialist dialectic of Marx.[3]

In the West, comment has basically limited itself to equally barren acknowledgements of Lukács' emphasis upon the constitutive importance of the concept of labor in Hegel's development and the role which the entrenchment of Marx in the Hegelian tradition can play in freeing Marxist ideology of its banal dogmatism.[4] To linger on such general pronouncements is as unnecessary as it is tiresome. Lukács has sought to strip away the hesitation paralyzing the discussion of Hegel and Marx, and it is high time to take up the systematic question itself.

In recognition of the need to finally ground the discourse of *Capital*, Lukács has indeed taken the magistral course of trying to specify the immanent relation of the dialectical method to the thematization of social production.[5] Yet, *The Young Hegel* ultimately fails in this important attempt because its own inadequate conception of dialectical determination finally undermines the sought-after interactive specification of labor.

This root deformation of the dialectic is Lukács' notion of the Subject-Object whose *Entäusserung* or externalization is to constitute the unqualified process of determination where universality and particularity no longer fall asunder. After having well documented the young Hegel's successive rejections of the egological positing of Kant, Fichte, and Schelling, Lukács seizes this self-mediating identity of the concept and its reality as that with which Hegel overcomes the standpoint of reflection. Yet in so doing, Lukács has actually given a Schellingian misinterpretation of Hegel's concept of *Geist* (or intersubjectivity) that effectively maintains the distinctions of consciousness, of subject and object, within their primordial identity, instead of advancing to the threshold of self-determining interaction through which Hegel will actually accomplish the thematization of self-consciousness. In this sense, the notion of the Subject-Object and its *Entäusserung* (which already occupied center stage in *History and Class Consciousness*) remains subject to the same criticism that the young Hegel levied against Schelling's resurrection of intellectual intuition—that the purported presuppositionless self-activity still begins with an assumed reflective determinacy.

The source of such error lies in that same reduction of the Hegelian inquiry to an egological positing which Marx performed in his *1844 Manuscripts*' discussion of the *Phenomenology of Spirit* and which Lenin repeated in his notebooks on Hegel's *Logic.* Just as these two predecessors had done, so Lukács loses sight of the systematic role that the *Phenomenology of Spirit* fulfills as the deduction of the concept of Science,[6] as that necessary introduction to the presuppositionless beginning from which the dialectical logic can begin. Rather than heeding Hegel's own strictures on the matter, Lukács has tended to interpret the *Phenomenology of Spirit* as a work that not only observes a given subject matter (i.e., consciousness) examining its own truth claims, but that also presents the determinations *per se* of such varied topics as labor, commodity exchange, and world history. For this reason, Lukács is led to mistakenly identify the structure of the *Phenomenology* with the divisions of the *Encyclopedia* conflating the System with its propadeutic.[7] The crucial result of all this is that Lukács understands the *Phenomenology of Spirit* to culminate in a specification of the Subject-Object Totality itself, and thereby to take on the dimension of a doctrine of the dialectical method. Like most commentators, he fails to recognize that the final movement of the *Phenomenology* renders the moments of *in itselfness* and *for itselfness* (the generic distinctions of consciousness) indistinguishable, so that we are left not with the concept of an intellectual intuition, nor even of the spiritual (*geistige*) unity of interaction, but with the utterly unanalyzable indeterminate immediacy of Being; which *is* determinateness freed of the presupposition of a knowing self.

Instead of grasping the significance of this result, Lukács traps the dialectic within the confines of self-reflection, turning from the concrete determining of Hegel's *Science of Logic* back to the abstract identity of subject and object. What this entails for the social determination of production is so evident that Lukács can waste no time with any mediating argument. *The Young Hegel* proclaims: the most readily graspable and the most essential embodiment of the Subject-Object *Entäusserung* is nothing other than labor itself. Indeed, if determination is to be an egological positing, then production cannot escape being subsumed under categories of reflection. Yet, Lukács goes beyond the implied reduction of production to technique to celebrate labor as that primordial praxis accomplishing the interpenetration of universality and particularity that grounds self-consciousness.

Following the example of the *1844 Manuscripts*, Lukács construes labor to be the rudimentary real *Entäusserung* whose own existence is a pure self-positing. However, because Lukács conceives the laboring activity as the monological relationship of the self-conscious individual and nature, he presupposes both the intentionality of the agent and the facticity of the object of his formative action. Thus, the sought-after Subject-Object identity is actually a *conditioned* instrumental process where agent, act and product fall asunder. Almost despite himself, Lukács makes this patently obvious when he seizes upon certain isolated determinations from the *System der Sittlichkeit* and the *Jenaer Realphilosophie* to declare that Hegel has revealed the *Entäusserung* of labor by describing the teleological nature of its act. Lukács' understanding of this relationship, however, has little in common with the determination Hegel gives Teleology in the *Logic*. For here *The Young Hegel* rather presents a purposive laboring akin to the process of *Techné* that Plato and Aristotle had developed in order to account for the imposition of a *given* form upon some entity.[8] That "teleological" formative action can result in nothing other than an utterly *external* union of universality and particularity, where the presupposed subject subsumes the object under the represented form leading his act.

Lukács' attempt to determine labor in terms of a "dialectic" of intellectual intuition finally resolves into this reduction of production to a monological technique. Although he still claims that labor's *Entäusserung* is the *Urform* of social relations (as he will continue to do in *Zur Ontologie des gesellschaftlichen Seins*), it is clear that such labor has actually excluded itself from interaction altogether. This is not due to any mere oversight on Lukács' part. It rather stems from the fundamental inability of categories of reflection to grasp labor as a moment in the constitution of social reality.[9]

If Lukács had instead remained true to his original questioning, there would have been little possibility of identifying dialectical determination with Subject-Object *Entäusserung* and of depicting labor in corresponding egological terms. For, as Lukács himself asserts time and again, *the* problem demanding the dialectical method is not on the order of realizing the autonomy of reflection, but of determining the self-specifying process of *interaction* that can comprehend the dilemma of modernity. *The Young Hegel* argues conclusively on this point: Hegel achieves the epoch-making insight that bourgeois society encompasses a sphere of interaction where the private individual is actually constituted in indifference to natural, given determinations, and wholly in and through intersubjectively defined mediations of need and labor; he realizes that the Practical Reason of reflection can no more contain the heterogeneous particularity of the bourgeois' self-seeking than it can overcome the hypothetical character of a formal positing. What, then, is the theoretical framework able to conceive of an *existing* social reality whose system of production individuates itself in the particular subjectivity of the modern private individual? What, then, if not a dialectical method superseding the aporetic distinctions of consciousness with the intersubjective self-activity of *Geist*?

Here, in this turn to the threshold of reciprocal recognition, of self-developing interaction, of social determination; in the departure from egological positing, we have the basis for the immanent bond between the dialectic and the problem of social production.

Again, Lukács leads us inexorably to this point, only to let go the implied specifications of both the dialectical method and the concept of capital. But the young Hegel did not let this issue drop. Nor did he limit his grasp of bourgeois society to unromantic *observations* of the brutal life of a burgeoning capitalism, so that latter-day Marxists could pardon him for the redeeming realism within the mystical shell. Lukács would link the argument of the *System der Sittlichkeit* and the *Jenaer Realphilosophie* to Adam Smith, but no, Hegel does not incorporate the teachings of the *Wealth of Nations* any more than he does those of Steuart. For, unnoticed if not unknown to both Marx and Hegel scholarship, it is Hegel who first carries out the Critique of Political Economy. By bringing the dialectical method to bear upon the thematization of bourgeois society, Hegel has been able to distinguish and transcend the limits of classical political economy by overcoming all reductions of social production to either natural relations or an egologically informed technique. He has instead embarked upon an intersubjective formulation of the System of Needs. And it is to this endeavor that one must turn in order to confront the grounded determination of capital.

Lukács never draws his inquiry to the point of examining that actual specification of bourgeois society which the presuppositionless self-developing determination of Hegelian Science comes to accomplish. If he had, he would have brought *The Young Hegel's* argument to a discussion of the particular inadequacy that marks the *System der Sittlichkeit* and the *Jenaer Realphilosophie* as errant forerunners of the *Philosophy of Right's* principled program for the determination of social production.

An account of Hegel's development that distinguishes the *Philosophy of Right* from his earlier writings on social theory would normally meet this challenge by focusing attention upon Civil Society's liberation of the production process from the traditional subsumption under categories of the Household, the political regime, or Natural Law. With this orientation, Manfred Riedel draws upon many of Lukács' own remarks to observe that in Hegel's early writings, "the analyses of the labor process generally either stand uncomfortably under titles such as 'the People' or 'Government,' or issue forth independently from one another within the framework of the 'practical' process of the living with Nature. The young Hegel places the rock-hard facts of Modernity—work and the division of labor, machinery, money and the commodity, wealth and poverty—almost untrimmed next to the overwhelmingly gripping and vital cultural tradition of antiquity, without examining these in themselves or even being able to join them systematically in relationship with one another."[10]

We find, for example, that in the *System der Sittlichkeit* the process of production is limited to the activity of a particular Estate (*Stand*),[11] and is in general subordinated within the political sphere of Government (*Regierung*).[12] In the *Jenaer Realphilosophie* this tendency is maintained, since the System of Needs still falls under the political designation of the State[13] even though it maintains a relative independence as a special sphere of existing recognition (*Anerkanntseins*).[14]

It is, of course, no small wonder that the *Philosophy of Right's* departure from such positions has important consequences for a Marxist theory of the State. Yet, when the dialectic of the system of production is itself at issue, still another distinction must be addressed. This concerns the relation between the intersubjectively specified determinations of Abstract Right and the System of Needs. For whereas the mature system elaborator operates a radical demarcation of Abstract Right from the self-constitution of social production, the young Hegel is unable to hold the two spheres apart, and articulate the actual specificity of the commodity determination and its underlying labor process.

A work that is to bring into relief the bond between the dialectic and the thematization of bourgeois society in Hegel's philosophical development cannot turn its eyes from this problem, particularly when the confusion over relations of Abstract Right and those of Civil Society has so penetrated Marxist discussion. *The Young Hegel's* discussion of the *System der Sittlichkeit* and the *Jenaer Realphilosophie* utterly fails in this respect, and must be supplemented.

To begin with, one cannot overlook how the *System der Sittlichkeit* introduces Abstract Right after *machine labor (Maschinearbeit)* has posited the possession of a product that is no longer in relation to the particular need of its owner, but is universally related to the need of others.[15] There Hegel writes:

"The relation to an object which an individual acquires for the sake of need and use so that it is here posited that he has not himself produced it for his personal consumption, a consumption in which he accordingly does not negate his own labor,—this is the beginning of rightful (*rechtlichen*), formally ethical (*sittlichen*) satisfaction and possession."[16] The implied derivation makes the maintenance of the bond of the worker to *his* product that *he* does not consume the real source of the abstract universality of Property, the Person, and Contract. This signifies, however, the effective negation of the very notion of *machine labor* with which the young Hegel has taken a first step towards describing a socially determined labor process.

For Hegel has just shown that the *machine labor* upon which the separation of *possession* from *use* is based actually subjugates the individual worker to the universal labor process, where "the universal itself is governing in the singular or particular."[17] On the one hand, "this labor, which is absorbed by the object as a whole, divides within itself to become an individual laboring activity,"[18] and on the other hand, through the machine process "the unrest of the concept's subjectivity is itself posited outside the subject."[19]

To be consistent with this determining, one would correctly observe that the *subjective* relation of the laboring individual to both the object that is worked upon and to the finished product *is* no longer. Here the laborer is posited as a participant in a commodity circulation to which his labor *as his own* maintains no specific abiding relationship.

Yet, when instead Hegel makes Abstract Right the immediate result of *machine labor*, he destroys that context of social production. A standpoint of reflection is reinstated to inform the labor process with the subjective determining of the individual laborer. The universal realm of commodity circulation must then give way to the opposition of a free will set against a rightless world of the *factor (die Sache)*.[20]

Lukács also passes over the fact that the *Jenaer Realphilosophie* brings this nascent repulsion of Abstract Right from out of Civil Society yet farther, for here the System of Needs has come still closer to its concrete form. From the very moment that the argument of the *Realphilosophie* reaches *actual intersubjectivity (wirklicher Geist)*, the overcoming of the abstract will is proclaimed.[21] "The *being of recognition is immediately* reality and within its element the Person has the actuality of its *being-for-self* for the first time; that is, the Person is laboring and satisfying its needs. *Here desire first attains the right to come forward*, for it is *actual*, i.e., it itself has *universal intersubjective (geistige) being*: the laboring of all and for all, as well as satisfaction and the satisfaction of all. Each serves the other and provides help; the individual as particular first here achieves determinate being."[22]

This is the system of interdependence of needy private individuals in its most general form. The self-seeking acquisition of commodities through individual labor has yet to differentiate itself as a system of social production: for only when commodity circulation has posited abstract need by realizing *need as abstract for itselfness in universal exchange* can the process of production break through the limit of the *self-objectification of consciousness* and become the industrial labor process producing commodities for the market.[23]

Yet, just when the already established sphere of commodity circulation is now being reproduced through the system of production, the young Hegel suddenly introduces Abstract Right, breaking open the context of Civil Society, and reintroducing the formality of the willing individual.[24] Under the aegis of the movement to connect the abstract production process with the concrete needs of the individual,[25] Hegel goes one step farther than in the *System der Sittlichkeit* to undermine the developing relationship of the System of Needs. For here, *property* emerges upon the reduction of production to the self-objectification of consciousness of subjective Spirit,[26] *as well as* upon the reduction of an *existing* commodity exchange to simple contract, where the recognition of abstract need no longer is a factor.[27] The identification of the quality of the product as an object of production with the designation of the individual worker in relation to *his* labor (which already appeared as the basis of *property* in the *System der Sittlichkeit*) is now joined by the abstraction of an exchange embodying "the same externalization (*Entäusserung*)"[28] of the presupposed individual, in order to posit the relations of Abstract Right.

The *Jenaer Realphilosophie's* genesis of the *Person, property,* and *contract* thus annihilates both the social determining of the laboring act and that specific intersubjective character of commodity exchange which has allowed the process of social production (*gesellschaftliche Arbeit*) to first emerge.

The upshot of these early unresolved attempts is that the young Hegel has effectively demonstrated at his own expense the necessity of a demarcation of the realms of Abstract Right and Civil Society.

In the *Philosophy of Right* this radical separating finally becomes an acknowledged theme, with the result that all reference to any individual willing independent of the self-distinguishing of the System of Needs is at last excluded from the determination of the social labor process. Although the temptations may seem inescapable to make the *Person* constitutive of the bourgeois, *property* the basis of the commodity, and *formative action* (*Formierung*) the essence of labor, the mature Hegel emphatically removes these moments of Abstract Right from *all* involvement in the specification of the system of production. This critical transformation in the conception of bourgeois society marks the passage beyond the unresolved tension in the social theory of the young Hegel, just as it marks a final preparation for Marx's thematization of the concept of capital. All the same, Lukács' *The Young Hegel* does not begin to extend its reach this far, even though its announced project would demand at least this last precision.

Without going into detailed analysis of the *Philosophy of Right's* argument for the System of Needs, it will here suffice to fill this gap by indicating the special formality that excludes the determinations of Abstract Right from the realm of social production.

First and foremost, the *Person* is both in itself and in its relation to externality distinct from the individuation constitutive of the System of Needs.

As the singular form of freedom in its pure being-for-self,[29] the Person is the completely abstract willing that has its particular content not within itself, but in an external immediately given factor (*Sache*), which exists for it as the simple receptacle of its will. [30] The particularity of the individual falls asunder from this determining, and the process of the Person is thus in principle entirely indifferent to Need and its satisfaction.[31]

The complete rightlessness of the factor furthermore eliminates any talk of interaction with an object *already* related to the will *and* need of others.[32] This is not altered by the fact that in his domination of the factor, the Person is self-related only because other Persons recognize the objective existence of his will in his subsumption of this pure external thing.[33] The reciprocal recognition of this relation neither informs the Person's act upon the factor, nor does it constitute an *existing* social structure which posits the individual in his free personality as a self-differentiation of the whole. Abstract Right cannot encompass such a *social* process which is central to the determining of the system of production, and which is first realized at the level of the self-distinguishing of Ethical Life (*Sittlichkeit*).

The correlative determinateness of *property* is tainted by the same formality. As Hegel writes, "The rationale of property is to be found not in the satisfaction of needs but in the supersession of the pure subjectivity of personality."[34] The object of property is, as such, entirely indifferent to production, exchange and consumption. Accordingly, all reference to the different value determinations that characterize the commodity are in principle excluded.[35]

The relationship of property has nothing more to say than that the Person has made its free will objective in the ownership of a factor.[36] Those who affirm the right to equality in the amount or type of property have missed this point just as much as those (including none other than the young Hegel and the young Marx) who would derive the property determination from a realm of commodity relations.[37]

Given the great importance of not thus conflating the Person with the bourgeois, and property with the commodity, it is still in specifying the abstractness of formative action (*Formierung*) that Hegel makes most obvious how the demarcation of Abstract Right from Civil Society has placed the determining of the labor process beyond the self-objectification of a given self-conscious individual and into the realm of interaction. This is all the more true since here Hegel gives precisely that process of externalization that the young Marx would later use as the touchstone for his unsuccessful determination of the system of production, and that Lukács would then pick up as the basis of Subject-Object *Entäusserung*. The difference in Hegel's intention, however, is immediately clear—for he refuses to call this formative action *labor*, and instead shows how it is *not* a labor process of the System of Needs.

"When I impose a form on something, the thing's determinate character as mine acquires an independent externality and ceases to be restricted to my presence here and now and to the direct presence of my awareness and will. To impose a form on a thing...implies a union of subject and object, although it varies endlessly with the qualitative character of the objects and the variety of subjective aims."[38]

Such determinateness is not only indifferent to all relation of need and its satisfaction, but entirely removed from any context within which the thing that is worked over has in itself a relatedness to other subjects or within which the formed product has an immediately social character. The Person who here transforms the factor (*Sache*) is not engaging in the satisfaction of human needs in a system of universal interdependence. And the product that emerges as the indifferent objectivity of his will has no quality that can stamp it as a commodity.

The *Formierung* of the subject by himself in no way escapes this formality either. The Person's working upon his physical and spiritual capacities to cast them in the form of the factor and make his own subjective possibility an external reality where his will is recognized[39]—this transformation stands entirely outside the self-determining of the private individual of Civil Society, who acquires universal needs and skills in the earning of his satisfaction within a network of commodity exchange. That the ability (*Vermögen*) of the Person takes the shape of the factor in no way places it in relation to need and will in general, as is the case with the *commodity*, labor power.

When these distinctions are completely grasped, the departure from the problematic of the young Hegel has been accomplished, even if only through a negative characterization of social production. To come to the positive determining of that sphere of interaction, however, it is necessary to enter the immanent process of the System of Needs. Only in this way will the promise of Lukács' *The Young Hegel* be realized, and *Capital* provided with a sure foundation.

## Notes

1. Long out of print in its East German edition, *The Young Hegel* has still not appeared in Hungarian translation. Cf. Tibor Hanak, *Lukács war anders*, (Meisenheim am Glan, 1973), p. 104.

2. Bela Fogarasi, "Marxistischer Historiker der Philosophie," *Aufbau*, Vol. 11, (1955), p. 362. In his Hegel book, *Subjekt-Objekt*, Ernst Bloch similarly gives *The Young Hegel* merely passing mention for having conscientiously brought out the progressive side of Hegel's youthful development. Cf. Ernst Bloch, *Subjekt-Objekt: Erläuterungen zu Hegel* (Frankfurt: Suhrkamp Verlag, 1972), pp. 51ff.

3. Rugard Otto Gropp, "Die marxistische dialektische Methode und ihr Gegensatz zur idealistischen Dialektik Hegels," *Deutsche Zeitschrift für Philosophie*, Vol. 1, No. 2 (1954).

4. As examples, see Iring Fetscher, "Georg Lukács: Der junge Hegel," in *Philosophischer Literaturanzeiger*, Vol. 2, No. 2 (1950), and Hermann Lubbe, "Zur marxistischen Auslegung Hegels," *Philosophische Rundschau*, Vol. 2 (1954–1955).

5. Social production is here used throughout to denote that sphere of bourgeois society where the private self-seeking person obtains social individuation by means of capital's intersubjective specification of the factors of need and labor.

6. For a discussion of how the *Phenomenology of Spirit* should be understood as this kind of a deduction, see Kenley Dove's article, "Hegel's Phenomenological Method," in *The Review of Metaphysics*, Vol. 23, No. 4 (Issue 92—June, 1970), and also by the same author, "Hegel's Deduction of the Concept of Science," *Boston Studies in the Philosophy of Science*, Vol. 23.

7. Habermas openly appropriates this incorrect description of the *Phenomenology's* structure within his discussion of Hegel. Cf. Jürgen Habermas, *Knowledge and Human Interest* (Boston, 1971), p. 19.

8. See M. B. Foster, *The Political Philosophies of Plato and Hegel* (Oxford, 1968), for a masterly account of why the concept of *Techné* cannot be used in the thematization of modern capitalist society.

9. For a brief discussion of this inability, see Richard Winfield, "The Dilemma of Labor," *Telos*, Vol. 24 (Summer 1975), pp. 115–128, Chapter 10 in this book.

10. Manfred Riedel, *Studien zu Hegels Rechtsphilosophie* (Frankfurt am Main: Suhrkamp Verlag, 1970), p. 152.

11. *Ibid.*, p. 85.

12. *Ibid.*, p. 82.

13. *Ibid.*, p. 96.

14. *Ibid.*, p. 93.

15. The possession of the product "...no longer expresses need for the same, but rather...(i.e.) in relation to the use of others," Hegel, *System der Sittlichkeit* (Hamburg: Felix Meiner Verlag, 1967), p. 26.

16. *Ibid.*, pp. 28–29.

17. *Ibid.*, p. 25.

18. *Ibid.*

19. *Ibid.*, p. 26.

20. Following Dove, I have used "Factor" as a translation for *die Sache* rather than "thing" in order to maintain Hegel's systematic distinction between *die Sache* and *das Ding*.

21. Hegel, *Jenaer Realphilosophie* (Berlin: Akademie Verlag, 1969), p. 213. The task is "here to sublate the abstract will or, to produce it, as sublated, in the element of the universal being of recognition, this intersubjective (*geistige*) reality." *Ibid.*, p. 214.

22. *Ibid.*, p. 213. Hegel here uses the term *Person* much as he will later use that of *Mensch* to name the private man of the System of Needs.

23. At the level of *subjective Spirit* within the *Jenaer Realphilosophie* work "is the *self-objectification of consciousness*. However, in the element of universality it becomes an abstract laboring...Since labor takes place for need as abstract being-for-self, so is this laboring itself abstract." *Ibid.*, p. 214.

24. In *Theory and Practice* Habermas incorrectly describes this process. According to his account of this section of the *Jenaer Realphilosophie*. "Only when the *division of labor* has produced abstract labor, and the *commercial exchange* has produced abstract enjoyment, when both make possible the labor of all for the satisfaction of the needs of all, does *contract* become the principle of bourgeois commerce." Cf. Jurgen Habermas, *Theory and Practice* (Boston, 1973), p. 187. What Habermas refuses to recognize is that *social labor* and *commercial exchange* do not originally stand side by side like his categories of *labor* and *interaction*. It is through the specification of commodity circulation that the process of production is first posited. Both the *Philosophy of Right* and *Capital* develop the System of Needs in this manner.

25. "A movement must now take place between these various abstractly produced objects whereby they are once again related to *concrete* needs, that is, to the needs of the individual." Hegel, *Jenaer Realphilosophie*, p. 215.

26. Subjective Spirit is here referred to as Hegel develops it in the *Jenaer Realphilosophie*, and not as it finally appears within the *Encyclopedia*.

27. "Here the accidentality of the taking of possession is sublated: I have everything through *labor* and through *exchange* in the being of recognition...The

spring, the source of property is here that of labor, my *act* itself—immediate self and being of recognition, *Ground*...I have *willed* in exchange, posited my factor as value, that is to say, an inward movement, an internal act, as labor is submerged in being; (it is in both cases) the *same externalization*...a) I make myself immediately into a thing, a form that is being, in labor. b) I just as much externalize this my determinate being, make it alien to me and yet maintain myself therein. For even there I intuit my existing guaranty." *Ibid.*, p. 217.

28. *Ibid.*, p. 217.

29. "In personality it is of myself alone that I am aware. A person is a unit of freedom aware of its sheer independence." Hegel, *Philosophy of Right*, trans. by T. M. Knox (New York: Oxford University Press, 1967), p. 235.

30. "488. Mind, in the immediacy of its self-secured liberty, is an individual..a *person*, in whom the inward sense of this freedom, as in itself still abstract and empty, has its particularity and fulfillment not yet on its own part, but on an external *thing*." Hegel, *Philosophy of Mind*, trans. by W. Wallace and A. V. Miller (Oxford: Oxford University Press, 1973), p. 244.

31. "Since, in personality, particularity is not present as freedom, everything which depends on particularity is here a matter of indifference." Hegel, *Philosophy of Right*, p. 235.

32. Through *contract* the factor does acquire internally the quality of being related to other free wills. This takes place, however, only within *contract*, which itself depends upon the particular act of the single will for its existence.

33. "491. The thing is the *mean* by which the extremes meet in one. These extremes are the persons who, in the knowledge of their identity as free, are simultaneously mutually independent." Hegel, *Philosophy of Mind*, p. 244.

34. Hegel, *Philosophy of Right*, p. 235.

35. So "subsistence is not the same as possession and belongs to another sphere, i.e. to civil society." *Ibid.*, p. 44.

36. "But I as free will am an object to myself in what I possess and thereby also for the first time am an actual will, and this is the aspect which constitutes the category of *property*, the true and right factor in possession." *Ibid.*, p. 42.

37. Hegel criticizes the Jacobin demand on this basis: "Of course men are equal, but only *qua* persons...But this equality is something apart from the fixing of particular amounts, from the question of how much I own. From this point of view it is false to maintain that justice requires everyone's property to be equal...since right is that which remains indifferent to particularity." *Ibid.*, p. 237.

38. *Ibid.*, p. 47.

39. "57...It is only through the development of his own body and mind, essentially through his self-consciousness's apprehension of itself as free, that he takes possession of himself and becomes his own property and no one else's. This taking possession of oneself is the translation into actuality of what one is according to one's concept, i.e. a potentiality, capacity, potency. In that translation one's self-consciousness for the first time becomes established as one's own, as one's object also and distinct from self-consciousness pure and simple, and thereby capable of taking the form of a 'thing'." *Ibid.*, pp. 47–48.

# 12

# The Logic of Marx's *Capital*

"It is impossible completely to understand Marx's *Capital*, and especially its first chapter, without having thoroughly studied and understood the *whole* of Hegel's *Logic*. Consequently, half a century later none of the Marxists understood Marx!!"[1]

## i) Introduction

So lamented Lenin in 1914, as world war began to quicken the ground for socialist upheaval. He had turned to Hegel, annotated the *Science of Logic* and given this private exclamation to its revelation of *Capital*. Unfortunately, the nature of the new understanding was never made clear, and the only time Lenin tried to show how the *Logic* could make Marx's work more intelligible, he merely compared the commodity with Hegel's "Being."

Nonetheless, Lenin's aphorism is still valid today, because neither Marx nor his commentators provide a systematic clarification of *Capital's* methodology. Marxist discussion has accepted the authority of its classics without even being able to ground the discourse of *Capital*. One looks in vain for a remedy to legitimate the work's starting point, to establish critically the adequacy of the argument, or to at last provide the guidelines for not only *completing* Marx's *unfinished* thematization of capital, but also determining the rest of social reality.

What compounds the problem is that throughout Capital's unfolding, an amalgam of historical example and general commentary interweaves with the strictly "scientific" argument. Although Marx occasionally warns his reader that a certain topic can receive its *systematic* treatment only at some later point, he presents most material without explicitly discriminating between necessary and merely supplementary discussion. No standard is provided to distinguish rigorous determination from congenial reflection and secure the passage from one element of the discourse to the next. Furthermore, Marx's frequent empirical examples can easily mislead one into considering his concepts as generalizations related to the same given object. This, however, only reduces Marx's conceptual system to the usual theoretical *model*, isolating his categories so that contradictions arise between various sections. The famous debate on the value-price transformation is a result of this confusion, to cite only one example.

Thus, to understand Marx's later writings, the well-worn claims of *dialectical* science must be elaborated. It must be shown *how* dialectical determination is immanently related to the conceptualization of capital, and how Capital actually does proceed dialectically. It is here that Hegel's *Logic* enters to elucidate the dialectical method, and reveal how the constitution of capital's realm is part of its specific philosophical project. For despite all the hue and cry over the specificity of the Marxist dialectic (Althusser's clamour included), Hegel's *Logic* does not stand over and against Marx's *Capital*, but *is* indeed its inseparable logos. This truth bares itself in the basic thrust of each work.

To begin with, Marx's thematization of capital is a *social determination* of production. The *Grundrisse* and *Capital* complete the critique of political economy originally outlined by Hegel in his discussion of the "System of Needs" in the *Philosophy of Right*, where "need" and "labor" are rescued from all reduction to an anthropological metabolism between Man and Nature or to a monological technical process. Production is instead developed as the intersubjective process of *capital's* self-constitution into that social sphere of interacting bourgeois. In this manner *Capital* accounts for production wholly through the social process of Interaction. The concept of capital is thereby a conception of modern bourgeois society precisely because only with the capitalist epoch does economic life emerge as an independent sphere of social reality, freed of all natural character just as it is freed of all subordination to the household or to feudal political designations.

Of course, Marx came to this position only in his mature systematic writings. In the *1844 Manuscripts* he had characterized labor in terms of the monological reflective categories of objectification (*Entäusserung*) and alienation (*Entfremdung*). In the *German Ideology* he retained the assumptions of classical political economy, first discussing production as a natural metabolism, and then conceiving Civil Society (*bürgerliche Gesellschaft*) as a given, suprahistorical condition of man's existence. Further, in *Wage-Labor and Capital* (1848), Marx formally distinguished forces of production from relations of production, thus implicitly reducing production to a technical process external to its social organization.[2] Not until he began the specific program of the *Grundrisse* and *Capital* could Marx discard these inadequate notions and articulate an intersubjective reality whose moments have the particular autonomy realized by the self-seeking bourgeois. Only when he became able to determine this social individuation of Interaction could Marx actually thematize capital. At that point the argument of the *Grundrisse* and *Capital* was able to emerge in its characteristic *self-developing immanence*, eschewing all reference to an external reflective standpoint for securing its advance, and thus eschewing all attempt at model-building or ideal-typical construction.

It is Hegel's *Logic* that provides the framework for such *social*, that is, *dialectical* determination. Unlike all previous inquiry, the *Logic* departs from indeterminancy to establish inter-individuality as the totality of determination.

Hegel realizes that Science must be presuppositionless, that all determination involves mediation, and that discourse must begin with the indeterminate immediate, Being. Yet, he is aware that such an absolute beginning is possible only if freed of the presupposition of a knowing self. For this reason, the *Logic* actually begins from the accomplished *supersession* of the standpoint of consciousness, and, therefore, of epistemology as such. The *Phenomenology of Mind*, is the "deduction of the concept of Science" because it observes the whole of experience overcoming the characteristic distinction of conscious knowing, that of in-itselfness and for-itselfness. Thereby knowing is no longer an instrument that comes to its object as to something ready-made apart from thought. Instead, determinateness is freed from the problematic limitation of a presupposed reflection. What results is nothing but the presuppositionless beginning of absolute indeterminancy with which the *Logic* must begin.[3]

On this basis the *Logic* proceeds from the thoroughgoing refutation of the primordiality of self-consciousness.[4] Unlike the major figures of German Idealism, Hegel is aware that Kant's transcendental apperception, Fichte's absolute synthesis of the *Ich* and the *Nicht-Ich*, and Schelling's Subject-Object identity of intellectual intuition, not only presuppose categorical determinations, but demand grounding in an *intersubjective*, process.[5] Hegel recognizes that the ego is fundamentally a unity of universality and singularity, whose autonomy *is* only in an through its individuation over and against others. The identity of the ego comprises itself not merely by unifying immediately given determinations so as to inform them as objects of knowledge. The ego is what it is by being a structure of self-consciousness common to every subject, yet individual and excluding all others.[6] For this reason the ego is determinate only in its unity and difference to a plurality of egos, whose own identity is a function of their dual relation to others.

As a result, consciousness cannot stand as the irrevocable and irreducible vantagepoint of discourse. Its process of reflection is constituted in intersubjectivity, whose elementary form is reciprocal recognition. In this basic interaction self-consciousness has its actuality. Here, as Hegel writes, "Each is the mediating term to the other, through which each mediates and unites itself with itself; and each is to itself and to the other an immediate self-existing reality, which at the same time, exists thus for itself only through this mediation. They recognize themselves as mutually recognizing one another."[7]

This grounding of conscious knowing in Interaction indicates the possibility of social determination, and with it, the possibility of a sphere of capital realizing the individuality of the bourgeois. What has yet to be shown, however, is that inter-individuality is the real forum of all determination. Although the *Phenomenology* frees discourse from the standpoint of consciousness, it provides only the most negative characterization of what supersedes it.

What provides the positive statement is the *Logic*. It shows how determination achieves totality by bringing the form of inter-individuality to such concreteness that no categorial specification fall outside of it. From the Logic of Being to that of Essence and finally to that of the Concept, there is an immanent succession where interrelations of a plurality come to comprise a more and more self-informed and inclusive sphere of determinancy. Thus, in the specification emerging out of Being, Hegel shows how *something* has its proper character only in relation to other correlatively determinate entities. This identity of being-within-self (*Ansichsein*) and being-for-other (*Sein-für-Anderes*) has its corresponding development in the Logic of Essence with the identity of *inner* (*Innerlichkeit*) and *outer* (*Ausserlichkeit*), where generally positedness and its positing are each what they are only through one another. At the threshold of the Concept, dialogical relationship acquires further determinateness in the identity of universality and singularity, where being-in-and-for-itself (the pure form of the ego's self-relation) *is* in so far as it *is* positedness, as an individuality contrasted with others. Finally, in the Idea reciprocity achieves its absolute, unconditioned concreteness in the mutual adequation of the Concept and Reality.[8]

By becoming this totality of determination out of the presuppositionless starting point of indeterminancy, Hegel's *Logic* establishes inter-individuality as the real foundation and arena of discourse. Its immanent self-determination positively replaces the monological standpoint of consciousness. This result is crucial both for the *Logic's* method and its relation to the *Realphilosophie* to which *Capital* belongs.

Since the *Logic's* self-determined process has eliminated all external reflection in constituting determination, form and content no longer fall asunder, but are so united that the very articulation of a specification is its own proof. Thus, the method of the *Logic* is not independently given, but must be constituted as a reiteration of the *Logic's* entire path of determination *qua* the self-development of the whole.[9]

In fact, the final determination of the *Logic*, the "Absolute Method," is precisely this complete retrospective unfolding, and not just the process of double negation that many identify with the dialectical method. This retrospection begins with a recollection of Being as "*in itself the concrete totality*, though that totality is not yet posited,"[10] as thus containing an implicit contrast that does unfold through double negation. However, once a new content arises out of this operation of double negation, the new determination has been proven,[11] so that, as Hegel writes, "the *content*...now belongs to the method. The method itself by means of this moment expands itself into a system,[12] where the Method's knowledge of the necessity of the advance is at each moment the entire system of determinations in the *Logic* confronting one of its phases.

If Hegel's *Logic* is to serve as the general foundation of *Capital* and as the methodological guide to the particular stages of Marx's argument, it is necessary to look for a correspondence with the self-development of determination in the *Logic*. The entire project of the *Logic* is subverted if particular categories are individually extracted and formally applied to Marx's work. Unfortunately, this is precisely what Hans-Jürgen Krahl and Helmut Reichelt do when they take Hegel's determinations of Essence and Appearance out of their proper context, and relate them to different levels of discussion in *Capital*.[15]

Hegel's *Logic* cannot be reduced to an externally introduced tool for investigating *Capital*. In order to maintain the *Logic's* supersession of all egological determining, the relation between its process and that of Marx's concept of capital must be far more immanent.

In point of fact, what follows from the *Logic's* result is precisely the required internal connection between the two sciences. The *Logic* can inform *Capital* without interfering with either of their independent self-developments because the totality with which the logical Idea consummates must be *particular* in order to be what it is.[14] Just as every determination has been shown to have an implicitly inter-individual structure, so too the entire *Logic* cannot remain alone in its universality, but must achieve its own identity as an individuality, that is, in its being-for-other. For this reason, Hegel's logical Idea necessarily develops immediately out of itself as a realm of Nature, and then, more concretely, as a self-informing world of intersubjectivity where Interaction (*objektiver Geist*) emerges to consummate itself in History.

On the basis of these further determinations, it is possible to maintain Hegel's claim that the *Logic* presents the Concept as such, and that the determinate concepts of the *Realphilosophie* are immanently related to it as specific forms of the logical oneness that must develop from itself as a totality.[15] Thus, the *Logic* is not a surrogate that permits *Capital's* particular subject matter to unfold. The Determinate Science progresses in its own freedom, just as the logical form of dialectical reason is independent of its interactional embodiments.[16] Nevertheless, the pure articulation of a particular science such as that of capital will reveal the determinateness of what Hegel calls the *Logic's* realm of shadows.[17] If the specification of the "Absolute Method" is definitive, then the systematic nature of any part of the Science will correspond with the development of the *Logic*.

Thus, the following discussion attempts to demonstrate how the rigorous argument of the first section of *Capital* (and the corresponding passages within the *Grundrisse*) avoids the dilemmas of egological knowing and instead fulfills the promise of immanent social determination. It should become apparent that Marx's concept of capital develops in the successive forms of the logical Idea without ever presupposing an independent knowing self to describe and order the determinations. For the content of Marx's discourse will turn out to be a *process* of specification in which the object of investigation comes about in the self-development that produces its realized determination. Thereby Marx overcomes the dogmatic idealism of his earlier work, where conscious reflection held sway instead of dialectical logic.

As Hegel writes, "Quantity...is a stage of the Idea: and as such it must have its due, first as a logical category, and then in the world of objects, natural as well as spiritual."[18] The very beginning of *Capital* seizes this pure determination within the intersubjective realm of Civil Society's System of Needs,[19] proceeds to embody its process of specification up through the positing of Money, and then continues to develop in the shadow of Measure towards Capital itself.

## ii) The Logic of Commodity Exchange

Pure quantity is "being, where the mode or character is no longer taken as one with the being itself, but explicitly put as...indifferent."[20] This is the category with which *Capital* begins.

In its immediate determination the commodity is an object of need and of will. As such, its qualitative material existence is something superseded in this its relation to need and will. As an object of specific utility the commodity is comparable to other things with similar utility, and as an object of a certain will, the commodity is likewise comparable to all other objects that exist for that will. Similarly, the specific need and specific will to which the commodity is related are respectively comparable to need in general and will in general. The commodity's quantitative determination as an object of need is use-value, and as an object of will, value.[21]

The determinations use-value and value are continuous magnitudes for they specify simple undifferentiated sameness for commodities at this stage.[22] At the same time, however, use-value and value are both discrete magnitude, since they specify the *single* commodity in its continuity with all others of like determination.

Just as "quantity contains the two moments of continuity and discreteness"[23] together, so the commodity's material existence immediately limits its dual universal specifications, posing it as a quantum of use-value and a quantum of value.[24] The commodity now has a determinate being that makes clear the distinction between its continuity and discreteness by *distinguishing* its sameness. Use-value and value here exist as a something, as *this* commodity. However, as such, these universals do not have simply one determinate being.

They rather exist as a plurality of such commodities. Each something of use-value and value is only a determinate quantity through its continuity and opposition to other similarly specified commodities. Therefore the limit on the commodity's discrete magnitude of use-value and value is not its simple unity as an isolated object, but instead is constituted in its specific relation to others.

The *movement of quantum to number* is here embodied, as commodities are placed in relation to each other in the structure of simple exchange. In this meeting of need and need and will and will, the commodity sustains itself as an object having magnitude of value through its relation to another commodity. The commodities are both alienated and appropriated by two contracting wills who face each other as owner of the commodity desired by the other. Rendered socially equal thanks to the diversity of their particular needs, these two subjects recognize each other as free property owners. "What...remains identical throughout as the property implicit in the contract is distinct from the external things whose owners alter when the exchange is made."[25] This "universal in which the subjects of contract participate"[26] is exchange value, and it is through its agency that the moments of the number determination concretize themselves.

The limit of number is not the abstract determinacy that it was with the simple quantum. In number this limit is posited as a manifold within the quantum itself, enclosing the specific aggregate of the other discrete magnitude to which it is related. The continuity of this *amount* is the *unit*, the form in which the quantum relates back to the opposing discrete magnitude that provides it with its limit. These two moments of number, *amount* and *unit*, are respectively embodied in the simple exchange of two commodities as the equivalent and relative forms of value.

The determinate being of use-value and value has led to the exchange of some commodity A for some other commodity B. In their participation in the universal of exchange-value, A and B distinguish themselves just as number has come to consist in its two aspects. The exchange of A for B is first manifest as the alienation of A as a value and the appropriation of B as a particular use-value. Here A presents itself as the relative form, and B as the equivalent form of value. A expresses its value in B, whose bodily form has become its equivalent. B is *immediately* presented as a quantity of A, for B's material existence as a particular use-value has become the independent embodiment of the value-form of A. As Marx writes, B's own value "acquires no quantitative expression''[27] since the underlying identity of exchange value has rendered B's value at one with its use-value. The contrast of use-value and value has been made evident for A, however, because its value has manifested itself in the material existence of *another* commodity, B. The value of commodity A has here obtained ''independent and definite expression,''[28] entirely apart from A's existence as a use-value.

This expression of the commodity A's value is a number that has the aggregate magnitude within it (as the manifold of its limit) the equivalent value form that B embodies. B's material existence as particular use-value is here the *amount* in this statement of number. This equivalent form *finds its continuity* in the relative value form of A, which so to speak encloses this *amount* in itself. B is ''an amount of one and the same *unit*,[29] and this *unit* of the number determination is commodity A in its relative form of value. Here ''the limit is an external one...the amount to be aggregated, is contingent, arbitrary.''[30] This ''accidental and purely relative''[31] nature of the exchange allows B to be any commodity whatever, and the exchange relation as a whole can only be brought about by the external act of the two contracting subjects.

However, this purely accidental character is overcome, because quantum as number actually ''has *within itself* the externality, the relation to other.''[32] In the self-relation of number to its amount, this moment collapses itself into the unit, and the limit of the quantum is posited as unitary and identical with the quantum itself. ''Number as a one, being posited as self-reflection reflected into itself, excludes from itself the indifference and externality of the amount and is self-relation *as relation through itself to an externality.*''[33]

This movement arises in simple accidental commodity exchange for the reason that what is the alienation of commodity A as a value and the appropriation as use-value is at the same time the appropriation of commodity A as use-value and the alienation of commodity B as a value. The result is exactly the reverse of the preceding: commodity A now figures as the amount, and commodity B as the unit in this number determination of value. Commodity B appears in the relative form as a mere use-value, while commodity A shows itself in the equivalent form as an exchange value whose use-value and value remain undifferentiated in independent form.

In either case, it is the commodity whose value is being expressed which ''figures directly as a mere use-value, while the commodity in which that value is to be expressed figures directly as a mere exchange value.''[34]

As a whole, then, this embodiment of the number determination presents each commodity as *both* an amount and a unit, as *both* the pure use-value and independently embodied value that together comprise the relative value form, and the pure exchange value that is the equivalent form of value. Here amount and unit have immediately passed into one another, and the individual commodity has shown itself to be determined as quantum of use-value and value by being external to both these specifications as a pure exchange value. The commodity has excluded the externality of its opposition to other commodities, for now its appearance as a magnitude of use-value and value has nothing to do with the particular determinacy of the other commodity exchanged with it. The completely accidental nature of the value relation has been superceded. The individual commodity has its relation to others reflected into itself, and no longer is this rapport determined by the chance meeting of the commodity with a *particular* other one. The limit of the commodity's value expression no longer rests upon a relation to a specific commodity B. The determination of the commodity has now been posited as an infinite series of exchange relations with all other commodies distinct from itself.

This transition to the expanded form of value is a movement from the determinacy of number to that of degree. From being in itself multiple, the limit in the quantum has passed over to become "in itself *simple* determinateness."[35] This "*independent* indifferent limit is absolute *externality*,"[36] for the self-relation of the quantum is at the same time interrelated to its determinacy as outside itself. Degree is related "through itself to its other"[37] in a continuous uninterrupted progress of self-external determinacy.

Degree manifests itself as that exchange relation where the individual commodity (let us call it A) expresses its value in the equivalent form of all other commodities. The value of A is "placed in contrast under all possible shapes with the bodily form of"[38] A, and all other commodities appear as "particular equivalents differing in kind."[39] The magnitude of A's value is an independent limit, indifferent to the determinate existence of each of the particular commodities opposing it. Its external expression is an absolute gathering of countless pure exchange values that altogether comprise an infinite expanse of "fragmentary equivalent forms, each excluding the others."[40] No contingent meeting of contracting subjects is called for to sustain the value relation. The continuous series of self-external determinacy is something that proceeds through commodity A itself. The expanded form of value posits the individual commodity as indifferent to its particular equivalent forms in their isolation, yet self-related in the continuity of their continual overcoming as fragmentary value forms.

As such, this degree determinacy is actually an immediate union of the quantitative aspect of absolute externality with the qualitative character of independence.[41] The degree is in the amounts that it has excluded "as its *own* amount,"[42] for it has revealed itself to be a "unity which is self-related through the *negation of its differences*."[43] In the expanded form of value, the determinate being of A's value is a limit which *becomes* in the continuous overcoming of the particular equivalent values related to it.[44]

This repulsion of determinacy from itself is the degree actually producing its otherness by impelling itself beyond itself.[45] Therefore, in this progression "quantity returns to itself,"[46] and shows itself to have "its infinity."[47] This self-determinacy is no longer beyond and outside the quantum, for the quantum now finds itself in other quanta as the quantitative infinity. These other quanta have their determinacy in it, and their determinacy as such gives this universal quantum its quality as the element and unity of the specification of all others.

In this manner the pure determination of the expanded form of value passes over to the general form. The individual commodity A is a universal equivalent in which all other commodities differentiate their value from their particular use-value. As their values are all expressed in this same commodity, A sustains its own infinite self-relatedness by finding itself as the substance in which every single commodity shows its individual value determination. This universal equivalent is the element and unity of all value forms by its very independent being. Although any commodity can be the equivalent of the general form of value, whatever commodity *is* determined as such immediately repels all other commodities from assuming its role, just as all other commodities exclude it from appearing in the relative form of value. The qualitative character of the particular universal equivalent is inseparable from its proper role as the medium in which all other commodities are rendered commensurate exchange values. Therefore the universal equivalent becomes limited to a specific commodity, and the general form of value has made its transition to money.

When the independence and indifference of quantitative infinity have finally combined, the qualitative quantum, measure,[48] has emerged. This immediate unity of quality and quantity is a specific quantum with a specific quality belonging to it. Therefore its magnitude constitutes its specific nature. As Hegel writes, "an alteration of the magnitude would alter the quality of the something."[59] At the same time, however, the measure is also a quantum with "an indifferent limit which can be exceeded without altering the quality."[50] The qualitative quantum has this immediate distinction of being on the one hand an intrinsically determinate magnitude, and on the other, an overcoming of the indifference of its external alterations in other quanta.[51]

Specifying measure is that determination in which these two moments are explicitly expressed.

This is first the qualitative quantum that has come to be a standard by which other quanta are determined as amounts of its unit. It is the rule by which other somethings are measured according to this external comparison, where the intrinsically determinate magnitude of the specifying measure remains an arbitrary amount.

This rule is given spiritual embodiment in money which stands opposed to the world of commodities as *measure of value* and *standard of price*.[52] Commodities quit their bodily shape and present their exchange value in an imaginary amount of money that fixes their value as a particular price. Individual commodities can no longer directly confront each other as use-values or exchange values. Their price determinations make their exchangeability dependent upon the external comparison to money.

At the same time, however, this specification of price actually negates this one-sided contrast of money and commodity. In its determination as price, the individual commodity comes to embody the universal equivalent, and the money appears itself in this particular form. The individual commodity here emerges as the essential, comparing itself to the money equivalent. Yet since money *is* price in-itself, the universal form of the entire world of exchange-value, all individual commodities are equally *its* particular substances.[53]

What is manifest is that in the price determination of exchange value, money and the commodity each exist in and through the other, and their difference is merely formal.[54] Money has shown itself to be intrinsically related to the individual commodity that it measures. In its determinate being as standard of price and measure of value, money *is* for itself the measure that the opposing commodity has given itself in price.

The determinacy of money has passed from that of the rule to that specifying measure which is not an external standard, but a qualitative quantum that is related to its own self in the specific quantum that it has measured.[55] Here, rather than the qualitative moment being determined on the side of the intrinsically determinate magnitude, it is now related to the alterable, external aspect of the amount belonging to the opposing quantum. The measure is no longer a bare quantum whose determinate being can change without upsetting its rule.

This assimilating determinacy is realized in Money's emergence as the medium of circulation. In the structure of commodity—money—commodity exchange, money comes to be a *specific* relation of exchangeability as the middle term of two commodities. Through the mediation of *this* amount of money, these two commodities are inextricably bound together. Money has assimilated the individual commodity that was its externally imposed amount, and specified itself in this otherness by relating this commodity to another through the agency of *this* money's specific magnitude.

The immediate determinacy of this process has two moments: the exchange of the first commodity ($C_1$) with the money, $C_1$-M, and the exchange of this money with the second commodity ($C_2$), M-$C_2$. Although both commodities "are. . .qualitatively related. . .each is on its own account a qualitative determinate being."[56] Just as the pure determinacy of measure has become "the *immanent* quantitative relationship of *two* qualities to each other,"[57] so these two commodities express their determination both as particular substances assimilated in money's self-determination and as determinate beings in their *individual* relation with the money.

Each of the two metamorphoses distinguishes itself in a dual way.

First, in both $C_1$-M and M-$C_2$, the commodities $C_1$ and $C_2$ each realize their price in M, which appears as the identical equivalent form of the two exchange values. In this way M allows each commodity to realize its price by posing its own exchange value in that of the other.[58].

Secondly, $C_1$-M and M-$C_2$ distinguish themselves *from* each other. In the first metamorphosis, it is the subtance of the exchange value, $C_1$ that leaves the circulation to be consumed. On the other hand, when M is exchanged for $C_2$, "exchange value disppears,"[59] since it is the money that is replaced by $C_2$ in its bodily use-value form.

In this second case the direct identity of the value determinations of $C_1$ and $C_2$ is broken. Sale and purchase are no longer identical, and money appears as a transient equivalent form.[60]

With this differentiation it has become evident that either moment C-M or M-C is the reverse of itself for another commodity. The stable identity of the first contrast (in which each commodity realized its price by posing its own exchange value in that of the other) is now ruptured. Instead, it is apparent that the exchange of a particular commodity A for its equivalent M is equally the exchange of some other commodity B's exchange value (also expressed in M) for commodity A as a use-value. The closed unity of the C-M-C exchange is overcome, and money has emerged as a specific magnitude related to an entire series of measure relations that form an ever-extending web of exchange circuits. In this "circulation of commodities"[61] money's determinacy is no longer limited to its bind with the two particular commodities of the former $C_1$-M-$C_2$ specification.

Here money "first shows itself to be a real measure; for it now appears as a determinate being which is both one and the same. . .and also quantitatively varied."[62] Its determination has passed from specifying quantity to real measure.

When money showed itself as the medium that let each commodity realize its price by posing its own exchange value in that of the other, it manifested being-for-self by negating the distinction between its qualitatively determined sides, $C_1$ and $C_2$.[63]

However, in so doing, the self-determination of the relation was also superseded in this negative unity. As Hegel writes, "a self-subsistent whole of this kind, just because it is a real being-for-self, is at the same time a repulsion into *distinct self-subsistent* somethings."[64] When $C_1$-M and M-$C_2$ distinguished themselves from each other, money became placed into relation with an entire network of commodity exchange, which replaced its own single measure determination with a whole series of measures. Here, "measure itself. . .has shown that it is unstable in its own self, and like the quantum as such, has its determinateness in other measure relations."[65] The circulation of commodities is this web of measures that "have become in themselves relations of measures which are themselves specified."[66]

The qualitative quantum is therefore reduced to an element of this sphere of exchange, and "it preserves itself through the presence of its indifferent, quantitative character and at the same time functions as a specifying moment of a new measure relation."[67] Money thus assumes a negative relation to the individual commodities facing it in each of its manifold exchange determinations. Now it seems always ready to remove commodities from circulation according to the M-C circuit. The path of circulation has become a constant movement of money away from its starting point. Money functions as "a transient and objective reflex of the price of commodities," [68] always within circulation. As such, money's quality becomes masked in its quantitative element,[69] sublating its character as a material object of human need. The bodily form of money collapses into its exchange value, and money has become a symbol of itself, a mere symbol of value. As this *currency*, money *posits* its use-value as exchange value, and instead of being a means of exchange, money has become a means of payment. "Its qualitative side falls and its *relationship to its other* becomes that quantitative mode of relationship which constitutes the specific determination of this self-subsistent measure."[70]

Money as means of payment embodies the determinacy of the self-subsistent measure which is related to a plurality of other measures that it excludes from itself. Since this relation remains quantitative, the self-subsistent measure also continues itself into these opposed quanta, and their overcoming is separable into the two moments that united to produce it. "This measure, based on such a relation, is thus infected with its own indifference; it is in its own self something external and alterable in its relation to itself."[71]

What this means with respect to money is that first, money stands as an *ideal* means of purchase that allows commodities to realize themselves as use-values *before* realizing their price in their actual exchange with money. Secondly, money converts itself into the material form of the commodity before this use-value has undergone the exchange metamorphosis that presents it in the value form.

Together, these two moments reveal a pattern of circulation that has become money-commodity-money. Instead of being a transient value form, money poses itself in the commodity to then return to itself in this its other. Whereas previously it had served as the mediation of the extremes of commodities' exchange value and use-value, money now makes this relation the mediation of its very own self.[72]

Money is first only advanced, rather than being spent as the converted value form of the commodity. The commodity appears as a particular use-value that directly embodies the particular exchange-value specified by its price. When the commodity actually changes places with the money (the commodity-money moment of money-commodity-money), this commodity has already realized both its use and exchange values, leaving the money as a self-subsistent general exchange value without any enduring reference to this opposing article. Here "money and the commodity represent only different modes of the existence of value itself, the money its general mode, and the commodity its particular. . .mode."[73] With this determinacy, money has become the universal commodity that is in its own self this beyond where it becomes differentiated into general and particular forms whose relation once again posits money as the independent form of exchange value.

This persistent presence of money is "an affirmatively present, qualitative foundation which, as also the continuity of the measure *with itself* in its externality, must contain in its quality the principle of the specification of this externality."[74] The determinacy that this M-C-M exchange embodies is an exclusive measure that is for itself in its beyond as both "another measure relation and also as another merely quantitative relation; it is determined as in itself a specifying unity which produces measure relations within itself."[75] However, this exclusive measure contains within it the moment of quantitative determinate being that is open to alteration. The magnitude of the relation is variable, and this *indifference* to the qualitative substratum is also the negation of the qualitative moment and the positing of a new something. This leads the determinacy to impel itself into the *measureless*.[76]

Here the specification of the universal commodity is first a self-preservation into its beyond that surpasses itself in a manner that is indifferent to its quality. In the relation $M_1$-C-$M_2$, $M_1$ and $M_2$ distinguish themselves by the difference of their magnitude. By being a greater amount of money, $M_2$ is the continuity of $M_1$ in its otherness. This alteration is an external distinction that is immediately given, and whose actual magnitude remains unspecified—the particular and general form of value emerge groundlessly from the substratum of the univeral commodity. However, this quantitative progress posits "the negation of the qualitative moment contained therein and hence of the merely quantitative externality too."[77] A new measure relation emerges, for $M_2$ is qualitatively the same as $M_1$, being itself another exclusive measure that also constitutes the independent form of exchange value.

As Hegel writes, "this transition of the qualitative and the quantitative into each other proceeds on the basis of their unity, and the meaning of this process is only to *show* or to *posit* the *determinate being* of such a substrate underlying the process, a substrate which is their unity."[78]

The external differentiation of $M_2$ from $M_1$ is actually a determination of the unity of the universal commodity that conserves and maintains itself. This quantitative distinction is something that the independent form of exchange value has *in itself*. Even though this quantitative progression establishes $M_2$ as an independent value, opposing the circulation that produced it, its negative relation to this process is a positive moment for the essential substance that has *conserved* itself in this opposition. "The alteration is only a change of a *state*, and the *subject* of the transition is posited as remaining the *same* in the process."[79]

Money's abstract unity of quality and quantity is overcome in this infinite substance that has its moments in *both* quality and quantity. "Value is here the active factor in a process, in which, while constantly assuming the form in turn of money and commodities, it at the same time changes in magnitude, differentiating itself by throwing off surplus-value from itself"[80] and *determining* this its self-expansion.

The movement $M_1$-C-$M_2$ has emerged as a self-determined, self-subsistent process whose moments are not indifferently related, but immanently specified by the process itself. Measure is reduced "to the status of a moment"[81] and the "determinateness of exchange value itself, or the measure of price, must now itself disappear as an act of circulation."[82]

The determinacy of Essence has finally been arrived at. The sphere of commodity exchange has realized itself in "the totality in which every determination of being is sublated and contained."[83] Capital has emerged as the exchange value that conserves and perpetuates itself in and through circulation at the same time that it presupposes itself.[84] It posits itself against itself in this act of value production, all the time remaining "at one with itself in this its own difference from itself." Commodity and money are simple elements in its process, and capital is in each one as its connection with its other, its opposite.[85]

The movement of determination has overcome the simple being of circulation, and now the deeper realm of the sphere of production has come to reveal itself in its necessary unfolding. The self-development of determinacy from quantity to essence is embodied in this all important transition, where the capitalist mode of production proceeds to show itself as the ground for the relations of commodity exchange.

The process of determination of the so-called Labor Theory of Value lifts the curtain.

### iii) The Self-Development of the Labor Theory of Value

Capital has emerged from the structure of commodity exchange as the immediate unity of commodity and money that has its own mediation in their process of valorization. The entire world of commodities is contained in ideal form within it, for capital is the product of its own movement as circulation at the same time that it faces this circulation as its presupposition.

The self-development of capital here proceeds in the pure language of the determinations of Essence. As Hegel writes, Essence "*differentiates* the determinations which are *implicit (an sich)* in it. . .it sets itself over against itself and is infinite being-for-self only in so far as it is at one with itself in this its own difference from itself."[86] At first, Essence is this simple negativity that is indifferent to the determinacy of being whose very sublation as otherness is equally essence's being for self. Because of the coincidence of this indifference towards the determinate, and the necessary supersession of it, essence "has to posit in its *own* sphere the determinateness that is only implicit in it, in order to give itself determinate being, and then being-for-self."[87]

In just this way, capital is first an immediate identity that must abolish itself as the unity of commodity exchange so that this act of circulation becomes a simple determinate relation that emerges as an element of capital itself.[88] By way of the process of production, this self-development is made clear.

With the world of commodities and money being the appearance in which capital poses itself, there is a distinction in this identity that presents capital as an ideality of the whole sphere of exchange that is in immediate relation to it. This is found in the simple enunciation that capital is merely a different being from the totality of exchange-value from where it has emerged and in whose process it conserves itself. However, this sphere in which capital appears or shines forth is not simply distinct from the unity of capital. It is rather distinguished from it as a being that is non-capital. As the independent exchange-value that preserves and perpetuates itself in and through circulation at the same time that it presupposes itself,[89] capital is a reflection in itself that renders its otherness a negative posed by capital in opposition to itself.

Labor-power is precisely this otherness that is stripped of all objective existence in the totality of exchange-value. It is the non-being of independent value, which nonetheless is the beyond in which capital produces itself as universal wealth. As such, labor-power is merely the possibility of exchange value in general. In a purely negative, subjective form, labor-power reflects the same totality and abstraction of individual exchange-values that is contained in capital's ideality. Labor-power presents itself as a purely formal *capacity* to realize capital in its self-valorization. [90] "General wealth (in contrast to capital in which it exists objectively, as reality)" is the "general possibility" of labor.[91]

This positing of labor-power is an embodiment of the advance from Essence to Illusory Being in the process of pure specification. Here, the simple difference between essence and the being to which it immediately is related emerges as an indifferent relation contained in essence's own reflection. What is contrasted to essence as the unessential *is* an immediacy that is essence's own. This being is not an other, whose difference falls outside of the indeterminate relation of the essential and the unessential and into a third entity, but an "immediate that is *in and for itself* a nullity. . . *illusory* being."[92] Its otherness is precisely essence's own negation of its determinate being. It has its nullity as its very essence, while "illusory being is not. It is the negative posited as negative." [93] Furthermore, this negativity and reflected immediacy of illusory being are not only constituted *by* essence, but *are* the moments of essence itself.[94] The posited and simple determinacy of illusory being is essence's own immediacy, as the "self-subsistent, which *is* as self-mediated through its negation." [95] Illusory being is not a nullity within essence's reflection, but rather is this reflection itself where essence's *own* immediacy and negativity are in identical union.[96]

Within the discourse of Capital, this self-development is constituted by the presentation of labor-power as the non-being of capital that is also capital's immediate existence as the negativity of independent value. The nullity of labor-power is maintained only through its negative relation to capital. Since labor is the non-being of capital that is posited by capital as its negative, it is the formal possibility of exchange value in which capital also realizes itself as universal wealth. The pure subjectivity of labor power, represented as the potentiality of the totality of exchange value, is immediately a positive relation, for labor-power is only as capital's own living source of value.[97]. And capital *is* only as self-mediated through its negation, labor-power. Labor-power is thus a reflection of capital within itself that must realize capital's existence.

As such, labor-power is no longer simply the non-being of capital—it has now emerged in positive relation to capital, acquiring the determination of pure use-value in its opposition to capital. Capital must bring labor-power back into relation with itself as part of its process, in order to affirm itself as capital.[98] It must face labor-power as an equivalent exchange value, equivalent in that it is sufficient to pose labor-power in opposition to itself. In this manner capital enters into an exchange with labor-power, trading what exchange value is necessary to sustain its opposite as the pure capacity to realize value. Capital presents itself as value existing for itself, just as the labor-power facing it has being for self in the laborer.[99]

This coming to be of the sale of labor-power has proceeded upon the determinacy of reflection, as it has emerged from the specification of illusory being. With the development of illusory being as a relation of essence's own reflection, the self-related negativity of essence has become the negating of its *own* self. Since essence is now "immediacy as a returning movement, as a coincidence of the negative with itself, it is equally a negative of the negative as negative. . . reflection-into-self is essentially the presupposing of that from which it is the return."[100]

In just this manner, capital relates to labor-power as its own pure use-value, grasping itself in both negation and simple equality. However, because this reflection has risen above simple difference, and acquired the determinacy of labor-power's positive relation to capital, capital faces the pure use-value labor-power both as immediately opposed to it, and as the presupposition of its own development. Labor-power opposes it as something external, determined in its own right. This is the worker, formally posed as a person existing for himself, separate from his capacity to work,[101] and stripped of all objectivity beyond his immediate existence.[102]. This is labor power as self-related, yet facing capital. On its own side, capital presents itself as value existing for itself, related to the free laborer as a capitalist, such that their opposition is external to each other's self-related determination. For the worker, his labor-power is a use-value only in that it *is* exchange value, and not an element in capital's self-affirmation. For the capitalist, labor-power has an exchange value because it *is* pure use-value in its relation *with* capital.[103] The basis of these immediate self-relations is, however, capital's presupposing of labor-power. And this is concretely achieved in its opposition to labor-power as an equivalent exchange value whose determination is such that its value is sufficient to pose and maintain labor-power in opposition to itself. Because of this, the identity of labor-power and capital is posited, and through the free exchange between worker and capitalist, what was an external relation between universal wealth and labor-power is now reflected into each of these two entities. With the completion of the sale of labor-power, it is now capital that divides itself according to its form and substance, embodying each element *as well* as their relation.[104] The immediate opposition of capital and non-capital is now explicitly mediated by capital itself. With this, the actual labor process has been posited.

Here the embodiment of external reflection has passed into the determinacy of determining reflection, to culminate its self-development of determinate essence. As the outcome of illusory being, external reflection presupposed its opposing being as a self-related immediacy whose determinacy was only an external moment to its act of reflection.[105] In so doing, however, the externally reflecting essence and the self-related being were both established as identical in the same indifference of their content to the form of the relation. Since the external reflection was the basis of their opposition, its identification is nothing other than the immanent reflection of the self-related determinacy of the essence and its being.[106]

This is just how the opposition of worker and capitalist, presupposed by capital in its appearance as the equivalent exchange value of labor-power, is an identity that emerges from the very content of worker and capitalist, whose existence for themselves is based on meeting and recognizing each other's will in the free exchange of labor-power. So is expressed the process of determining reflection that emerges when the positedness of external reflection has shown itself to be "*only* a positedness with respect to essence."[107] Here what were external self-related determinations have shown themselves to be in perfect unity with the external reflection that actually had absolutely presupposed them as determinations of its own return-to-self. Through the exchange of labor-power, capital is this determining reflection that really posits the character of worker and capitalist as well as their relation of contract. This is reflection that *is* as "the relation to its otherness within itself."[108] Both the content of reflection and the form in which this content is determinate are contained within essence itself. Essence is related to an other such that the related term and its relation are no longer distinct.[109] Determining reflection really overcomes the distinguishing it is based upon. Essence has emerged as a determinate essence, or *an essentiality*, where otherness and relation-to-other have collapsed into each other within essence's pure equality-with-self.[110]

Within such process of determinacy, the exchange of labor-power with capital has now posited capital as a determinate essence distinguishing itself in function of its content as a simple process of production, and, in function of its form, as a process of autovalorization.[111] However, although capital has emerged as the substantial relation of its differentiation as form and content, it is at first merely a unilateral relation within this distinction. Capital has appropriated its opposite, labor-power, and made it one of its constituent elements, but it has done so only by absorbing it as an *activity* that conserves and augments capital as its finality.[112]

As a result, capital has immediately realized its substance of self-subsistent exchange value and its form of self-expansion as distinct elements of its content alone. Labor concretely embodies capital as formal process, and what opposes it is capital as pure passive object of this process, material.[113] Capital's substantial aspect here appears as a function of labor.[114] It has been reduced to its pure substance, and all relation to its form has disappeared. The work process has become the activity of labor itself, and capital finds itself as raw material and instrument of labor, as abstraction of itself in movement.[115]

In the language of pure specification, what is before us is that equality-with-self that is *essential* identity, having brought itself to unity. [116] Determinate essence, or essentiality, differentiates itself such that what is distinguished is "a non-being which is the non-being of itself.[117] Reflection has become an internal repulsion that is identity by immediately drawing itself inward, collapsing within itself, and distinguishing nothing. The contrast of labor as a formal activity facing capital as the pure passive object of its process is just this determinacy of an essentiality whose self-equality "is the passage beyond itself into the dissolution of itself."[118] With capital doubling itself as labor and simple object of labor, it is presenting itself as its own non-being, distinguishing itself so as to reduce itself to a bare substance negated by its own non-being, labor.

This relation of essential identity is nothing other than absolute difference, for it presents an absolute negativity that is self-related through this very identity.[119] This difference gathers together essentiality and the identity through which it asserted itself. Because here identity is immediately self-reflection, and the other element is difference in itself, "The distinguished terms *subsist* as indifferently different towards one another because each is self-identical."[120] The resulting diversity consists of self-related moments, indifferent to each other, as well as to their own determinations.

This self-development of determinacy becomes the unfolding of capital within itself as simple substance abolishing the opposition active worker—passive object of labor,[121] reuniting the passive substance of capital with the pure form of labor. Here absolute difference manifests itself in *labor*'s active relation with itself as a process of production. As difference in and for itself, labor consumes the bare stuff that is capital, impressing it with form, discarding its own pure subjectivity, and objectifying itself in this substance that it works upon.[122] In so doing, however, labor has united the difference in itself of its negating work with the essential identity that a passive capital embodied. This unity has taken place within labor's own act of determination, and the self-relatedness of each moment subsists indifferent to the other as distinct objective forms that embody for labor its own aspect of identity and difference.

The labor process now develops under two aspects. On the one hand, raw materials are impressed with the substance of labor, objectifying the finality of its activity as reaffirmation of capital. On the other hand, the instrument of labor takes on subjective activity, becoming "the objective means which subjective activity inserts between itself as an object, as its conductor."[123] In other words, the raw material is that substance consumed by labor and the instrument of labor is that substance consuming the pure subjectivity of labor itself.

The raw material and the instrument of labor stand respectively as external identity and external difference, or as likeness and unlikeness, in relation to labor's reflection-into-self. In the raw material labor finds identity by negating the inert formlessness of its object; through the instrument of labor, labor is related to itself negatively, passing its own reflection into this tool.

Nonetheless, in both moments, the reflection-into-self of labor is the negative unity of both, for "The independent self-reference which each of them is, is in fact the self-reference that sublates their distinctiveness and so, too, themselves."[124] This being the case, these indifferent sides of diversity are in *opposition* as moments of this single negative unity.[125]

Labor in process, working on its raw material through the instrument of labor, contains these two aspects within the unity of its act, and each of these aspects *is*, as concomitant elements of a single activity absorbing them both. This relation realizes the determinacy of "positive and negative. . . self-subsistent in that they are the reflection of the *whole* into themselves."[126] And this specification renders each moment positive and negative in its own self, since each maintains itself in so far as its opposite *is*, and in so far as it itself is in identical relation with this its opposite.[127]

However, since determinacy is here a positing of positive and of negative as a single reflection, there is the contradiction of a positing of self-identity that is in opposition to identity.[128] As embodied in the reality of the labor process, this specification comes into being in labor's active engagement with its instrument of labor and raw material. In this movement each aspect asserts itself in helping absorb and eliminate the other relation. Labor's negative relation to the raw material is also the consuming use of its relation to the instrument of labor and vice versa. Here the labor process actually pushes beyond labor and the two concrete recipients of its self-relation. Their unity in labor's activity has them vanish in an identity that is their destruction as self-subsistent relations.

The pure specification of such contradiction, however, does not halt at a unity that is the null. What perishes is only "the *positedness* of the self-subsistence"[129] that positive and negative constituted. What remains and perseveres is a self-subsistent unity that has returned to itself through the negation of its own posited form as the opposition of positive and negative.[130] This unity is itself posited, excluding itself from itself as the unity of positive and negative.

The product of the labor process emerges within this pure determinacy thrust forward by the self-annulling relation of labor to itself in its transformation of the raw material through the agency of the instrument of labor. Here is incorporated the given form impressed by the labor, as well as the substance materializing the labor itself. This result is indeed a material object that has been created, and yet no empty thing. The product has emerged as an excluding unity of reflection, that is capital reinstating itself as an active essential relation, now determining itself as *Ground*.

Capital has immediately restored itself as the positor of its own determinacy in the *created* use-value that is the result and sublation of the labor process. The elements of this labor process have had their use-value *determined* as substance of exchange value, and their former mode of existence (as capital reduced to pure content) has now been consumed.[131] In the product, capital has reflected itself back into its bare content, and reaffirmed itself as value that is subject, and for whom the labor process as a whole is the form of its self.[132]

This is essence determining itself as ground, posing a self-sublating positedness as its reflection of self-identity. Here reflection determines itself as the negative that is essence's *in itself*.[133] An immediate has emerged as the restored identity of essence that is just as much determined by essence's self-excluding reflection.[134] In this manner, immediate determinate being essentially *presupposes* a ground, and as such, essence has a two-fold determinacy—

that of *ground* and the *grounded*. Essence is first *not-positedness*, setting itself over against positedness. Secondly essence is positedness *qua* positedness. Thus essence as ground is an identity of positedness with itself, just as the grounded's "reflection-into-self is the identity of the ground."[135] Here is united the ground's determinate self-identity with the negative identity of the grounded.

In this unity essence is distinguished from its mediation, for the two reflections are both determinate, and different from their simple identity. Together they constitute *form* that faces essence, being "the indeterminate, which, in its determinations, is indifferent towards them."[136] Here form's determinations subsist in a dissolution that is the ground of the subsistence they give to themselves. At the same time, essence constitutes itself "as the *simple substrate* which is the *subsisting* of form."[137]

Thus form is just as much related to the "other" in which form subsists as sublated, and simple essence is only an "*inactive* substrate in which the form-determinations subsist and are reflected into themselves."[138] In this *determining* form, sublated positedness has become self-related, *presupposing* its identity in the indeterminate, formless essence to which it is an other. Essence is thus "*determined* as formless identity; it is *matter*."[139]

As embodied in the discourse of capital, this self-development emerges from the material product of the labor process, which is a created use-value that presupposes capital, the process of valorization, at the same time that it sublates the immediate labor process. On the one hand, capital sets itself over against the object as self-expanding value. On the other hand, capital has here developed as the becoming of exchange value whose substance is now constituted by such created use-value.

In uniting its self-identity as process of reproduction of exchange-value with the negative identity of created use-value, capital emerges as a process of production whose elements are themselves the results of its own formative process. This unity of product and elements of production renders capital distinct from its own ground-grounded mediation. There now emerges a simple identification of capital with itself where capital's material constituents appear as self-identical embodiments of invariable value that realize their simple sum in the final product which is their result.

Altogether, these elements comprise a form facing capital. They subsist as indifferently related quantities of value in the very process of production that transforms and negates their determinate existence.

On its own side, capital is the presupposed independent value that has now become its own result, in an unchanged form.[140] It is simply the bare inactive substrate of its own decomposition into quantitative values.

Thus the product and the elements of production actually presuppose this empty formless substance that capital has become. In effect, they determine capital as the simple *matter* of their *formal* existence as an equation of equivalent quantitative sums. As Marx writes: "The only process, as regards value, [is] that it sometimes appears as a whole, a unity; then as a division of this unity into certain amounts; finally, as sum."[141] The process of production has emerged as the constitution of the value of capital in its simple sum.

This relation of the addition of self-identical quantitative elements of value and the formless capital that is their substrate proceeds as a self-development of determinacy that emerges out of this distinguishing of form and its matter to become the new relation of form and content. With the appearance of matter as an absolute susceptibility to the form that is posed relating itself to this other as its subsistence, the illusory indifference of form and matter is removed. Now the whole relation is a unity of form and matter wherein each reciprocally presupposes the other. In this manner form sublates its own formless self-subsistence by rendering matter as something posited. At the same time, however, it has overcome its own relation to matter as a posited form, and it produces its subsistence on its own account.[142] This movement is no less a transformation taken on by matter itself. For when form has "sublated itself, the determinateness which matter has as against form also disappears, namely, to be an indeterminate subsistence."[143] Matter no longer relates to form in an indeterminate self-identity. Matter is now self-determined in a posited unity with form. In this unity form and matter withdraw, overcoming the subsistence they maintained externally in each other. Here form *is* a material subsistence, and matter *has* a necessary form.[144] Their unity is the *determinate basis* of formed matter "which is at the same time indifferent to form and matter, these being sublated and unessential determinations."[145] This posited unity of form and matter is *content*.

The formal division of capital into elements of value whose simple sum achieves their unity develops itself within the just described process of determination by realizing a union in the determination of abstract labor time. The indifferently related quantities of value that are the elements of capital's process of identification take up into themselves their presupposition of capital's activity, and acquire a determinate existence as specific quanta of abstract labor time, individual coagulations of capital's bare motion. Alongside this development, capital is no longer a formless substrate, but a whole that embodies and poses a definite sum of values that are inherently related to its own process by finding their measure in amounts of abstract labor time. The product and the elements of production no longer subsist in a formless matter whose simple presence as self-identical independent value grants them life. And nor is capital a formless subsistence in relation to the independent values constituting its process. The specific measures of abstract labor time pose themselves the determinate value of capital as a whole, just as capital posits itself in unity with the product and elements of production by having the expression of its bare activity of valorization, abstract labor time, inform these individual values in a particular manner. In values of abstract labor time the formal moments of capital find material subsistence, and capital itself acquires a necessary form. The determination of abstract labor time is the *content* of this process.

The pure process of specification of such a content relation first develops itself as content that is the posited unity of matter and form, as well as something standing opposed to the form of its positedness. The latter form has come to embrace form and matter, just as content is their determinate substrate. In this manner content has in fact withdrawn into its ground, by being the identical element in form and matter that is indifferent to their external determinations. The self-identity of content is not only that unity indifferent to its form; it is also its *essential* form, and thus the identity of a ground relation.[146] Nevertheless, content remains distinct from its ground. Being "determinate in its own self...content is the essential identity of ground with itself in its positedness...[and also] the posited identity over against the ground relation."[147] The immediate determinacy of the content is precisely the negative relation of the form to itself. Ground is therefore a *formal* mediation, since here it "relates itself negatively to itself and makes itself into a positedness."[148] The determinate content is posited both as ground and as the grounded, all the time indifferent to this two-fold form, and in both cases, only one determination.[149] Thus form and content are no longer really distinguishable, since now "*there is nothing in the ground that is not in the grounded, and there is nothing in the grounded that is not in the ground.*"[150] The ground has become the exact same content, once as something posited, and again as an essentiality, determinate being reflected-into-self.[151]

This process of self-development from *form* and *content* through *formal ground* acquires spiritual reality with the emergence of living labor as a simple means to capital's self-valorization. When abstract labor time provides the posited unity of capital's simple division as a relation of matter and form, this content also stands outside the form of this entire process. Although abstract labor time is the identical content in both the specific values of the elements of production and the product, and the whole equation grasped in its total aggregate of specified value, it also is indifferent to the external determinations that characterize each of these moments as elements of production, product, and capital (as embracing their process). As something distinct, abstract labor time is the essential identity of capital with itself in its posited relation as an equation of specific created values, and also is itself a posited identity over against this entire process of valorization.

In this way, the immediate existence of this content is actually the negative self-relation of abstract labor time as essential form. The relation of abstract labor time has now developed into a subjective movement that becomes by being submerged in its own determinations as process in the service of capital's self-valorization. Labor is here a value-creating activity by informing already existent elements of abstract labor time with capital's movement of created value. As Marx writes, "living labor is no more than a means to imbue existing value with value; in other words, to make it into capital...this process appears as that of the auto-valorization of capital."[152] Abstract labor time actively communes with itself as capital's own forceful self-relation that throws itself forward as a production of specifically created value. As materialized social labor that conserves itself and grows by absorbing living labor, capital has become value creating value, itself in movement.[153]

The content of the elements of production, abstract labor time, now engages in active opposition to them, acquiring living vitality as labor that conserves and reproduces their value by its simple *act.* The former labor time embodied by the raw materials and instrument of labor is replaced and preserved in the product and the instrument of production that remain at the process' end, not by the expenditure of the labor, but rather through *capital's* self-identity, which is *only* activated by labor's appearance as an active abstract labor time. Labor itself establishes its own value upon the abstract labor time that it has expended in realizing itself, and this value is swallowed up as well into the created product that completes capital's self-affirmation. The process of living labor as simple means of the process of valorization is a motion that is both the foundation of capital and its own creation. It is no longer possible to distinguish capital's existence as elements of value in process and the unity of this movement itself. Living labor's activization of created value as value that creates value is capital in its posited development, as well as in its essential form.

This is the tautological relation of formal ground. Here ground is the same determination of content, once as something posited, and again as essentiality, determinate being reflected-into-itself. Nevertheless, since this simple determinacy of the content does not contain the form of the ground relation within itself, and is indifferent to it, it is external to this form, and distinct from it.[154] The ground and the grounded are both in *their specific character* the identity of the whole with itself, and these immediate, self-identical determinations constitute the difference within the form of the relation. Because of this utter simplicity of their difference, the unity of the ground and the grounded is an empty, countentless relation—"a *one* or a *something* as an external combination of them."[155]

Here, formal ground has passed over into the relation of real ground. This determinacy is two-fold. First, the content of the relation is in continuity with itself in the positedness that renders it the simple identical element of ground and the grounded. Secondly, this relation comprises the additional determination of an unessential form, that is free from the ground and is an immediate manifoldness.[156] This latter element, the non-ground aspect of the relation, is "an external bond which does not contain the unessential manifold content as *posited*; it is therefore likewise only a *substrate*."[157] Thus the immediate identity of ground and the grounded, and the something which relates their distinct content, is the emergence of two different substrates. They in turn present a new relation of an external ground which is related to an immediate content that it has not posited, but whose diversified determinations it does bring into combination, determining "which is ground and which is posited by the ground."[158]

Thus real ground has withdrawn into *another* ground, making itself a positedness. This new ground is the complete ground, which is identical with the real ground that it now is grounding. This "new ground into which that merely posited, external 'togetherness' has sublated itself is, as its reflection-into-self, the *absolute relation* of the two determinations of the content."[159]

This process of pure specification becomes capital's self-development through the emergence of the production process as a creation of a surplus value contained in the resultant product.

The coincidence of ground and grounded in living labor's informing of materialized abstract labor time as value that creates new value is a determinacy of content that is really external to the form of this whole relation. Living labor's process and capital's auto-valorization are the immediate self-identical determinations that, as such, make up the empty difference in their identity as ground and grounded. The thing that combines them in their diversity is simply the surplus value to be found through the created product. Both elements, living labor's process and capital's auto-valorization, are in continuity with themselves in this posited value that *is* their additional specification whose immediate particular measure is first unrelated to the ground. This indifference leaves surplus value merely a bare substrate of the relation of labor's expenditure as capital's means of valorization. However, this leaves both the realization of labor and surplus value as different contents related to a ground which has not posited them, but does bring their specifications into a combination in which the surplus value is now posited by the expenditure of labor.

This new ground is the restoration of the immediate labor process, here incorporated in capital's determinate auto-valorization. Here are joined the two aspects of the entire movement of production, grasped in their immediate unity: on the one hand, the simple process of production in which the activity of labor conserved the use-value quality of past labor by transforming the material substance of the passive capital facing it, and giving it a new form; on the other hand, the process of valorization which has just emerged when capital's identification with itself through the absorption of living labor had conserved the quantity of objectified abstract labor time found in its elements of production.

The contrasting unity of these two moments reveals that the newly created product contains a specific surplus value, whose quantitative determination derives from the difference between the exchange value that capital has paid to the worker for his labor-power, and the exchange value that the abstract labor time of his work has realized. The relation of living labor to surplus value is now concretely posed in this determinacy of complete ground. The identity contained in this contrast of the two aspects of capital's process of production completes the self-development of the so-called "Labor Theory of Value."

## Notes

1. Lenin, *Collected Works*, Vol. 38: *Philosophical Notebooks* (Moscow: Foreign Languages Publishing House, 1963), p. 180.

2. For a critical analysis of these conceptions, see Chapter 10 of this volume.

3. For a discussion of this systematic relation of the *Phenomenology* and the beginning of the *Logic*, see Kenley Dove, "Hegel's 'Deduction of the Concept of Science'," *Boston Studies in the Philosophy of Science*, Vol. 23.

4. Thus, the Hegelian Dialectic moves by rejecting the Frankfurt School's empty subjective Negative Dialectic of external reflection. Again, the *Phenomenology* accomplishes the job better than Adorno, Horkheimer *et al.*, by characterizing them as that shape of consciousness described under the heading: "The law of the heart, and the frenzy of self-conceit."

5. For this reason, Bloch's and Lukács' characterization of Hegel as a philosopher of the Subject-Object Identity is false. See Bloch, *Subjekt-Objekt* (Frankfurt am Main: Suhrkamp Verlag, 1962); and Lukács, *Der junge Hegel* (Neuwied and Berlin: Luchterhand Verlag, 1967).

6. "But the *I* is, *first*, this pure self-related unity, and it is not immediately but only as making abstraction from all determinateness and content and withdrawing into the freedom of unrestricted equality with itself. As such it is *universality*;....Secondly, the *I* as self-related negativity is no less immediately *individuality* or is *absolutely determined*, opposing itself to all that is other and excluding it—*individual personality*." Hegel, *Science of Logic*, trans. by A. V. Miller (New York: Humanities Press, 1969), p. 583. This point has been developed by Dieter Henrich in *Hegel im Kontext* (Frankfurt am Main: Suhrkamp, 1971), p. 97, and by Jürgen Habermas in *Theory and Practice*, (Boston: Beacon Press, 1973), pp. 145–146.

7. Hegel, *The Phenomenology of Mind* (New York: Harper and Row, 1967), p. 231. It must be noted that this description of the concept of recognition is not itself part of the argument of the *Phenomenology*, which considers reciprocal recognition not as it is *per se*, but only as it appears *for consciousness*. Thus, within the shape

of consciousness of Master and Slave the problem is described in these terms: "This pure conception of recognition, of duplication of self-consciousness within its unity, we must now consider in the way its process appears for self-consciousness." *Ibid.*, p. 231.

8. "That something also has *within it* the same character that it is *in itself*, and, conversely, that what it is as being-for-other it also is in itself—this is the identity of being-in-itself and being-for-other....This identity is already formally given in the sphere of determinate being, but more expressly in the consideration of the Idea as the unity of the Notion and *actuality*." Hegel, *Science of Logic*, p. 120. "Because being that is in and for itself is immediately a *positedness*, the Notion in its simple self-relation is an absolute *determinateness*...thus the Notion is the *individual*." *Ibid.*, p. 582.

9. In *Hegel im Kontext*, Dieter Henrich develops this point (pp. 102–103) only to contradict it, by discussing the thematization of double negation in a particular set of determinations of the Logic of Essence as an *externally* applicable *metalogic* for the *Logic* as a whole.

10. Hegel, *Science of Logic*, p. 829.

11. *Ibid.*, p. 838.

12. *Ibid.*

13. See "Zur Wesenslogik der Marxschen Warenanalyse" in Hans-Jürgen Krahl, *Konstitution und Klassenkampf*, (Frankfurt am Main: Verlag Neue Kritik, 1971), and Helmut Reichelt, *Zur logischen Struktur des Kapitalbegriffs bei Karl Marx*, (Frankfurt am Main: Europaische Verlagsanstalt, 1970).

14. See Henrich, *Hegel im Kontext*, pp. 164–165.

15. "...a Notion is first, in its own self, *the* Notion, and this is only one and is the substantial foundation; secondly, a Notion is *determinate* and it is this determinateness in it which appears as content: but the determinateness of the Notion is a specific form of this substantial oneness, a moment of the form as totality, *of that same Notion* which is the foundation of the specific Notion." Hegel, *Science of Logic*, p. 39.

16. *Ibid.*, p. 586.

17. *Ibid.*, p. 58.

18. Hegel, *The Logic* from the *Encyclopedia of the Philosophical Sciences* (London: Oxford University Press, 1968), p. 187.

19. See paragraphs 189–208 of Hegel's *Philosophy of Right*.

20. Hegel, *Werke*, Vol. 8: *Enzyklopädie der philosophischen Wissenschaften* (Frankfurt am Main: Suhrkamp Verlag, 1970), paragraph 99, p. 209.

21. Hegel, *Werke*, Vol. 7: *Grundlinien der Philosophie des Rechts* (Frankfurt am Main: Suhrkamp Verlag, 1970), pp. 135–136.

22. Hegel, *Werke*, Vol. 5, p. 212.

23. *Ibid.*, p. 228.

24. Hegel, *Werke*, Vol. 7, p. 137.

25. *Ibid.*, pp. 159–160.

26. *Ibid.*, paragraph 77, p. 160.

27. *Marx-Engels Werke* (MEW), Vol. 23: *Das Kapital—Erster Band* (Berlin: Dietz Verlag, 1972), p. 70.

28. *Ibid.*, p. 75.

29. Hegel, *Werke*, Vol. 5, p. 251.

30. *Ibid.*, p. 235.

31. MEW, Vol 23, p. 51.

32. Hegel, *Werke*, Vol. 5, p. 251.

33. *Ibid.*, pp. 252–253.

34. MEW, Vol. 23, p. 76.

35. Hegel, *Werke*, Vol. 8, p. 216.

36. *Ibid.*, p. 218.

37. Hegel, *Werke*, Vol. 5, p. 253.

38. MEW, Vol. 23, p. 80.

39. *Ibid.*, p. 78.

40. *Ibid.*

41. Hegel, *Werke*, Vol. 8, p. 228.

42. Hegel, *Werke*, Vol. 5, p. 254.

43. *Ibid.*, pp. 254–255.

44. *Ibid.*, p. 259.

45. *Ibid.*, p. 260.

46. Hegel, *Werke*, Vol. 8, paragraph 110, p. 228.

47. Hegel, *Werke*, Vol. 5, p. 278.

48. Hegel, *Werke*, Vol. 8, paragraph 107, p. 224.

49. Hegel, *Werke*, Vol. 5, p. 395.

50. *Ibid.*, p. 398.

51. *Ibid.*

52. MEW, Vol. 23, p. 113.

53. Marx, *Grundrisse*, trans. by Martin Nicolaus (NY: Vintage Books, 1973), p. 229.

54. *Ibid.*, p. 301.

55. Hegel, *Werke*, Vol. 5, p. 399.

56. Hegel, *Werke*, Vol. 5, p. 402.

57. *Ibid.*, p. 403.

58. Marx, *Grundrisse*, p. 212.

59. *Ibid.*, p. 260.

60. MEW, Vol. 23, p. 125.

61. *Ibid.*, p. 126.

62. Hegel, *Werke*, Vol. 5, p. 403.

63. *Ibid.*, p. 409.

64. *Ibid.*, p. 412.

65. *Ibid.*, p. 416.

66. *Ibid.*, p. 413.

67. *Ibid.*, p. 417.

68. MEW, Vol. 23, p. 143.

69. *Ibid.*, p. 417.

70. *Ibid.*, p. 419.

71. *Ibid.*, p. 436.

72. Marx, *Grundrisse*, p. 331.

73. MEW, Vol. 23, p. 168.

74. Hegel, *Werke*, Vol. 5, p. 436.

75. *Ibid.*

76. *Ibid.*, p. 442.

77. *Ibid.*, pp. 443–444.

78. *Ibid.*, p. 444.

79. *Ibid.*

80. MEW, Vol. 23, p. 169.

81. Hegel, *Werke*, Vol. 5, p. 445.

82. Marx, *Grundrisse*, p. 235.

83. Hegel, *Werke*, Vol. 5, p. 456.

84. Marx, *Grundrisse*, p. 262.

85. *Ibid.*, p. 261.

86. Hegel, *Werke*, Vol. 6, p. 15.

87. *Ibid.*

88. Marx, *Grundrisse*, pp. 332–333.

89. *Ibid.*, p. 262.

90. *Ibid.*, p. 296.

91. *Ibid.*

92. Hegel, *Werke*, Vol. 6, p. 19.

93. *Ibid.*

94. *Ibid.*, p. 22.

95. *Ibid.*

96. *Ibid.*

97. Marx, *Grundrisse*, p. 296.

98. *Ibid.*, p. 274.

99. *Ibid.*, p. 303.

100. Hegel, *Werke*, Vol. 6, pp. 26–27.

101. Marx, *Grundrisse*, p. 289.

102. *Ibid.*, p. 296.

103. *Ibid.*, p. 306.

104. *Ibid.*, pp. 301–302.

105. Hegel, *Werke*, Vol. 6, pp. 28–29.

106. *Ibid.*, p. 29.

107. *Ibid.*, p. 33.

108. *Ibid.*, p. 35.

109. *Ibid.*

110. *Ibid.*, pp. 38–39.

111. Marx, *Grundrisse*, pp. 310–311.

112. *Ibid.*, p. 209.

113. *Ibid.*, p. 302.

114. *Ibid.*, p. 298.

115. *Ibid.*, p. 303.

116. Hegel, *Werke*, Vol. 6, p. 39.

117. *Ibid.*, p. 40.

118. *Ibid.*, p. 44.

119. *Ibid.*, p. 46.

120. *Ibid.*, p. 48.

121. Marx, *Grundrisse*, p. 298.

122. *Ibid.*

123. *Ibid.*, pp. 298–299.

124. Hegel, *Werke*, Vol. 6, p. 51.

125. *Ibid.*, p. 52.

126. *Ibid.*, p. 57.

127. *Ibid.*

128. *Ibid.*, pp. 66–67.

129. *Ibid.*, p. 67.

130. *Ibid.*, p. 68.

131. Marx, *Grundrisse*, p. 316.

132. *Ibid.*, p. 311.

133. Hegel, *Werke*, Vol. 6, p. 80.

134. *Ibid.*, p. 82.

135. *Ibid.*, p. 84.

136. *Ibid.*, p. 85.

137. *Ibid.*, p. 86.

138. *Ibid.*, p. 87.

139. *Ibid.*, p. 88.

140. Marx, *Grundrisse*, p. 315.

141. *Ibid.*, p. 314.

142. Hegel, *Werke*, Vol. 6, p. 90.

143. *Ibid.*, pp. 91–92.

144. *Ibid.*, p. 92.

145. *Ibid.*, p. 94.

146. *Ibid.*, p. 94.

147. *Ibid.*, p. 95.

148. *Ibid.*, p. 96.

149. *Ibid.*, p. 97.

150. *Ibid.*

151. *Ibid.*

152. Marx, *Un Chapitre Inédit du Capital*, unpublished in German original, Trans. by Roger Dangeville (Paris: Union Générale D'Éditions, 1971), p. 139.

153. *Ibid.*

154. Hegel, *Werke*, Vol. 6, p. 98.

155. *Ibid.*, p. 103.

156. *Ibid.*, p. 104.

157. *Ibid.*

158. *Ibid.*, p. 105.

159. *Ibid.*, pp. 109–110.

# 13

# The Social Determination of the Labor Process from Hegel to Marx

If two centuries of war and revolution have given catastrophic testimony to the practical problem of constituting the social domain of economic life, the corresponding theoretical problem of conceiving need and labor in social terms has proven to be no more facile. Leaving aside the shortcomings of the proposed resolutions, one finds that of the three principal social philosophies, the *polis* conception of classical Greece, contractarianism, and the theory of Interaction established by Hegel, only the last has even allowed the question to arise.

What has made production so problematic a theme for social theory is the twofold difficulty of excluding all presocietal relations from economic life, and having social bonds accommodate the seemingly inscrutable particularity of need and its attention provisioning.

On the one hand, if production is not to be cast outside social existence proper, it must somehow avoid being reduced to either a natural metabolism between man and the physical world or a sphere of technique, where theoretical reason subjugates natural objectivity on casual terms.

On the other hand, if production is to have an eminently social reality, then society must itself be so conceived as to encompass interrelations of individuals with respect to their own particular neediness.

Lacking the categorial means to accomplish either of these specifications, the best representatives of both classical Greek philosophy and contractarianism have simply had to exclude production from their practical sciences.

For Plato and Aristotle the ethical life of the *polis* begins precisely where concern with need and work ends.[1] Those activities dealing with particular satisfactions and productions are either relegated to slaves incapable of aspiring to the self-sufficiency of the citizen, or to that array of artisan pursuits which oversteps the natural limits of the *oikos* to become a material presupposition of city life that is yet excluded from the ways of *praxis*. The polity cannot incorporate these functions within the emphatically social dimension of its good life because *chrematistic*, whether in its household boundary or in its unnatural measurelessness at the interstices of the *polis*, contains an irreducible reference to particular ends. The ethical unity of the *polis* rather realizes itself in a governed *paideia*, where the social individual comes to determine himself only in so far as he assumes a definite character of virtuous conduct that is already found within the city. Any subjective activity that independently *creates* the determinacy of its own end, whether as a free willing or as a self-seeking private pursuit, is in principle incompatible with the substantial life of the city.

Plato explicitly recognizes this contradiction, and constructs his ideal *polis* in conscious opposition to all manifestations of a self-determining particular agency. He leaves behind the limited pursuits of the City of Pigs to instead conceive a political unity banning every conceivable womb of private endeavor. Aristotle, on the other hand, preserves mention of the *oikos*, by distinguishing the utterly "non-economic" *praxis* of household management from the asocial *poiēsis* of slave work, just as he indicates the material existence of monetary exchange and craft industry only to distinguish these from the essential felicitous conduct of the citizenry. In both cases, the principle of social life remains the actual self-informing bond of the *polis*, which grounds itself by realizing a naturally determined objectivity whose element is the citizen of definite character. Although Plato and Aristotle have conceived a genuinely concrete social reality, its specific individuation cannot comprehend the independent particularity required for the social determination of production.

Contractarian theory, on the other hand, grounds social relations in the structure of autonomous self-consciousness that Plato had begun to recognize as the very principle spelling dissolution for the substantial bond of the *polis*. Kant brings the contractarian tradition to its fruition by first purging its self-determining subject of all psychological, anthropological, and otherwise naturally determined content, and then providing a framework where all specifications are to be systematically engendered through the ego. The practical dimension here emerges as the positing of the individual free will that has its own self for its content. Because this autonomy is immediately taken as an absolute starting point, with objective reality falling beside it as a limit yet to be overcome, the self-determination of the practical subject remains an inherently *formal* application of a categorical imperative. Such moral striving forever seeks a recognizable actuality for its own activity within a hypothetically construed civil order. This regulative society's sole activity is to legislate the coexistence of individual wills once it has itself emerged through their mutual contract. Because such social life has no other content than the empty abstract identity of individual willing, all reference to the particularity of need and its satisfaction falls outside the relations of free selves to one another. As Kant himself explicitly indicates, the activity of work must here be conceived as a technical process, expressing a causal domination of natural objects in response to man's empirically conditioned side. Accordingly all economic action is essentially indifferent to social life, and merely embodies a monological application of the laws of theoretical reason.[2]

Needless to say, it is on this formal basis that economics has developed as a modern "social" science, constructing models for the technical allocation of scarce resources in relation to psychologically determined needs. This effective refusal to conceive production in social terms may indeed be a prevalent orthodoxy, but it is hardly a final disposal of the problem.

For when the two systematic exclusions of production from social philosophy are examined together, the means for superseding their complementary refusals are at least indicated. One sees that whereas in the classical Greek conception the naturally determined concrete association of the *polis* can not contain the independence of particular subjectivity, the free individual willing of the contractarian inquiry is unable on its part to ground a social order with a real particular content—that other prerequisite for socially specifying the heteronomy of need and its satisfaction. To rise above each respective one-sidedness would seem to demand eliminating their mutual opposition and somehow integrating their two principles. What is thus required is nothing other than a process uniting the determinate social reality given a natural embodiment in the *polis* with the self-determining individuality immediately given in the egologically developed free practical subjectivity.

The theoretical resolution of this task is first posed by Hegel in his concept of Objective Spirit, which receives its most complete development as the entire subject matter of the *Philosophy of Right*. According to this notion, the social dimension is a totality of interaction, or, to use Hegel's expression, the Idea of the will, freedom that realizes itself in constituting an existing world of interrelated subjects.[3] This is not the willing of an individual autonomy beset with opposition to natural desire and an externally given objectivity, nor the concrete rule of a naturally defined *polis*, but rather the reality of an irreducibly *intersubjective* willing where a plurality of individuals objectively determine themselves in and through mutually constitutive relations to one another. Instead of postulating self-consciousness in its immediate opposition to otherness, Objective Spirit presents a reciprocal individuation that already constitutes the objective practical structures facing its recognized subjects. Therefore they relate not to a natural world, but to a realm of Interaction of which they themselves are the appearing elements. Consequently, Interaction signifies social substance that is individuality and its arena, an arena entirely comprised of willed bonds of mutual recognition stricken of all predetermined, natural character.

In this framework of Objective Spirit, the most rudimentary structure of social reality is that interrelationship where the existing medium of reciprocity and its individuated subjectivity are least determinate. This is the utterly *abstract* right of a plurality of subjects who relate to each other simply as *persons*, as freely willing agents with no other distinguishing mark than the external medium embodying each of their wills in a respected individual realization. This medium, however, is itself just some thing or other whose only socially constitutive determinacy is that it *is* the receptacle of their recognized willing. With all its given, natural concreteness reduced to the mere matter of an intersubjective *determinable*, this entity is what Hegel calls the *factor*,[4] *die Sache*, the generic objectivity wholly informed by Interaction.

As such, it allows for an actual plurality to freely interact through a real, yet purely social object. Nevertheless, the elemental immediacy of the factor just as much impels Interaction to advance beyond the bare form of Abstract Right. For if Interaction is to become the actual reciprocity that builds the complete content of a social world, it cannot remain limited to the all too indeterminate interrelation of *persons* through the factor. On the one hand, the factor must cease to be a mere intersubjective *determinable* and instead develop into *all* objectivity that is finally determined within Interaction. On the other hand, the individuality constituted in reciprocity must lose the bare abstractness of Personhood and acquire the greatest concreteness containable by a particular subject.

What the entire argument of the *Philosophy of Right* attempts to demonstrate is that Interaction does indeed come to constitute the social totality by developing itself into the successive shapes of Abstract Right, Morality, the Family, Civil Society, the State, International Relations, and finally World History. These do not comprise different modes of consciousness in their apprehension of "social" values, but a series of universal forms of interrelation, each constituting a characteristic individuality within its particular structure of reciprocity.

Whereas Interaction begins with the ideterminacy of Abstract Right, where *persons* recognize each other as single free wills through the factor of their immediate *property*, Morality supplants this external receptacle with the medium of the recognized inwardness of individuals who accordingly interact as *moral subjects*. In the family the *personality* of the *family member* arises in a concrete interrelation operating through the factors of birth, sexuality, and love. With the immanent dispersal of the family unity, Interaction further comprises the constitutive arena of *private* individuality, a Civil Society of self-seeking, yet interdependent *bourgeois*. In the state Interaction steps beyond the relativity of civil association to become a body politic that is an end in itself, having *citizens* as its mutually individuated actors. However, because even the state can have its own *determinate* individuality only in the context of a plurality, Interaction impels itself beyond political sovereignty to entail the field of international relations where *individuated states* interact through the recurrent procession of mutual treaty and war. Finally, the endemic immediacy of this reciprocity is superseded by the interaction of World History, where the interrelation of particular social totalities becomes a universal self-determining succession of *individual epochs*. This process brings the practical dimension to its farthest reach by realizing the self-generation of an Interaction so universal that it incorporates the entire content of practical life.

Here in the sweep of epochs that Hegel outlines, historical realms progressively purge themselves of natural, predetermined relations until the point is reached where nothing is left that has not been constituted through bonds of recognition. Consequently, the development of successive social systems does not remain the progress of a *particular* people and tradition existing over and against some foreign, ahistorical residue. History rather makes itself world encompassing, "westernizing," desacralizing, revolutionizing all that stands in the way of the establishment of a practical realm wholly comprised by Interaction. As Hegel asserts, it is the modern world that finally gives objective legitimacy to *all* the determinations of the idea,[5] bringing the totality of Interaction to the light of day.

Although History thus comes to universally realize the entire breadth of interaction, it is within the specific sphere of Civil Society that the social determination of production actually emerges as a theme. Here in the constitutive arena of the bourgeois, society differentiates itself into the particular subjectivity whose self-seeking individuality no less resolves itself into the bond of an existing social interdependence. What Hobbes portrayed as the *bellum omnium in omnes* is here no natural condition, but the particular structure of interaction where the bourgeois proceeds from his or her own self interest only to find that its realization requires a reciprocal engagement with other private individuals. In this context of interrelated private pursuit Hegel develops the social reality of economic life as a System of Needs building the rudimentary foundation of Civil Society.

Because the determinacy of World History incorporates far more than the internal structure of Civil Society, the social determinations of production are not historical categories, but relations of economic interaction per se. Nevertheless, since World History presumably culminates in the generation of a world embodying nothing but the pure structures of Interaction, the social determination of production would accordingly emerge historically as a constitutive sphere of *modern* society. This, of course, is precisely what Marx suggests, when he notes that the categories of economic life first actually come to exist in their universality within the capitalist epoch, where not only labor exists as such, but all the determinations of production are realized independently of the natural limits that had previously obscured their essential social form.[6]

Thus neither presupposing history nor making historical claims, Hegel systematically formulates the System of Needs by solely considering how need and its satisfaction can irreducibly involve social relations. Starting with Civil Society's most elementary and indeterminate structure of private pursuit *qua* relation to other, Hegel recognizes that this interrelated self-seeking must be of such a character that although its aim derives entirely from personal preference, the means of its fulfillment are necessarily outside the bourgeois' own private sphere and only to be had through others.

The great insight of Hegel that first allows the social determination of production to proceed is that economic *need* is precisely this immediate other-directed self-interest of the bourgeois. As such, economic need is no natural desire yearning for objects untouched by Interaction, but the social want for what is neither one's own possession nor freely available from Nature. What the bourgeois therefore *needs* are essentially *commodities*, goods expressly acquired from other private individuals whose own neediness renders them equally interdependent.

Because this specific factor of consumption is not some naturally given scarce resource, but a private possession intrinsically related to the need and will of all other bourgeois, the commodity bears use value and possession value, the respective social qualities of its universal existence for these two emblematic sides of private individuality. On this basis, as Hegel argues, the all-sided assertion of neediness necessarily develops into an interaction of commodity exchange, where goods exhibit the further social character of their universal equivalence, namely exchange value.[7]

Thus, when it becomes a matter of considering the production process as a constitutive moment of the civil community of private pursuit, Hegel correctly concludes that laboring must somehow transcend technique and produce the commodity with the full complement of its social qualities of use, possession and exchange value. In his treatment of the "Kind of Labor," however, Hegel proves unable to actually account for this social production. Although his brief remarks suggest that commodity fabrication is a private earning where labor transforms a possessed, yet naturally predetermined material into a new commodity for sale, Hegel never details how labor's particular agency can posit the social universality of value and thereby secure the livelihood of the laboring bourgeois. Consequently, Hegel's groundbreaking attempt to socially determine economic life founders at the very point where labor is first set the task of producing commodities for the interrelated neediness of the bourgeois.

Despite the genuine significance of the posed problem, only one philosopher has since addressed it and sought to establish the production process as a legitimate theme of social philosophy. This is none other than Karl Marx, whose systematic writings, the *Critique of Political Economy*, the *Grundrisse*, and *Capital*, provide the unique elaboration of the social philosophy of Interaction originally introduced by Hegel. Marx's development of the concept of capital in these works is nothing but an attempt to bring the determination of the System of Needs to its systematic completion.

The specific moment at which this general thrust reveals itself most clearly is in Marx's discussion of the immediate production process. Here, in answer to Hegel's failure, the intersubjective determination of the laboring act is again made thematic, to definitively deprive both asocial *poiēsis* and technical reason of any irreducible hold on production.

Unfortunately the one presentation of this matter that Marx himself published, Chapter VII of the first volume of *Capital*, provides no more than a bare indication of an actual argument. Here he instead relies on a collection of external reflections and natural assumptions to characterize the capitalist labor process. What one has in effect is a virtual restatement of that very reduction of social determination to given relations of Man and Nature for which Marx had long pilloried classical political economy. Instead of following out capital's emergence from the system of commodity exchange as that independent value informing the circulation of which it is no less the result, Marx follows up on the uncritical baggage that already encumbered the opening Commodity section of his work.

There he had contradicted his own basic argument with extraneous discussions asserting the presocial character of use value and need,[8] reducing the universality of labor and abstract labor time to empirical generalizations,[9] and advancing a labor theory of value based on a universal exchange between private non-capitalist producers.[10]

When Marx so claims that there is an eternal metabolism between man and nature defining need and utility prior to all interaction, it indeed follows that use value can only be a given matter unessentially related to the abstract social form of exchange value. Yet such a concept immediately abrogates the notion of social production, by conditioning the laboring activity to an end (the produced use-value and its satisfaction of need) independent of all intersubjective determination. Here Marx regresses from the theoretical advance of Hegel's System of Needs, where need and use value were already socially specified through the interaction of therein constituted private individuals.

Similarly, when Marx accounts for the universality of labor and its measure as a result of some presupposed reflection's *abstracting from* the *given* array of particular work situations, he leaves the universal dimension externally specified through the structure of an observing consciousness while the concrete empirical starting point is itself technically differentiated. At least Kant would have had the rigor to admit that such determining has excluded the labor process from the field of social philosophy.

And just so antithetical to his acknowledged project is Marx's grounding of exchange value in the "labor" of private producers. For not only does this derivation obliterate the capital-labor relationship, but it above all restricts the laboring act to the technical relation of an individual and nature within an externally given division of labor *à la* Adam Smith.

It is not hard to see how the fruit of these misconceptions serves to obfuscate and mystify *Capital's* account of the labor process.

Marx goes first awry in his positing of abstract labor power. Without further ado, he here attempts to reconcile the analytic equivalence of exchange with capital's self-expansion (*qua* M-C-M′) by simply discovering in the market the available presence of labor power, that commodity whose consumption creates additional value.[11] Such reasoning, however, is fallaciously circular. In order to characterize labor power through its *subsequent* value-producing consumption by capital, Marx must effectively presuppose the entire labor theory of value whose proper theme is none other than the labor process. Of course, that cannot *already* be legitimately referred to, since the labor theory of value's own determination of value production is first able to proceed only *after* labor power and its sale have both been specified.

When Marx nevertheless then advances upon this false basis to further specify labor power itself, he gives it a purely natural determination as that innate anthropologically defined capacity to expend human muscle power in general.[12]

This regression to presocial specification continues unabated, once capital has absorbed this completely *extrinsic* factor and somehow made it an element of its social process. For the unfolding of the labor process here proceeds as that familiar metabolism of man with nature that effectively excludes all notion of social production. Instead of maintaining the activity of labor upon its material as a self-informing of *capital*, Marx turns the actual agency into a technical formative act essentially unrelated to all social interaction.[13]

Nevertheless, he still claims that such presocial action not only posits a use value as its product (which is itself no natural given, but a social relation) but an exchange value as well.[14] Characteristically, the only way that Marx is able to introduce this reduction of value production to an anthropological assertion is by harking back to his earlier "derivation" of the labor theory of value, and letting it deliver *ex nihilo* the very relation that is here being analyzed.[15] Of course, it then becomes trivially self-evident that the value of every product is determined by the abstract labor time expended upon its production, and that the technical labor process posits value in the same manner. We are really simply left gaping before gifts of nature that bestow living labor with the capacity to both preserve value and create it anew.[16] As a result, the necessity of capital's social determining of production is removed, so that only under the *incidental*, particular *circumstance* of a sufficiently long expenditure of labor time does capital's own identity as self-expanding value result from the labor process.[17]

The upshot of this wholly inadequate conception is that here, at the very place where Marx's philosophical program should be most boldly announcing itself, the social determination of production instead has the ground knocked right out from under it. Without a doubt, the confusion infesting contemporary Marxist discussion has much of its root in this utter obfuscation within the heart of the cherished tome itself. For only with respect to this imperfect heritage could labor remain excluded from social philosophy and be conceived as an epistemological category, as a key to a philosophical anthropology of liberation, as an egologically informed structure of alienation and revolution, or as a formal technical notion expressed in the contrast of forces and relations of production and of base and superstructure.[18]

With the publication of the *Grundrisse*, however, the last excuse has fallen away for these misadventures in the name of Marxism. It must finally be seen that in the various recesses of this immense manuscript there lie the bases of that actual argument giving the social determination of the labor process.

Where *Capital* strays from its own program, the *Grundrisse* does not veer from the task at hand. The determinations are there to be taken, although with considerable difficulty. What makes for the great impenetrability of the *Grundrisse's* presentation is not so much the haphazard scattering of bits and pieces of the self-developing specification, as the intense technicality of Marx's language. As nowhere else in his corpus, Marx here explicitly informs his discussion with the pure process of determination of Hegel's *Science of Logic*. In order to unravel the immanent development of the labor process as it proceeds through all its transitions, it is hard to avoid a constant recourse to the argument of the *Logic*. One finds, in fact, that the *Grundrisse's* delineation precisely embodies the entire path from Essence through Complete Ground in the *Logic*.[19] Nevertheless, to indicate how such a self-development of capital *is* a social determining of labor does not require such a complete study of the inner necessity (a study for which the *Logic* is the indispensable guide). What is at issue is whether or not the entire determinacy of the immediate production process does indeed emerge through a dialectic of Interaction in radical independence from all presocial specifications.

The *Grundrisse's* argument speaks for itself:

i) Our point of departure is that moment where, according to the *Grundrisse*, the process of money-commodity-money transaction has resulted in the emergence of capital as the independent self-renewing exchange value that immediately manifests itself in and through the continuous flux of circulation. Although the self-identity of capital is thus directly apparent in the composite movement of money and commodity, there is yet a distinction in this unity. This simply consists in capital being something more than the system of commodity exchange out of which it arose and in which it maintains itself.

Given this immediate difference, however, the totality of exchange value wherein capital appears is not merely something other than the unity of capital. By preserving and perpetuating itself through the sphere of exchange while simultaneously affirming its own independence, capital effectively relegates its determinate manifestation to the status of something whose external existence has no other significance than that of being posed by capital in opposition to itself. What capital stands distinguished from is therefore an entity specifically determined as non-capital.

Through its relation Marx is able to account for the intrinsic, socially determined emergency of labor power. For as the *Grundrisse* argues, labor power is precisely what comprises this negative of capital's unity.[20] Deprived of any existence in the totality of exchange value, it is the non-being of independent value that is just as much the very beyond through which capital is able to posit itself as universal wealth. The same totality and abstraction of individual exchange value contained in capital's self-identity here has its purely negative, subjective reflection.[21] "As the existing *not-value*,"[22] labor power is thus not some anthropological endowment to exert formative action, but rather the purely formal capacity to realize nothing other than capital in its self-valorization.[23] Accordingly, one cannot even speak of labor power without reference to the interactive process of capital.

ii) As is evident, labor power here has its constitutive nullity not simply by itself, but by being opposite capital. Labor power only is the mere potentiality of exchange value in which capital asserts itself as universal wealth *because* capital has posited it as the non-being of itself. The pure subjectivity of labor power *is* only as capital's own "*living source* of value,"[24] just as capital *is* only as self-mediated through its negation, labor power.

As a consequence of this affirmative specification, labor power ceases to be just the non-being of capital, and instead assumes the character of the pure use value generically facing capital as that through which capital secures its own constitutive self-expansion. Accordingly, as the *Grundrisse* argues, capital must now bring such labor power *back* into relation with itself in order to assert itself *as* capital.[25]

iii) Having engendered labor power exclusively in terms of the interactive process of capital, the argument of the *Grundrisse* now proceeds to socially determine the very individuation of worker and capitalist in their relation of free contract. Marx has shown how capital has come to relate to labor power as its own pure use value, and thereby achieve realization. However, in so far as this confrontation is equally labor power's *own* affirming relation to capital, what capital here faces is not just some use value immediately opposing it, but an entity comprising the very *presupposition* of capital's own development.

Labor power thus opposes capital as an independent other, determined in its own right. Here is the proper immanent emergence of the worker, socially constituted as a private individual existing for himself, able to present his capacity to realize capital as an exchangeable commodity,[26] yet stripped of any other objectivity constitutive of the capital facing him.[27] As such, this social individuation refers to no anthropological or egological parameters, but only to labor power as independent, yet intrinsically facing capital.

On its own side, capital stands as value existing independently, facing the free laborer as the specifically correlative economic agent, the capitalist.

Taken together, both parties oppose one another such that their confrontation is something external to each other's autonomous identity. Accordingly, the labor power of the worker is a use value for himself not as the essential element of capital's self-realization, but as an exchange value pure and simple. Conversely, labor power has an exchange value for the capitalist only because it *is* pure use value in its relation *with* capital.[28]

Nevertheless, the root of these two immediate relations to self extends beyond each, for it is capital's presupposing of labor power that first establishes the Interaction making them possible. This becomes actually manifest in capital's opposition to labor power as an equivalent exchange value whose sole determination is that its value be sufficient to purchase labor power as a commodity from its autonomous bearer. Unlike *Capital*, the *Grundrisse* thus does not indulge in the circular reasoning that introduces abstract labor time as a measure for the value of labor power ever before value production has itself been specified.[29] Instead of making that unsystematic claim, Marx here recognizes that simply the mutually agreed equivalence of labor power and capital is explicitly posited. What results is nothing other than an immanently developed free exchange between worker and capitalist. Through this, the former external relation between capital and labor power is superseded by an internal connection.

The opposition of worker and capitalist has here revealed itself to be actually a correlative relation establishing their very character. For not only has capital presupposed the worker-capitalist distinction in its appearance as the equivalent exchange value of labor power, but so have the protagonists had their own characteristic roles for themselves only in so far as they met and recognized each other in a free exchange of labor power. As a result, what was the immediate confrontation of capital and non-capital has now become a contrast explicitly mediated by capital itself. With the exchange of labor power, capital has effectively shown itself to have really established the generic individualities of worker and capitalist as well as their constitutive relation of commodity exchange. Whereas in *Capital* Marx tended simply to *find* available subjects in the market to qualify as the necessary protagonists, here in the *Grundrisse*, he reveals the actual *emergence* of the specific economic agencies that stand opposed as worker and capitalist within the self-distinguishing interactive structure of capital.

With the execution of this social relation, the completion of the sale of labor power, the actual labor process begins.

iv) Marx now proceeds to develop the activity of labor as an inner working of *capital*. The worker-capitalist exchange has left capital an encompassing whole into which the externality of labor power and the relation to the worker have collapsed and been absorbed.[30]

With this internalization, capital has effectively divided itself according to its valorizing form and value content, embodying each element *as well* as their relation.[31] As the *Grundrisse* portends, capital now generally embarks on specifying itself in function of its content as a simple labor process, and in function of its form, as a process of self-realizing value.[32]

However, although capital has here become an *inner* determining of its own substance *qua* self-positing value, it is initially just the unilateral relation where this movement takes place exclusively on the part of the newly appropriated element within capital which is not yet explicitly constituted as a mere dependent *component*. This is necessarily the case for no other reason than that capital has incorporated labor power only by absorbing it as an *activity* able to realize value's self-expansion.

Consequently, capital now stands with its substance of independent exchange value and its form of self-realization both determined as distinct elements of its content alone. In conceiving this self-specification of *capital*, the *Grundrisse* has come to introduce labor without recourse to the vagaries of *Capital*'s presocial notions of formative activity. For here an *emergent* labor is precisely what has its specific character concretely embodying capital as formal valorizing process in opposition to capital as pure passive material of this process.[33] Capital has reduced itself in its inner appearance to this lifeless object of labor, and all relation to its independent form has been masked. What development awaits now stands ready to unfold as a function of labor, where generally speaking "capital's *distinction from labour* appears only in the material character of *raw material* and *instrument of labour*. . . an abstraction which takes place within the process itself."[34] Doubling itself first, however, as merely labor and simple object of labor, capital here determines its inner workings more precisely as a self-reduction to a bare substance transformed by its own specific otherness, labor.

v) The *Grundrisse* has brought us to the threshold where the self-development of capital has become the laboring act itself. Here capital unfolds as the rudimentary process eliminating the opposition, active worker-passive object of labor by uniting the inert material of capital with labor's determining form.[35] Needless to say, this action proceeds through labor's agency not in some technical sense independent of social relations, but only *as* a specific component of capital.

The *Grundrisse* can not bother with that familiar metabolism of man and nature, either, for here labor processes a bare stuff that is *essentially* capital, discarding its own pure subjectivity by objectifying itself in this passive matter it impresses with new value form.[36] In so doing, labor has effectively united the otherness of its negating work with the underlying identity of capital embodied in the inert object. However, since this union has occurred within labor's process, it achieves concrete existence as such only when these two aspects actually emerge as distinct objective relations within the unitary movement of labor's activity.

vi) On the basis of this intended development, the *Grundrisse* comes to develop an essentially social determination of the raw material and instrument of labor. For as Marx argues, here the laboring activity constitutes itself on the one hand by impressing raw materials with the form of labor so that labor's finality as a reaffirmation of capital attains an objective presence. On the other hand, the labor process simultaneously proceeds in the contrasting act where labor's own agency is embodied in an instrument of labor determined as "the objective means which subjective activity inserts between itself as an object, as its conductor."[37] Within the unity realized by the labor process as a whole, these two components distinguish themselves by positing the raw material as that substance consumed by labor and the instrument of labor as that substance consuming the pure subjectivity of labor itself. With respect to the raw material, labor affirms its subjective character by negating the passive formlessness of its object, whereas through its instrument, labor relates negatively to itself, passing over its own activity to this tool.

In each case, however, labor's self-assertion is actually the mutually eliminative unity of both. For the independent character of these two co-existent sides of labor is such that their different agencies cancel their respective distinctiveness by consuming their very own existence.[38] Although labor certainly contains both these aspects in transforming the raw material through its instrument, each of them actually exists as a concomitant element of a single process absorbing them both.

Indeed, the working upon the raw material proceeds only in so far as its opposite, the working through the instrument of labor, *is*, just as this latter agency *is* only in so far as the former *is*.[39] Nevertheless, at the very same time each distinct agency thus manifests itself by helping absorb and eliminate the other relation. Labor's informing of the raw material is actual only through the consuming use of its relation to the instrument of labor, just as this latter operation can proceed only with the completion of the raw material's transformation.

The real unity of these coincident assertions thus constitutes a production process that impels itself beyond labor and the dual objective forms of its expenditure. For here the laboring activity has led its own contrasting components to vanish in an identity that annihilates their independent determinations.

vii) This resulting identity is none other than the product of the labor process, thrust forward by labor's self-annulling engagement. The transforming of the raw material through the instrument of labor has collapsed into this result, which immediately incorporates both the given form impressed by labor and the substance materializing labor itself. Although what has been produced thus stands as a material object, it is yet no empty thing. For the *Grundrisse* has already led us beyond all traces of egological formative action and its technique. The product is not the receptacle of an individual act, but the concrete commodity realization of a socially determined process. As this social factor, the created object has emerged as nothing less than capital's reinstatement of itself as an active unity, explicitly restored as the abiding positor of its own inner working by the produced use value that is result and sublation of the labor process. As Marx notes, the elements of the laboring activity have thereby had their existence consumed as capital's own inner reduction to a pure content animated by labor's independent form. Furthermore, now that labor's agency has thus been revealed to be a mere component of capital, their use value is no less *redetermined* as substance of capital's self-subsistent exchange value.[40]

The argument of the *Grundrisse* now reaches the point where the labor process resolves itself into value production. Avoiding the shallow artifice of the "transition" from Section 1 to Section 2 of Chapter VII in *Capital*, Marx has here established capital's own immanent development out of its inner working as an activity of labor into an inner life visibly animated by capital's own agency.

viii) The apparent independence of the laboring activity has been shown to be illusory, and labor has been explicitly relegated as a component of capital. Accordingly, the product now stands as the accomplished supersession of the labor process that equally presupposes capital's *self*—valorization. On its part, capital here presents itself in distinction from the mere *positedness* of the created use value as the reaffirmed independent self-expanding value. However, because capital has reemerged as value subject by so consuming labor, capital's persisting value substance is nevertheless comprised of nothing other than the material result of the labor process, namely the castoff instrument of labor and the product.

Consequently, what was the passage of the concrete factors of the labor process into the created use value and discarded means has here become the vehicle of capital's self-assertion as independent value. Instead of remaining materially distinguished through labor's process, these elements now have their specific character as values differentiated in terms of capital's self—valorization.

Thus, as the *Grundrisse* rightly indicates,[41] capital's inner diremption into object, instrument, and labor has impelled itself into a simple division of capital's given value into distinct portions. As such, these redetermined value quanta stand differentiated only in terms of their diverse value magnitudes. Accordingly, labor here has its distinguishing mark through the measure of the previously established exchange value of labor power, whereas the former object and instrument of labor have their distinguishing magnitudes on the basis of the given exchange values they incorporated as separate parts of capital's original value.

Although the respective proportions between these predetermined value quanta are arbitrary, their aggregate value is equal to that of the product and discarded instrument in so far as these two totals comprise the two sides of capital's abiding identification with itself as the self-same autonomous value. Accordingly, the factors of the labor process and their results stand together merely as given quantities of value within a tautological unity.

By immediately decomposing itself into such unrelated value quanta so as to assert its own identity, capital here becomes no more than the bare substrate of a rote addition. As the *Grundrisse* observes, capital now stands as nothing but the presupposed value that becomes its own result in an utterly unchanged form.[42] For as Marx writes, "The only process as regards value, [is] that it sometimes appears as a whole, unity; then as a division of this unity into certain amounts; finally as sum."[43]

ix) However, the emergent inner working of capital's valorization can not remain this mute addition of indifferent measures. Once capital has achieved self-identity through the value equivalance of the factors and results of production, it has posited itself as the universal value that returns to itself without being bound to the particular limit of its given value. Accordingly, capital's reaffirmed value necessarily poses its own augmentation in just the same manner as the resultant universality of M-C-M exchange gave rise to the further social realization of M-C-M′ exchange.

Thus, no sooner is capital's value summation achieved, than the aggregate value of the product and discarded instrument becomes determined as a greater magnitude than the total given exchange values of the factors of production. Since the resulting value increment here proceeds from capital's unlimited universality as an increase per se, its actual dimension is basically unspecified.

Be this as it may, the determination of the product's exchange value is not an utterly groundless affair. For although the factors of production have had their value quanta set prior to the operation of capital's inner working, the product has its particular exchange value established only as a consequence of the specific trajectory of capital's valorization. To begin with, the created use value has first been determined as an exchange value only in and through the value equation of production. Furthermore, it has there been given its actual value measure through the sum of capital's predetermined value constituents, minus the reappearing value of the former instrument of labor, and plus the realized increment of capital's value augmentation, whose actual size will be established through the eventual sale of the product.

Thus, capital has effectively passed beyond the inactivity of its initial value differentiation now actually to posit the specific exchange value of the product, whatever it turns out to be in the product sale. As such, capital's inner working has finally become an explicit value *production*, breaking through the formality of its tautological division and addition by genuinely positing a new exchange value containing capital's added, surplus value.

x) What formerly had been labor's transformation of the object through the instrument of labor is now the value reproduction and production process constituting capital's self-expansion. Accordingly, labor's agency here becomes the value-positing act of capital's own valorizing unity.

xi) As this subordinate, yet moving force of capital's active mediation of its own inner working, labor necessarily develops under the two aspects of capital's value informing.

1) First of all, because capital's reaffirmation of its value being underpins the unity of value production, labor realizes this reassertion by preserving the predetermined exchange values of the factors of capital with which it functions. This exchange value reproduction occurs immediately and with no particular effort on labor's part. For as the *Grundrisse* correctly indicates, from the very moment value production is set in motion by labor's simple contact with its object and instrument, these factors become promptly activated as objective elements of the abiding self-equality of capital that accordingly secures the conservation of their exchange values in the resulting product and discarded instrument.[44] Thus, it is not some natural quality of labor that gives it the facility to reproduce value, as *Capital* erroneously suggests,[45] but rather labor's social determinacy as the explicit vehicle of capital's self-identity.

Under the banner of this self-preserving power of *capital*, labor's reproduction of the respective exchange values of its object and instrument further distinguishes itself only according to how the product and the discarded instrument variously incorporate these given value quanta. On the one hand, since labor's object gets completely transformed into the created use value without leaving a trace, all of its exchange value reappears in the product exchange value. On the other hand, since labor's instrument is susceptible to wear and tear from its material operation upon the object, the discarded implement will embody only what remains intact. Because whatever loss is suffered by the instrument is here redetermined in exchange value terms, the discarded means will accordingly contain less exchange value than it originally possessed. However, since the predetermined exchange value of the instrument is necessarily reproduced in any case, the value no longer within the discarded means has nowhere else to reappear than in the product. Consequently, the exchange value of the product contains this depreciated fraction of the instrument's value in addition to the entire exchange value of the object of labor.

What is not so effortlessly reproduced, however, is the predetermined exchange value of labor power. For although capital's tautological division and addition had preserved the exchange value of labor power together with that of labor's object and instrument, now that labor has assumed its active value-positing role over and against the elements of capital's given exchange value, it has lost all objectlike value substance of its own and rather has become a valueless, pure value-reproducing and producing agency. As a result, in order for the presupposed exchange value of labor power to be preserved, labor must replace it with a specific effort on its own part.

xii) 2) What effects this replacement, as well as capital's self-expansion, is the other side of value production, namely, labor's value-creating agency. Its boundary is already defined by what capital's valorizing unity encompasses over and beyond the perfunctory reproduction of the values of labor's object and instrument. In a word, all that capital's self-expanding form still leaves labor to produce are those portions of the product-value replacing labor power's predetermined exchange value and building the added value of capital's increment.

So situated and prescribed, labor now operates as the manifest activity with which capital enlivens its own predetermined value constituents in order to create new value and thereby realize the self-expansion establishing capital's unbounded universality. Because labor here proceeds in open subordination to the valorization it precipitates, the act of production no longer gets differentiated through labor's own agency *qua* the process of an object and instrument *of* labor. Now labor rather acts in a manner utterly external to itself, not only reproducing the given exchange value portions of capital through its mere contact with them, but producing new value in explicit abstraction from its own particular agency. As this manifest component, indifferent to its very own transforming act, labor posits the value sealing capital's self-expansion by virtue of nothing more than the sheer expenditure of its operation. For this reason the only constitutive content of labor's value production is the abstract labor time comprising its bare duration.

Admittedly, not even in the *Grundrisse* does Marx actually detail the foregoing social determination that has accounted for the emergence of the proper sense of abstract labor time. Nevertheless, the argument of the *Grundrisse* does not hesitate to take up this legitimate social relation without further ado. On its basis, Marx correctly recognizes that the exchange value objectified in the product now stands determined through capital's self-valorization by being no less defined by the specific measure of labor's actual duration. It follows that the expended abstract labor time here immediately translates itself into the particular exchange-value measure of the produced exchange value portion of the product, which, needless to say, both replaces the previously established exchange-value of labor power and builds the added exchange value of capital's self—expansion.

Unfortunately, instead of correctly grasping this result, Marx oversteps the limit of abstract labor time's contribution to the product-value, and restates Hegel's erroneous suggestion that labor posits the entire value of the product. In both the *Grundrisse* and *Capital* Marx repeatedly claims that the value of the product is measured by the abstract labor time expended in its own production plus that already expended producing the object of labor and the depreciated part of the instrument of labor, while the produced surplus value is measured by the difference between labor's duration and the labor time expended in "producing" the purchased labor power.[46] It should be clear, however, from the *Grundrisse's* own development of the production process wherein labor time itself gets constituted, that neither the object and instrument of labor, nor labor power itself are already determined as products, incipiently bearing objectified abstract labor time. Their exchange values have rather all been established prior to the engagement of value positing labor. Indeed, in the case of labor power, one has a commodity that can not possibly be a product, since it appears on the market not by issuing from any inner working of capital, but simply by the potential laborer deciding to offer his or her capacity to valorize capital as a commodity for sale. Marx' own tendency to consider exchange value as the phenomenal form of embodied labor contradicts the very reality of labor power, as well as that of other non-produced commodities, such as land, money and works of art, all of which bear exchange values without being products of any capital-labor relation.

Furthermore, it must be recognized that the entire foregoing exchange value production of labor is itself purely *ideal*, in that what alone *actualizes* capital's self-expansion is the subsequent sale of the product at a price sufficient to bring capital a return of an exchange value greater than that advanced in the product's manufacture. That this sale occur at all, and how much money be received, are matters determined not by what happens in the production process, but by the actual agreement of the parties to the producer-consumer exchange finalizing capital's M-C-M′ circuit. Because this market realization of the product does not automatically follow from its production, the resulting purchase price is whatever the buyer and seller freely agree to, which can of course reflect any number of factors external to production, as is the case in any commodity transaction. Indeed, it is precisely this endemic variability in both price and sales volume that makes competition possible.

Consequently, if the product sale be achieved at a price granting capital its constitutive M-C-M′ form, then and only then has the production process been a production process *of capital*, actually producing new exchange value. In that case, the *potential* value production of labor stands retroactively as a production of an actual exchange value whose measure lies determined in the price at which the product has been sold. Given, the M-C-M′ formula encompassing capital's production process, the labor time expended in producing the new commodity stands retroactively responsible for that portion of the product's exchange value that is over and above the price paid for the object of labor and whatever exchange value has been lost by the instrument of labor between the time of its engagement in production and the time of the product sale. The magnitude of this depreciation can only be determined according to the price at which the instrument of labor can be sold at the end of the production process, and this lost exchange value must reappear in the product price if capital's M-C-M′ relation is to be achieved.

Since the actual surplus exchange value is here finally determined by the price at which the product gets sold, there can be no prior derivation of any part of the product's exchange value from the labor time expended in its production. Rather, the reverse holds—namely, because labor's ideal value production becomes actual only through the product sale, it is that sale which sets the amount of exchange value to which labor time gets referred.

For these reasons, Marx's Labor Theory of Value must be amended to accommodate the *ideal* and *indeterminate* character of labor's exchange value producing role within capital's inner working.

In this connection, it is important to note that insofar as the immediate labor process is something common to all capital production processes, however else they be distinguished, it does not itself provide the specific structure by which capitals individuate themselves in their relation to one another. In other words, not only is labor's value-positing something ideal and indeterminate for capital in general, but it has no relevance to the actual determination of prices and profits within the competitive process, where the conditions of price-setting, realized sales and resulting profits are dependent upon the existing system of market relations *between* capitals rather than upon the mere inner workings of each capital's immediate labor process. This, of course, is something Marx has failed to recognize properly in the theory of competition he develops in the third volume of *Capital*, a theory that proceeds from a value-price transformation where price and profit relations of the plurality of individual capitals are inappropriately derived from the relations of the labor process.[47]

Nevertheless, what has been established regarding the labor process itself remains an accomplishment of fundamental importance. With simple correction and supplement, the *Grundrisse*'s argument has revealed how the social reality of capital develops as a production process, constituting the economic roles of laborer and capitalist, determining the laboring act entirely in terms of capital's own socially specific structure, and producing the commodity with all its social features. Through this deed, Marx has not only robbed *poiēsis* and technique of their status as irreducible alternatives, but contributed to the solution of the theoretical problem first raised in Hegel's System of Needs. Thus, however, unresolved be the struggle in practice, at least thinking the social determination of production need not be problematic.

## Notes

1. Reference is here made to the argumentation of Plato's *Republic* and Aristotle's *Nicomachean Ethics* and *Politics*.

2. Kant writes that economics, whether of the household, agriculture, or the state, cannot "be reckoned as practical philosophy...For all these contain only rules of skill (and are consequently only technically practical) for bringing about an effect that is possible according to the natural concepts of causes and effects, which, since they belong to theoretical philosophy, are subject to those precepts as mere corollaries from it (viz. natural science) and can therefore claim no place in a special philosophy called practical." Kant, *Critique of Judgment*, trans. by J. H. Bernard (New York: Hafner, 1951), p. 9.

3. Hegel, *Philosophy of Right*, trans. by Knox (New York: Oxford University Press, 1967), pp. 35–36.

4. I have here used Kenley Dove's suggested translation for *"Die Sache"* in order to maintain Hegel's systematic distinction between *"das Ding"* and *"die Sache,"* a distinction that Hegel's English translators do not always maintain.

5. So Hegel writes, "the creation of civil society is the achievement of the modern world which has for the first time given all determinations of the Idea their due." *Op. cit.*, p. 226.

6. Marx, *Grundrisse*, trans. by Martin Nicolaus (New York: Vintage Books, 1973), pp. 103–107.

7. See paragraphs 190–195 of Hegel's *Philosophy of Right*.

8. "Use-values. . .constitute the substance of all wealth, whatever may be the social form of that wealth." Marx, *Capital*, Vol. 1, (New York: International Publishers, 1970), p. 36.

9. "The labour-time socially necessary is that required to produce an article under normal conditions of production, and with the average degree of skill and intensity prevalent at the time." *Ibid.*, p. 39. See also *ibid.*, p. 323.

10. See *ibid.*, pp. 73ff.

11. *Ibid.*, p. 167.

12. "By labour-power or capacity for labour is to be understood the aggregate of those mental and physical capabilities existing in a human being, which he exercises whenever he produces a use-value of any description." *Ibid.*

13. "Labour is, in the first place, a process in which both man and Nature participate, and in which man of his own accord starts, regulates, and controls the material re-actions between himself and Nature. He opposes himself to Nature as one of her own forces. . ." *Ibid.*, p. 167.

14. "All labour is, speaking physiologically, an expenditure of human labour-power, and in its character of identical abstract labor, it creates and forms the value of commodities." *Ibid.*, p. 46.

15. "Let us now examine production as a creation of value. We know that the value of each commodity is determined by the quantity of labor expended on and materialised in it, by the working-time necessary, under given social conditions, for its production. This rule also holds good in the case of the product that accrued to our capitalist, as the result of the labour-process carried on for him." *Ibid.*, p. 186.

16. "The property therefore which labour-power in action, living labour, possesses of preserving value at the same time that it adds it, is a gift of Nature. . . ." *Ibid.*, p. 206.

17. "If we now compare the two processes of producing value and of creating surplus-value, we see that the latter is nothing but the continuation of the former beyond a definite point. If on the one hand the process be not carried beyond the point, where the value paid by the capitalist for the labour-power is replaced by an exact equivalent, it is simply a process of producing value; if, on the other hand, it be continued beyond that point, it becomes a process of creating surplus-value." *Ibid.*, p. 195.

18. For a critical discussion of these false notions see Richard Winfield, "The Dilemma of Labor," *Telos*, No. 24 (Summer 1975), and Richard Winfield, "The Young Hegel and The Dialectic of Social Production," *Telos*, No. 26 (Winter 1975–1976), Chapters 10 and 11 of this volume.

19. For a detailed discussion of this congruence see Richard Winfield, "The Logic of Marx's *Capital*" *Telos*, No. 27 (Spring 1976), Chapter 12 of this volume.

20. Marx, *Grundrisse*, p. 296.

21. "Since capital as such is indifferent to every particularity of its substance, and exists not only as the totality of the same but also as the abstraction from all its particularities, the labour which confronts it likewise subjectively has the same totality and abstraction in itself." *Ibid*.

22. *Ibid*.

23. *Ibid*.

24. *Ibid*.

25. *Ibid*.

26. *Ibid*., p. 289.

27. *Ibid*., p. 296.

28. *Ibid*., p. 307.

29. "The value of labour-power is determined, as in the case of every other commodity, by the labour-time necessary for the production, and consequently also the reproduction, of this special article." Marx, *Capital*, Vol. 1, pp. 107–171.

30. Compare Hegel, *Science of Logic*, trans. by A. V. Miller (New York: Humanities Press, 1969), p. 411.

31. Marx, *Grundrisse*, pp. 301–302.

32. *Ibid*., pp. 310–311.

33. "The relation is the material relation between one of capital's elements and the other; but not *its own* relation to both. It therefore appears on one side as merely *passive object*, in which all formal character is extinguished; it appears on the other side only as a simple *production process* into which capital as such, as distinct from its substance, does not enter." *Ibid*., p. 302.

34. *Ibid*., p. 303.

35. *Ibid*., p. 298.

36. *Ibid*.

37. *Ibid*. 298–299.

38. Compare Hegel, *Science of Logic*, p. 421.

39. *Ibid.*, p. 425.

40. "The elements of the production process are not preserved in their material character, but rather as *values*, while the mode of existence which these had *before* the production process is consumed." Marx, *Grundrisse*, p. 316.

41. *Ibid.*, pp. 316, 691–692.

42. *Ibid.*, p. 315.

43. *Ibid.*, p. 314.

44. *Ibid.*, p. 356.

45. Marx, *Capital*, Vol. 1, p. 200.

46. *Ibid*, p. 195; Marx *Grundrisse*, pp. 337, 356, 359.

47. For a more thorough consideration of these questions, see David P. Levine, *Economic Theory* (London: Routledge and Kegan Paul, 1978), and Richard Dien Winfield, "The Social Determination of Production: The Critique of Hegel's System of Needs and Marx's Concept of Capital", (Ph.D. dissertation, Yale University, 1977).

# 14

# Hegel's Challenge to the Modern Economy

## i) Economic Relations as a Problem of Social Justice

Throughout all the major upheavals of modern times, economic relations have been treated as vital matters of social justice to which politics cannot be indifferent. Although little agreement has been reached over what these relations should be, the proper order of the economy has everywhere become a contested issue of public affairs.[1] Nevertheless, the premise that economic relations are normative social structures to which citizens must attend if they are to live in justice has not found general acceptance in modern theory. On the contrary, a great many modern thinkers have rejected the idea that economic relations are social in character and denied that they have any normative content at all. Instead of granting the economy the status of a sphere of social justice involving its own relations of right, they have conceived economic activity as either a natural function or a monological affair involving the single self.

The natural account of economic relations views them as a metabolism between man and nature comprising an ineluctable feature of the human condition. On this basis, the economy gets construed as a sphere of necessity, lying outside all considerations of right and wrong. With its relations given by nature rather then determined by the free volition of its participants, it comprises a domain for which no actions are responsible and in which no questions of justice can arise.[2]

The monological account, for its part, arrives at the same consequence by determining economic relations through some function of the self. This can involve a psychological principle, as in marginal utility theory, where the values of commodities are determined by estimates of psychological desire. Alternatively, it can entail conceiving economic activity as a technical process, where a single agency acts upon objects according to causal laws. This technical framework can be restricted to production, rendering it a process where a laboring self uses an instrument to impose some new form upon a given material, or it can be equally extended to distribution, making it a unilateral assignment of goods to consumers who are treated as ordered objects as well. In either instance, the economic relations concerned are deprived of any normative content; for all they involve are relations between a self and objects, rather than relations between individuals wherein justice can enter.[3]

This common outcome of the natural and monological conceptions of economics was, of course, already perceived by the classical representatives of practical philosophy. Aristotle, for one, well recognized that if economic relations were understood to consist in *technê* and *poiēsis,* that is, in instrumental action and making, then they could not involve the just activity of *praxis.* So construed, economic activity would not be performed for its own sake as universally valid conduct, but for resultant products and satisfactions that would themselves be predicated upon purely particular needs rooted in either nature or arbitrary appetite.[4] Kant, on the other hand, observed that if economics concerned a technical working upon nature, in response to psychologically determined needs and not normative relations between autonomous selves, then it would have to be excluded from practical theory and relegated to a positive science applying causal rules of the understanding to an empirical subject matter.[5]

What these conclusions underline is how—contrary to the common concern of modern practice—the natural and monological conceptions both rule out any normative significance for economic activity by determining it independently of the relations between individuals that are specific to their plurality and enacted through their willing. The natural and monological theories therefore can offer no critique of existing relations, for they address their subject matter as something consisting in relations of nature and the self that no common action can alter. Accordingly, if their concepts were not to correspond to the reality they putatively describe, what would warrant change would be their theoretical construct.

If, however, economic activity is not reducible to natural or monological functions, but can comprise normative social relations, then a prescriptive rather than a descriptive economic science is called for—an economics that falls within the theory of justice, and that can call into question the legitimacy of the existing order of the economy. In that case, if the economy does not accord with the concept of just economic relations, what should be altered is not theory, but economic reality. This possibility, which has been effectively assumed by the makers of modern history, presents imposing theoretical challenges.

First, if economic relations are to be social, they must not be constitutively determined independently of society. This requires that economic relations not be specified in terms of either natural or monological relations, which by definition have no social content. It further entails that economic relations not be characterized as belonging to some normative sphere other than society, such as the household or the state. If economic activity is relegated to their domains, then the economic order ceases to be a social question. What these requirements mean in positive terms is that economic relations must have their entire character accounted for through what is involved in social relations alone.

If, however, the economy is to have a *normative* social being realizable through political action, then the reality of justice must be shown to incorporate a sphere of society distinct from such other structures as property relations, morality, the family, and the state. Then, it must further be demonstrated that the specific social bonds of that sphere do accommodate economic need and the activities securing its satisfaction.

### ii) Hegel's Mandate for Prescriptive Economics

The figure in the history of thought who has most seriously addressed these challenges and attempted to conceive economic relations as proper matters of social justice is Hegel. In his discussion of the "System of Needs" in the *Philosophy of Right,* Hegel draws economic relations into the realm of right and undertakes to develop the normative economics that can determine what economy the just society should have.

In taking this step Hegel is hardly the first to consider the economy as a sphere of justice. Political economy, classically represented by Adam Smith, had already sought to conceive the wealth of nations as a system of economic relations distinguishing proper civilized society from the unjust life of savages.[6] Indeed, Hegel introduces his own treatment of economic relations by praising the political economists for succeeding in using their understanding to discover laws of motion within the vast array of economic activity before them.[7]

Employing the understanding to describe the lawful motion of an observed economy is, however, an entirely different enterprise from using reason to conceive what order the economy should have. Although Hegel is willing to acknowledge the descriptive accomplishments of the political economists, his prescriptive economics is radically different from theirs.

Unlike Smith, Steuart, and Ricardo, Hegel is concerned with conceiving a strictly social rather than political economy. This reflects his understanding that normative social relations can neither be natural, monological, nor political, but must belong within a civil society. It is certainly true that political economy also situates economic relations within what it calls a civil society. However, its civil society is such that the economic relations falling within it are equally natural, monological, and political in character. This is due to the fact that political economy operates within the framework of the liberal theory of Hobbes, Locke, and Rousseau. For liberal theory, just public life consists in a civil order whose society and state have the common end of realizing a liberty whose content derives from the capacity natural to the self of choosing freely among given alternatives. Here civil society figures as a sphere of justice where individuals enjoy the naturally grounded liberty to dispose over property and pursue their particular interests under the regulation and protection of a government limited to securing that liberty's harmonious exercise. Political economy adopts this characterization of civil society, and its concomitant reduction of politics to civil government, by conceiving economic relations as features of a society whose pursuit of particular interest is equally the end to which government is subordinated.[8] Since politics here consists in protecting the same liberty at play in the market relations in this civil society, the economy can be called political. Furthermore, because individuals participate in this "political economy" by exercising the natural liberty to pursue particular ends of one's own choosing, the society of the economy is composed of action both natural and monological in character. Thus, however much political economy wishes to sanction the economy as a normative sphere setting off civilized society from savagery, it undermines the justice of economic activity by deriving its structures from normatively neutral relations of humans and nature.

Hegel, on the contrary, holds that if economic relations are to be matters of justice falling within a civil society, then both they and that society must consist in nonnatural, intersubjective structures of freedom. What leads Hegel to make this decisive break with the natural and monological aspects of political economy is the dual insight underlying his entire *Philosophy of Right*. By working through the dilemmas in traditional practical philosophy, Hegel comes to realize that (1) justice must have no foundations, and that (2) justice can have this foundation-free character only if it consists in the reality of freedom, whose own structures are determined by free willing rather than by any independent factors such as natural law or the given nature of the self. Hegel arrives at these conclusions by following to its radical consequences the common truism that justice involves only what lies within the power of voluntary action and not what occurs independently by nature. Although this means that what should be *is* only through convention rather than natural necessity, Hegel recognizes that the distinction between "ought" and "is" prohibits given convention from automatically providing the content of justice.[9] Although justice may exist only by convention it is just only if its relations are such that they should hold irrespective of what simply is.[10]

Hegel reasons that, since given convention cannot prescribe what is just, the relations of justice must be in their entirety both universal and unconditioned—universal insofar as they must hold for every particular situation, and unconditioned insofar as they cannot be relative to any condition lying outside justice. This does not mean that justice loses the particularity of content that has been recognized to be basic to action ever since Aristotle. It rather signifies that the only particular features that can legitimately affect a relation of justice are other relations of justice, whose own right to enter in can follow solely from justice itself. Otherwise, justice would be bound to independently given factors, leaving it no more justifiable than any other convention of ordered behavior. Accordingly, justice itself conditions and particularizes its own relations, which is precisely what allows them to be universal and unconditioned with regard to what lies outside them. Only by being determined through itself can justice escape the hold of givenness and achieve its own constitutive, unconditioned universality. Accordingly, Hegel concludes, justice can have no foundations, for it must be its own ground and standard. Consequently, the theory of justice, including any prescriptive economics, must not derive the relations of justice from prior principles or procedures of construction.

Furthermore, Hegel argues, justice must consist in enacted relations of freedom among individuals; for only an entirely self-determined convention can satisfy the foundation-free requirements of normativity. Therefore, the theory of justice is not a theory of the Good, but the theory of right to the degree that right designates—as Hegel indicates—nothing but the reality of freedom.[11] If this is so, then a prescriptive economics is properly a theory of economic right devoted to conceiving that economic order that consists entirely in structures of freedom.

When Hegel proceeds to develop the theory of justice as a theory of the reality of freedom, he does follow the lead of liberal theory, which first made the freedom of liberty the basis of justice, in place of the prescribed norms of virtue. Nevertheless, Hegel radically departs from the liberal path by recognizing that the freedom of justice can neither be conceived as liberty, nor as a prior principle of justice.

Whereas just action cannot be determined by exogenous factors, liberty is afflicted with a heteronomy involving not only the content of its ends, as Kant critically observed, but also its form. Rather than being determined by the will itself, liberty's own form of choosing derives from the given nature of the self, just as its ends are chosen from among alternatives independently supplied by outer circumstances or separate inner faculties of desire or reason. As a result of this dual bondage to givenness, liberty lacks the unconditioned universality justice requires. Furthermore, when the naturally defined liberty is made the principle from which the institutions of justice are derived, through such procedures as the social contract, liberty becomes the determining ground of justice. This undermines the identity of freedom and justice by robbing the latter of the foundation-free, self-determined character it requires.

For these reasons, the economic freedom that prescriptive economics must address cannot be founded on the exercise of liberty, so dear to political economy.

The normative inadequacy of liberty indicates to Hegel that justice must instead be sought in a freedom whose form and content are both determined by willing, and whose self-determination is concrete enough to comprise the entire reality of justice. Although Hegel does not deny that the choosing will of liberty is a capacity that all individuals possess as part of the nature of their selves,[12] he argues that the freedom of justice must involve an artificial agency that acts in terms of a normative framework that its own willing brings into being. Only then can the structure of willing and all the particulars of its action be truly self-determined and coincide with the enacted order of justice.

What leads Hegel to the positive conception of justice containing his prescriptive economics is his understanding that the will can exercise the mandated freedom of justice only by interacting with other wills, and not by acting on nature or its own self. So long as the will restricts itself to technical or some other monological activity, the parameters of its action remain defined by factors of nature and the self that are no more products of willing than structures of justice. If, however, individuals act towards one another so that how and what they will is determined solely in reciprocity with how and what others will, they will all exercise an autonomy whose specific character completely derives from their freely entered relationship. In such a mutual interaction, the content of their willing is not supplied by independently given factors, but rather by ends whose particular differences are specific to the relation between individuals comprised by their concomitant actions. This relationship is not something imposed upon them, leaving how and what they will ordained by a structure thay have not willed into being. On the contrary, this relationship is their self-determination; for each participant wills her relation to others through an act of her choice that nevertheless can proceed only in virtue of these others willing that same relation through their own voluntary action. Hegel appropriately calls the interaction of freedom a reciprocal recognition process insofar as within its enacted structure each individual wills her own end and relation to others by respecting the self-determinations that they will as part of the same relationship.[13] He further observes that such freedom is itself a relation of justice; for not only is it wholly self-grounded, but the complimentary self-determinations comprising it proceed in a conjunction of right and duty giving each normativity. Due to the reciprocity of the interaction, each act is an exercise of right and duty—both enjoying the respect the other individuals afford through their concordant actions and showing respect for their self-determinations by not violating their respective limits. Accordingly, each participant here exercises an *objective* freedom, whose very form of mutual respect provides an intersubjective validity assuring its reality.[14]

Although the right and duty of objective freedom thus make it an existing structure of justice rather than a regulative ideal, Hegel is well aware that the unity of justice and freedom requires that freedom not consist in a single relation of interaction, incapable of containing all the different institutions of right.[15] The reality of freedom must instead comprise a system of interactions incorporating all institutions of justice. Furthermore, if the self-grounded character of justice is not to be violated, then the unity of this system must be imposed from within by a particular structure of interaction whose freedom unites and orders the whole as a self-ordered system. Hegel recognizes that the freedom of civil society cannot play this role insofar as social action confines itself to addressing particular interests and welfare and never engages in determining the total structure of justice as the end of its activity. Politics does, however, constitutively attend to ordering the whole framework of right of which it is a part. Therefore, Hegel reasons, the system of right must be crowned by a sovereign state, institutionalizing a political freedom that determines the whole by ruling over all the other spheres of right so that their respective freedoms are secured in unity with its own self-governing activity. Only when politics achieves this preeminence can the entire reality of justice ground itself and enjoy unconditioned universality. If, on the contrary, the state collapses public freedom with free enterprise, or reduces government to management of public welfare, or champions proletarian interest so as to cause itself to wither away, then politics becomes an instrument of independently given, nonpolitical ends, instead of the self-ordering interaction whose rule allows right to rest on its own freedom.

Because justice, however, must have a sovereign political unity, politics must be for its own sake—which can only be the case if no other institutions of right challenge its supremacy. This means that no economic order can be just that acts as the determining base of a political superstructure. More generally, it signifies that all the nonpolitical structures of right must be determined both in their own integrity as specific modes of freedom, and as subordinate institutions incorporated within the free state. These dual considerations provide the basic mandate for Hegel's prescriptive economics. Given the project of the *Philosophy of Right,* the question of what the economy should be can only be answered by determining the economic order that is a structure of freedom, and by establishing the relation it has to the free state as well as to the other institutions of freedom over which politics holds sway. Since Hegel locates the just economy within civil society, his normative economics must be evaluated by examining (1) how civil society figures as a normative sphere of freedom, (2) why just economic relations consist in the freedom specific to civil society, (3) whether Hegel has properly developed them in these terms, (4) how the justice of the economy relates to other civil institutions, and finally (5) how the just economy stands under the rule of self-government.

### iii) The Legitimacy of Civil Society and the Civil Character of Economic Freedom

If Hegel's prescriptive economics is to have legitimacy as a normative science of a social, rather than a political, economy, the justice of freedom must be shown to require a civil society containing economic relations. In the *Philosophy of Right* Hegel addresses this task in the course of arguing that right has its exhaustive reality in the interactions of freedom of persons and property, morality, the family, civil society, and the state. Hegel conceives civil society after property relations, morality, and the family, but before the state for two important reasons. First, though Hegel's civil society is not determined by any natural liberty, it consists of relations between individuals who do already interact as persons, moral subjects, and family members, without, however, pursuing their civil relations in terms of any political involvement. Consequently, civil society can only be conceived if the concepts of personhood, morality, and the family already lie at hand. Second, in Hegel's view, the just state cannot exist without there being civil freedom with all the social institutions that comprise its exercise. Thus, if civil society is to have any justification, it must provide a mode of freedom presupposed by politics that neither property, moral, nor household relations can supply.

What satisfies this requirement, giving civil society its mandate, is the freedom to realize particular ends of one's own choosing in reciprocity with others. This right is something lacking in property relations, morality, and the household, even though it can only be exercised by individuals enjoying the rights of persons, moral subjects, and adult family members. Indeed, personhood is a prerequisite for all further freedoms, since without ownership of one's own body, there is no way one's actions can be recognized as one's own. Nevertheless, as Hegel points out,[16] disposing over property does not realize an individual's particular ends in reciprocity with others; for the property-holding will of the person has no particular end lying in itself, but first acquires determination by embodying itself in some external entity. Simmilarly, although morality underlies all ethical institutions by making individuals responsible for realizing right through their own actions, the end of moral action is not the mutual realization of particular interests, but whatever conscience determines to be just. In contrast, the household does provide an existing association whose members enjoy the right and duty of acting for its common good. However, although this gives them a private realm on whose basis they are free to enter society, the family unity is destroyed if its own members interact within the household in terms of individual interests.

If this indicates that the freedom of interests requires more than property, moral, and household relations for its realization, then what necessitates a separate civil sphere devoted to its exercise is the role of such freedom as a precondition of free politics. As Hegel suggests,[17] if the state were to allow for no civil society to realize the reciprocal pursuit of individual interests, state rule would stand in irreconcilable opposition to the interests of its citizens. Instead of securing the totality of freedom, the state would then exclude a whole dimension of their autonomy and so forfeit its own legitimacy. Therefore, Hegel concludes, there should be a civil society to provide the sphere of freedom for the reciprocal realization of individual interests.

Although this line of argument points to the legitimacy of a civil society, it tells neither what civil society actually is, nor how economic relations fall within it. Rather, it raises the questions of what types of institutions can realize interest as a right and make "civil society" more than a wishful slogan.

As Hegel discovers, the immediate answer to this question establishes prescriptive economics as a science of a social economy; for what provide the minimal institution of freedom in which interests are reciprocally realized are none other than commodity relations. Hegel comes to this insight by thinking through the basic mandate of civil society, not as naturally construed by liberal theory and political economy, nor as conditioned by some historical necessity, but in accord with the foundation-free requirements of justice.

On these terms, the task of civil society consists in providing the institutions that allow individuals to realize their interests through a normative interaction of freedom rather then in an exercise of natural liberty where all pursue whatever they choose without any mutual recognition of right. Hegel recognizes that if civil society is to save the pursuit of interest from an *omnium bella omnium*—a war of all against all—that pursuit must somehow be so determined that each individual can achieve his freely chosen ends by realizing and respecting the similar pursuit of others. In that case, action towards others for the particular ends of one's own choosing will be a matter of justice; for it will proceed as part of a mutual observance of right and duty where each interacting participant determines himself in view of his own interest with the agreement of others by simultaneously honoring their concordant exercise of that same freedom. Such an interaction will thus allow for a normative community of interest in which the free realization of each member's particular ends figures as a right that all are duty-bound to respect, to the degree that only in so doing can they engage in their own respected pursuit of interest.

Participation in this minimal relationship of civil freedom accordingly consists in willing particular ends of one's own choosing where those ends are attainable only by action towards others entailing the concomitant fulfillment of their respective ends. For this to be so, these ends must be independently pursued interests that their bearer cannot realize with what nature directly provides, what already lies within that individual's household and private property, or what others may furnish without thereby realizing an interest of their own. If the pursuit of interest is to be a normative civil interaction, the interests at stake must instead require something that can only be supplied by other individuals, who can do so themselves only by voluntarily obtaining in return what satisfies their own chosen ends.

Hegel's entire prescriptive, social economics proceeds from his insight that the particular ends meeting these requirements of civil justice consist in needs whose content is completely a matter of personal preference, yet which can only be satisfied by what someone else has to offer under the condition that the bearer of the first need possess and agree to offer in return something satisfying a similarly advanced need of the latter. Hegel recognizes that such need can be determined neither naturally, as a physical want for what the body requires, nor monologically, as a psychological yearning for what the soul might desire. Although, as Hegel grants in his discussion of the right of distress *(Notrecht)*,[18] every person has a right to satisfy his or her subsistence needs, insofar as the maintenance of life is a precondition for any exercise of freedom, that maintenance does not comprise the specific justice of civil freedom, where what further achieves legitimacy are reciprocally realized interests free of any natural limit. The same is true for psychological needs, whose satisfaction may be a precondition for the sanity required to interact as a recognized person, but whose content cannot prescribe what can figure as a need in civil society.

Accordingly, Hegel understands that what does characterize civil need is that it is directed upon means of satisfaction that can only be obtained from correlatively needy individuals. Although the particular content of such need is a matter of personal preference and may well coincide with some physical or psychological wants, what makes it an object of civil right is that it is pursued in reciprocity with the needs of others. Only this social relatedness—consisting in the correlative pursuit of interest of a plurality of individuals—can mandate what figures as a need within the normative relations of civil freedom.[19]

Consequently, what comprises the exclusive objects satisfying need that is civil in character are *commodities*—goods expressly owned by other individuals who are willing to exchange them to satisfy their own correlatively determined wants. Only within a context of a plurality of commodity owners can need enjoy the legitimacy of being the particular end pursued within the reciprocal relation of civil freedom. Conversely, only within the interaction of individuals who need what others have and have what others need, can property function as a commodity—related not only to the will of its owner, but also to the civil need of others with commodities of their own. What this signifies is that the needs at play in the minimal interaction satisfying the mandate of civil society are economic needs in the specific normative sense of needs for commodities, needs that by that very character can only be satisfied with the analogous needs of others.

Hegel therefore concludes that civil society directly entails a system of needs comprising a market economy of commodity relations. This social economy is the institution providing the freedom of particularity with its basic reality; and for this reason, it commands the normativity making it the subject matter of prescriptive economics. If this reveals why Hegel addresses what the economy should be by conceiving a social economy of commodity relations forming the basic institution of civil society, it leaves open whether

Hegel has adequately developed the system of needs as the elementary structure of civil freedom.

### iv) The Key Matters of Debate in Hegel's System of Needs

Hegel's account of the internal structure of the system of needs is marked by four overriding features that are of as much importance for determining social and political justice as a whole, as for prescribing the just economy.

First, Hegel conceives commodity relations as legitimate interactions of freedom proper to civil society. Second, he works out their total structure without subsuming them under a system of capitals whose profit derives from wage labor commodity production.[20] Third, although Hegel grants legitimacy to commodity relations, he nonetheless argues that they cannot secure for every individual the actual exercise of the very right they make possible, namely, the respected freedom to satisfy needs of one's own choosing in reciprocity with others. Fourth, Hegel conceives classes as necessary elements of the just economy, but characterizes them in terms more appropriate to estates.[21]

The significance of the first two features is set in relief by Marx's critique of commodity relations and of the civil society that rests on them. In contrast to Hegel, Marx rejects the legitimacy of commodity relations, and with them civil society, because he considers them to be bound up with capitalism, which he judges to be a non-normative historical formation resting on the exploitation of labor and subjecting society and politics to bourgeois rule in the interest of capital. As a consequence, Marx analyzes commodity relations not in a prescriptive economics but in a descriptive theory of capital; there he determines them as relations swallowed up within the accumulative process of capital that comprises not the elementary structure of a normative civil society, but the determining base of a historically given, bourgeois society whose overthrow is a necessary prelude to the realization of justice.

If Hegel's prescriptive economics is to have any validity, Marx's critique of commodity relations must be refuted by showing that the system of needs is indeed a structure of freedom, not only irreducible to capital, but containing none of the bonds of domination that Marx ascribes to it. Such a refutation will equally demonstrate that civil society is not a bourgeois society in Marx's pejorative sense.

Freeing the system of needs from the taint of "capitalist exploitation" will not, however, exonerate the unbridled free enterprise of the market, if the third feature of Hegel's account is justified. Hegel's idea that commodity relations cannot automatically realize the freedom in whose exercise they consist contradicts the classic view of political economy that the market commands itself with an invisible hand, ensuring the welfare of all. If, on the contrary,

Hegel's argument can be shown to be valid, it will mandate the addition of further institutions of freedom to resolve the problem of justice that the market introduces.[22]

Finally, Hegel's justification and depiction of a class society rooted in the system of needs has decisive significance, both for his own conception of the just society and state, and for justice today. If it can shown that Hegel's characterization of social classes does not result from the economic dynamic of commodity relations, this will entail major reworkings of Hegel's class division, as well as of his conceptions of the corporations and the state—both of which rest heavily upon estate relations.

All these issues can be resolved only by turning to the internal structure of the system of needs as presented by Hegel and as rethought where necessary to give justice its due.

### v) Capital and the Legitimacy of Commodity Relations

Hegel appropriately begins his account of the system of needs with the most elementary relationship of need and the means of its satisfaction, allowing for the reciprocal realization of self-interest that civil society requires. This consists in nothing other than a market in which a plurality of individuals face one another simultaneously as bearers of personally chosen needs for the commodities of others, and as owners of some commodity that others similarly need. This dual relationship forms the starting point of all further normative market relations because an individual can participate in this society of interest only by both choosing to need a commodity belonging to someone else, and owning a good that that other individual needs.[23]

It is here, then, that Hegel's prescriptive economics must begin to establish the structure and legitimacy of commodity relations. The first step in this direction is provided by Hegel's argument in paragraphs 190 and 191 of the *Philosophy of Right* that both the needs and the commodities comprising the correlative elements of market interaction stand in an artificial multitude and diversity, which may incorporate certain naturally given wants and objects as well as conform to the possibilities of material reality, but which nevertheless cannot be prescribed by any natural principles. Unlike political economists and Marx, who have tended to view economic need and use value as anthropological factors of the human condition.[24] Hegel recognizes that the utility sought by civil need is as social as the want it addresses. Both have their specific character solely in terms of the just convention of the reciprocal realization of particular ends, which utility can enter into only by being born by commodities satisfying not the wants of human nature, but the specifically social need of individuals who have a commodity of their own to exchange.

On the basis of this enacted structure of interaction, the variety and plenitude of utilities is no more restricted by the given requirements of life than that of the needs individuals choose to have and realize in reciprocity with others. Because both need and its object are matters of preference limited only by what others concomitantly choose to need and own, the possible refinement and number of either is as measureless as it is capricious.[25]

This aspect of the multiplication and discrimination of needs and commodities is of central importance to social justice and the legitimacy of commodity relations. In effect, it establishes a whole new domain of right by liberating need from the set bounds of natural subsistence and reconstituting it as a civil need as unlimited in magnitude and variety as the commodities required to satisfy it. Since the content of need is determined by how commodity owners freely interact rather than by the physical requirements of individuals and the natural scarcity of those things that satisfy bodily wants, the need for commodities is itself a factor of freedom, enjoying the normativity common to self-determination. Consequently, with commodity relations the right of need to be satisfied is no longer restricted to what a person requires to exist and act towards others. Because satisfying the need for commodities realizes the freedom of interest in a relation of right and duty, the justice of freedom extends to whatever needs figure within it.

This immediately makes social justice a problem of much more formidable challenge than that of securing everyone's person and property. Due to the unavoidable multiplication and refinement of needs and commodities, what must be treated as a civil right of each individual is the reciprocal satisfaction of an endlessly multifarious and discriminating neediness whose means of satisfaction are all already owned by others in an equally unnatural plenitude and variety. Although each individual here has the opportunity to choose from a mass of luxury beyond all physical requirement, he does so in a dependent poverty without end; for as Hegel notes, not only is his need without limit, but it can be satisfied only by what others own and willingly relinquish for something satisfying their own needs.[26] Consequently, to realize the right of satisfying civil need, one does not confront the obstacle of nature's niggardliness, which technical activity can overcome, but rather the barrier of entitled commodity ownership, which may be violated by theft, but which can be removed only in conformity with civil reciprocity through the free consent of the owner. The unsatisfied need for commodities therefore comprises the socially specific poverty of a boundless want for an artificial plethora of goods justly unobtainable without a commodity of one's own that others want in return.

If this civil predicament makes the continuance of such poverty a social wrong, it also mandates how it can be righted: Given a market of needy commodity owners, the only way they can obtain what they need in a mutual exercise of freedom is by entering into commodity exchange with one another. Accordingly, the basic interaction realizing the community of interest of civil society is the freely entered relation of commodity exchange, where individuals acquire a good they need from someone else by voluntarily giving in return a commodity of their own that that other individual needs. Having identified the factors that form the components of this relation, Hegel's prescriptive economics appropriately proceeds to consider the exchange process itself and what is entailed in its operation.

The decisive point that Hegel's argument here establishes is that, within the mutual relationship of exchange, the traded commodities acquire a further social quality consisting in the equivalence of exchangeability of one good for the other as realized in their actual exchange.[27] Although Hegel does not give this quality a name of its own, distinguishing it from the social utility or use value that each commodity bears as the object of a certain civil need, what he is addressing is exchange value—the equivalent exchangeability of two traded commodities. What is of crucial importance is that Hegel recognizes that this quality is something neither intrinsic to the natural qualities of the exchanged commodities, nor rooted in a psychological estimation of them, nor determined by anything preceding the mutually agreed exchange act setting them in their actual relation of equivalence. The voluntary bilateral character of commodity exchange requires that this be so, since what makes two commodities exchangeable is the concurring decisions of their respective owners, who, being independent individuals in the market, need not be swayed by any particular external factors, nor conform to any stipulated model of "economic rationality." The only constraint they face is the necessity of reaching agreement with other commodity owners, who themselves act under the same condition of having to accommodate the needs of others in order to satisfy their own.

This means that any market situation where goods are traded at proportions fixed independently of the choices of the parties to exchange would violate the constitutive freedom of commodity relations and represent a social injustice *unless* it occurred out of considerations for matters of right, such as political sovereignty or public welfare, having priority over particular exercises of market freedom, but not entailing their complete annulment.

Accordingly, any labor theory of value that determines the exchange values of commodities by the conditions of their production misconstrues commodity relations by ignoring that every commodity exchange is determined by the free mutual agreement of the exchange partners. It is precisely this reciprocal freedom constitutive of commodity exchange that makes it possible for nonproduced items, such as labor, power, and land, to have exchange value as much as any product—so long as some individual agrees to trade another commodity for them.[28] Consequently, when prescriptive economics turns to exchange value as it arises in commodity exchange, what it addresses is a relation of commodities in general rather than something specific to the particular class of commodities comprising products. Hegel understands this, and therefore properly analyzes commodity exchange prior to and independently of his consideration of commodity production.

Admittedly, when Hegel subsequently discusses the labor process entailed by the market, he does speak of labor impressing its product with value.[29] However, Hegel does not thereby fall into the trap of the labor theory value; for he nowhere claims that labor's act sets the exchange value at which products are actually bought and sold, or, for that matter, furnishes surplus value that appears in transformed form as profit. Hegel's reference to labor's production of value instead properly signifies that, when a commodity is produced, the labor expended on its manufacture gives the material on which it acts a new form and utility, allowing it to have a new exchangeability whose actual measure will finally be determined not in production, but in the interaction of the market place.

All this bears directly on the justice of commodity relations: for what Hegel here uncovers in thinking commodity exchange effectively rules out the principle objections Marx has directed against them.

In *Capital,* Marx first challenges the legitimacy of commodity relations by arguing that commodity exchange results in a fetishism of commodities where the social relations between individuals proceed as relations between things ordering their actions.[30] Hegel's analysis has revealed, however, that commodity exchange involves an exercise of freedom completely the reverse of what Marx laments. In the first place, the goods individuals exchange are not things of a merely natural character but commodities bearing the socially determined qualities of use and exchange values in function of the interdependent willing of their owners. What allows these goods to be exchanged rather then unilaterally seized is that their owners agree to treat one another both as free persons, with entitled ownership of their respective commodities, and as independent bearers of interest entitled to exercise the civil right of satisfying needs of their own choosing in reciprocity with others. Consequently, when individuals enter into an exchange, they interact not as the subjects of things that rule their lives, but as masters of commodities—utilizing them as subordinate means to satisfy their civil needs, and thereby exercise the honored freedom of achieving those particular ends of their own that advance the interests of others.

Neverthless, even if exchange relations do proceed in a freedom and equality according them the justice of a civil right, their justice would be purely formal if, as Marx further argues, exchange value derives from expended labor, and commodity production involves a capital-labor relation where labor is exploited. These two claims are the core of Marx's critique of commodity relations; but, as in the case of "commodity fetishism," Hegel's concept of exchange unmasks their untenability.

Following the political economists, Marx introduces his labor theory of value in *Capital* by arguing that commodities could not be exchanged if they did not share some prior factor giving them all a commensurable exchange value. Since they have different physical properties and utilities, Marx concludes that the common feature allowing for their exchangeability must lie in the labor embodied in them, which forms the commensurable basis of their exchange equivalence when reduced to its quantitative character as abstract labor time.[31] Like all labor theories of value, however, Marx's argument not only assumes that all commodities are produced, but contradicts the voluntary character of commodity exchange. As Hegel has shown, because exchange occurs solely through the free agreement of the owners of the traded commodities, their equivalent exchange value is actually determined by the common resolve of these individuals to exchange them. As a consequence, the exchanged commodities need not be produced, nor can the production process of traded products have any binding effect on the proportions at which they are bought and sold. Factors of production can only determine the minimum price that must be met if the product is to be sold without a loss in relation to the cost of its manufacture.

Hegel accordingly recognizes that prescriptive economics can further conceive of exchange relations involving money and the earning of profit prior and without reference to commodity production and expended labor.[32] As he indicates, all that is needed for a commodity to function as money is for commodity owners to honor it in their exchange as the universal equivalent and standard of measure of the exchange value of all other commodities.[33] Although money can thereby operate as a means of exchange, facilitating the trade of two particular goods (represented by the schema C—M—C), individuals can equally advance money to receive more in return simply by finding someone willing to sell them a commodity (M-C) that they can resell at a higher price to some other willing individual. The free reciprocity of exchange makes this all possible, which is why profit can be made through speculation without any engagement in production.

Marx, however, bases his whole theory of the exploitation of labor on the idea that profit cannot arise out of exchange alone, but must be accounted for by a creation of new exchange value taking place within the process of commodity production. When he analyzes the sequence of two commodity exchanges (represented by the formula M-C-M′), where one individual buys the commodity of another (M-C), and then sells it for more money than he paid (C-M′), Marx reasons that the added exchange value received at the end of the second transaction would contradict the constitutive equivalence of commodity exchange if it had no other origin. Consequently, he concludes, an individual who advances money to receive more in return must obtain his increment by engaging in an intervening production of commodities where he pays the hired laborer less for his labor power than the exchange value his labor produces.[34] This discrepancy between payment received and value produced comprises the "exploitation" of labor, which Marx admits involves no juridical wrong since the laborer is paid the equivalent exchange value of his labor power and does not own his labor, which is not a commodity with exchange value, but only the form in which the labor power already purchased by his employer is consumed.[35] Nevertheless, since for Marx the rate of this exploitation determines the rate of surplus value upon which profit and capital investment ultimately depend, commodity relations would stand determined by a factor relatively independent of reciprocal willing, condemning the principle of civil freedom to an empty formality.

The fatal flaw in Marx's concept of the exploitation of labor is that it rests completely upon the claim that commodities have their exchange value determined by the quantity of abstract labor time embodied in them. Once, however, one follows Hegel's insight that exchange value can be determined only by the mutual agreement of the parties to exchange, it is evident not only that profit can arise through an M-C-M′ exchange sequence without intervening commodity production, but that there can be no exploitation of labor in Marx's sense of the term. The latter is precluded simply because the exchange value of any product bears no necessary relation to the amount of labor expended in its production, but rather depends upon the wills of its prospective buyers, whose independence entails all the variation in sales volumes and price settings that make capital's realization of profit anything but an automatic consequence of its internal organization of production.

If this brings Marx's theory to the point of collapse, it also has central consequences for capital and commodity relations as a whole—consequences that Hegel's prescriptive economics must, and largely does, take into account.

To begin with, insofar as capital realizes its constitutive M-C-M′ circuit of exchange with neither exploitation of labor nor any necessary engagement in commodity production, capital must be conceived in its proper universality instead of being reduced, as in Marx's *Capital,* to a social structure based upon the capital-labor relation specific to privately owned, industrial capital employing wage laborers. Although capital can certainly take that particular form, as history testifies, it can equally produce commodities and consummate its M-C-M′ exchange sequence without any wage labor at all, if, for example, it operates as a workers' cooperative whose members draw dividends rather than wages. So too, capital can just as well be publicly as privately owned, without in any way altering its interaction in the market in pursuit of profit. Whatever the case, whether a unit of capital engages in production, pays wages, or is owned by an individual, a corporation, the state, or a workers' cooperative, it will still face the same market predicament that defines the logic of its constitutive accumulation. Furthermore, since there is nothing about capital that prevents its internal organization from being constructed through the same sort of voluntary agreement comprising the exchanges in which its M-C-M′ realization of profit consists, capital in no way undermines the legitimacy of commodity relations. On the contrary, capital shares their justice, as well as their limitations, inasmuch as capital involves the same exercise of right at work in any other market activity. As a result, the theory of capital does not just describe a merely historical mode of production, but falls within prescriptive economics as the conception of a structural element of the just economy.

Hegel accordingly introduces traces of the profit-earning relation of capital into the system of needs, mentioning the M-C-M′ form of exchange and production for profit.[36] Certainly Hegel's treatment is far too scanty to provide the required conception of capital; but his brevity does reflect the important fact that capital is but an element, rather than the unifying structure, of commodity relations. They cannot be reduced to relations of capital because exchange value does not derive from embodied labor of any sort, let alone from labor exploited by capital—just as commodities can be traded without their exchange resulting in a profit for either participant.

This means that exchange relations do not resolve themselves into the accumulation process of capital, as Marx tends to suggest, but rather involve produced and nonproduced commodities whose exchange may, but need not, form part of any M-C-M′ capital circuit. Hegel's conception of exchange properly takes this into account by leaving open these possibilities without giving any one hegemony over the rest.

The subordinate character of capital has similar consequences for commodity production. If goods can bear exchange value as commodities without issuing from capital, then commodity production can figure within the reciprocal satisfaction of needs, with or without profit as well as with or without wage labor. Prescriptive economics must therefore conceive the forms of commodity production so as to allow for all these options. Hegel achieves this himself by differentiating the basic modes of commodity fabrication without expressly limiting them to capital or any other alternative arrangements. In paragraphs 196-98 of the *Philosophy of Right* he instead presents in succession the elementary labor process where the act of laboring produces a whole new commodity, manufacturing where mass production is achieved by both simple duplication of laboring acts and a division of labor where each act completes only one step in the product's formation, and finally mechanization where machines under the supervision of technicians step in to replace the rote work of detail labor. What makes all these forms of production normative relations specific to civil society is that they produce commodities for the market, and that those engaged in this production do so in such a way as to satisfy their own needs in reciprocity with others. As such, every one of these forms can just as well be pursued on a non-profit basis as serve the accumulation of capital, with or without the payment of wages.

Nonetheless, it might appear that Hegel does not maintain the secondary position of capital within the system of needs, for when he proceeds to conceive the total process of commodity relations in its inclusive unity of all commodity exchange and production, he develops his analysis under the heading "Capital" *(das Vermögen)* and outlines how the "capital" of society involves the acquisition of particular "capitals" of its members.[37] In doing so, however, Hegel does not reduce the system of needs to a system of capitals; for what he understands under the rubric of "capital" *(Vermogen)* is simply the general wealth of the civil economy as it is composed of all the particular commodity ownerships and earning activities at play in it. Here the total capital of society does not designate an ever-accumulating, aggregate exchange value consisting in the competitive system of particular profit-seeking enterprises. It rather signifies the amalgam of all commodity relations, in whose network of interdependence individuals acquire and dispose of particular capitals, simply comprising the commodities they own that allow them to satisfy their needs in exchange by way of all those earning activities that they are free to choose from in the system of needs.[38]

If this total network does not result in the hegemony of capital, it does entail the formation of social classes, which Hegel appropriately considers as the next theme of his prescriptive economics.

### vi) The Justice of Class Society and the Injustice of Estates

Hegel's account of commodity relations has already indicated how the reciprocal satisfaction of need involves a variety of ways of engaging in exchange and production, where different types of earning are linked to different types of commodity ownership and need. For instance, whoever pursues the M-C-M′ circuit of exchange needs capital to advance in the market to earn a profit. By contrast, an individual interacting as a landlord needs landed property or some other rentable commodity in order to obtain rent as his form of income, whereas a laborer needs a marketable labor power and whatever else allows him to enter someone else's employ and earn a wage. Consequently, whenever an individual participates in commodity relations, he does so by exercising one mode, or possibly several different modes, of earning shared by whoever have chosen to satisfy their needs in a similar manner. This means that commodity relations entail classes consisting in those different groups of individuals who have chosen to pursue a common type of earning with its associated needs and goods.

Since, as Hegel's arguments have indicated, commodity relations involve no exploitation, the economic relation between classes is not one of domination, but of the same mutual exercise of freedom characterizing all activity in the system of needs. Furthermore, since each class pursues its mode of earning only in a voluntarily entered interdependence with the others, no class will have any automatic command over a privileged amount of earnings in relation to the others.

Belonging to a class is thus in all respects an act of freedom on the part of its members. They belong to a class not by birth or some other factor independent of their wills, but through exercising their civil right to satisfy freely chosen needs in reciprocity with others. Due to the interdependence of classes, each individual's freely entered class affiliation equally involves relating to members of other classes entirely through recognition and respect of their exercise of that same freedom. Consequently, the class division issuing from the system of needs is nothing but a realization of civil freedom, which is to say that the just society is a class society.

The Marxist ideal of a classless society is, in contrast, utterly unjust, since it requires conceling the civil freedom to choose both one's needs, and how one will satisfy them in reciprocity with others. These freedoms would have to be curtailed; for their exercise is precisely what creates class differences in the first place. The only way a classless society could be achieved would thus be by imposing a regime forcing individuals to restrict their needs to a certain type,[39] and to limit the type of exchange and modes of earning in which they engage. Since such a regime is entirely possible, a classless society is not some wistful utopia but a real threat to social justice and its institutions of freedom.

Hegel begins his discussion of classes by properly pointing out the features that give them their civil legitimacy. He observes that classes directly issue from the workings of commodity relations insofar as different modes of earning tied to different needs and commodity ownerships are automatically pursued by common groups of individuals, given the variety of engagements in exchange and production in which market activity consists.[40] He accordingly emphasizes that individuals become affiliated with a particular class solely in virtue of how they freely choose to participate in commodity relations.[41] He further argues that, since classes issue from commodity relations, what differentiates them from one another must be nothing other than distinct modes of earning specific to the system of needs.[42]

Nevertheless, when Hegel proceeds to identify and characterize the actual classes of just economy, he falls back upon conventional descriptions of estates, whose combination of natural foundations and political privilege completely violates the justice of civil society. Turning a blind eye on differences rooted in commodity interaction, he instead introduces a "substantial" class of peasants and nobles, a ''reflective'' class embracing market activity as a whole, and a ''universal'' class primarily consisting of civil servants. The anomaly of this breakdown is obvious.

To start with, Hegel characterizes his substantial class in terms of a naturally bounded livelihood that not only operates wholly outside the system of needs, but has its existence threatened by the spread of commodity relations. Instead of engaging in a particuler mode of earning commodities in reciprocity with others, the substantial class lives directly off the land, satisfying a purely household want with produce wrested from the earth independently of exchange. [43] Dependent upon the variable condition of seasonal changes, fertility, and so forth—rather than the social necessity of the market—consuming gifts of nature's alien power instead of commodities won through free activity, this entire class subsists in a naturally limited autarchy, free of the insecurity of trade, the search for profit, and the caprice of others[44]—free, in other words, from any involvement in the constitutive interdependence of commodity relations and the modalities of earning characterizing classes. Almost despite himself, Hegel admits the incompatibility of a peasantry and nobility with the system of needs by repeatedly describing how the spread of commodity relations undermines the natural basis of the substantial class by liberating the economy of the land from household autarchy and privileged birthright, and turning agriculture into a factory industry producing for the market.[45]

By contrast, what disqualifies Hegel's universal class are not natural features—such as those that exclude peasants and nobles from civil society—but an occupational identity deriving from the sphere of public office, rather than from the forms of earning rooted in commodity relations themselves. Instead of pursuing particular interests specific to the system of needs, the universal class is characterized as devoting itself to the aims of government.[46] Although Hegel variously describes it as a body of civil servants,[47] a military class,[48] or the entire panoply of soldiers, lawyers, doctors, clergymen, and scholars, [49] what unites its members is action for the universal end of the state—action that therefore requires political rather than market institutions for its exercise. As a consequence Hegel is compelled to admit that the activity of the universal class does not comprise a private earning and that its members must instead be provided with either some *given,* private wealth or state support to relieve them of having to attend to their own needs.[50] If this were to leave both their class activity and their livelihood unencumbered by engagement in the interdependent earning of the system of needs, then they would fail to practice a distinct mode of economic activity, as required to qualify as a social class. If, on the other hand, their independent wealth and state subsidy were taken in their purely economic form, then the members of the universal class would lose their common bond and fall instead into the distinct group of those individuals living off unearned wealth and wages, respectively.

Insofar as this leaves the characteristic identity of the universal class as exogenous to commodity relations as that of peasants and nobles, it is not surprising that Hegel characterizes his remaining "reflective" class as if its earning involved all activities of the system of needs. The members of this class consume only what they earn through their own diligence and free choice, treating nature as a wholly subordinate material, and premising their activity upon the needs and labor of others.[51] Unlike the substantial and universal classes, the reflective class directs itself upon the particular through relations of mutual dependency where its members engage in commerce and trade, manufacture commodities, and advance capital[52]—in a word, doing everything commodity relations call for. As a result, the reflective class does not represent one mode of earning but rather contains the entire genuine class division within itself. Hegel effectively shows this by subdividing the reflective class into three groups differentiated, as social classes should be, by their types of engagement in commodity relations.[53]

What all this indicates is that Hegel's characterization of classes must be rejected and replaced by a class division wholly endogenous to commodity relations. This needed revision also entails, however, fundamental changes in the structure of civil society and the state. As the above arguments have shown, for there to be a just civil society, peasants and nobles must be excluded, civil servants must lose their social status as a separate class and be incorporated instead into the types of groups Hegel subsumes under his reflective class, and these groups must themselves cease to be sections of a single class and rather comprise the classes in their entirety. Furthermore, since the corporations consist in the voluntary associations formed to advance the particular shared interests arising out of the common forms of earning of the system of needs,[54] they can no longer be the special prerogative of a single class. Hegel makes the reflective class the corporations' privileged soil[55] insofar as he subsumes all commodity interaction under it: but with a true class division, corporations become a matter for every class.

These alterations in society have equally significant ramifications for the state since Hegel's classes bear distinct political privileges that are the other side of their state identity. This is most evident when Hegel conceives the estate element of the legislative power. Here his suspect class division assumes a political role, producing government institutions incompatible with not only the proper class structure of civil society, but the independence political freedom should achieve through the demarcation of civil society and the state. Although the political function of the legislature requires an assembly representing *political* opinion about what laws should be enacted to realize the constitution in the face of changing circumstances in society, government, and foreign affairs,[56] Hegel calls for a bicameral estate assembly, where the lower chamber represents the universal interest of state authority as something somehow rooted in civil society itself.[57] Because Hegel effectively subsumes the entire system of needs under the reflective class, he assigns it the lower chamber, even though civil interest could properly be represented only if all *social* classes were admitted.[58] Conversely, Hegel makes the upper chamber a house of lords precisely because the nobility is totally extraneous to the system of needs and therefore suited to masquerade as that element "of" society that stands aloof from social interest and so supposedly provides the civil foundation for the universal ends of politics.[59] Since, however, the nobility has no place in civil society, and the classes are properly defined by purely social pursuits, their mediation with the state cannot occur from within themselves, but must take place from the side of the state through a rule *over* civil society that protects and enforces its social justice in conformity with the exercise of political freedom. Consequently, the legislative assembly should have no class representation of any sort, for the universal ends it addresses are common to all individuals in their capacity as citizens.

### vii) The Limits of Commodity Relations and the Realization of Social Justice

If Hegel introduces, but improperly characterizes, the class division inherent in civil society, he does succeed in uncovering the intrinsic inability of commodity relations to realize for all the exercise of right in which they consist. As Hegel indicates, this endemic limit to the justice of the economy has two sides that call for two different remedies.

On the one hand, all commodity interaction presupposes, but cannot enforce, the property relations allowing for commodity ownership, civil need, and exchange. Just as the abstract right of persons is subject to conflicts of nonmalicious wrong, fraud, and outright crime that it has no means to adjudicate and punish in an objectively binding manner,[60] so the just economy cannot secure the person and property of its participants through its own relations of commodity exchange. Since they can only proceed themselves so long as property rights are not violated, commodity relations are incapable of guaranteeing either the preconditions of every exchange, or the altered commodity ownership in which it results. Therefore, Hegel concludes, the just economy must be supplemented by a public administration of civil law enforcing property rights with a recognized and effective authority to adjudicate disputes, punish offenders, and retribute their victims.[61]

Although the institutions of this public administration of civil law can secure what individuals own before, during, and after engaging in economic activity, it cannot remove the inability of the civil economy to insure the reciprocal satisfaction of the needs generated within commodity relations as matters of social right. This remains a problem that the civil protection of property cannot resolve for two reasons duly indicated in Hegel's discussion.

To begin with, precisely because the just economy consists in commodity relations operating through mutual agreements of exchange, its members can never be assured of meeting others in the market who not only have needs and commodities correlating with their own, but also the will to enter into exchange.[62] Whether the commodities involved be produced or nonproduced; whether their exchange be part of a circuit of capital; and whether that capital be advanced by an individual, a private corporation, a worker cooperative, or a state enterprise, each party's ability to satisfy its particular commodity needs still depends upon the free and accordingly arbitrary decision of others to market the needed goods in return for what that party offers—be it money, labor power, capital, or some other commodity. So long as commodity relations have free sway, no participant in the market can count on encountering consumers or producers able and willing to conclude any sought exchange.

What compounds this contingency in entering exchange is the development of disparities in wealth that result from commodity relations, but create barriers for the less wealthy to satisfy their needs in the market. The very freedom of commodity relations always allows for some economic agents to amass commodities through exchange of such great exchange value as to enable them to engage more easily in further transactions, while prejudicing the opportunity of others to do the same. Because such specifically social inequality requires nothing more than commodity exchange to come into being, its existence does not depend on what type of commodity ownership predominates. Since nothing in the internal structure of a participant in the market can free it from operating through mutual agreements with other independent participants, neither nonprofit nor profit-making corporations, private nor public enterprises, corporate nor worker self-managed firms can prevent differences in wealth from arising that undermine the equal opportunity of individuals to satisfy their chosen needs in reciprocity with others.

As a consequence, there can be no invisible hand where commodity relations order themselves so as to guarantee the economic welfare of all, as political economists would like to believe. On the contrary, because the opportunity to participate in the civil economy is left unsecured by the commodity relations comprising the exercise of that right, any "free enterprise" system entails social injustice and must be rejected. This applies not only to a system of unregulated private capital but to any social order that seeks to resolve the problem of economic welfare through a principle of organization internal to the economy, such as worker self-management or public ownership of individual enterprises.

On the other hand, social justice cannot be achieved by replacing the market with a totally planned economy, where either a centralized state authority or decentralized communes determine the occupation and received goods of each individual. Even if this ordering were accomplished through democratic procedures, as in a radical kibbutz, it would eliminate the freedom of particularity that requires commodity relations to enable individuals to choose independently what they need and how they will earn a corresponding living in conjunction with others. After all, it is precisely the inability of some to exercise this *freedom* that is the social wrong that should be righted. Accordingly, the solution to social injustice does not consist in eliminating commodity relations, but in providing all the opportunity to participate in their reciprocal satisfaction of freely chosen needs.

Hegel understands this far better than those who stand him on his head: and, therefore, he recognizes that the remedy to social inequality lies not in the overthrow of commodity relations, but outside the economic order altogether in two separate civil institutions that he calls the corporations and the police. Their task is not preempted by the public administration of civil law, because the latter's protection of property only preserves the given distribution of wealth, instead of altering it so that all can actually satisfy their need through action of their own choosing.

Hegel introduces corporations because he recognizes that civil society gives its members the right to form economic interest groups to advance jointly their common needs as long as they do so in conformity with the market and civil law. These groups, which can issue from any of the classes,[63] enjoy civil legitimacy because they are voluntary; they forward particular interests that can only be realized in reciprocity with those of others; and thus they can only pursue their common cause by participating in, rather than supplanting, civil institutions. This mandates that their field of action lies in the market and the institutions of civil law and thereby sets the limit of their ability to right the social wrong endemic to the just economy.

On the one hand, the members of economic interest groups can take legal action together to protect their property with greater effect, but that alone cannot secure the satisfaction of their needs. In the market, on the other hand, they can collectively decide under what terms to enter into exchange so as to facilitate transactions in their interest through the pressure of their common front. Since, however, such activity does not unilaterally appropriate the commodities of others, but only aims to persuade them to agree to a desired exchange, it cannot overcome the dependence of its members' welfare upon the arbitrary exchange decisions of others—which is what calls for common corporate action in the first place. Because corporations are but particular groups that can only satisfy their members' need with the consent of other independent participants in the market, no corporation can guarantee the welfare of its members, nor need any success it might achieve benefit members of other corporations or unaffiliated individuals beyond what they may receive as opposite parties to exchange.

Although the activity of corporations does comprise a further mode of civil freedom, it thus cannot be counted on to remove social injustice, and may just as well worsen, as alleviate, the inequality of wealth.[64]

The plight of corporations thus reveals that, if social justice is to be achieved, the civil economy must be subject to an additional enforcement of welfare that is neither directed upon the members of a certain class, nor administered by private groups, whose efforts are constrained by the arbitrariness of others. The very rights founded in commodity relations require that economic interest group activity be supplemented by a *public* administration of welfare, addressing all members of society and issuing from a universally respected civil authority empowered to guarantee them the chance to satisfy their freely selected commodity needs through economic activity of their own choice. Hegel introduces his "police" to carry out just this task, duly aware of its decisive role in setting the economy in its proper subordinate position within the just society.

Here once again Marx's ideal of communism falls short of the requirements that prescriptive economics ordains. Since social justice concerns realizing the legitimate freedom of commodity relations, it extends beyond the imperatives of human species being and the normative neutrality of monological action. Accordingly, the public administration of welfare cannot subscribe to the motto "From each according to his ability; to each according to his needs," which leaves both work and need matters of liberty, without the mutuality of right and duty that grants each normative validity. Instead, it must aim at the much more ambitious goal of guaranteeing the reciprocal satisfaction of freely chosen needs through freely entered exchange relations.

Although Hegel's account of the "police" is brief at best, his conception of commodity relations already prescribes the twofold way in which public authority must secure the welfare of all as an exercise of civil freedom: At one and the same time, public authority must insure that the commodities needed by individuals be in adequate and affordable supply in the market and that they all have the commodities they require to obtain through exchange what they need.

As Hegel notes, this cannot be achieved through a public dole, unilaterally allotting individuals' goods to consume and jobs to perform, for that would eliminate, rather than secure, their civil freedom to choose what they need and how they will earn a corresponding livelihood.[65] Similarly, the civil authorities cannot impose an absolute equality of wealth, stipulating either the specific goods or total exchange value each is to have; for that would not be identical with the enforcement of everyone's right to realize independent interests, which would involve completely different commodities and levels of wealth due to the varying preferences of individuals.

Nevertheless, the unrestricted character of civil need and the inequality endemic to commodity relations require public regulation quite radical in scope. Since, as Hegel has shown, commodity relations entail the limitless multiplication and refinement of needs, public authority must cope with ever possible inadequacies in the supply of commodities by both restricting the need whose satisfaction it guarantees, and regulating the actual resources of the economy to furnish the market with as much of the needed goods as possible. These dual impositions are just, insofar as they apply to everyone and enable them to satisfy needs of their own choosing in reciprocity with others—albeit within limits determined solely as to allow all to engage in that reciprocal satisfaction itself.

Analogously, wherever inequality of wealth reaches such a magnitude as to create social disadvantage, civil authority must act to ensure that all do have adequate means to earn the livelihood they desire through action of their choice, given the capabilities of the economy. Since inequality is not a wrong unless it presents barriers to someone's desired participation in the market, enforcing the welfare of the disadvantaged need involve an administered redistribution of wealth only when other options are lacking.[66] When redistribution is required, the right of civil society would mandate that it be accomplished through monetary taxation and payment, rather than by dispossession and receipt of specific goods, for as Hegel argues, the former method preserves the freedom of particularity by letting each individual choose what to relinquish or acquire.[67] Although Hegel does not explicitly comment on the limits of such redistribution, the mandate of his police would suggest that whatever is necessary to eliminate social disadvantage is justified to the extent that the freedoms of commodity relations are upheld.[68]

In these ways the right of interest brought into being by commodity relations entails a perennial regulation of the economy, where civil authority enforces both the property rights and welfare of individuals in accord with the varying condition of the market, and the unalterable norms of economic freedom. Since this enforcement consists in an intervention *upon* commodity relations rather than in their removal, the just economy remains the institutional base of civil society, both presupposed and referred to by all other civil relations. Nevertheless, because the justice of commodity relations mandates their public regulation, the civil economy is the *subordinate* and not the determining base of the just society. If, on the contrary, society stands under the sway of the market—be it ruled by private capitalists, worker self-managed cooperatives, or government enterprises—there will be an unfree society, lacking the public subordination of the economy that can alone realize everyone's civil freedom to satisfy needs for commodities through freely chosen activity.

Significantly, these considerations of social justice do not lead Hegel to adopt the view of social democracy that the state should be a welfare state devoted to administering the public welfare with the consent of the governed.[69]

He instead recognizes that for there to be a just society and state, the civil subordination of the economy must be supplemented by a political subordination of civil society that frees self-government from relegation to a management of the economy. This is due to the inherent dependency of civil institutions and contrasting independence of just politics. By themselves the civil administrations of law and public welfare cannot provide the necessary conditions for their own existence. They lack not only the legislative power to furnish the laws they apply and obey, but also the source of authority to give their activities obligatory force for all individuals. On the other hand, if the state were restricted to functions of civil regulation, politics would be bound to independently determined interests, leaving government unable to set its own aims and exercise the genuine sovereignty that makes the reality of right a self-grounding order.

Hegel therefore places civil society under the rule of constitutional self-government that realizes political freedom as an end in itself, but also secures the other freedoms to the degree that they comprise its own prerequisites.[70] The sovereign state thus grants civil administration the law, power, and authority it needs on the political basis of the constitution and government legislation. Since, however, politics must remain supreme or forfeit its constitutive sovereignty, government must not only insure the social regulation of the economy, but exercise a political regulation of its own to prevent economic interest from undermining political freedom. Hegel raises this issue primarily in reference to wartime measures that restrict civil freedom for the sake of defending national sovereignty.[71] Because peacetime politics requires economic means to conduct political activity,[72] the state must also intervene to insure that all citizens have adequate resources to engage in politics, so that economic power does not become a basis of political privilege.

If Hegel has not provided a full account of these political tasks, his prescriptive economics has set a challenge to the modern economy of abiding social and political relevance. This challenge presents three imperatives of justice: first, that the economy be made a sphere of right offering everyone the full array of commodity relations; second, that civil authority regulate the economy to guarantee all their exercise of economic freedom; third, that government act to prevent economic power and interest from obstructing political freedom. In face of the capitalisms and socialisms of today, these imperatives remain everywhere matters for all.

## Notes

1. With the rise of industrial society, its global expansion through colonialism, imperialism, and revolution, the development of socialist and fascist movements, and

the rivalry of communist and capitalist blocs, virtually all sides in the political arena have come to regard economic relations as a normative concern of the highest order. Whether it be under the banner of bourgeois independence from serfdom, civilizing industry for the non-Western world, free enterprise versus totalitarianism, or the free association of producers to end all exploitation and class division, the economy has recurringly been ascribed a constitutive place within the just society that political action should seek to secure.

2. When classical political economy conceives need to be naturally determined by human physical requirements, derives exchange from a natural inclination to barter, and defines capital as the stock of goods required to sustain the laborer's life during production (see Adam Smith, *The Wealth of Nations* [New York: Random House, 1937], pp. 13, 259) it is effectively adopting this position as much as does neoclassical economics when it defines the factors of production as naturally scarce resources (David P. Levine, *Contributions to the Critique of Economic Theory* [London: Routledge and Kegan Paul, 1977], pp. 198, 236) or as do such thinkers as Marx (Karl Marx, *Capital*, Vol. 1 [New York: International Publishers, 1970], pp. 46, 167) and Hannah Arendt (Hannah Arendt, *The Human Condition* [Chicago: University of Chicago Press, 1958], p. 96ff.) when they characterize production as an anthropological factum of man's species being.

3. When marginal utility theorists draw their demand curves, when Martin Heidegger (*The Question Concerning Technology and Others Essays*, trans. by W. Lovitt [New York: Garland Publishing, 1977], pp. 3–35) and Jürgen Habermas (''Labor and Interaction'' in *Theory and Practice* [Boston: Beacon Press, 1973], p. 142ff.) reduce production to technique and instrumental action, or when econometricians and socialist planners attempt to guide economics with schemes for technically allocating given resources, the result is the same exclusion of any normative, let alone social, dimension from the economic realities at hand.

4. Aristotle, *Politics*, 1254a1–8, 1258b.

5. Kant, *Critique of Judgment*, trans. by J. H. Bernard (New York: Hafner, 1951), p. 9.

6. Smith, *The Wealth of Nations*, p. 14.

7. G. W. F. Hegel, *Philosophy of Right*, trans. by T. M. Knox (New York: Oxford University Press, 1967), remark to paragraph 189. This work is subsequently referred to as PR, with the following number being the paragraph number.

8. The example of Rousseau shows that the conflation of social and political domains can go either way in defining ''political economy,'' depending on whether civil society or civil government is emphasized. In Rousseau's *Discourse on Political Economy*, he reduces all legitimate social activity to that of civil government and accordingly characterizes political economy as the business of public administration.

9. Operative practice may indeed be the order to which action conforms, but that only signifies that that conformity has the quality of being and not that it has legitimacy.

10. If, for example, an economic order were relative to certain cultural factors that were not themselves structures of justice, commanding unconditional respect, that economy would be determined by a convention that was not just and thereby lack legitimacy.

11. Hegel, PR, 1 and 29.

12. Hegel treats it as a theme in his theory of Subjective Spirit under the heading "Practical Spirit."

13. Hegel, PR, 71 remark.

14. *Ibid.*, 261 remark.

15. If that were so, freedom and justice would remain apart, forfeiting their common normativity and ruling out any philosophy of right, let alone one developed as the theory of objective freedom.

16. Hegel, PR, 37.

17. *Ibid.*, 260 and 261 remark.

18. *Ibid.*, 127.

19. If, for example, individuals happen to satisfy certain physical or psychological needs, such as for air or affection, without interacting as proprietors of what the other needs, these needs play no role in the social relations of the community of interest.

20. Although Hegel does make brief mention of the relationship of capital and labor, he treats it as a subordinate element within the system of needs rather than as a privileged, determining structure that envelopes and orders all commodity relations within its process of capital accumulation.

21. As a result, two of his three classes, the so-called substantial and universal ones, have identities entirely unrelated to commodity relations, whereas the remaining class, the so-called reflective one, pursues all the types of earning specific to the system of needs.

22. The terms of this mandate will naturally have fundamental significance for evaluating the competing claims of laissez-faire capitalism, social democracy, and communism.

23. As Hegel's own example indicates, any consideration of commodity production, the total wealth of the market, or class relations presupposes this relationship of reciprocally needy commodity owners, and must be treated subsequently.

24. See n. 2; Marx, *Capital*, Vol. 1, p. 36.

25. In his *Vorlesungen über Rechtsphilosophie* (Karl-Heinz Ilting, ed., Vol. 4 [Stuttgart-Bad Cannstatt: Frommann-Holzboog, 1974], p. 475) Hegel accordingly observes that what needs should be satisfied and what should be the means of their satisfaction cannot be preordained, for an individual's civil need can have any content so long as what satisfies it is owned by someone else, just as a commodity can be anything as long as it is property needed by someone other than its owner.

26. Hegel, *Vorlesungen über Rechtsphilosophie*, Vol. 4, p. 605; PR, 195.

27. Hegel foreshadows this in PR, 77 and treats it thematically in PR, 192.

28. In his essay "Zum Abschluss des Marxschen Systems" (in *Aspekte der Marxschen Theories 1: Zur methodischen Bedeutung des 3. Bandes des "Kapital,"* ed. by F. Eberle [Frankfurt-am-Main: Suhrkamp, 1973]) Eugen V. Bohm-Bawerk rightly points out how the exchange value of nonproduced goods poses an insoluble problem for Marx's labor theory of value.

29. Hegel, PR, 196.

30. Marx, *Capital*, Vol. 1, p. 71ff.

31. *Ibid.*, p. 38ff.

32. Thus, in his *Vorlesungen über Rechtsphilosophie*, Vol. 4, pp. 630–631, Hegel lists three principal forms of exchange: (1) the exchange of particular commodities, (2) the exchange of commodities for money, and (3) the exchange of money for more money, leaving aside all mention of whether the commodities involved be produced or not.

33. PR, 204 and 299, 63 addition. Hegel, *Vorlesungen über Rechtsphilosophie*, Vol. 4, pp. 228–229.

34. Marx, *Capital*, Vol. 1, p. 166ff.

35. *Ibid.*, Vol. 1, Chapters 6 and 7.

36. See n. 32; Hegel, PR, 199; *Vorlesungen über Rechtsphilosophie*, Vol. 3, pp. 619–620, and Vol. 4, pp. 626–627.

37. Hegel, PR, 199 and 200.

38. For this reason, T. M. Knox would have done better to translate "Vermögen" as "wealth" rather than as "capital."

39. For instance, needs could be limited to consumer goods, rather than capital or rentable commodities.

40. Hegel, PR, 201; *Vorlesungen über Rechtsphilosophie*, Vol. 1, PP. 314–315; Vol. 3, p. 621; Vol. 4, p. 511.

41. Hegel, PR, 206; *Vorlesungen über Rechtsphilosophie*, Vol. 1, p. 322; Vol. 3, pp. 635, 638.

42. Hegel, PR, 201; *Vorlesungen über Rechtsphilosophie*, Vol. 3, pp. 624–632.

43. Hegel, PR, 203.

44. *Ibid.*, 203, 305, 306, and 204 addition; *Vorlesungen über Rechtsphilosophie*, Vol. 3, p. 628.

45. Hegel, PR, 203 addition. Significantly, Hegel notes that this occurs through the activity of the reflective class, whose pursuit of business deprives the peasantry and the nobility of their substantial foundation in the land and pulls them down to the ranks of factory operatives (*Vorlesungen über Rechtsphilosophie,* Vol. 3, p. 626). Such a relation of one-sided annihilation, so at odds with civil interdependence, is only to be expected, for the class embodying the spirit of commodity relations can solely come upon the substantial class as a vestige of pre-civil relations to be uprooted and done away with. Hegel makes this unambiguously clear when he remarks that the peasantry and nobility are necessarily confronted with force and compulsion by the *introduction* of commodity relations (*Vorlesungen über Rechtsphilosophie,* Vol. 4, p. 515), which, far from containing the natural ties of the substantial class, actually leaves no room for them. In this connection, Hegel also observes that the entailed forced elimination of the substantial class has indeed occurred in the country with the most developed civil society of his day—England, where land exists only as a material for factory-like employment and use (*Vorlesungen über Rechtsphilosophie,* Vol. 4, p. 517).

46. Hegel, PR, 303.

47. Hegel, *Vorlesungen über Rechtsphilosophie*, Vol. 3, p. 632.

48. Hegel, PR, 296 addition.

49. Hegel, *Vorlesungen über Rechtsphilosophie*, Vol. 4, p. 521.

50. Hegel, PR, 205.

51. *Ibid.*, PR, 204 and 203 addition.

52. *Ibid.*, 250; *Vorlesungen über Rechtsphilosophie*, Vol. 3, p. 629; Vol. 1, p. 315. Hegel, *The Philosophy of Mind*, trans. by W. Wallace (Oxford University Press, 1971), paragraph 528.

53. Hegel, *Vorlesungen über Rechtsphilosophie*, Vol. 4, pp. 630–631; Vol. 4, p. 520. In place of estates of peasants and nobles and civil servants, these groups comprise a handicraft class, making individual goods to satisfy singular needs, a factory class mass-producing commodities for socially differentiated needs, and a commercial class, having exchange as its business and exchange value as its end (Vol. 3, pp. 628–631, Vol. 4, p. 520; PR, 204). It can thus come as no surprise that when Hegel does use

the term *Klasse* instead of *Stand*, it is to describe either the proletariat (PR, 243), whose identity rests entirely on its role in commodity production and so forms a genuine social class rather than an estate, or the "wealthier classes" (PR, 245) whose identity is equally economic in character.

54. Hegel, PR, 251.

55. *Ibid.*, 250.

56. Hegel indicates this himself in *ibid.*, 298 and 301.

57. *Ibid.*, 303–312.

58. *Ibid.*, 308.

59. *Ibid.*, 305–307.

60. *Ibid.*, 82ff. and 102.

61. *Ibid.*, 209–229.

62. *Ibid.*, 200, 230, 236, and 237.

63. See p. 248.

64. This applies as much to labor unions, business associations and consumer groups as to federations of communes or worker self-managed enterprises.

65. Hegel, PR, 245.

66. For example, adequate self-financing public works could serve this purpose, providing both work opportunities and needed commodities *if* they did not exacerbate already existing overproduction in certain branches of industry, a circumstance Hegel warns against in PR, 245.

67. Hegel, PR, 299 remark.

68. Due to the endemic contingency of market relations, the measures of the public administration of welfare have to be continually revised in reaction to the changing situation of the economy.

69. Hegel, PR, 258 remark.

70. *Ibid.*, 260 and 261.

71. *Ibid.*, 323 and 324.

72. This includes resources not only to fund political organizations and mount political campaigns but to have access to the public through the media.

# 15

# Rethinking Politics: Carl Schmitt versus Hegel

Recently, a slew of Carl Schmitt's political writings have been translated into English, making newly available his *Concept of the Political, Political Theology, The Crisis of Parliamentary Democracy,* and *Political Romanticism.*[1] Addressing the theory and practice of modern politics, these slim monographs at once tantalize and frustrate with their bold strokes, whose sweeping connections are more intimated than systematically developed. All four studies are united by a critique of liberal political theory and the depoliticization of modern institutions, a critique that has found subsequent resonance among thinkers as diverse as Martin Heidegger, Hannah Arendt, Leo Strauss, Michael Oakeshott, and Jurgen Habermas. This dual critique has as its counterpart a positive doctrine of politics that Schmitt traces in reaction to the political crisis of our times. Both in its critique of liberalism and modern politics and in its affirmation of the political, Schmitt's work lends itself to a confrontation with Hegel, that other modern thinker who repudiated liberalism and its political embodiments in an effort to reestablish the primacy of politics.

## i) Schmitt's Critique of Liberal Political Thought

Schmitt's critique of liberal theory centers upon liberalism's alleged failure to conceive what characterizes politics in distinction from other institutional spheres. Although liberal thinkers address the nature of the state as if they were thereby laying hold of the political dimension, their equation of state and politics becomes deceptive because the state they analyze is penetrated by society, rendering affairs of state social concerns and social matters state functions.[2] This identity of state and society is realized to an extreme in the "total state" of totalitarianism, where every domain is subsumed by the state in a "politicization" of nonpolitical spheres. As much as the "total state" may seem to render everything political, it achieves a thorough depoliticization by collapsing all institutional boundaries so that the state can no longer possess any politically distinctive features.[3] Schmitt maintains that the seeds of this depoliticization are introduced by liberal theory in its derivation of political institutions from private rights and interests, as well as in the identification of state and society underlying its embrace of democracy.

This is reflected in how, on liberal grounds, political conflict becomes reduced to struggles over prepolitical rights and interests, where opponents face one another more as moral and social competitors than as political foes.[4] Here political institutions are not the decisive factor, but rather instruments for achieving aims determined in other spheres.[5] The state is at the service of society, where society has an order of its own instrumental to its members' individual liberty.[6] This, however, undermines the authority of the state as a particular association. Grounded on the private rights and interests of its members, the liberal state can no more coherently demand that they sacrifice their life and property than can economic enterprises.[7] Nor can the state impose any special entitlements and obligations upon members of its particular domain if it is a vehicle for realizing rights and interests that are common to all individuals. By virtue of its national boundary, the state must differentiate between citizens and foreigners. Yet the interests and rights of persons to which liberal theory appeals transcend such distinctions, being more at home in social institutions of universal scope, like the market.[8] On both counts, liberalism fails to provide an affirmative political doctrine, offering instead a critique of politics, whose basic concern is negating the power of the state, restricting government from interfering with individual liberty and property.[9] All that is left is administering an economic-technical system, whose universal reach elicits a pacifist internationalism in which all trace of the state's individuality fades away.[10] Alas, Schmitt observes, this liberal conclusion has become a harbinger of the modern onslaught against politics, where capitalists, Marxist socialists, syndicalists, and technicians have all joined hands in seeking to supplant political problems with technical and economic challenges.[11]

All this may be true, but why it condemns liberal theory is another matter. Some argument must be added to show that the liberal characterization of the state is deficient on either descriptive or normative grounds. In the first instance, Schmitt appears to adopt a descriptive perspective, maintaining that liberal theory upholds an extermination of politics that simply cannot be. Just as Marx cannot suppress the question of who will rule a communist society, where the state has withered away and associated producers seek to balance their needs and applied abilities, so, Schmitt suggests, the liberal subordination of politics to society and an internationalist humanism cannot prevent struggles over power by politically divided opponents, including wars to end all war and national division.[12]

If this is so, then the depoliticization of liberal institutions can be only partial, engendering a political system at war with itself. The task of political thought would then be to diagnosis the indwelling crisis of the liberal state and provide a remedy whose legitimacy would reside in its consistent realization of the nature of politics. In this way, Schmitt would lead us to an affirmative political theory without need of any ethics. A normative approach would be superfluous, since all that would be required is conceiving a noncontradictory embodiment of what politics is. This would supply a guide for political practice, directed at safeguarding the internally consistent political order from those who would introduce depoliticizing contradictions.

Nietzsche followed a similar strategy in affirming the political order of the superman. Nietzsche had little choice, given his claim that values are rooted, not in reason or nature, but merely in an arbitrary will whose positing of norms amounts to no more than a will to power imposing its particular perspective upon others. On this basis, the only way an affirmative politics can be retained is if one regime uniquely enjoys a consistency in its will to power eluding all others. It is in this respect that Nietzsche ascribes preeminence to the new aristocracy of the superman. It escapes the inconsistencies of democratic and socialist embodiments of slave morality, which claim universal legitimacy for what, in Nietzsche's view, is actually nothing but norms imposed by a particular standpoint in expression of a will to power. By contrast, the new aristocracy is perfectly consistent by imposing an order unabashedly arbitrary and perspectival in character.

This congruence in strategy may make more comprehensible how Schmitt could embrace Nazism after having appeared to be its theoretical adversary. Nevertheless, Schmitt departs from Nietzsche in identifying both the contradictions of liberalism and the affirmative core of politics.

## ii) Schmitt's Critique of the Liberal State

Schmitt's critique of the liberal state focuses upon the contradictions underlying the crisis of parliamentary democracy so starkly evident in the final days of the Weimar Republic. Two problems stand out: how the liberal constitutional state undermines its own political sovereignty and how parliamentary democracy operates so as to make parliament itself a superfluous institution.

According to Schmitt, political sovereignty is undercut in the liberal constitutional state by the division of powers, which limits the prerogatives of every branch of government, and by constitutional limitations upon emergency powers.[13] Both features subordinate every political decision to given legal norms, a subordination assumed to be endemic to rule by law and constitutional government. Yet, Schmitt suggests, this subordination is an anomaly on several counts.

To begin with, it contradicts a basic feature of legality, that legal norms cannot realize themselves.[14] They cannot independently translate themselves into juridical reality because all that legal prescriptions designate is how decisions should be made, leaving out of account who should decide and apply the law.[15] Consequently, the objective necessity of laws must lie not in their content but in a command that ensures their competence and authority.[16] In other words, the legal order itself rests on a decision that only a sovereign power can make, the decision that determines when a normal situation prevails, first permitting legal norms to have their jurisdiction.[17] Since such a decision simultaneously establishes when an emergency situation exists, it follows, contrary to the constitutional restraints of the liberal state, that a sovereign power alone has the prerogative to decide when an emergency begins and ends, as well as what can be done while it endures.[18]

By contrast, the liberal subordination of political power to legal norms, epitomized in Kelsen's theory of how a legal order rests on a basic norm,[19] deprives the state of the very sovereign decision making it needs to defend itself from its domestic and foreign foes. Hamstrung by a balance of powers and constitutional restrictions on emergency powers, the liberal state simply cannot resist the sort of internal enemies who would dismember the Weimar Republic. In embracing these constraints, the liberal state becomes the political equivalent of deism, excluding the direct intervention of the sovereign in the constitutional order, as if its legal machine could run by itself.[20] Just as deism committed the inconsistency of banning God from the world while retaining belief in his existence, so liberal politics paralyzes the head of state while retaining him at the apex of rule. Clothed with the trappings of an independent prerogative, inviolable and above parties, the liberal head of state is equally reduced to a mere executive organ, beholden to parliament, the consent of the cabinet, and the constitution.[21] In so doing, the liberal state not only contradicts its own sovereignty, but undermines its very viability.

Parliamentary democracy, Schmitt maintains, is afflicted by an analogous dilemma. The democratic element of parliamentary democracy, expressed in the identity of ruler and ruled, embodies the same conception of immanence at work in the identifications of state and sovereignty, sovereignty and the legal order, and state and the legal order with their balance of powers and constitutional limits on emergency powers. Like them, it excludes any sovereign decision making that transcends the limited organs of the state.[22] In the case of parliamentary democracy, this presents a particularly acute problem, for not only does it impede political sovereignty, but it brings parliament into crisis with itself.

Schmitt expounds this dilemma at length in *The Crisis of Parliamentary Democracy*, which offers the most sustained argument of his recently translated monographs. Here Schmitt focuses upon the tension between the principles of liberal parliamentarism and mass democracy, exploring an area often overlooked by political philosophers who all too readily equate democracy and parliamentary rule.

Although the oldest justification for parliament is that it derives from the democratic principle as applied to modern conditions where direct democracy is no longer possible, Schmitt points out that this derivation makes little sense. That a modern citizenry can neither assemble together nor individually address every detail of legislative policy does not mandate that there be an elected parliament, acting as a representative committee of the people, with a government that is a committee of parliament. These technical considerations may allow for representatives to decide for the people, but they equally permit a single trusted representative to supplant parliament with a Caesarian rule.[23] Moreover, no matter how extended suffrage may be, parliament is not representative of the whole people since it depends only on current voters,[24] whereas no matter how short its electoral term, parliament is independent of them and the whole people between elections and recall initiatives.[25] Hence, if parliament is to have a justification, it must lie somewhere other than in representative democracy.

Schmitt instead identifies the essential principles of parliament in the centrality of discussion and openness.[26] They entail such cardinal features of parliamentary rule as the publicity of parliamentary proceedings, the freedom of speech and immunity of representatives, and the independence of representatives from any binding mandate by their constituents or party.[27] What makes these provisos imperative is the meaning of parliamentary discussion. It seeks to determine laws, not through a battle of interests, but by an exchange of political opinion aiming to persuade and be persuaded with arguments for the truth and justice of legislative proposals. If these features of parliamentary debate are to be upheld, then members of parliament cannot function as representatives of particular social groups, local constituencies, or political parties, bound by instructions from those who have made them their delegates. Instead, the openness and rational character of parliamentary discussion require that representatives be independent participants in debate, concerned for the justice of the entire state and free to persuade and be persuaded by the most cogent arguments.[28] Laws enacted by parliament are accordingly not in essence commands based only on authority but general rational principles issuing from informed discussion.[29]

Since it could be questioned whether parliamentary debate is still by nature more prone to sophistry than reason, Schmitt maintains that parliament's affirmation of public deliberation rests on the general liberal principle that truth results from the unrestrained competition of opinion, where the best opinion ordinarily wins.[30] This assumption allegedly underlies the liberal commitment to the openness of political life and to the division of powers, with its distinction between legislative and executive branches of government and prevention of the gathering of state power at any one point.[31] These features all have legitimacy, not as mainstays of representative democracy, but as bulwarks for the free competition of opinions from which political truth is born.[32] To this end, parliament must be not only balanced against the other branches of government but also internally balanced, supplementing the openness of debate with federalism or bicameral arrangements, within which the balancing of opinions is secured through the presence inside each chamber of a recognized opposition.[33] Without these divisions of power, the very constitutionality of the parliamentary system ceases to be, which is why dictatorship stands as an antithesis of parliamentarism, representing the suspension of the liberal constitution and its distinction between legislative and executive powers.[34]

Admittedly, as Schmitt points out, the rationalism at the heart of liberal parliamentarism has a limited character. On the one hand, it concentrates itself in the workings of parliament, where, granted that legislation is deliberation, an assembly for the exchange of different opinions is appropriate. By contrast, in the executive branch, where action must be quick and forceful in response to such contingencies as war and civil disturbances, a unity of decision is required that is best achieved by a single individual who can act immediately.[35] On the other hand, even within parliament, the truth of political debate is recognized to be relative, deciding not absolute principles of ideology but political issues that are relative by nature. For these, the proper remedy is a relative truth attained through a discussion involving multiple participants.[36]

In analyzing how such government by discussion lies at the core of liberal parliamentarism, Schmitt is primarily concerned with showing how it is undermined by modern mass democracy and, more theoretically important, how it is incompatible with the requirements of democracy. Despite the parliamentary trappings of the mass democracies of our day, they have allegedly reduced public debate to an empty formality, making superfluous the cardinal parliamentary features of the independence of representatives and the openness of parliamentary sessions. This has been achieved by a party system, where parties oppose one another, not as participants in an open discussion devoted to truth and justice, but as social and economic power groups, jostling for control in the legislature and in electoral campaigns by appealing to the immediate interests and passions of voters. In this struggle for domination, parliamentary representatives relinquish their independence by accepting the binding mandates of party and local supporters, and the openness of parliamentary debate becomes superfluous now that discussion is merely a device for imposing predetermined agendas.[37] Rendered a technical means for political victory, the parliament of mass democracy demonstrates its own dispensability as an institution of rational debate, forfeiting the only rationale for its own retention.[38]

What makes, in Schmitt's eyes, the fate of parliament in mass democracy more than an historical accident is the fundamental opposition between parliamentarism and democracy. Whereas parliamentarism depends upon the exchange of different political opinions, democracy rests on an identification of ruler and ruled that requires achieving a homogeneity involving the eradication of social and political pluralism.[39] This homogeneity, it must be understood, is an equality restricted to the particular sphere of the individual body politic, since a universal democracy of mankind would obliterate the basic political distinction between the treatment of citizens and foreigners.[40] Although modern mass democracy may sometimes aspire to the humanitarian ethic of a world democracy, as the League of Nations and United Nations might suggest, what is essential to democracy is the requirement of domestic homogeneity.

Rousseau's concept of the 'general will' is instructive in this regard, for, as Schmitt points out, Rousseau's ideal of a true state whose citizens are subject to self-imposed law can only be sustained without the compromise of delegation and unheeded minorities if the people are so homogeneous that all unanimously combine into a univocal general will. Were there to be divisions producing an out-voted minority, its will would still be identical to the will of the majority, since it is the majority that determines the general will in which everyone's genuine freedom should reside. Yet, those who were out-voted would discover that their particular wills did not conform to the willing of self-imposed laws in which true freedom consists. They would therefore remain unfree.[41] To avoid this outcome, a homogeneity is needed, which itself requires, as the *Social Contract* details, that there be no religious differences, no economic divisions, no special interests, and no political parties that could separate the people from one another. It further entails that laws be made without discussion, because of the absence of contending political opinions, and even that judges and parties to a legal suit all seek the same outcome.[42] Only by achieving unanimity by obliterating all heterogeneity can the general will realize the identity of governed and governing that makes for a truly consequential democracy. Yet, in so doing, Rousseau's concept of the general will undermines the social contract argument on which it rests. As Schmitt points out, since a contract rests on differences between its parties, a social contract is unnecessary when there is the unanimity required by the general will, whereas when the heterogeneity is at hand for a social contract to be entered, this precludes the formation of a univocal general will.[43]

Whereas this suggests that democracy must seek its legitimation elsewhere than in the hands of contractarians, it equally indicates how democracy suffers from a crisis of its own that may aggravate the crisis of parliamentarism but that has an independent character.[44] In attempting to realize the identity of governed and governing, democracy chafes against parliament as an outmoded relic whose reliance upon discussion by independent representatives loses all justification in its opposition to the will of the people. Accordingly, Schmitt observes, bolshevism and fascism, as antiliberal as they are, need not be antidemocratic. Dictatorial and Caesaristic techniques can be a direct embodiment of democratic power, not simply through referenda and similar devices of a more "direct democracy," but above all in the sphere of publicity where the people alone exist in their democratic homogeneity, so at odds with liberal individualism.[45] Yet if democracy is driven to emasculate and eventually dispense with parliament, this makes only more acute the problem of how democracy is to retain legitimacy and avoid being devoured by totalitarian movements for whom it is, in its turn, a useful but dispensable ornament.

Democracy's dilemma, Schmitt maintains, lies in the series of identities on which it logically rests. These identities, of governed and governing, sovereign and subject, people and their representatives, and law and the people's will, find expression in the extension of suffrage, the reduction of electoral terms of office, and in the introduction of voter initiatives and referenda, all of which aim at approaching the ideal of direct democracy where ruler and ruled are literally one.[46] In each case, however, there is room for the people to be manipulated and deceived, so that the out-voted minority might be the keeper of the genuine will of the people. Of themselves, the democratic identities are formal, for unless the will of the people is properly formed, they do not enjoy legitimacy. This introduces the problem confronting Schmitt in the final days of the Weimar Republic: when enemies of democracy threaten to employ democratic institutions to win over a majority for the purpose of overthrowing democracy, then the loyal democrat must choose whether to save democracy by opposing the majority with antidemocratic measures. This choice comes to the fore, because what is of paramount importance is ultimately who controls how the people's will is constructed.[47] In order to insure that the people will in the proper way, the popular will must be educated, much as Rousseau proposed with his appeal to the Legislator and Civil Religion as needed cultivators of the general will. Taken to its logical conclusion, this program results in an educational dictatorship that suspends the rule of the majority for the sake of a true democracy awaiting creation after the dictatorship has sufficiently cultivated the will of the people.[48] Democracy thereby reaches an impasse, where political power is needed to form the people's will to the point where it can govern, while at the same time political power is held to come only from the will of the people.[49] This outcome sets in relief how dictatorship and democracy are hardly antitheses, as well as how democracy and parliamentarism can exist apart.[50]

The foregoing analysis provides a powerful tool for an immanent critique of modern politics, unmasking contradictions and inconsistencies afflicting the liberal democratic state. However, immanent critique does not provide any affirmative alternative by itself. It is here, in inquiring into the normative lessons of Schmitt's discussion, that things are far from clear. Although Schmitt is concerned throughout with retrieving the affirmative dimension of politics that modern conditions threaten, his own efforts at identifying it are meager and problematic.

### iii) Schmitt's Positive Doctrine of Politics

Having told us much of what politics is not, Schmitt offers little more than two positive theses on which an affirmative doctrine of the state might be built. First, he maintains that political association constitutively rests upon an opposition of friend and foe. Second, he identifies political sovereignty with the power to decide when a normal, rather than an emergency, situation prevails. These are the two pillars of a doctrine of the state that is to avoid the contradictions of liberal theory and practice, as well as provide a barrier to the totalitarian undertakers of parliament and democracy. Yet, Schmitt's dual theses furnish little indication of what his political alternative comprises and less sense of what normative legitimacy it can command.

Schmitt's first thesis, that the friend-foe opposition is constitutive of politics, might seem reminiscent of Hobbes's vision of the war of all against all from which issues the founding covenant of the commonwealth. Yet, whereas Hobbes applies this opposition to individuals in the state of nature and then only secondarily to individual states that have arisen from the former opposition through covenant, Schmitt introduces the friend-foe distinction from the outset as an opposition between the citizenry of one state and their public enemies, who are preeminently other states but may also be domestic subversive groups. Unlike in the Hobbesian picture, Schmitt's alliance of friends is a specifically political one, resting on shared citizenry in a particular state, just as his enmity between foes opposes members of one body politic to those of another (either real or represented in the subversive imagination) who threaten its political existence.[51] By making such a friend-foe opposition constitutive of political association, Schmitt adopts the novel strategy of advancing a doctrine of politics wherein the state is a particular body politic irreducibly defined in relation to others. Most traditional political theories address the relations of citizens to one another and their government before turning to international relations and their impact upon the domestic life of each state. Schmitt's first thesis instead suggests that the doctrine of the state must conceive every aspect of politics in terms of a plurality of particular states.[52]

Even granted that this strategy is adopted, it is still unclear how it leads to any institutional ramification other than the same provisions for defense and the conduct of foreign relations that other political theories have commonly incorporated. In light of Schmitt's insistence on the political centrality of the friend-foe opposition and his polemical critique of how the liberal state roots its politics in conflicts of interest that corrupt the friend-foe divide, one would expect other consequences pervading domestic political affairs.

There is one major consequence, which is equally arrived at by Aristotle and Hegel on very different bases: namely, Schmitt's emphasis upon the friend-foe distinction represents an affirmation of both the autonomy and the supremacy of politics. By defining the political in terms of the opposition uniting citizens agains public enemies who jeopardize their common political life, Schmitt is seeking to free politics from subordination to any nonpolitical factors and their associated antitheses.[53] By describing this opposition in terms of the potential of war, Schmitt is emphasizing how politics is fundamental to all other domains, given how their whole existence hangs in the balance the moment political association is engaged.[54] Thus, whereas courage, for Hobbes, is denied the status of a virtue insofar as the state can only demand obedience conditional upon preserving each subject's life,[55] Schmitt's opposition of friend and foe gives politics the power of life and death over individuals because political association is only at hand when all is ready to be mobilized in its defense.

Advancing the friend-foe opposition may help affirm how politics is an autonomous domain presiding over all others, but by itself it neither dictates the internal structure of government and political activity nor provides any norms for evaluating different regimes. Schmitt's second positive thesis on the nature of sovereignty might appear to concretize the friend-foe distinction in this direction. In arguing that sovereignty is tantamount to having the power to decide when there is a normal situation in which law is valid, Schmitt is applying the friend-foe opposition insofar as what distinguishes a normal from an emergency situation is the degree to which the political foe threatens the body politic. When a community lacks a figure empowered to make this decision, Schmitt suggests, it cannot organize itself in terms of the friend-foe opposition that would make it a political association for whom all nonpolitical considerations are secondary. However, having a true sovereign is not the privilege of any particular form of government. The free decision of the sovereign to begin and end emergency situations can coexist with parliamentary government, democracy, or dictatorship as long as adjustments are made to give the sovereign power this its constitutive prerogative. Thus, although Schmitt can begin by urging the Weimar Republic to take emergency measures to curtail its totalitarian domestic foes, he can readily acknowledge the sovereignty of *Der Führer* when a victorious Hitler takes decisive measures of his own.

This very leeway is indicative of a formality in Schmitt's two principles of politics. Although the centrality of the friend-foe opposition may affirm the autonomy and supremacy of politics, this can simply reflect the normatively neutral fact that political power is structurally dominant over all other forms of association. Predominance in power does not, however, confer supreme authority if any distinction is to be retained between the fact and legitimacy of rule, contrary to the doctrine that might makes right. By itself, therefore, the thesis of the autonomy and supremacy of politics establishes neither that politics has any normative priority over nonpolitical associations nor any basis for ranking the validity of different forms of political association. The same can be said of Schmitt's thesis that sovereignty is rooted in the prerogative to decide when the political situation is one of normalcy or emergency. It, too, leaves undetermined whether political association is of any value, as well as whether any normative evaluation of different regimes is possible.

Schmitt seems to fall into the same quandary that afflicts Nietzsche's politics of the will to power. By reducing all normative systems to perspectival impositions of arbitrary values, Nietzsche leaves himself with no other resource for ranking political regimes than their respective consistency in giving political embodiment to the will to power. However, acknowledging the superior consistency of the new aristocracy in comparison to the contradictory universalism of liberal democracy and socialism does not provide any basis for championing the new aristocrats and castigating modern proponents of slave morality. If all values are posits of a will to power, then consistency deserves no more authority than any other factor. Schmitt himself hints at such an outcome, observing how counterrevolutionary political philosophers end up dissolving the notion of legitimacy from which they set out by heightening the moment of decision to an extreme.[56] As Schmitt chronicles, this engenders a political romanticism for which politics is a mere plaything for aesthetic self-indulgence but not an affirmative domain in its own right.[57] Schmitt fails to recognize that, by the same token, if all that politics rests upon is a friend-foe opposition and an authority empowered to decide when normalcy gives way to political emergency, then his unveiling of the contradictions of the liberal state cannot serve as a normative critique. In the absence of any justification of either politics in general or particular forms of state, the inconsistencies of parliamentarism and mass democracy are of undecided value.

But is Schmitt's positive doctrine of politics merely descriptive in character? It certainly seems to be when he, like Nietzsche, roots the affirmation of politics upon an ultimate natural presupposition—in Schmitt's case, the dangerous character of man.[58] Yet, as Leo Strauss observes in his critique of Schmitt, this assumption does not figure as a binding ground, for if it did, politics would be an inescapable fate that modern developments could not menace. If Schmitt is to be defending a threatened body politic, then the affirmed essence of the political cannot lie in any natural given but must have some ethical character.[59] And then, the critique of the depoliticizations of modern conditions would retain a normative bite.

Does this ethical character lie simply in a moral embrace of the bellicosity of human groups, which, if repressed, eliminates the underpinnings of politics?[60] But what could be moral about this bellicosity on which the opposition of friend and foe resides? Is it as Strauss suggests, that the threat to the political is a threat to the seriousness of life, in that the autonomy and supremacy of political association makes the friend-foe conflict one in which all relative concerns, be they personal interests, managerial goals, or technical and economic aims, are suspended in deference to the absolute end of maintaining the body politic? To flee the friend-foe opposition would then represent a willingness for agreement and harmony at any price, an abandonment of all commitment to what is right, a betrayal of the effort to retain an objective meaning for human life.[61] If the question of ethics, of what is right, is to be taken seriously, then politics, as lying in the division of friend and foe, is something justified and worthy of protection.[62]

Yet if the affirmation of the political consists in this general upholding of ethics, we are left once again with a political formalism in which all political associations, together with all their accompanying friend-foe oppositions, stand on a par. All equally challenge the instrumental spirit of technology and the hegemony of private interests insofar as all are equally serious in defending the convictions they embody. As Strauss suggests, Schmitt's affirmation of the political turns out to be an inverted world of liberalism, for whereas liberalism tolerates all sincere convictions as long as they respect peace and legality, Schmitt's positive doctrine of politics grants equal respect to all convictions that are held with the earnestness involving the potential of going to war.[63]

### iv) The Pitfalls of Schmitt's Political Doctrine

The failure of Schmitt's doctrine of politics to provide a normative affirmation of political association suggests that his two theses may not only be insufficient bases for capturing the essence of politics, but simply wrong. And if this is so, then Schmitt's critique of the liberal state may equally be in need of rethinking. Although Strauss proposes that a critique of Hobbes is where we must turn to remedy Schmitt's difficulties,[64] a far better choice is to turn instead to the affirmation of the political that Hegel has undertaken.

If we examine Hegel's argument, we find that he repudiates both of Schmitt's cardinal theses. To begin with, Hegel does not start his political theory with a plurality of states, as is required to make sense of Schmitt's thesis that the friend-foe opposition is constitutive of political association. Although Hegel later introduces international relations and analyzes how the interaction of states entails domestic provisions for national defense, the regulation of foreign trade and investment, and the conduct of foreign diplomacy, he begins by introducing the minimal determination of the state per se. Of course, if political association is minimally determinate independently of international relations, then what distinguishes politics must be found in something other than a friend-foe opposition. But why should the character of political association be given prior to the interaction of states, whereas personhood, moral subjectivity, the family, and economic agency are all determined by Hegel in terms of the interaction of a plurality of agents?

There are two possible reasons. On the one hand, an argument like Schmitt's may well fall into the vicious circularity of taking for granted political association. If the friend-foe distinction is to be constitutive of politics, then the unity of friend and foe must not already reside in political groupings whose formation is antecedent to their encounter. Yet can the groups colliding in the friend-foe opposition be coeval with their interaction in the way in which individuals exist as owners only in and through the process of mutual recognition by which their correlative property entitlements are established? What provides a negative answer to this question is the other reason for rejecting an interstate starting point for political theory: namely, that what minimally defines political association are domestic features of the body politic.

Hegel's account of politics provides several such domestic factors that define the state in distinction from the other spheres of right. To begin with, political association is, in contrast to property relations and morality, a structure of ethical community. Instead of relating individuals in terms of rights and obligations given independently of any shared convictions of the good and membership in an existing community, the state constitutes an association whose participants exercise a political agency defined by belonging to the state that provides a common framework whose reproduction is precisely what their political activity aims at and achieves. Whereas moral agency seeks to realize a good that neither already exists nor is common to every conscience, political association removes the gap between ought and is and between subjective willing and objective right. The state does so by constituting a community whose members aim at realizing shared rights and duties already actualized in the political institutions within which their political participation can alone occur.

However, political association is not unique in exhibiting the cardinal features of ethical community, since, if we follow Hegel, so do the family and civil society, once reconstructed as institutions of self-determination. One can only exercise household rights and their coordinate duties by belonging to a home whose welfare and autonomy is the common aim of its members, just as one can only participate in the regulated market of civil society by pursuing interests whose realization is tied to the satisfactions of others within the existing web of commodity relations. Therefore, political association must be minimally determinable not just as ethical community but as that form of ethical community distinct from family and civil society. Hegel provides us with several differentia by which political ethical community can be domestically distinguished in this way.

First, there is the autonomy and supremacy of political association in relation to property relations, morality, family, and civil society. Contrary to Schmitt, this autonomy and supremacy are defined, not in terms of the relation between states, but in terms of the relation between the state and the nonpolitical practices it incorporates and oversees. On this basis, political association is distinguishable as the type of ethical community that rules over all other spheres of right, doing so preeminently in pursuit of aims that are defined independently of these other domains. Although, as Hegel duly emphasizes, the integrity of these prepolitical spheres demands that political activity maintain their freedoms in conformity with its own, political association is primarily concerned with realizing the self-governing autonomy of citizenship that no other practice can provide.

What characterizes the activity by which politics is both autonomous and supreme are two interconnected factors: its unique reflexivity[65] and the universality of its aims. Unlike family participation and civil activity in the economy and courts of law, political engagement involves acting so as to determine the very totality of right within which one's own agency as citizen proceeds. To participate in self-government, whether as campaigner, voter, or official, is thus to engage in an activity that acts upon itself. By contrast, household activity operates within strictures of family rights and obligations that are never laid down by the acts that conform to them. Similarly, economic activity is always concerned with particular satisfactions and never directed at determining the workings of the economy itself.

Intimately tied to the unique reflexivity of political activity is the universality of its aims. Simply by being an engagement in self-government, political practice always involves willing an end that is universal in respect to the jurisdiction of the body politic. Family members constitutively aim at maintaining the particular welfare of their household, and economic agents always aim at satisfying their particular needs. Only in their capacity as citizens do individuals make the goal of their activity the common order of the entire political community. Although their political actions may be influenced by particular interests rooted in family or economic involvements, the very fact that they engage in self-governing means that they will a policy applying to the order of the entire state as well as issuing in the name of the whole.

If these features provide distinguishing marks of political association, then the friend-foe opposition becomes at best an ingredient in international relations but no longer a necessary constituent of political life. Since the autonomy, supremacy, reflexivity, and universality of politics are all determined independently of a plurality of states, political association can be conceived without starting with the contrast of one body politic to another, just as a state could conceivably exist without standing in relation to any other politically organized communities.

Not surprisingly, Schmitt's second thesis, identifying sovereignty with the power to decide when there are states of emergency or normalcy, is beset with difficulty. As we have seen, this thesis is polemically directed at the immanence conception of sovereignty, whose most radical practitioner is quite correctly identified by Schmitt as Hegel. Hegel brings this conception to an extreme by conceiving of an organic division of powers in which no branch of government can will anything determinate in the name of the state without acting in consort with the other two branches. Here, the head of state is primarily limited to authorizing legislation voted on by parliament.[66] Although this leaves the head of state with little more to do than dot the "i" on enacted legislation, without this authorization legislative proposals do not have the force of law and the executive branch has nothing to execute. Hegel's point is to achieve precisely what Schmitt repudiates, namely, insuring that no particular will substitutes itself for the will of the state. Only when acts of state require the codetermination, direct or indirect, of all citizens can constitutionality be preserved, providing the existing framework of shared rights and duties by which politics can operate as a form of ethical community.

If, by contrast, a figure within the state is able to stand above the law and decide political questions without the codetermination of other citizens, political sovereignty is actually destroyed. For if, as Hegel argues, sovereignty consists in the autonomy and supremacy of political association over nonpolitical practices, where this is achieved through a mode of ethical community distinguished by reflexivity and universality, then conferring to any citizen the power to declare situations of normalcy or emergency would subordinate politics to a unilateral will whose exercise could no longer realize political freedom. Instead of willing the reproduction of the constitutional framework in which all nonpolitical and political rights and duties are realized, such a decision-making authority would exercise the same fundamentally nonreflexive, prepolitical making that a founding will exercises in willing into being a constitutional order to which its own activity cannot belong. Such activity is not action for its own sake, in the way in which political self-determination reproduces the body politic that self-government needs in order to operate. It is rather action for the sake of retrieving an order that only functions after such decision-making has expended itself. Just as the activity by which a constitution is established is antecedent to the sovereign agency of the founded state, so the decision-making by which emergency powers are conferred and exercised falls outside the actuality of the state, unless strictly limited by the constitution and the balance of powers by which constitutionality maintains itself. In the latter case, the agency exercising emergency powers constitutes what Schmitt calls a "commissary dictatorship." As Schmitt's terminology explicitly acknowledges, such dictatorship remains subject to constitutional law, bereft of that power to introduce or suspend legality in general with which he wishes to identify sovereignty. In the former case, which Schmitt identifies as sovereign dictatorship, there is no real sovereignty either. There the decision-making that seems to substitute personal rule for rule by and under law is not an ingredient in political association but rather figures as an interim expediency, at play only so long as the conditions of genuine politics are wanting.[67]

When Schmitt still insists that the power to decide on the exceptional circumstance transcending law is a general constituent of politics not tied to interim emergencies,[68] arguing in support that law always rests on an antecedent decision, he ignores the reflexive character of the ethical community of the state. The law of political association does not exist apart from the activities by which it is authorized and enforced. In the state's constitutional system, rule by law exists only by virtue of the decision-making of citizens, just as this decision-making depends upon the constitutional framework within which it alone can proceed. By appealing to an unencumbered political authority standing above law and the balance of powers, Schmitt is fleeing rather than redeeming political sovereignty.

### v) Rethinking the Crisis of the Liberal State

If Schmitt's affirmation of the political is fundamentally flawed, so too are major features of his critique of the liberal state. This is particularly true of Schmitt's analysis of the crisis of parliamentary democracy and the tension pitting parliamentary rule against democratic self-government.

Largely because of his rejection of the immanence conception of sovereignty, Schmitt construes democracy in terms of how it is conceived and legitimated in the social contract theory of Rousseau. Even though Schmitt is manifestly aware of the incoherencies in Rousseau's justification of democracy,[69] he accepts the Rousseauian conclusion that democracy requires homogeneity and that the legitimacy of democracy depends upon how the will of the people is cultivated. Both of these views presume that democracy is to be thought of as the self-assertion of a unitary will, defined independently of the institutions of political plurality, and that what is subject to democratic decision-making are matters subject to prior determination by reason, these being in Rousseau's case the traditional liberal commitments to uphold the person and property of individuals as given apart from political community in the state of nature. So long as democracy is so construed, it will conflict with parliamentarism's affirmation of the exchange of diverse political opinions and its correlative commitment to the openness of discussion and the independence and concern for political truth and justice of representatives. However, if democracy is not defined by homogeneity nor concerned with affairs susceptible of rational prescription, then the tension between parliamentarism and democratic government can be overcome.[70]

Although Hegel subverts the role of democracy and parliamentarism in his political theory by allowing social interests to be directly represented in a corporate legislature and by having this parliament be an instrument for politically educating the citizenry in line with the rational edicts of the head of state, his basic account of the political provides the resources for reconciling parliament and democracy. Hegel's concept of the just state as an ethical community whose mode of self-determination is autonomous and supreme, as well as reflexive and universal, situates legislative activity in several key respects. To begin with, it renders the legislature subject to a constitutional order committed to realizing the rationally transparent principles of property, moral, family, social, and political rights and obligations. This subjection is institutionally achieved by an organic balance of powers charging the legislature to realize the principles of the constitution in the face of contingent circumstances by formulating laws whose enactment depends on the authorization of the head of state. Constitutional principles may be determined by reason in the way in which the Philosophy of Right conceives the different structures of self-determination and the political community uniting them in a self-ordered whole. The legislature, however, has the task of drafting legal proposals that apply these principles to particular political conjunctures that can only be known through observation and interpretation. Hence, legislative activity involves a political judgment whose deliberations are always perspectivally limited and never more than an "educated" opinion. What legislation addresses are thus matters that are inherently insusceptible to rational prescription. Legislative proposals are rather always matters for debate, where no standpoint has special privilege and where the only appropriate final arbiter is the weight of political opinion as it results from the free exchange of competing judgments. What gives legislative debate its rational, yet relative, character is that it concerns the implementation of rationally determined principles of right, principles that are already embodied in the household, social, and political structures in relation to which legislative activity proceeds.

Democratic decision-making is particularly appropriate to legislative deliberation in two respects. Since the drafting of law is ultimately a matter of determining the weight of opinion subsequent to an open exchange of political judgments, majority decision is the procedure most suited for formulating legislation. This appropriateness of democracy within the legislature does not of itself say whether legislators should be selected by lottery, election, examination, executive appointment, birth, or some other means. What calls for an election of legislators is the reflexive and universal character of political activity, which entails that acts of state be mediated by the codetermination of all citizens. A participatory democracy in which all citizens legislate in person is excluded on two grounds. On the one hand, such an arrangement would require limiting active citizenship to the few so that other necessary functions could be carried out, disrupting the reflexive character of self-rule by introducing rule over the politically inactive. On the other hand, such an arrangement would disrupt the balance of powers by allowing the same body to preside over the drafting, authorization, and execution of law. If, however, parliament is a legislature of elected representatives, politics can provide a sphere of self-determination wherein citizens codetermine the realization of the totality of right, exercising an autonomy predicated on the very framework their actions knowingly reproduce. Given the autonomy, supremacy, and universality of political aims, such parliamentary representation cannot be subordinate to particular interests, as may well be the case in mass democracies such as Schmitt decries, where politics is at the mercy of competing social powers. Far from conflicting with democracy, the openness of parliamentary debate and the independence of representatives are a precondition for voters to exercise any role in distinctly political affairs. For if representatives are subject to binding mandates, by which particular interests assert themselves, the aims of legislative activity are deprived of the autonomy, supremacy, and universality that make them properly political. This does not mean that representatives are elected into office without any political commitment to their constituency, reducing electoral contests to competitions of leadership qualities rather than political programs. The genuine political grounds for selecting representatives do lie in the political opinions to which they subscribe. However, because of the relativity of legislative debate and the corresponding contingency of political conjunctures, a legislator's commitment to a particular legislative program cannot be absolute, where deviations entail automatic recall or the like. On this count as well, democracy is reconcilable with parliamentarism.

Where then does this reconciliation leave the critique of liberal institutions? Essentially it shifts our attention from any principled conflict between democracy, parliamentarism, and political sovereignty to the contest between civil society and the state in which regimes of east and west and north and south remain embroiled. It can be shown, employing the categories of Hegel's philosophy of right, that civil society and the state can be reconciled, provided that social inequalities are counteracted through a pervasive public regulation of market activity and that social factors are prevented from becoming bases of political privilege.[71] However, when social and political institutions fail to meet these requirements, a critique can be made, as applicable to the liberal state, where an inequitable civil society challenges the autonomy and supremacy of politics, as to communist regimes, where struggles in civil society contest the social and political hegemony of the ruling party; and to ''underdeveloped'' nations, where traditional practices compete with distorted realizations of civil society and the state.[72] To this end, the insights of Hegel can help redeem the abiding contributions of Schmitt and cut through the fog of the modernity-postmodernity debate.

## Notes

1. Carl Schmitt, *The Concept of the Political*, trans. by George Schwab (New Brunswick, NJ: Rutgers University Press, 1976); *Political Theology: Four Chapters on the Concept of Sovereignty*, trans. by George Schwab (Cambridge, MA: MIT Press, 1985); *The Crisis of Parliamentary Democracy*, trans. by Ellen Kennedy (Cambridge, MA: MIT Press, 1985); *Political Romanticism*, trans. by Guy Oakes (Cambridge, MA: MIT Press, 1986).

2. Schmitt, *The Concept of the Political*, p. 22.

3. *Ibid*., p. 24.

4. *Ibid*., p. 28.

5. *Ibid*., p. 43.

6. *Ibid*., p. 60.

7. *Ibid*., p. 48.

8. *Ibid*., p. 55. Ronald Dworkin adopts this argument in *Law's Empire* (Cambridge, MA: Harvard University Press, 1988), Chapter 6.

9. Schmitt, *The Concept of the Political*, p. 71.

10. *Ibid*., p. 72.

11. Schmitt, *Political Theology*, p. 65.

12. Schmitt, *The Concept of the Political*, pp. 57, 79.

13. Schmitt, *Political Theology*, pp. 11, 12.

14. *Ibid*., p. 28.

15. *Ibid*., pp. 32–33.

16. *Ibid*., pp. 20, 33.

17. *Ibid*., p. 10.

18. *Ibid*., p. 12.

19. *Ibid.*, p. 19.

20. *Ibid.*, p. 37.

21. *Ibid.*, pp. 59–60.

22. *Ibid.*, pp. 50–51. Significantly, Schmitt identifies Hegel as the greatest systematic architect of this immanence philosophy (*ibid.*, p. 50).

23. *Ibid.*, p. 34.

24. *Ibid.*, p. 98.

25. *Ibid.*, p. 34.

26. Schmitt, *The Crisis of Parliamentary Democracy*, p. 2.

27. *Ibid.*, p. 3.

28. *Ibid.*, p. 6.

29. *Ibid.*, p. 43.

30. *Ibid.*, p. 34, 38.

31. *Ibid.*, p. 36.

32. *Ibid.*, p. 39. This argument sheds light on Habermas's difficulty in tying his appeal to an unconstrained communicative speech situation as the procedural basis for ethics to his substantive commitment to democratic institutions.

33. *Ibid.*, pp. 40–41.

34. *Ibid.*, p. 41.

35. *Ibid.*, p. 45.

36. *Ibid.*, p. 48.

37. In this light one can better comprehend the common critique of parliamentarism cited by Schmitt, namely, that proportional representation and the party list system destroy the proper relation between voter and representative, making parliamentary factions of decisive importance, leaving key decisions to the secret meeting of faction leaders, where parties and economic interests rule at the expense of openness and of the correlative principles that members of parliament represent the whole people and are responsible to their own independent conscience (*ibid.*, pp. 19–20). Schmitt's analysis allows us to see that this critique may be germane to parliament as it is distorted under conditions of mass democracy but not necessarily applicable to parliamentarism as such.

38. *Ibid.*, pp. 7–8.

39. *Ibid.*, p. 9.

40. *Ibid.*, p. 12.

41. *Ibid.*, p. 27.

42. *Ibid.*, p. 14.

43. *Ibid.*

44. *Ibid.*, p. 15.

45. *Ibid.*, p. 17.

46. *Ibid.*, p. 27.

47. *Ibid.*, p. 29.

48. *Ibid.*, p. 28. The bolshevik affirmation of democracy is a prime example of this outcome, Schmitt suggests, since it regards the popular will of bourgeois democracy to be falsely educated because of capital's domination over political parties and the press, and advances communism as the first true democracy (*ibid.*, p. 29).

49. *Ibid.*, p. 29.

50. *Ibid.*

51. Leo Strauss, "Comments on Carl Schmitt's *Der Begriff des Politischen*," in Schmitt, *The Concept of the Political*, p. 88.

52. H. L. A. Hart is one of the few political theorists who follow Schmitt's lead in taking the state to be defined in terms of the plurality of body politics. Hart does so, however, on the very different basis of having what defines states be empirically determined by whatever international law happens to leave as the prerogative of individual nations. See H. L. A. Hart, *The Concept of Law* (Oxford: Oxford University Press, 1982), p. 209.

53. Schmitt, *The Concept of the Political*, p. 27.

54. *Ibid.*, pp. 47, 88.

55. *Ibid.*, pp. 46, 89.

56. Schmitt, *Political Theology*, p. 65.

57. Schmitt, *Political Romanticism*, p. 125.

58. Schmitt, *The Concept of the Political*, p. 61.

59. *Ibid.*, pp. 93–95.

60. *Ibid.*, p. 95.

61. *Ibid.*, p. 101.

62. *Ibid.*

63. *Ibid.*, p. 103.

64. *Ibid.*, p. 105.

65. The conceptual ramifications of this feature are focused upon in Michael B. Foster's *The Political Philosophies of Plato and Hegel* (Oxford: Oxford University Press, 1967) and in Richard Dien Winfield's "The Logic of The State," in Richard Dien Winfield, *Overcoming Foundations: Studies in Systematic Philosophy* (New York: Columbia University Press, 1989). Robert Bruce Berman discusses reflexivity in Hegel's theory of the state in terms of the self-referring purpose of political action. See Robert Bruce Berman, *Categorial Justification: Normative Argumentation in Hegel's Practical Philosophy* (Ph.D. dissertation, New School for Social Research, NYC, 1983), pp. 168–172.

66. Admittedly, Hegel violates the spirit of his own division of powers in two fundamental ways. On the one hand, he undermines the autonomy and supremacy of political association, violating the demarcation of state and civil society by turning parliament into an estate assembly, whereby social factors dictate political functions. On the other hand, he emasculates the legislative powers of parliament by reducing its activity to one of largely cultivating the political spirit of the citizenry in accord with the rational insights of the head of state.

67. Norberto Bobbio makes this point in "The Rule of Men or the Rule of Law" in his essay collection, *The Future of Democracy*, trans. by Roger Griffin (Minneapolis: University of Minnesota Press, 1987), pp. 152–153.

68. Schmitt, *Political Theology*, p. 5.

69. See Richard Dien Winfield, *Reason and Justice* (Albany, NY: SUNY Press, 1988), pp. 263–265, for a further discussion of these incoherencies.

70. Admittedly, as we have seen, Schmitt does acknowledge that the truth at stake in parliamentary debate is relative in character. Nevertheless, his opposition of parliamentarism to democracy is based on an emphasis upon the rational character of parliamentary deliberation.

71. Arguments to this effect are made in Richard Dien Winfield, *The Just Economy* (New York: Routledge, 1988) and in Richard Dien Winfield, *Reason and Justice* (Albany, NY: SUNY Press, 1988).

72. For an example of such a critique, see "Capital, Civil Society and the Deformation of Politics," in Winfield, *Overcoming Foundations*.

# 16

# Political Freedom and Territorial Rights

## i) The Practical Importance of Territorial Rights

Few would dispute the central place of territorial rights in human affairs. When it comes to international relations, nothing figures more fundamentally than the claimed boundaries of nations. Territorial rights underlie all intercourse between nations, setting the very limits at which international concerns begin and end. Perennially a prime source of international hostilities,[1] territorial claims are equally the precondition of all cooperation among nations in peace as well as in war. Yet the importance of territorial rights is hardly breached unless their role in domestic affairs is understood, a role reflecting the significance of international relations for the life of each citizen in every nation.

Admittedly, international relations would count for little in the lives of individuals if political life had no affirmative value of its own or if the body politic had a self-sufficiency making relations between nations of no bearing upon the just order of the state. Were property relations, family matters, or economic and social concerns all that had intrinsic value, then international affairs and territoriality would be of secondary importance, since borders could shift and conquerors come and go without blemish to these nonpolitical affairs. If, however, the political life of the citizen has its own value, as both ultimately determining the design of nonpolitical institutions and providing its own good of self-rule, then international relations can only be ignored if the state has such self-sufficiency as to be impervious to external threat and without need of any foreign ties. Only then can the entire political life of individuals not be at risk in foreign affairs, where recognition of territorial rights first provides for a domain in which to exercise political independence.

History amply confirms, however, how rare a luxury is indifference to territorial rights and foreign affairs. Far from being self-sufficient, states are neither invulnerable to foreign dangers nor free of dependence upon other nations for economic or military support. Nor do states belong to a benign international society in which some preestablished harmony reigns, allowing them to forget their neighbors and turn all energies inward. Nor can the affirmative value of political independence be held in abeyance, especially in view of the modern quest for self-government.

Given the fragility of national self-sufficiency, the unequal power of different states, the lack of order characterizing the society of nations, and the corresponding jeopardy of national independence, it is no exaggeration to call foreign affairs, and hence concern for territorial rights, the most important issue for a state, save, perhaps, civil war.[2] Thus Diodotus in Thucydides' history can rightly view freedom from foreign domination as the greatest of things, for without the territorial claim of the nation enjoying respect, its citizens forfeit their political autonomy together with its power to mould and safeguard their nonpolitical lives.[3] By the same token, the demands of attending to foreign affairs and territorial claims may well put a lower ceiling on the aspirations of any state towards justice than that entertained by the classical reveries of political self-sufficiency.[4] At the very least, the state's need to mobilize in defense of its own territory brings to consciousness the supremacy of national sovereignty over every particular concern.[5] In this respect, the nurturing of domestic freedom through the maintenance of peace among nations can appear as the highest political good, indeed, as the entire end of justice.[6]

### ii) The Theoretical Problems of Territorial Rights

Despite this practical importance, which brings with it an urgent need to adjudicate international disputes over territory, the very possibility of a theoretical solution is far from secure. As with any problem of right, the challenge of nihilism must be countered. If, as the nihilist maintains, no ethical standards are rationally justifiable, theories of territorial rights must resign themselves either to describing how territorial rights are and have been operative or to the metaethical task of deconstructing the rationally groundless but pragmatically comprehensible assumptions underlying various positions on territorial entitlements.

What is particularly troublesome in the case of territorial rights is that, even if a normative political theory is possible, prescribing objective standards of justice applying within the boundaries of the sovereign state, this by no means insures that there are any objective norms pertaining to international relations and territorial entitlements. In order to establish a normative theory of territorial rights, it must further be demonstrated either that international norms are derivable from domestic principles of justice or that relations between nations contain their own nonderivative rights and duties. Nothing less can chase nihilism from the international arena, since not only may no international norms be derivable from domestic rights, but international relations may be such as to preclude any inherent norms of their own.

The questionable status of international law suggests the considerable challenge posed by these two sources of doubt. To the extent that the society of nations lacks an international legislature, courts with compulsory jurisdiction, or centrally organized sanctions,[7] international relations well appear to be both incommensurable with the relations between individuals within the state and without any proper laws of their own. Hence, far from being able to assume the objectivity of territorial rights, we must face the problem in its full generality.

How then is a normative theory of territorial rights to be conceived? The answer falls within the broader question of how a normative theory of international relations should be constructed. First of all, where within the theory of right should international relations be treated? Are they to be conceived subsequent to and apart from the conception of the just state, or do international relations comprise a context constitutive of the individual nations they contain, requiring treatment in tandem with what could be called internal sovereignty? Naturally, the answer to this question has implications as much for domestic as for international relations.

The first option, which could be called "national atomism," is the most common choice among both ancient and modern political philosophers. Aristotle, for one, embraces the route of imagining a solitary state happy in itself and in isolation, living under a good constitution, whose scheme has no regard to foreign affairs and war.[8] Although he dismisses the goodness of the life of the individual hermit for lacking the benefits of the household, friendship, and political association that make life worth living, Aristotle grants the state a normative self-sufficiency that permits political justice to be addressed in abstraction from international relations. In a similar vein, Rawls sees fit to formulate a reasonable conception of justice for the basic structure of society conceived as a closed system.[9] Although the complete theory of right will also contain principles for individuals and for the law of nations, as well as priority rules for deciding conflicts between these three spheres,[10] these are to be treated subsequently to the principles of social and political justice, whose prior derivation will make the other spheres' determination more tractable.[11]

Needless to say, if a normative theory of international relations, including territorial rights, is to follow the route of deriving international from domestic norms, then it must be possible to determine the justice of the state prior to a consideration of international relations, which is precisely how national atomism proceeds. Opposing this strategy is the view that the conception of the state is parasitic upon an account of international relations. H. L. A. Hart presents this in its most radical form, arguing that, insofar as sovereignty simply refers to the area of conduct in which a state is autonomous, how and to what extent a state is sovereign can only be determined by first ascertaining the rules governing the relations between states, rules that set the limits on the freedom of each.[12] Similarly, Leo Strauss emphasizes how political society always is a partial and particular society, so that, although its highest task may be its self-improvement, its primary task is its self-preservation, involving all the internal ramifications of being part of the society of nations.[13] Hence, Aristotle himself will admit that legislators should regard neighboring countries and construct a constitution with a view to military strength.[14]

Despite their contrast, these approaches are more complementary than contradictory. The structures of right constituting the domestic life of the just state, such as property, family, social, and political relations of justice, may have essential features given independently of international relations at the same time that international relations entail strictures of justice bearing upon certain other aspects of their existence. Conversely, although international relations impose institutional requirements within the just state, most immediately in regard to the political institutions for conducting foreign affairs and organizing the national defense, international relations cannot even have any determination without there being at hand structures of nonpolitical and political association that first make possible a plurality of nations. Hence, the just state has a dimension given independently of international relations, whereas relations between nations do determine certain other features constitutive of states as members of the community of nations.

Admittedly, those features endemic to states in their plurality might or might not be normatively neutral. If they were normatively indifferent, then the theory of justice could begin and end with a treatment of domestic affairs, with an allowance made for an inquiry into those features of morality that are independent of institutional arrangements. If, however, justice does involve features dependent upon relations among nations, then the theory of justice must advance from first addressing those dimensions of right that pertain to domestic relations independently of international relations to a consideration of whatever normative ramifications arise from the plurality of nations, including prescriptions for reorganizing domestic life and norms governing external affairs.[15]

Granted that a normative theory of domestic relations is possible, it is hard to imagine how international relations could be without normative significance at least in regard to the maintenance of domestic rights in the face of the threats to their security that foreign relations introduce. Thus, even were international relations bereft of any normative concern beyond asserting the rightful welfare of each just state, they would have to be incorporated within the scope of the theory of justice. Accordingly, a normative theory of territorial rights will be a sine qua non for any comprehensive philosophy of right, given how fundamental territorial claims are for relations between nations.

### iii) National Atomism and Liberal Theory

That the plurality of nations requires additional measures to be taken for the sake of domestic rights might suggest that the norms of international relations are wholly derivative of domestic justice, as it is determined independently of foreign affairs. If this is so, the normative theory of territorial rights proceeds from a given plurality of individual states, each of which contains structures of right that not only possess their legitimacy logically prior to any foreign intercourse but also figure as the privileged source for the specification of international norms. This atomistic starting point bears strong resemblance to the state-of-nature construct of liberal theory, which presumes that individuals are subject to no obligations that do not derive from the rights they bear prior to any interpersonal conventions.

It thus should come as no surprise that liberal theorists have seized upon this resemblance and sought to conceive the norms of international relations in analogy to the social contract argument. Although not all liberal theorists have followed this analogy to the point of constructing an international civil order arising from a covenant among nations,[16] figures such as Hobbes, Locke, Kant, and Rawls have all accepted its basic premise that international and personal rights are rooted in the same atomistic logic. In order to arrive at a satisfactory account of territorial rights, it is important to explore the pitfalls of their common strategy.

By conceiving international relations as if they exhibited the same basic structure as personal rights, liberal theory engages in a dual remapping that underlies its whole conception of justice. On the one hand, the liberal conflation of international with interpersonal relations translates the problem of domestic justice into the distinctly international terms of war, whereby individuals get disembedded from all institutional relations and confront one another in the predicament of independent nations, bearing rights constituted in their own domain but facing one another without being subject to any governing authority. On the other hand, the same conflation of the situation of states and individuals transforms the problems of international justice into mere extensions of private right writ large.

That these consequences represent a dual confusion becomes apparent when liberal theorists apply their social contract atomism to international affairs. Even though the analogy is not without some plausibility, it engenders anomalies suggesting that territorial rights can no more be modeled after the natural right conception of personhood than domestic justice can be derived from a state of war. This is best seen by examining the similarities and differences between persons and states that liberal theorists themselves acknowledge in investigating the laws of nations.

To begin with, the liberal standard-bearers all agree that persons and nations stand in the same state of nature and are governed by the same natural law. For Hobbes this signifies that both individuals and states find themselves in a war of all against all, where, if the parallel be observed, there is no recognized property nor justice and injustice, and where, as a consequence, the passions and reason should impel persons and sovereigns alike to seek some route of escape from a condition so brutish and mean.[17] For Locke, this leaves states, like individuals, in a condition of all-sided license, where, nevertheless, property can be instituted and promises made binding, thanks to the natural laws of God evident to the right reason of persons and princes.[18] Hence, both maintain that the state of nature cannot be dismissed as idle fiction, for so long as independent nations exist, the world can never be without such a state.[19] For Kant, the same parallel holds, insofar as nations face one another as moral persons in a condition of natural freedom.[20] Thus states, like individuals, enjoy the right to wage war, but equally the right of compelling one another to leave behind the state of war and erect an order of lasting peace.[21]

While citing such similarities, these same thinkers acknowledge certain key differences. Kant, for example, admits that international law involves, not merely relations between states, but relations between individual persons and foreign citizens or entire states.[22] Although Kant claims that this disanalogous feature can be readily comprehended from the concept of the state of nature among individuals,[23] it suggests how the state's internal structure as an independent system of different ethical associations sets it significantly apart from the individual. Even if one were to picture the composition of the state in analogy to the soul (following Plato) or the embodied individual (following Hobbes), the body politic would still contain right-bearing legal subjects and normative institutions categorially distinct from any psychological or anatomical factors.

Hobbes notes another central difference: whereas the natural liberty of particular men condemns them to a misery from which only a covenant instituting a sovereign can relieve them, individual states are able to uphold the industry of their subjects and hence enjoy a degree of self-sufficiency that permits them to endure their state of nature without suffering as persons do.[24] Similarly, Locke observes that, although conquered states are like victims of robbers in a state of nature, having no court on earth to appeal to, conquering nations are too mighty for the weak hands of justice in this world, in contrast to individual thiefs, who not only are vulnerable to other individuals in the state of nature but subject to punishment in civil society.[25]

The significance of these differences is well brought out by Hume and Hart, who, despite repudiating social contract from their respective utilitarian and legal positivist standpoints, incorporate much of the atomistic logic defining liberal theory. Hume observes that, whereas individuals by nature cannot subsist without association and that their association cannot survive without observance of laws of equity and justice, nations can subsist not only without foreign dealings, but even to some degree in a state of general war. Hence, their observance of justice, though useful, is not as much a necessity for them as for individuals.[26] This helps explain why nations may ignore treaties and alliances harmful to themselves in a way in which individuals may not ignore contracts and property entitlements,[27] whether or not we accept Hume's justification of this practice by appeal to a utilitarian concern for harm and benefit.

Hart draws out the key point that underlies the above observations. It is not simply that states have a greater self-sufficiency than individuals. What decisively matters is that states, unlike individuals, are not approximately equal in strength and vulnerability.[28] For this reason, states are not in common need of external sanctions to maintain their security, as would be the case of individuals born free and equal in a state of nature.[29] By the same token, even if external sanctions were countenanced in international affairs, they would not have the same efficacious employment that civil sanctions can enjoy. Given the unequal power of states and the public character of aggression, any initiation of war is much more risky than personal crime, since there can be no guarantee that the conflict will remain localized nor that the combined strength of one side or the other will prevail. Consequently, long periods of international peace may intervene, even though the use of sanctions involves great risks of its own, making the threat of sanctions a meager deterrent in comparison to the efficacy of arrest, conviction, and punishment in deterring individual crime.[30]

Although neither Hart nor Hume dwells upon how these differences disrupt the analogy between the liberal idea of the natural rights of individuals and the rights of nations, the results are plain when liberal theorists press their analogy in the face of the irremovable contrasts between persons and states. Essentially, there are two outcomes. Liberal theorists are forced to admit either that nations can never cease confronting one another in a state of nature or that the establishment of an international civil order retains a problematic character fundamentally distinct from domestic justice. One way or the other, the project of a normative theory of territorial rights arrives at an impasse.

Hobbes and Locke exemplify the former alternative in ways reflecting their complementary conception of the state of nature. For Hobbes, the identification of international relations as a state of nature signifies that nations are in a war of all against all,[31] where every sovereign has the same right to procure the safety of his people as every individual has to safeguard his own body.[32] Because there is no earthly legislator, tribunal, or executive of natural justice, but only the court of conscience, and because there is no law or injustice or property where there is no common power,[33] nations, like individuals, are free to use force and fraud to protect their domains, whose extent is determined by no more than what they can get for as long as they can keep it.[34] Properly speaking, nations thus have no territorial rights in this state of nature, for, like individuals in their war of all against all, possession rests exclusively upon unilateral force.

Here, however, the analogy breaks down. In respect to individuals, Hobbes reasons that they, because of their roughly equal power and corresponding equal vulnerability, are led by the fear of death and the prudential calculations of reason to follow the articles of peace and make covenant to institute a commonwealth whose sovereign alone has the power to initiate separate property entitlements.[35] In respect to nations, Hobbes can make no parallel argument. As he has himself observed, states are able, thanks to the industry of their subjects, to maintain a relatively comfortable self-sufficiency that saves them from the misery[36] that gives individuals a motive for making peace and instituting civil government. Similarly, the lack of equality between states removes the key precondition for either the passions or reason to compel all nations to enter a covenant and subject themselves to a world sovereign lording over them. In terms of Hobbesian calculations of self-preservation and liberty, the inequality and self-sufficiency distinguishing nations from individuals leaves nations with no reason to relinquish their "natural" independence and erect an international commonwealth, for many will do better relying on their own power. As a result, sovereigns remain at all times in a state of war,[37] leaving territorial rights a contradiction in terms.

Even if nations were to make a covenant and establish a commonwealth, the territory of their new combined state would be in the same predicament. Although provinces could have territorial rights issuing from the will of the new federal sovereign, the territory of the federation would once again be a possession resting on nothing but force as regards any other terrestial or extraterrestial states to which contact might be made. Hence, on either score, the Hobbesian argument is unable to provide for a normative theory of territorial rights.

Locke comes to similar conclusions even though he allows for property entitlements and contractual obligations arising in the state of nature. Princes do owe unexemptible subjection to the same laws of God and nature that bind individuals in the state of nature.[38] Insofar as individuals are entitled to take ownership of whatever unclaimed object their labor improves, provided that so doing does not jeopardize the survival of others, one would expect that nations would enjoy the same prerogative with regard to territory. Nonetheless, this opportunity is of little meaning since, in the absence of a recognized governing authority, each property owner has equal judicial and executive powers to settle disputes, leaving no property entitlement with an objective determination. However, whereas individuals are instructed by right reason of the divine command to make peace by agreeing to unite into a civil society whose appointed government shall secure their person and property, Locke admits of no parallel route for nations. Even when they are in league with one another, nations remain in a state of nature. They may well have entered alliances, but only a compact establishing one community and one body politic puts an end to their state of nature.[39] So long as states retain their independence, they lack objectively binding territorial rights, whereas if they do unite into a single encompassing nation, its territory remains just as much without an objective entitlement once other states are encountered, either by secession or external discovery.

It might be objected that Hobbes and Locke do both acknowledge territorial rights when they address the rights of conquest. Hobbes maintains that conquerors acquire dominion through the consent of the vanquished, since the fear under which the conquered consent is no different than the fear of death under which individuals unite to form a commonwealth.[40] Locke, by contrast, argues that an unjust aggressor never acquires right over the conquered, since men are never bound by promises extorted by unlawful force, whereas a victor in a lawful war acquires dominion over the lives of those who were unlawful aggressors but not over their possessions, save for reparation for damages received and war expenses, with reservation made for the support of the aggressor's dependents.[41] In each case, what is at stake is the sovereign's right of dominion over the life and property of individuals and not the right of one state to have its territorial claims recognized by another.

The opposite extreme is exemplified by Kant, who pursues the liberal analogy to its radical conclusion, arguing that states are bound to erect a league of nations following the idea of social contract.[42] Proceeding from the common liberal assumption that states are from nature in a condition of war akin to the natural state of individuals, Kant presumes that the rationale for social contract holds equally true for nations, despite their inequalities of strength and relative self-sufficiency. Kant can do so insofar as he roots the reason for leaving the state of nature not in any passions or prudential calculations but in a moral imperative to establish an order in which the autonomy of all members is duly respected. In this regard, states, like individuals find themselves from nature in an illegitimate condition, a condition of war where what reigns is the license of the more powerful.[43] Following Hobbes, Kant reasons that in both states of nature all property claims, be they personal or national, are merely provisional, lacking the objective recognition that only a higher governing authority can provide.[44] Hence, all peoples, like all individuals, stand originally in a community of land, comprising not a legal community of ownership, but one of a physically possible interaction from which separate entitlements can only emerge after moving to a civil condition, uniting all peoples under an administration of universal laws.[45] Accordingly, the same inconvenience that compels individuals to enter into civil relations compels each state to form a common community,[46] not just to realize their self-interests, but to be able to interact in a universally lawful manner, as right demands. In following the imperative to unite into a league of nations, each state can expect its security and right to be guaranteed by the lawful decision of the states' united wills and the united power of the established league, instead of relying upon individual power and judgment.[47] Just as a civil government is necessary to protect the autonomy and property of individuals, so a league of nations is necessary to insure that states do not interfere with each other's internal affairs and to defend them against external harm.[48] Indeed, since civil government cannot insure the rights of its citizens unless its own national rights are upheld by the peace-keeping world government of a league of nations, the imperative to erect a league of nations is of paramount importance.[49]

Yet, having come so far, Kant cannot help admitting that a league of nations can never be fully analogous to a civil government. On the one hand, such an association of states is not an indissoluble union grounded on one constitution, like the United States of America. Only if it were could it actually settle the disputes of peoples in a civil, judicial way. A league of nations is essentially but a confederation of independent states which, because of their abiding independence, represents an arbitrary, always dissolvable association with no sovereign power of its own.[50] As a result, the league's world government is more of an ethical ideal than an effective reality. Kant even confesses that the perpetual peace at which it aims is an unrealizable idea because a too great extension of a league of nations makes the protection of each part impossible, whereas a plurality of such leagues reinstates a state of war.[51]

The essential problem is that only if the league of nations obliterates the national independence of its members can it secure their rights, whereas if it achieves such a union it eliminates their character as states and renders itself nothing more than a civil government. Since territorial rights in the Kantian scheme depend upon the international legality of a league of nations in which national sovereignty is not submerged, the territorial claims of states remain just as provisional as they did in the state of nature. For, as Hegel points out, the Kantian vision of a league of nations presupposes the agreement of states, which always rests on their particular sovereign wills and thereby remains trapped in contingency.[52] This problem, so evident in respect to states, equally afflicts the social contract among individuals. There, too, one must presuppose both the unanimous commitment to peace and justice whose absence provides the very rationale for uniting under a common sovereign, and the obligatory force of contract, which equally is absent in the state of nature where individuals are subject to no commands that do not issue from their own will.[53] The dual confusion of the liberal analogy thereby becomes plain: just as international relations cannot be understood on the model of natural relations among individuals, so justice between persons cannot be conceived on the model of peace and war among nations.

One further problem of key importance for moving beyond the liberal analogy is that if a league of nations were to succeed in outlawing wars of aggression in accordance with a principle of the self-determination of nations, this would only make sense on the assumption that all current boundaries are just[54] and that each of the member nations had the sort of internal constitution making it deserving of international legal equality. Even though Kant's moral basis for uniting nations into a world government allows him to ignore the differences in power and self-sufficiency between nations that have crucial bearing for Hobbesian prudential calculations, Kant must presume a normative equality between nations for which there can be no guarantee, especially when he himself distinguishes between those nations that are organized in conformity with liberal principles of freedom and equality and those that are not. Although liberal theory may see fit to treat all responsible individuals as equal, assuming that all teleological ends are without foundation and that liberty alone has affirmative value, liberal theory cannot maintain the same for nations without abandoning its efforts to determine what distinguishes valid civil government from illegitimate despotism. Hence, the principle of the right of self-determination of nations, which might appear to be liberal theory's logical foundation for assessing the territorial rights of states, remains invidiously formal, failing to tie national self-determination to the domestic autonomy of citizens.

Rawls's procedural reformulation of the liberal argument is no better at removing these obstacles to a coherent ethics of territorial rights. In transposing the choice procedure of his original position from individuals to nations,[55] Rawls might be thought to have established a framework for determining the principles of international justice without embracing the incoherencies of an international social contract. Certainly, his argument in no way depends upon the institution of a world government. Nevertheless, by imposing a veil of ignorance upon the representatives of different nations, depriving them of knowledge of their own and other societies and commissioning them to agree upon principles of international justice that will best serve their interests without possibly prejudicing the interests of others, Rawls is not simply nullifying the contingencies of historical fate in pursuit of international fairness.[56] He is also following his liberal predecessors in ignoring how nations are unequal in regard to not only wealth and power but also to the justice of their domestic institutions. This should not be surprising, since the whole basis of procedural justice is that the parties to its privileged choice procedure are of equal desert and have no aims and interests that already possess any differential ethical value. Hence, when Rawls proceeds to derive a principle of the equal liberty of nations as the basic proviso of international law, he commits the same petitio principii that he did in deriving his domestic principle of equal liberty. In each case, the resulting principle is already presupposed by the choice procedure from which it issues. Interestingly enough, Rawls makes no mention of an international difference principle, which, in analogy to his domestic difference principle, would ordain that nations are obliged to redistribute their wealth, arms, and territory so that the economic and military inequalities of states are diminished until the least advantaged nations cease to derive any benefit. Such a principle would be no more admissible than that of equal liberty, since it too would presuppose the equal right of each nation to maintain itself, something that procedural justice cannot establish, and would ignore the comparative justice of its domestic institutions.

### iv) Legal Positivism and Territorial Rights

With the liberal analogy between individual and international relations leading to an impasse, must the project of a normative theory of territorial rights be abandoned in favor of the descriptive analysis championed by legal positivism? Often legal positivism is opposed to natural right theory as if the two exhausted the possible strategies for addressing domestic and international relations. If this were true and the liberal approach were emblematic of natural right theory, then territorial rights would have to be left to the legal positivists.

Of course, there are natural right theorists, such as St. Thomas Aquinas, who identify international law with natural law without embracing the liberal strategy of social contract. Aquinas suggests that international law is natural law both because all law is either natural or positive and the law of nations is not positive law, given the absence of an international legislature, and because the law of nations is what all nations observe and what all agree to is what is natural.[57] Although Aquinas equally maintains that the law of nations is natural by being dictated by reason, his appeal to existing features of reality involves the generic confusion of natural right theory, which characteristically roots what ought to be in something that is, conflating normative legitimacy with what is given by nature.

Legal positivism aims to avoid this mistake in the first instance by maintaining that the essence of law lies not in the conformity of its content to any givens but in being the command of a sovereign will backed by the threat of organized sanctions. On this basis it follows that, since there is no international sovereign nor any system of international sanctions, there can be no international law, properly speaking, and that hence each national sovereign is immune from all external obligations, including the observance of any territorial rights of other nations.

This version of legal positivism, classicly advanced by John Austin, is plagued by its own appeal to the given reality of a sovereign will, whose existence is presumed to provide the privileged source of legal norms. It also falls prey to the natural right objection that any observance of international law refutes legal positivism by showing that the essence of law does not lie in being the coercive command of a sovereign and that sovereigns are not immune from all legal obligation.[58] In recognition of such problems, subsequent legal positivists, such as Hans Kelsen and H. L. A. Hart, have eliminated the foundation of a sovereign will and instead conceived the essence of law to lie in a system of rules whereby a basic norm or so-called secondary rules grant authority to the making and application of positive laws. What makes this a purely positive conception is that it roots the basic norm or rules neither in reason nor nature but simply in convention. In this formulation, legal positivism can grant that the absence of an international sovereign and effective international sanctions does not preclude international law, and indeed Kelsen is willing to identify, as the basic international norm, the principle that *pacta sunt servanda*. On this basis, territorial rights, like all other international matters, would issue from treaties and no other consideration would be relevant, given the absence of any other source of norms.[59] Hart rejects Kelsen's characterization, both because not all obligations recognized under international law arise from treaties and because there is no necessity that the rules of international law be systematically united under a basic norm.[60] Instead, he claims that international law resembles customary law in form (by lacking a legislature, courts with compulsory jurisdiction, and officially organized sanctions) but municipal law in content (by involving demands for compensation, threats of retaliation, and ethically indifferent and alterable rules, all inappropriate to morality), with the implication that territorial rights and other international entitlements have no special origin or status other than whatever nations happen to recognize in their regard.[61]

Unless there is a normative alternative to natural right, it is difficult to avoid judging the legal positivist option on its own terms by asking whether it is descriptively accurate. This, however, is the wrong question to pose because there is a third theoretical option that avoids the appeals to privileged givens undermining natural right without embracing the conventionalism of legal positivism. It provides a framework for avoiding the pitfalls of the liberal conflation of individual and national rights, for taking into account the inequality of nations, and for comprehending the special role of treaties in the law of nations without reducing all territorial rights to matters of treaty or other international conventions.

### v) Political Self-Determination and Territorial Rights

What allows for a normative theory of territorial rights is the basic insight that relations of justice cannot have foundations. If justice were to be juridically determined by any antecedent ground, such as independent givens of nature or privileged procedures of construction, conduct and institutions would derive their validity from something outside of and lacking justice itself. Justice, like reason, must be self-grounding, and the sole way that conduct and institutions can free themselves of juridical foundations is to be self-determined. Only by comprising an objective reality of freedom can practice free itself from given foundations, owe its valid character to itself, and achieve the self-legitimation required for normative justification. The freedom in which justice must thus consist is not the natural liberty that rational agents must possess as the precondition of responsible action. Such liberty is itself a given capacity, antecedent to every chosen action, having a form that is natural rather than self-determined. Only by participating in the practice of enacted institutions of freedom and thereby exercising the artificial agencies of property owners, moral subjects, family members, civilians, and citizens can individuals achieve the genuine self-determination satisfying the self-grounding character of normativity. Hence, the theory of justice is not a theory of the embodiment of an antecedently given form of the good or of the outcome of some deliberative process, but a theory of a self-ordered system of institutional freedom, conceiving the organized practices that give self-determination an objectively recognized reality.[62]

On these terms, the legitimacy of a state lies in the extent to which it realizes self-government in conformity with the nonpolitical institutions of freedom that property, moral, household, and social relations can constitute when organized as distinct modes of self-determination. What counts, normatively speaking, is therefore not the genesis of the nation, nor its conformity to independent natural or cultural givens, but the self-determined actuality of its own institutions.

Accordingly, the territory of a legitimate state is one that provides it with the domain in which its free institutions enjoy their reality. National territory is not simply real estate belonging to the state but rather the realm of its exclusive political jurisdiction, within which public, private, and foreign ownerships may coexist. Hence, the right to national territory belongs to one and only one type of subject, not a property-owning person, a moral individual, a family member, or an economic agent, but a politically organized citizenry. Conversely, what gives a citizenry its identity is not such prepolitical factors as ethnic or racial identity, a history of occupying a common land, or religious community, but the political convention of being subject to the same constitution. Consequently, Aristotle is right in maintaining that the identity of the state is not constituted by its borders or the group that inhabits it but by the criterion of its constitution, which allows the state to remain the same even when the composition of its territory and population change.[63] By the same token, Kant is equally correct in holding that citizens possess the territory of their fatherland through their constitution, and not through any other factor.[64]

Accordingly, the right of a people to self-determination, proclaimed during the French Revolution, adopted by Lenin as the anticolonial slogan of the Comintern, and brought to its radical conclusion by Nazism, is bogus. It mistakenly roots the political right to independent sovereignty in the prepolitical given of a people, whose identity resides, not in governing itself under a common constitution, but in cultural or racial factors. Furthermore, by treating the people's will, and not the constitutionally limited voice of the citizenry, as the source of political right, it contaminates the state with a power standing above all constitutional restraint, threatening the sort of tyranny imposed by the most passionate zealot of a people's self-assertion: Adolf Hitler.[65] Because, however, the just state is for its own sake, providing a self-governing association essentially free to incorporate a population of diverse races, ethnic backgrounds, and territorial history, the right to political self-determination is enjoyed by a politically defined citizenry that can only incidentally be a people.

What provides a non-natural and nonconventional basis for territorial right is that national territory gives a citizenry the domain it needs for exercising its right to political self-determination. Hence, a citizenry enjoys a territorial right in function of its basic political right to live under a just political constitution. This territorial right is relative to the conditions of domestic political self-determination, conditions that pertain to all states and that are not particular international conventions varying through history.

The normative theory of territorial rights can therefore be developed by exploring how territory functions as a condition of political self-determination, which itself contains and is mediated by the institutions of nonpolitical freedom. This requires taking account of two interrelated factors that can both be conceptually specified. One is the domestic structure of the just state as it mandates the prerequisites of valid political activity and the valid nonpolitical institutions of freedom that underlie and contribute to self-government. The other is the range of possible external relations that the just state may face.

National territory functions as a necessary condition of domestic justice first and most generally in that self-government requires some space within which its constitutive political and nonpolitical activities can operate. This minimal requirement does not, of course, mandate what kind or how large of a space is required. In fact, it leaves open the possibility that the just state may have no fixed territory but may wander about in nomadic fashion.

Nevertheless, purely domestic considerations do add the further requirement that the territory, be it fixed or changing, be hospitable and large enough to provide the means for sufficient health and economic opportunity, as well as the resources to support just social and political institutions. In addition, the territory cannot be so overpopulated, dispersed, or impenetrable as to make impossible the cohesive contact and communication on which both self-government and social justice depend.[66]

These requirements are all that count in the conceivable situation where a nation is so situated as to have no contact with other states or with any communities of rational beings who have failed to achieve political organization. Where the domestic prescriptions for national territory apply to only one such isolated state, the territorial rights of that nation have but one external limit. The nation is at liberty to incorporate whatever territory it needs for its own just institutions, provided that in so doing it does not unduly jeopardize the welfare of future generations. They must be taken into account because the right to political self-determination is not temporally limited.

However, the moment a just state loses such isolation, its territorial right takes on a more complicated character. Certain features hold regardless of what kind of foreign contacts it has. Whether it stand in relation to other just states, illegitimate regimes, or communities lacking political organization, and whether it or they have fixed borders or nomadic habits, two factors intervene to alter the territorial requirements of its own domestic justice.

First, the presence of other communities brings with it the possibility of economic and cultural interdependencies that may be significant for the flourishing of domestic institutions of freedom. Second, even if a nation can maintain its institutions of justice without foreign trade and cultural exchange, other communities pose a possible threat to the security of its domestic life. These considerations dictate, on the one hand, that the national territory be endowed with sufficient resources, climate, topography, and egress to allow the nation to trade advantageously with other communities yet be sufficiently self-sufficient to escape foreign economic and cultural domination detrimental to its domestic justice. On the other hand, they mandate that the national territory be sufficiently populated, rich, and strategically located to make it defensible against foreign military encroachment.[67] These requirements are each relative to the corresponding features of foreign territories and the current conjuncture of foreign alliances and hostilities. Yet, because they are common territorial conditions for the maintenance of domestic justice, any state with legitimate institutions is entitled to them. The same, however, cannot be said for communities that are unjust. Because their domestic life is without validity, there is no imperative to provide the territorial conditions for its perpetuation.

It is this normative differentiation between communities that entails a corresponding differentiation in territorial rights. There are three basic possibilities: relations between just states, relations between just states and communities lacking just political institutions, and relations between communities lacking just political institutions. Strictly speaking, all three cases may involve nomadic as well as territorially immobile communities, and communities of rational beings other than homo sapiens, granted that such communities may exist and come into contact with one another and/or human communities.

The relationship between just states presents the only case even remotely resembling the picture arising from the liberal analogy. Because just states are of equal desert, they do stand in a relation of equality whereby each is entitled to the territory enabling it to maintain its institutions of social and political freedom without foreign encroachment. In principle, such states warrant recognition as independent nations whose borders deserve respect, just as they are obliged to recognize the same entitlement of other legitimate states and observe a principle of nonintervention in their domestic affairs. In regard to uninhabited territory, such as ocean floors, arctic wastes, or extraterrestial bodies, each just state deserves an equal claim, to the extent that possession of such territories may affect their own rightful welfare. Furthermore, to the degree that differences in territorial size, natural resources, and strategic location may unequally jeopardize the stability and security of the institutions of equally just regimes, there is, in principle, a normative requirement for territorial readjustments that advance the general realization of justice.

When just states interrelate with unjust states or communities that have no political organization, such territorial reciprocity is inapplicable. Unjust and just states may enjoy a formal equality in that each is independent against the other,[68] but this feature does not translate into equal territorial entitlements. A legitimate and an illegitimate regime may each require respected territory to maintain their independence, but only the just state deserves its independence and the conditions that make it possible. This does not signify that the subjects of an illegitimate regime deserve to be conquered and deprived of the conditions of their own political self-determination. Rather, the very right of the inhabitants of an unjust regime to live under institutions of freedom warrants foreign intervention if it can contribute to domestic liberation, as well as territorial adjustments if they enable the inhabitants to win the institutions for exercising their due social and political rights. Since citizens can exercise political self-determination within a variety of borders, observing the historical boundaries of peoples or other linguistic and religious groups is secondary to the establishment of frontiers within which institutions of freedom can prosper. Consequently, a just regime is under no obligation to honor past territorial treaties with an illegitimate community if breaking treaty obligations advances the global cause of social and political justice. Similarly, communities with different degrees of domestic justice do not have equal entitlements to uninhabited territory. Once again, what determines how such lands should be used and acquired is how their disposition will promote the maintenance and expansion of the social and political institutions of freedom. Since territorial disadvantages may only contribute to the perseverance of domestic injustice, the above principle is not a prescription for keeping the inhabitants of illegitimate communities in the most inhospitable, least defensible territories.

Lastly, when nations with equally unjust domestic institutions interact, their territorial rights are not equivalent to those of just regimes. Once again, what counts is not a formal observance of national independence but the substantive claims of social and political justice. Hence, the only territorial entitlements unjust regimes have in regard to one another are those that promote the development of just institutions within each. Once again, past treaties and traditional boundaries have validity only by contributing to this end.

The sobering challenge of applying these principles is most evident in the relations between just states. Because the maintenance of national sovereignty makes effective world government an unrealizable ideal, just states have no other vehicle for realizing their equal territorial rights than in mutually recognizing each other's claims, be it through tacit or explicit treaty agreements, reached with or without prior hostilities. So long as the treaties in question do not subvert the domestic justice of either, they deserve to be observed.

Nevertheless, the domestic rectitude of states does not guarantee their mutual recognition of territorial entitlements. Just regimes may maliciously violate each other's borders, either for illicit advantage or as an inescapable measure of self-preservation in response to real or perceived foreign threats. Just regimes may also nonmaliciously ignore the perceived entitlements of others, by incorrectly estimating each other's legitimacy, by having conflicting interpretations of boundary agreements, or by disagreeing over what territorial adjustments are necessary to promote the independence and welfare of one another. In the absence of any higher authority to determine whether states are legitimate and deserving of recognition, whether borders are just, whether territorial violations have occurred, and whether border adjustments and penalties are due, and in the absence of any recognized enforcer of such judgments, the application of the principles of territorial rights remains captive to the particular arbitrariness of each state as it faces others in a struggle for recognition.[69] Hence, the affirmation of territorial rights among just states takes the form of a contingent alternation of peace and war, of treaty agreements and treaty violations,[70] where no will has binding discretionary power and where reason may mandate the general principles of territorial entitlements but not their particular applications. These remain matters of subjective estimation, since determining the legitimacy of states and their territorial claims depends upon empirical observation and subsumption of the observed particulars to rational principles, introducing ineradicable problems of interpretation that each state must confront on its own.

The basic predicament is common to all relations between states, be they just or not. As a consequence, territorial rights always remain mere imperatives, lacking the objectively recognized and administered reality that domestic institutions provide for the property, household, social, and political rights of their citizens. Nevertheless, no citizen can afford to ignore territorial rights, both because upholding them requires constant vigilance and because the space for a free public life is our most precious estate.

## Notes

1. Alexander Hamilton, *The Federalist*, No. 7, in *The Federalist*, ed. by Jacob E. Cooke (Middletown, CT: Wesleyan University Press, 1982), p. 36.

2. Leo Strauss, *The City and Man* (Chicago: University of Chicago Press, 1978), p. 239.

3. *Ibid.*

4. *Ibid.*

5. G. W. F. Hegel, *The Philosophy of Right*, trans. by T. M. Knox (New York: Oxford University Press, 1968), paragraph 323.

6. Immanuel Kant, *Metaphysik der Sitten*, in *Werke XI* (Frankfurt am Main: Suhrkamp Verlag, 1968), A235/B265–266.

7. H. L. A. Hart, *The Concept of Law* (Oxford: Oxford University Press, 1982), p. 209.

8. Aristotle, *The Politics*, trans. by Ernest Barker (New York: Oxford University Press, 1982), p. 286, 1325b23–32.

9. John Rawls, *A Theory of Justice* (Cambridge, MA: Harvard University Press, 1971), p. 8.

10. *Ibid.*, p. 108.

11. *Ibid.*, p. 8.

12. Hart, *op. cit.*, p. 218.

13. Strauss, *op. cit.*, p. 6.

14. Aristotle, *op. cit.*, p. 5, 1265a; p. 66, 1267a.

15. This route is followed, for example, by Hegel in the *Philosophy of Right*.

16. Whereas Hobbes and Locke reject this denouement, Kant accepts its logic, as does Rawls in his procedural reinterpretation of the social contract.

17. Thomas Hobbes, *Leviathan*, ed. by C. B. Macpherson (Harmondsworth, UK: Penguin Books, 1968), pp. 187, 394.

18. John Locke, *The Second Treatise of Government*, ed. by Thomas P. Peardon (Indianapolis, IN: Bobbs-Merrill, 1952), pp. 105, 109.

19. *Ibid.*, p. 10; Hobbes, *op. cit.*, p. 187.

20. Kant, *op. cit.*, paragraph 55, A216/B246.

21. *Ibid.*, A208/B238.

22. *Ibid.*, A216/246.

23. *Ibid.*

24. Hobbes, *op. cit.*, p. 188.

25. Locke, *op. cit.*, p. 100.

26. David Hume, *An Enquiry Concerning the Principles of Morals*, ed. by J. B. Schneewind (Indianapolis, IN: Hackett, 1983), p. 35.

27. *Ibid.*

28. Hart, *op. cit.*, p. 213.

29. *Ibid.*, p. 214.

30. *Ibid.*

31. Hobbes, op. cit., p. 187.

32. *Ibid.*, 394.

33. *Ibid.*, pp. 187, 394.

34. *Ibid.*, p., 188.

35. *Ibid.*, pp. 202, 295–296.

36. *Ibid.*, p. 188.

37. *Ibid.*, p. 187.

38. Locke, *op. cit.*, p. 109.

39. *Ibid.*, p. 10.

40. Hobbes, *op. cit.*, pp. 252, 255–256.

41. Locke, *op. cit.*, pp. 99, 101–104, 106.

42. Kant, *op. cit.*, A217/B247.

43. *Ibid.*

44. *Ibid.*, A227/B257.

45. *Ibid.*, A229/B259.

46. *Ibid.*, A398.

47. *Ibid.*, A399.

48. *Ibid.*, A217/B247.

49. *Ibid.*, A235/B265–266.

50. *Ibid.*, A217/B247, A227/B257.

51. *Ibid.*, A227/B257.

52. Hegel, *op. cit.*, paragraph 333.

53. For a further exploration of the dilemmas of social contract theory, see Richard Dien Winfield, *Reason and Justice* (Albany, NY: SUNY Press, 1988), Chapter 4.

54. Strauss, *op. cit.*, p. 6.

55. Rawls, *op. cit.*, pp. 378–379.

56. *Ibid.*, p. 378.

57. *St. Thomas on Politics and Ethics*, ed. by Paul E. Sigmund (New York: W. W. Norton, 1988), pp. 67–68.

58. A. P. d'Entrèves makes this argument in *Natural Law* (London: Hutchinson, 1981), p. 68.

59. Hart, *op. cit.*, p. 228.

60. *Ibid.*

61. *Ibid.*, pp. 222–226.

62. For a detailed presentation of this strategy for ethics, first introduced by Hegel, see Winfield, *op. cit.*., Chapter 8ff.

63. Aristotle, *op. cit.*, pp. 98–100, 1276a–1276b.

64. Kant, op. cit., A207/B237.

65. Hannah Arendt analyzes these ramifications in *On Revolution* (New York: Viking Press, 1976) and *The Origins of Totalitarianism* (New York: Harcourt Brace Jovanovich, 1973).

66. Aristotle describes how legislators and founders of states must take account of these considerations in the *Politics*, *op. cit.*, p. 99, 1276a.

67. See Aristotle, *op. cit.*, p. 293, 1326b–1327a.

68. Hegel, *op. cit.*, paragraph 322.

69. See *ibid.*, paragraph 331.

70. *Ibid.*, paragraph 333.

# Index


Absolute Knowing, 21–22, 50
Absolute Idea, 13, 27, 28, 29, 30, 44, 45, 46, 47, 48, 49, 172
absolutely good man, 109
abstract labor time, 191–195, 209, 210, 213, 219–221, 242–243
abstract right, 100–102, 104, 112, 119–124, 135, 138, 146–146, 148, 149, 152, 153, 160–164, 205–206
accumulation of capital, 244, 245, 256
administration of civil law, 82, 104, 128, 130, 249–250, 254, 255, 274
Adorno, T., 195
alienation, 137, 139–141, 147, 151, 211
Althusser, L., 170
analytic-synthetic distinction, 3, 7, 12, 26
Aquinas, St. T., 294
Arendt, H., 88, 105, 106, 119, 134, 255, 261, 303
Aristotle, 35, 109, 123, 158, 203–204, 228, 230, 270, 285, 286, 296, 303
atomism,
  ethical, 56, 65, 66, 69, 98–99
  national, 285, 287–294, 299
Austin, J., 294
authorizing power. *See* head of state
automation. *See* mechanization
autonomous reason, 3–12
Avineri, S., 149

balance of powers. *See* division of powers
base and superstructure, 120, 138, 143–144, 211, 233, 253
being, 23, 41–42, 45, 157, 172
Berman, R., 51, 58, 73, 74, 282
binding mandate, 266, 278
Bloch, E., 165, 195
Bobbio, N., 282
bourgeois, 206, 207
  *See also* civilian
bourgeois society, 148, 155, 159, 170, 237
Burke, E., 64

capital, 138, 139, 146, 159, 172, 183–195, 210, 211–222, 243–245, 250, 281
capitalism, 111, 130, 131, 159, 237, 254
capitalist, 140, 141, 186–187, 212–214, 222, 262
categorial totality. *See* Absolute Idea
categorical imperative, 99, 116, 117, 138, 204
child rearing, 81
citizen, 67, 83, 87, 105, 129, 131, 204, 206, 262, 275
civil freedom, 233, 234–236, 246, 252, 275
civil government, 85, 86, 96, 97, 98, 104–105, 116–117, 125, 129, 230, 255, 291–292, 293
civil religion, 268
civil rights, 77, 87, 95, 125, 127, 128, 239, 241
civil society, 95, 96, 104, 111, 112, 124–129, 131, 134, 138, 141, 142, 146, 148, 152, 160, 164, 170, 174, 206, 207, 233–237, 246, 253, 255, 258, 273, 274, 275, 278, 283

civilian, 105
classes, 104, 106, 121, 129, 145, 237, 238, 245–249, 251, 252, 256, 258, 259
  class interest, 126, 129, 133, 135
  class struggle, 130, 145, 152
  political classes. *See* estates
classless society, 246, 255
coherence theory of truth, 6
colonialism, 254
commodity relations, 82, 104, 111, 120, 126–127, 131, 133, 146, 148, 161–164, 166, 236, 238, 240, 244, 247, 250, 252, 253, 273
  commodities, 82, 126, 174–175, 208, 236, 257
  commodity exchange and circulation, 82, 127, 153, 161–164, 174–183, 184, 208, 209, 211, 239–242, 250, 257
  commodity fetishism, 127, 241, 242
  commodity production, 82, 126, 161–162, 241, 242, 244–245, 256
  inability to secure civil justice, 249–254
communism, 133, 136, 246, 252, 256, 268, 278, 280
communist society, 141–142, 246, 252
communitarianism, 61, 63–64, 65, 70, 72
competition, 221–222, 245
concept, 113, 172, 173
conscience. *See* morality
consciousness, 21, 29, 32, 143, 144, 171, 206
  as given subject matter of phenomenology, 4, 21–22, 42, 157, 171
  distinction of, 4, 157, 171
consequentialism, 63
constitution, 248, 264, 292, 296, 297
  constitutionality, 96–97, 254, 266, 275
  constitution-making, 275
contract, 141, 146, 161, 162, 166, 167, 175, 289
contractarianims. *See* social contract theory
cooperation, 145, 152
corporations. *See* economic interest groups
courage, 270
crime, 121, 249, 289
critique of epistemology, 150, 171

deconstruction, 19
definite description, theory of, 52
deism, 264
democrcay, 270, 276–278
  bourgeois democracy, 281
  and constitutionality, 263–264, 266
  direct democracy, 265, 268, 278
  justification of, 267
  mass democracy, 265, 266, 271, 278, 280
  parliamentary democracy, 263, 264–268, 270, 276–278
  participatory democracy. *See* direct democracy
  representative democracy. *See* parliamentary democracy
d'Entrèves, A. P., 303
deontology, 61, 62–63, 64, 65, 67, 68–69, 70, 71, 72, 73, 74
desacralization of nature, 120, 121, 123, 131
determinate negation, 7, 9, 12, 13
dialectical logic. *See* systematic logic
dialectical materialism, 155
dialectical method, 155, 156, 157, 159, 160
dictatorship, 266, 268, 270, 276
difference principle, 294
division of labor, 150, 166, 209
division of powers, 263–264, 265, 266, 275, 276, 277, 278, 282
dole, 131, 252
Dove, K. R., 165, 166, 195, 222
Dworkin, R., 279

economic determinism, 120
economic disadvantage. *See* inequality of wealth
economic freedom, 104, 125, 231, 253
economic interest groups, 128, 238, 251–252
economic rights, 82, 127
economics, 138, 205
prescriptive, 228, 229–233, 235, 237, 241, 243, 244, 252, 254
economy, 82, 125, 227, 283
edifying philosophy, 40
emergency and emergency powers, 263–264, 269, 270, 271, 275–276
empiricism, 61, 71
Engels, F., 156
Enlightenment, 72, 111
environmental ethics, 80
estates, 104, 135, 160, 237, 238, 245, 246–249, 256, 258, 259, 282
ethical community, 65, 69–71, 72, 123, 124, 132, 163, 273–274, 275, 276
exchange value, 176–177, 184–185, 208, 210, 212, 216, 217–221, 240–241, 244, 252
executive power, 266, 275
exploitation of labor by capital, 140–141, 237, 241–243, 244, 246

family, 67, 69–70, 81, 112, 124, 129, 206, 228, 234, 273, 274, 283
family freedom, 69–70, 81, 124
fascism, 254–255, 268
*See also* Nazism
federalism, 266
fetishism of commodities. *See* commodity fetishism
Fichte, J. G., 38, 147, 148, 157, 171
forces and relations of production, 137, 138, 142–143, 150, 170, 211
foreign affairs. *See* international relations
formal logic 8, 45
formalization, 28
Foster, M. B., 72, 73, 74, 75, 134, 165, 282
foundationalism, 3, 10, 19, 79, 80, 230–231, 295–296
foundational epistemology, 80
fraud, 103, 121, 249
free enterprise, 71, 233, 237, 250, 255, 256
free will, 89–91, 99, 100–101
freedom,
freedom and justice, 99, 108–109, 110, 119, 230–231, 256, 296
freedom and justification, 80, 108–109
freedom as interaction, 80, 99, 100–102, 109–110, 111, 114, 117–119
logic of, 89–91, 100–101
negative freedom, 90
French Revolution, 84, 111, 130–131, 297
friend-foe opposition, 269–272, 273, 274
future generations, 298

Gadamer, H. G., 40, 80
gender, 81, 84, 121
general will, 267
the Good, 89, 109, 231, 273, 296

Habermas, J., 106, 119, 144–153, 165, 166, 195, 255, 261, 279
Hart, H. L. A., 281, 285–286, 288, 289, 295
head of state, 275, 277, 282
Hegel, G. W. F., 3–4, 7, 9–13, 19–32, 33, 41–49, 51, 58, 64, 73, 91–92, 100–105, 106, 107–136, 144–153, 155–167, 169–170, 171–173, 174, 184, 203, 205–208, 209, 211, 220, 222, 229–254, 256, 257, 258, 259, 261, 270, 272–279, 280, 282, 292, 301, 303

critique of Kantian ethics, 111–117, 119, 122–123, 134
on civil society, 104, 124–129, 131, 137, 229–230, 233–237, 256, 258, 273
on consciousness, 42
on economics. *See* system of needs
on ethical community, 123, 124, 124–130, 153, 163, 273–274
*Jenaer Realphilosophie*, 144–145, 151, 152, 153, 158–162, 166
logic of being, nothing and becoming, 25, 26, 41–43
on master-slave relationship, 145
on modernity, 107–108, 111, 119, 123, 130–132
on morality, 73, 74, 112, 122–124, 273
*Phenomenology of Spirit*, 4, 13, 21–23, 25, 42, 50, 145, 152, 157, 165, 171–172, 195
*Philosophy of Nature*, 29–30, 32, 45, 50
*Philosophy of Right*, 64, 74, 100–105, 107–110, 147, 148, 153, 159–160, 162–164, 205, 229, 233, 234, 238, 244, 301
*Philosophy of Spirit*, 23, 32, 48–49, 50, 100
*Realphilosophie*, 29–30, 32, 172, 173
*Science of Logic*, 3–12, 19–32, 41, 44, 45, 50, 105, 147, 149, 157, 158, 169, 170, 171–173, 211
*System der Sittlichkeit*, 158–162
on spirit, 100, 147, 152, 166, 205, 256
on the state, 104–105, 124, 129–130, 272–279, 282

Heidegger, M., 255, 261
Henrich, D., 195, 196
history, 107, 110, 111, 144, 173, 206–207, 283
of the institutions of freedom, 110, 111, 120, 121, 133, 173, 207
Hitler, A., 84, 270, 297
Hobbes, T., 112, 207, 229, 269, 272, 287, 288, 289–290, 291, 293, 301
holism, 6, 39–40, 80
Horkheimer, M., 195
household. *See* family
human rights, 78, 83, 84, 85, 86, 87
humanism, 262
Hume, D., 73, 288–289
Husserl, E., 15–18, 38

Idea, 30, 172, 173
imperialism, 254
indeterminacy,
as outcome of phenomenology, 157, 171
as starting point of systematic philosophy, 10–11, 12, 20, 24, 41–42, 171
individuality, 51–58, 113
and universality and particularity, 51–55
logic of, 51–55, 172
of the free will, 90–91, 98–99, 101, 103, 105, 112–113, 115, 116
*See also* freedom, self-determination
inequality of wealth, 250, 251, 252, 253, 278
instrument of labor. *See* labor processes
intellectual intuition, 56, 157, 158
interaction, 138, 144–146, 150, 151, 152, 153, 156, 157, 158, 159, 163, 166, 170, 171–172, 205, 206, 207, 208, 211, 213
*See also* freedom as interaction
inter-individuality, 171, 172
international law, 281, 285, 288, 293, 294–295
international relations, 206, 248, 269, 272–273, 274, 283–301
intersubjectivity, 171, 173
*See also* interaction and reciprocal recognition
invisible hand, 250

Jacobins, 120, 167
judgment, 113, 116
  logic of, 55, 58
justice, 89, 228, 230–231, 296
  as the reality of freedom, 80, 89, 108, 230–231, 232, 256, 296
  teleological conception of, 89
  theory of, 107, 109, 231, 286

Kant, I., 15, 16, 17, 24, 26, 29–30, 37–38, 65–66, 74, 111–117, 118, 119, 122, 123, 124, 134, 135, 138, 144, 147, 157, 171, 204, 209, 228, 231
  epistemological theory, 15, 16, 17, 24, 26, 29–30, 37–38, 113–114, 115, 135
  ethical theory, 65–66, 74, 111–117, 118, 119, 122, 123, 124, 134, 138, 204, 209, 287, 288, 291–293, 297, 301
Kelsen, H., 264, 295
Kierkegaard, S., 11, 13, 41, 56, 66, 74
Knox, T. M., 257
Krahl, H. J., 173

labor, 137–148, 150–153, 155, 157, 158, 166, 188–189, 204, 208, 210, 214–222, 242–243, 144
laborer, 212–214, 222, 243, 245
labor power, 148, 164, 184–187, 195, 210, 212–214, 217, 219, 220, 243, 250
labor process, 186–195, 209, 210, 214–222, 241, 244
  instrument of labor, 188–189, 214–221
  object of labor, 188–189, 214–220
labor theory of value, 183–195, 209, 210, 218–221, 240–243, 257
laissez-faire. *See* free enterprise
language, 144, 151, 152
language games, 16–18
law, 70–71, 248, 263–264, 276, 277, 295
  civil law, 96, 251, 274
league of nations, 289, 290, 291–293, 300
legal positivism, 288, 294–295
legality, 70–71, 111, 117, 264, 276
legislature, 96, 248–249, 277
  *See also* parliament, parliamentarism
Lenin, V. I., 157, 169, 297
Levine, D., 135, 225
liberal state, 263–268, 271, 272, 276–278
liberal theory, 77, 80, 85, 86, 91–98, 99, 101, 102, 109, 112, 116, 126, 128, 136, 229–230, 231, 261–268, 269, 272, 276, 287–294, 295, 299
  and the defense of democracy, 86, 262, 265, 268
liberty, 66, 80, 86, 92–98, 105, 112, 113, 114, 115, 116, 119, 121, 125, 230, 231, 232, 234, 252, 268, 293, 296
Locke, J., 86, 112, 229, 287, 288, 289, 290–291, 301
logic, 4–12
  descriptive and prescriptive, 8, 9
  of the concept, 28, 58
  starting point of, 5, 20–27
  *See also* formal logic, systematic logic and transcendental logic
logical positivism, 34
Lukács, G., 58, 147, 149, 155–164, 195

MacIntyre, A., 40
marginal utility theory, 227, 255
market freedom, 67, 70
markets, 262
  *See also* commodity relations, system of needs
Marx, K., 41, 119, 126, 127, 129, 135, 137–144, 146, 155, 156, 157, 162, 163, 164, 169–171, 173, 191, 193, 208–222, 237, 238, 241–244, 252, 255, 257, 262
  *Capital*, 137, 139, 146, 148, 155, 156, 164, 166, 169–174, 208–211, 213, 214, 216, 218, 220, 221, 241–242

critique of commodity relations, 127, 237, 241–244
*Grundrisse*, 137, 139, 146, 148, 155, 156, 170–171, 174, 208, 211–222
theory of alienation, 137, 139–141, 170, 211
theory of base and superstructure, 143–144
theory of capital, 139, 155, 162, 166, 170–171, 174–195, 210, 243–244
theory of communist society, 136, 252, 262
theory of forces and relations of production, 137, 142–143, 150
Marxism, 110, 126, 128, 139, 146, 155, 160, 169, 211, 246, 262
mass production, 244, 258
mathematics, 20
mechanization, 244
medical ethics, 80
metaethics, 64, 73, 284
metaphysics, 20, 23, 34–36, 44, 45
modernity, 107–108, 111, 119, 121, 123, 124, 129, 130–132, 139, 159, 160, 165, 170, 207, 261, 271, 279
money, 174, 178, 184, 242
as means of payment, 181
as measure of value and standard of price, 178–179, 242
as medium of circulation, 179–180
monological approach, 98–99, 227–228
*See also* atomism
monotheism, 57, 58
morality, 64–72, 83, 111, 112, 122–123, 129, 130, 206, 234, 273
action and deed, 67, 74, 122
and community, 63, 65, 68, 70–71
and conscience, 66, 69–70, 71, 123, 129, 234, 273
and interaction, 64–70, 295
and legality, 70–71, 123
intention and welfare, 68–69, 122
purpose and responsibility, 67–68, 69, 74, 122
national boundary, 262, 267, 283, 296–301
*See also* territorial rights
natural determination, 109, 110, 117, 120, 121, 126, 131, 133, 135, 159, 210, 227, 246–247
natural law, 94, 96, 97, 160, 288, 290, 294
natural right, 77, 81, 87, 93, 95, 96, 97, 105, 289
theory of, 80, 85, 86, 294, 295
natural will, 92–93, 98
naturalized epistemology,
nazism, 84, 133, 263, 297
need, 163, 174, 203, 204, 209, 228, 257
civil need, 238–239, 253, 256, 257
market need, 174, 208, 229, 236, 238–239, 253, 256, 274
multiplication and discrimination of, 238–239, 253
natural need, 228, 238, 239
subsistence needs, 236, 239
neo-classical economics, 255
Neitzsche, F., 66, 263, 271
nihilism, 64, 80, 284
nominalism, 55, 58
non-malicious wrong, 103, 121, 249

Oakeshott, M., 261

parliament, 263, 264, 275, 280, 282
parliamentarism, 264–268, 271, 280, 282
participatory democracy. *See* democracy
particularity, 51–55
logic of, 51–55
parties and the party system, 86–87, 133, 264, 265, 266, 267, 280
paternalism, 68
people, 84, 85, 133
perpetual peace, 292–293

person, 163, 166, 167, 205–206, 234, 242, 249, 273, 287–289, 291
*See also* property relations
phenomenology,
as introduction to systemic philosophy, 157
as a form of transcendental philosophy, 16
philosopher-king, 109
philosophical anthropology, 31, 32
philosophy, 9, 11, 12, 21, 31, 40, 48–49
physics, 20
Plato, 35, 109, 123, 134, 158, 203–204, 288
Platonism, 55, 58
poiesis, 204, 209, 228
police. *See* public administration of welfare
polis, 125, 203–204, 205
political economy, 111, 125, 126, 159, 170, 229–230, 231, 242, 250, 255
critique of, 159, 170, 230
political freedom, 70, 77, 83, 86, 87, 95–96, 105, 111, 128, 129, 233, 248, 249, 254, 274, 275
and constitution-making, 275
and territorial rights, 295–301
political parties. *See* parties and the party system
political romanticism, 271
positive law, 277, 294, 295
and constitutionality, 277
positive science, 33–34, 37, 44
possession-value, 208
post-analytic philosophy, 19, 40
poverty, 82, 111, 127, 131, 149, 239
praxis, 89, 203, 228
procedural justice, 293, 296
production process. *See* commodity production, labor process
profit, 221–222, 241, 242, 243, 244, 247
proletariat, 133, 148, 259
dictatorship of, 233
proletarian interest, 133, 233
property relations, 67, 73, 81, 93, 95, 97, 100–103, 104, 119–124, 129, 140, 145–146, 148, 161–163, 206, 234, 241, 249–250, 253, 257, 262, 273, 275, 283, 288, 289, 290, 291
and morality, 67, 73
as the minimal structure of right, 100–102, 119–120, 135
civil enforcement of, 95, 239, 249–250
violations of, 103, 121, 249
psychologism, 17
public administration of welfare, 82, 128, 130, 131, 133, 252–254, 259
public opinion, 87
punishment, 288, 289
pure thought, 4, 6, 7, 21, 25, 31
Putnam, H., 40

Quine, W. V. O., 34, 49

race, 81, 83, 84, 121, 297
raw material, 188–189, 214–215
*See also* labor process
Rawls, J., 80, 134, 285, 287, 293–294, 301
reason, 113–114, 115, 116
recall initiatives, 265, 278
reciprocal recognition, 83, 100, 101, 102, 104, 106, 109, 118, 121, 144, 145, 153, 159, 163, 195, 205, 232, 273, 300
referendum, 268
Reformation, 111, 130
Reichelt, H., 173
relativism, 64
rent, 245
representational cognition, 4, 22
revenge, 121
revolution, 107, 110, 254
Ricardo, D., 125, 229
Riedel, M., 160
right, 77–87, 99, 106, 107, 231, 272, 277, 286

of distress, 236
right and duty, 57, 67, 68, 79, 80, 232, 239, 252, 273
Roman right, 121
Ritter, J., 134, 135, 136
Romanticism, 111
Rorty, R., 40, 80
Rousseau, J.-J., 112, 229, 255, 267, 268, 276

Sandel, M. J., 73
Schelling, F. W. J., 19–31, 38, 41, 157, 171
Schmitt, C., 261–279
self-consciousness, 57, 139, 140, 141, 144, 145, 157, 158, 168, 171, 205
self-determination,
and justice, 99
and normative validity, 10, 43, 70, 74, 79
logic of, 10, 11, 44, 46, 48, 89–91
of nations, 293
of peoples, 297
self-government. *See* democracy
self-thinking thought, 4, 6, 8, 12, 21, 25, 26
sense-certainty, 42
sexual orientation, 81
slavery, 203
Smith, A., 125, 159, 209, 229
social contract, 85, 86, 95, 97, 104, 105, 116, 117, 231, 267, 287–288, 291–293, 294, 301
social contract theory, 92–98, 104, 203, 204–205, 287–288, 291–293, 303
and the defense of democracy, 86, 95, 267, 276
social democracy, 133, 253, 256
social science, 138, 205
socialism, 128, 250–252, 254, 255, 262, 263, 271
Socrates, 35, 72
sovereignty and sovereign power, 264, 269, 270, 271, 275–276, 284
species being, 78, 79, 81, 83, 84, 86, 121, 135, 142, 252, 255
spirit, 145, 147
state, 82–83, 104–105, 112, 124, 129–130, 206, 233, 234, 247, 254, 261, 283, 286, 287–289, 296
genesis of, 296
relation between state and civil society, 95, 105, 124, 130, 131, 233, 248–249, 253–254, 261–262, 278–279, 282
relations between state and non-political associations, 83, 129, 233, 234, 270, 271, 272, 274, 275, 277, 283, 284, 296, 297
state of nature, 85, 92–95, 97, 101, 120, 269, 276, 287, 288, 289–291, 292
Steuart, J., 125, 159, 229
Strauss, L., 261, 271, 272, 286
subjectivity, 23, 29
substance, theories of, 52
surplus value, 183, 194–195, 217–221, 241, 242–243
syllogism, 114, 115, 116, 135
system of needs, 139, 142, 147, 155, 160–164, 166, 170, 174, 207, 208, 209, 222, 229, 236, 237–238, 244, 245, 247, 249, 273
systematic logic, 8, 28
systematic philosophy, 19, 26, 113

taxation, 253
Taylor, C., 72, 73
techné, 158, 165, 227–228, 255
technology, 272
territorial rights, 283–301
totalitarianism, 255, 261, 268, 269
transcendental philosophy, 15–18, 44, 46, 150–151
self-elimination of transcendental argument, 38–39, 50

transcendental condition, 15, 16, 17, 18, 23, 40, 150–151
transcendental logic, 8
transcendental ontology, 20, 24, 28, 29, 30, 31, 32
treaty, 206, 289, 295, 300

understanding, 113–114, 115, 116, 135
unemployment, 127, 131
universality, 51–55
logic of, 51–55
universe, 58
use-value, 126, 174, 185, 208, 209, 210, 212, 213, 216, 238–239, 242
utilitarianism, 61–62, 64, 65, 67, 68, 69, 70, 71, 72, 74, 114, 134, 288, 289

V. Bohm-Bawerk, 257
value, 174, 189
equivalent and relative forms of, 175–176
expanded form of, 177–178
general form of, 178
value-price transformation, 170, 221–222

wage labor, 243–244
war, 206, 254, 262, 266, 270, 272, 285, 287, 288, 289, 290, 291, 292, 283, 300
Weber, M., 138
Weimar Republic, 263, 264, 268, 270
welfare state, 129, 133, 233, 253
White, A., 19–32
Winfield, R. D., 13, 14, 73, 74, 88, 106, 135, 165, 223, 224, 225, 282, 303
Wittgenstein, L., 15–18, 80
worker. *See* laborer
worker self-management, 250, 253, 259
wrong, 102, 103, 121